THE SERPENT POWER

BEING THE

SHAṬ-CHAKRA-NIRŪPAṆA AND
PĀDUKĀ-PANCHAKA

TWO WORKS ON TANTRIK YOGA, TRANSLATED FROM THE SANSKRIT, WITH INTRODUCTION AND COMMENTARY

By ARTHUR AVALON

ISBN: 978-1-63923-464-6

Printed: July 2022

Cover Art By: Amit Paul

Published and Distributed By:
Lushena Books
607 Country Club Drive, Unit E
Bensenville, IL 60106
www.lushenabks.com

ISBN: 978-1-63923-464-6

CONTENTS

Preface

In my work "Shakti and Shākta" I outlined for the first time the principles of "Kundalī-Yoga" so much discussed in some quarters, but of which so little was known.

This work is a description and explanation in fuller detail of the Serpent Power (Kundalī Shakti), and the Yoga effected through it, a subject occupying a preeminent place in the Tantra Shāstra. It consists of a translation of two Sanskrit works published some years ago in the second volume of my series of Tantrik Texts, but hitherto untranslated. The first, entitled "Shatchakranirūpana" ("Description of and Investigation into the Six Bodily Centers"), has as its author the celebrated Tantrik Pūrnānanda Svāmī, a short note of whose life is given later. It forms the sixth chapter of his extensive and unpublished work on Tantrik Ritual entitled "Shrītattvachintāmani." This has been the subject of commentaries by Shangkara and Vishvanātha cited in Volume II. of the Tantrik Texts, and used in the making of the present translation.

The second text, called "Pādukā-Panchaka" ("Fivefold Footstool of the Guru"), deals with one of the Lotuses described in the larger work. To the translation of both works I have added some further explanatory notes of my own. As the works translated are of a highly recondite character, and by themselves unintelligible to the English reader, I have prefaced the translation by a general Introduction in which I have endeavored to give (within the limits both of a work of this kind and my knowledge) a description and explanation of this form of Yoga. I have also included some plates of the Centers, which have been drawn and painted according to the description of them as given in the first of these Sanskrit Texts.

It has not been possible in the Introduction to do more than give a general and summary statement of the principles upon which Yoga, and this particular form of it, rests. Those who wish to pursue the subject in greater detail are referred to my other published books on the Tantra Shāstra. In "Principles of Tantra" will be found general Introductions to the Shāstra and (in connection with the present subject) valuable chapters on Shakti and Mantras. In my recent work, "Shakti and Shākta" (the second edition of which is as I write reprinting), I have shortly summarized the teaching of the Shākta Tantras and their rituals. In my "Studies in the Mantra Shāstra," the first three parts of which have been reprinted from the "Vedānta Kesarī," in which they first appeared, will be found more detailed descriptions of such technical terms as Tattva, Causal Shaktis, Kalā, Nāda, Bindu, and so forth, which are referred to in the present book. Other works published by me on the

Tantra, including the "Wave of Bliss," will be found in the page of advertisements.

The following account of Pūrnānanda, the celebrated Tāntrika Sādhaka of Bengal, and author of the "Shatchakranirūpana," has been collected from the descendants of his eldest son, two of whom are connected with the work of the Varendra Research Society, Rajshahi, to whose Director, Sj. Akshaya Kumāra Maitra, and Secretary, Sj. Rādhā Govinda Baisāk, I am indebted for the following details:

Pūrnānanda was a Rahri Brāhmana of the Kashyapa Gotra, whose ancestors belonged to the village of Pakrashi, which has not as yet been identified. His seventh ancestor Anantāchārya is said to have migrated from Baranagara, in the district of Murshidabad, to Kaitali, in the district of Mymensingh. In his family were born two celebrated Tāntrika Sādhakas—namely, Sarvānanda and Pūrnānanda. The descendants of Sarvānanda reside at Mehar, while those of Pūrnānanda reside mostly in the district of Mymensingh. Little is known about the worldly life of Pūrnānanda, except that he bore the name of Jagadānanda, and copied a manuscript of the Vishnupurānam in the Shāka year A.D. 1448-1526. This manuscript, now in the possession of one of his descendants named Pandit Hari Kishore Bhattāchārya, of Kaitali, is still in a fair state of preservation. It was brought for inspection by Pandit Satis Chandra Siddhāntabhūshana of the Varendra Research Society. The colophon states that Jagadānanda Sharma wrote the Purāna in the Shāka year 1448.

This Jagadānanda assumed the name of Pūrnānanda when he obtained his Dīkshā (Initiation) from Brahmānanda and went to Kāmarūpa (Assam), in which province he is believed to have obtained his "Siddhi" or state of spiritual perfection in the Āshrama, which still goes by the name of Vashishthāshrama, situated at a distance of about seven miles from the town of Gauhati (Assam). Pūrnānanda never returned home, but led the life of a Paramahangsa and compiled several Tāntrika works, of which the Shritattvachintāmani, composed in the Shāka year A.D. 1499-1577, Shyāmārahasya, Shāktakrama, Tattvānandataranginī, and Yogasāra are known. His commentary on the Kālī-kakārakūta hymn is well known. The Shatchakranirūpana, here translated, is not, however, an independent work, but a part of the sixth Patala of the Shrītattvachintāmani. According to a genealogical table of the family of this Tāntrika Āchārya and Vīrāchāra Sādhaka, given by one of his descendants, Pūrnānanda is removed from his present descendants by about ten generations.

This work has been on hand some five years, but both the difficulties of the subject and those created by the war have delayed its publication. I had hoped to include some other plates of original paintings and drawings in my possession bearing on the subject, but present conditions do not allow of this, and I have therefore thought it better to publish the book as it stands rather than risk further delay.

ARTHUR AVALON.

RANCHI,
September 20, 1918.

"We pray to the Paradevatā united with Shiva, whose substance is the unmixed nectar of bliss, red like unto vermilion, the young flower of the hibiscus, and the sunset sky; who, having cleft Her way through the mass of sound issuing from the clashing and the dashing of the two winds in the midst of Sus*h*umnā, rises to that brilliant Energy which glitters with the luster of ten million lightnings. May She, Ku*n*dalinī, who quickly goes to and returns from Shiva, grant us the fruit of Yoga! She being awakened is the Cow of Plenty to Kaulas, and the Kalpa Creeper of all things desired for those who worship Her."—*Shāradā Tilaka*, xxv. 70.

The Six Centers and the Serpent Power

I. INTRODUCTION

The present works, Shatchakranirūpana ("Description of the Six Centers, or Chakras") and Pādukā Panchaka ("Fivefold Footstool"), deal with a particular form of Tāntrik Yoga named Kundalī Yoga, or, as some works call it, Bhūtashuddhi. These names refer to the Kundalinī Shakti, or Static Power in the human body by the arousing of which the Yoga is achieved, and to the purification of the elements of the body (Bhūtashuddhi) which takes place upon that event. This Yoga is effected by a process technically known as Shatchakrabheda, or piercing of the six Centers or Regions (Chakra) or Lotuses (Padma) of the body (which the work describes) by the agency of Kundalinī Shakti, which in order to give it an English name I have here called the Serpent Power.[1] Kundala means coiled. This Power is the Goddess (Devī) Kundalinī, or that which is coiled; for Her form is that of a coiled and sleeping serpent in the lowest bodily center, at the base of the spinal column, until by the means described She is aroused in that Yoga which is named after Her. Kundalinī is the Shabdabrahman—that is, Divine Cosmic Energy—in bodies (*v. post*). The Saptabhūmi, or seven regions (Loka),[2] are, as popularly understood, an exoteric presentment

---

[1] One of the names of this Devī is Bhujangī, or the Serpent.

[2] The seven "worlds" Bhūh, Bhuvah, Svah, Mahah, Jana, Tapah, Satya. See Introduction to my Mahānirvāna Tantra and "Wave of Bliss" (Comm. to v. 35). Lokas are what are seen (lokyante)—that is, attained—and are hence the fruits of Karma in the form of particular re-birth. Satyānanda's "Comm. on Īsha Up.," Mantra 2.

of the inner Tāntrik teaching regarding the seven centers.[3]

The Yoga is called Tāntrik for a twofold reason. It will be found mentioned in the Yoga Upanishads which refer to the Centers, or Chakras, and in some of the Purānas. The treatises on Hathayoga also deal with the subject. We find even similar notions in systems other than the Indian, from which possibly in some cases they have been borrowed. Thus, in the Risala-i-haq-numa, by Prince Mahomed Dara Shikoh,[4] a description is given of the three centers "Mother of Brain," or "Spherical heart" (Dil-i-muddawar); the "Cedar heart" (Dil-i-sanowbari); and the Dil-i-nilofari, or "Lily heart."[5] Other references may be found in the works of the Mahomedan Sufis. So some of the Sufi fraternities (as the Naqshbandi) are said[6] to have devised, or rather borrowed, from the Indian Yogis[7] the Kundalinī method as a means to realization.[8] I am told that correspondences are discoverable between the Indian (Asiatic) Shāstra and the American-Indian Māyā scripture of the Zunis called the Popul Vuh.[9] My informant tells me that their "air-tube" is the Sushumnā; their "twofold air-tube" the Nādīs Idā and Pinggalā. "Hurakan," or lightning, is Kundalinī, and the centers are depicted by animal glyphs. Similar notions have been reported to me as being held in the secret teaching of other communities. That the doctrine and practice should be widespread we might expect if it has a foundation on fact. This form of Yoga is, however, in particular associated with the Tantras or Āgamas, firstly, because these Scriptures are largely concerned therewith. In fact, such orderly descriptions in practical full detail as have been written are to be found chiefly in the Hathayoga works and Tantras which are the manuals, not only of Hindu worship, but of its occultism. Next, Yoga through action on the lower static center seems characteristic of the Tāntrik system, the adepts of which are the custodians of the practical knowledge whereby the general directions in the books may be practically applied. The system is of a Tāntrik character also in respect of its selection of the chief center of consciousness. Various people have in antiquity

---

[3] That is, the six Chakras and the upper cerebral center, or Sahasrāra. See as to Upanishads and Purānas, *post*, p. 39.

[4] "The Compass of Truth." The author was the eldest son of the Emperor Shah-i-Jehan, and died in A.D. 1659. Its teaching is alleged to be that of the secret doctrine of the "Apostle of God."

[5] Chapter I., on Alam-i-nasut: the physical plane, or what the Hindus call the Jāgrat state. Ed. Rai Bahadur Srisha Chandra Vasu.

[6] See "The Development of Metaphysics in Persia," by Shaikh Muhammad Iqbal, p. 110.

[7] Al-Biruni is said to have translated Patanjali's work, as also the Sāngkhya Sūtras, into Arabic at the beginning of the eleventh century.

[8] The author cited, however, says: "Such methods of contemplation are quite unislamic in character, and the higher Sufis do not attach any importance to them."

[9] A translation was, I am told, begun and not finished by the occultist James Pryse in *Lucifer*, the old Theosophical journal, which I have not seen.

assigned to various parts of the body the seat of the "soul" or life, such as the blood,[10] the heart, and the breath. Generally the brain was not so regarded. The Vaidik system posits the heart as the chief center of Consciousness—a relic of which notion we also still preserve in such phrases as "take it to heart" and to "learn by heart." Sādhaka, which is one of the five functions of Pitta,[11] and which is situated in the heart, indirectly assists in the performance of cognitive functions by keeping up the rhythmic cardiac contractions, and it has been suggested[12] that it was perhaps this view of the heart's construction which predisposed Indian physiologists to hold it to be the seat of cognition. According to the Tantras, however, the chief centers of consciousness are to be found in the Chakras of the cerebro-spinal system and in the upper brain (Sahasrāra), which they describe, though the heart is also recognized as a seat of the Jīvātmā, or embodied spirit, in its aspect as Prāna.[13] It is for the reasons mentioned that the first verse of the Shatchakranirūpana here translated speaks of the Yoga which is to be achieved "*according to the Tantras*" (Tantrānusāre*na*)—that is, as Kālīcharana its Commentator says, "following the authority of the Tantras."

This Yoga has been widely affirmed. The following review does not profess to be exhaustive, for the literature relating to Kundalī and Layayoga is very great, but includes merely a short reference to some of the Upanishads and Purānas which have come under my notice, and of which I kept a note, whilst engaged in this work.[14] It will, however, clearly establish that this doctrine concerning the Chakras, or portions of it, is to be found in other Shāstras than the Tantras, though the references in some cases are so curt that it is not always possible to say whether they are dealing with the matter in the same Yoga-sense as the work here translated or as forms of worship (Upāsanā). It is to be noted in this connection that Bhūtashuddhi is a rite which is considered as a necessary preliminary to the worship of a Deva.[15] It is obvious that if we understand the Bhūtashuddhi to here mean the Yoga practice described, then, with the exception of the Yogī expert in this Yoga, no one would be competent for worship at all. For it is only the

---

[10] *Cf.* the Biblical saying, "The blood is the life."

[11] See p. 11 of the Introduction to third volume of my Tāntrik Texts (Prapanchasāra Tantra).

[12] Kavirāja Kunjalāla Bhishagratna in his edition of the Sushruta Sanghitā. Another explanation, however, may be given—namely, that during man's history the importance of the various perceptive centers has in fact varied.

[13] According to some Indian views, the brain is the center of the mind and senses, and the heart that of life. Charaka says that the heart is the root from which spring all other parts of the body, and is the center of some of the functions or organs. According to Sushruta, the heart is the seat of all sensations.

[14] There are many others. Some references kindly supplied to me by Mahāmahopadhyāya Ādityarām Bhattāchāryya arrived too late for insertion.

[15] See Taranga I. of the Mantramahodadhi: Devārchā-yogyatā prāptyai bhūtashuddhing samācharet.

accomplished (Siddha) Yogī who can really take Kundalinī to the Sahasrāra. In the ordinary daily Bhūtashuddhi, therefore, the process is purely a mental or imaginary one, and therefore forms part of Upāsanā, and not Yoga. Further, as a form of worship the Sādhaka may, and does, adore his Ishtadevatā in various parts of his body. This, again, is a part of Upāsanā. Some of the Shāstras however, next mentioned, clearly refer to the Yoga process, and others appear to do so.

In what are called the earliest Upanishads,[16] mention is made of certain matters which are more explicitly described in such as are said by Western orientalists to be of later date. Thus, we find reference to the four states of consciousness, waking, and so forth; the four sheaths; and to the cavity of the heart as a "soul" center.

As already stated, in the Indian schools the heart was considered to be the seat of the waking consciousness. The heart expands during waking, and contracts in sleep. Into it during dreaming sleep (Svapna) the external senses are withdrawn, though the representative faculty is awake; until in dreamless sleep (Sushupti) it also is withdrawn. Reference is also made to the 72,000 Nādīs; the entry and exit of the Prāna through the Brahmarandhra (above the foramen of Monro and the middle commissure); and "up-breathing" through one of these Nādīs. These to some extent probably involve the acceptance of other elements of doctrine not expressly stated. Thus, the reference to the Brahmarandhra and the "one nerve" imply the cerebro-spinal axis with its Sushumnā, through which alone the Prāna passes to the Brahmarandhra; for which reason, apparently, the Sushumnā itself is referred to in the Shivasanghitā as the Brahmarandhra. Liberation is finally affected by "knowledge," which, as the ancient Aitareya Āranyaka says,[17] "is Brahman." "He, Vāmadeva, by his knowing self having left the world and having attained all delights in the world of heaven, became immortal."

The Hangsa Upanishad[18] opens with the statement that the knowledge therein contained should be communicated only to the Brahmachārī of peaceful mind (Shānta), self-controlled (Dānta), and devoted to the Guru (Gurubhakta). Nārāyana the Commentator, who cites amongst other works the Tantrik Compendium the Shāradā Tilaka, describes himself as "one whose sole support is Shruti"[19] (Nārāyanena shrutimātropajīvinā). The Upanishad (§ 4) mentions by their names the six Chakras, as also the method of raising of Vāyu from the Mūlādhāra—that is, the Kundalīnī Yoga. The Hangsa (that is, Jīva)

---

[16] For some references from the older Upanishads, see an article by Professor Rhys Davids in J.R.A.S., p. 71 (January, 1899), "Theory of Soul in Upanishads." See also Vol. I. of my "Principles of Tantra," referring amongst others to Prashna Upanishad, III. 6, 7.

[17] P. 236 (edited by Arthur Berriedale Keith) of "Anecdota Oxoniensia."

[18] Ānandāshrama Edition, Vol. XXIX., p. 593.

[19] The Tantra, like every other Indian Shāstra, claims to be based on Veda.

is stated to be in the eight-petalled lotus below Anāhata[20] (§ 7) where the Ishtadevatā is worshipped. There are eight petals, with which are associated certain Vrittis. With the Eastern petal is associated virtuous inclination (Punye mati); with the South-Eastern, sleep (Nidrā) and laziness (Ālasya); with the Southern, badness or cruelty (Krūra mati); with the South-Western, sinful inclination (Pāpe manīshā); with the Western, various inferior or bad qualities (Krīdā); with the North-Western, intention in movement or action (Gamanādau buddhi); with the Northern, attachment and pleasurable contentment (Rati and Prīti); and with the North-Eastern petal, manual appropriation of things (Dravyagrahana).[21] In the center of this lotus is dispassion (Vairāgya). In the filaments is the waking state (Jāgrad-avasthā); in the pericarp the sleeping state (Svapna); in the stalk the state of dreamless slumber (Sushupti). Above the lotus is "the place without support" (Nirālamba pradesha), which is the Turīya state. The Commentator Nārāyana says that the Vritti of the petals are given in the Adhyātmaviveka which assigns them to the various lotuses. In the passage cited from the Hangsopanishad, they, or a number of these, appear to be collected in the center of meditation upon the Ishtadevatā. In § 9 ten kinds of sound (Nāda) are mentioned which have definite physical effects, such as perspiration, shaking, and the like, and by the practice of the tenth kind of Nāda the Brahmapada is said to be attained.

The Brahma Upanishad[22] mentions in v. 2 the navel (Nābhi), heart (Hridayam), throat (Kantham), and head (Mūrdhā), as places (Sthāna) "where the four quarters of the Brahman shine." The Commentator Nārāyana says that the Brahmopanishad, by the mention of these four, indicates that they are the centers from which the Brahman may (according to the method there prescribed) be attained.[23] Reference is made to the lotuses at these four places, and the mind is spoken of as the "tenth door," the other nine apertures being the eyes, ears, nostrils, and so forth.

The Dhyānabindu Upanishad[24] refers to the hearing of the Anāhata sounds by the Yogī (v. 3). The Upanishad directs that with Pūraka meditation should be done in the navel on the Great Powerful One (Mahāvīra) with four arms and of the color of the hemp flower (*i.e.*, Vishnu); with Kumbhaka meditate in the heart on the red Brahmā seated on a lotus; and with Rechaka think of the three-eyed one (Rudra)

[20] This lotus is commonly confused with the Anāhata. The latter is a Chakra in the spinal column; the eight-petalled lotus is in the region of the heart (Hrid) in the body.

[21] Lit., "taking of things." The translation of this and some of the other Vrittis is tentative. It is not easy in every case to understand the precise meaning or to find an English equivalent.

[22] Ānandāshrama Edition, Vol. XXIX., p. 325.

[23] It will be observed that the two lower Tāmasic centers are not here mentioned.

[24] *Ib.*, p. 262.

in the forehead. The lowest of these lotuses has eight petals; the second has its head downwards; and the third, which is compounded of all the Devatās (Sarvadevamaya), is like a plantain flower (vv. 9-12). In v. 13, meditation is directed on a hundred lotuses with a hundred petals each, and then on Sun, Moon, and Fire. It is Ātmā which rouses the lotus, and, taking the Bīja from it, goes to Moon, Fire, and Sun.

The Amritanāda Upanishad[25] refers to the five elements, and above them Arddhamātrā—that is, Ājnā (vv. 30, 31). The elements here are those in the Chakras, for v. 26 speaks of the heart entrance as the aerial entrance (for the Vāyu Tattva is here). Above this, it is said, is the gate of liberation (Mokshadvāra). It is stated in v. 25 that Prāna and Manas go along the way the Yogī sees (Pashyati), which the Commentator says refers to the way Prāna enters (and departs from) Mūlādhāra, and so forth. He also gives some Hatha processes.

The Kshurikā Upanishad[26] speaks of the 72,000 Nādis, of Idā and Pingalā, and Sushumnā (vv. 14, 15). All these, with the exception of Sushumnā, can "be severed by Dhyāna Yoga" (*ib.*). Verse 8 directs the Sādhaka "to get into the white and very subtle Nāda (*Quære* Nādī) and to drive Prāna Vāyu through it"; and Pūraka, Rechaka, Kumbhaka, and Hatha processes are referred to. The Commentator Nārāyana, on v. 8, remarks that Kundalī should be heated by the internal fire and then placed inside the Brahmanādī, for which purpose the Jālandhara Bandha should be employed.

The Nrisinghapūrvvatāpanīya Upanishad[27] in Ch. V., v. 2, speaks of the Sudarshana (which is apparently here the Mūlādhāra) changing into lotuses of six, eight, twelve, sixteen, and thirty-two petals respectively. This corresponds with the number of petals as given in this work except as to the second. For, taking this to be the Svādhishthāna, the second lotus should be one of ten petals. Apparently this divergence is due to the fact that this is the number of letters in the Mantra assigned to this lotus. For in the six-petalled lotus is the six-lettered Mantra of Sudarshana; in the eight-petalled lotus the eight-lettered Mantra of Nārāyana; and in the twelve-petalled lotus the twelve-lettered Mantra of Vāsudeva. As is the case ordinarily, in the sixteen-petalled lotus are the sixteen Kalās (here vowels) sounded with Bindu or Anusvāra. The thirty-two-petalled lotus (Ājnā) is really two-petalled because there are two Mantras here (each of sixteen letters) of Nrisingha and His Shakti.

The sixth chapter of the Maitrî Upanishad[28] speaks of the Nādīs; and in particular of the Sushumnā; the piercing of the Mandalas Sun, Moon, and Fire (each of these being within the other, Sattva in Fire,

[25] *Op. cit.*, 43. The Amritabindu Upanishad at p. 71 deals generally with Yoga.
[26] *Ib.*, Vol. XXIX., p. 145.
[27] Ānandāshrama Edition, Vol. XXX., p. 61.
[28] Vol. XXIX. of same edition, p. 345; see pp. 441, 450, 451, 458, and 460.

and in Sattva Achyuta); and of Amanā, which is another name for Unmanī.

Both the Yogatattva Upanishad[29] and Yogashikhā Upanishad[30] refer to Hathayoga, and the latter speaks of the closing of the "inner door," the opening of the gateway of Sushumnā (that is, by Kundalī entering the Brahmadvāra), and the piercing of the Sun. The Rāmatāpanī Upanishad[31] refers to various Yoga and Tantrik processes, such as Āsana, Dvārapūjā, Pīthapūjā, and expressly mentions Bhūtashuddhi, which, as above explained, is the purification of the elements in the Chakras, either as an imaginative, or real process by the aid of Kundalinī.

I have already cited in the Notes numerous passages on this Yoga from the Shāndilya Upanishad of the Atharvaveda, the Varāha and Yogakundalī Upanishads of the Krishna Yajurveda, the Mandalabrāhmana Upanishad of the Shukla Yajurveda, and the Nādabindu Upanishad of the Rigveda.[32]

The great Devībhāgavata Purāna (VII. 35, XI. 8) mentions in a full account the six Chakras or Lotuses; the rousing of Kundalī (who is called the Paradevatā) in the Mūlādhāra by the manner here described, uniting Jīva therewith by the Hangsa Mantra; Bhūtashuddhi; the dissolution of the gross Tattvas into the subtle Tattvas, ending with Mahat in Prakriti, Māyā in Ātmā. The Dharāmandala is mentioned, and it and the other Mandalas are described in the manner here stated. The Bījas of Prithivī and other Tattvas are given. Allusion is also made to the destruction of the "man of sin" (Pāpapurusha), in terms similar to those to be found in the Mahānirvāna and other Tantras. A remarkable Dhyāna of Prānashakti is to be found in this chapter, which reads very much like another which is given in the Prapanchasāra Tantra.[33]

Lingga Purāna, Part I., Ch. LXXV., mentions the Chakras with their different petals, the names of which are given by the Commentator. Shiva is Nirguna, it says, but for the benefit of men He resides in the body with Umā, and Yogīs meditate upon Him in the different lotuses.

Chapter XXIII. of the Agni Purāna, which is replete with Tantrik rituals, magic, and Mantras, also refers to the Bhūtashuddhi rite wherein, after meditation with the respective Bīja Mantras on the navel, heart, and Ājnā centers, the body of the Sādhaka is refreshed by the flow of nectar.

Finally, an adverse critic of this Yoga whom I cite later invokes the

---

29 Same edition, Vol. XXIX., p. 477.

30 *Ib.*, p. 483; and as to the passage of Kundalī through the Brahmadvāra, see p. 485.

31 *Ib.*, p. 520.

32 These Yoga Upanishads have been recently translated as part of "Thirty Minor Upanishads," by K. Nārāyanasvāmi Aiyar (Theosophical Society of Madras, 1914).

33 See Ch. XXXV., Vol. III., of my "Tantrik Texts."

authority of the great Shangkara, though in fact, if tradition be correct, it is against him. Shangkara, in whose Maths may be found the great Tantrik Yantra called the Shrīchakra, says in his Commentary on vv. 9 and 10 of Ch. VIII. of the Bhagavadgīta: "First the heart lotus (Anāhata) is brought under control. Then, by conquering Bhūmi (Mūlādhāra, etc.) and by the upward going Nādī (Sushumnā), after having placed Prāna between the two eyebrows (see v. 38, Shatchakranirūpana), the Yogī reaches the lustrous light-giving Purusha." On this the Tīkā of Ānandagiri runs: "By the Sushumnā Nādī between Idā and Pinggalā. The throat is reached by the same way—the space between the eyebrows. By conquering earth (Bhūmi) is meant the process by which the five Bhūtas are controlled." Shrīdhara Svāmī says: "By the power of Yoga (Yogabala) Prāna must be led along the Sushumnā." And Madhusūdana Sarasvatī says: "The upward-going Nādī is Sushumnā, and the conquest of Bhūmi and the rest is done by following the path indicated by the Guru; and by the space between the eyebrows is meant the Ājnā chakra. By placing Prāna there, it passes out by the Brahmarandhra, and the Jīva becomes one with the Purusha." The famous hymn called Ānandalahari ("Wave of Bliss"), which is universally ascribed to Shangkara, deals with this Yoga (Shatchakrabheda); and in the thirteenth chapter of Vidyāranya's Shangkaravijaya the six lotuses are mentioned, as also the fruit to be gained by worshipping the Devatā in each Chakra.[34]

Pandit R. Ananta Shāstrī says:[35]

"Many a great man has successfully worked the Kundalinī to the Sahasrāra, and effected her union with the Sat and Chit. Of these stands foremost the great and far-famed Shangkarāchārya, a humble pupil of one of the students of Gaudapādāchārya, the author of the well-known 'Subhagodaya' (52 slokas). Having well acquainted himself with the principles contained in this work, Shrī Shangkarāchārya received special instructions based upon the personal experience of his Guru. And adding his own personal experience to the above advantages, he composed his famous work on the Mantra-shāstra, consisting of 100 slokas; the first forty-one of these forming the 'Ānanda-Laharī,' and the rest forming the 'Saundarya-Laharī'; the latter apostrophizes the Devī as a being who is beauteous from head to foot.

"'Ānanda-Laharī' may be said to contain the quintessence of the Samayāchāra. The work is all the more valuable because the author teaches it from personal experience. Lengthy commentaries are written on almost every syllable of the text. The value attached to the work may be adequately understood by the following theory. Some hold that

---

[34] See also Ānandagiri's Shangkaravijaya and Mādhava's Shangkaravijaya (Ch. XI.; see also *ib.* where Shrīchakra is mentioned).

[35] Ānandalaharī, 14. I have translated this hymn under the title "Wave of Bliss."

Shiva is the real author of 'Ānanda-Laharī,' and not Shangkarāchārya, who was but a Mantra-drashtā or Rishi—*i.e.*, one who realized the process and gave it to the world. No less than thirty-and-six commentaries on this work are now extant. Among them we find one written by our great Appaya Dīkshita. The commentaries are not entirely different, but each has its own peculiar views and theories.

"As for the text of 'Ānanda-Laharī,' it contains forty-and-one shlokas. According to some commentators, the shlokas are 35 in number; some recognize only 30, and according to Suddhāvidyotinī and others only the following shlokas constitute the text of 'Ānanda-Laharī': 1-2, 8-9, 10-11, 14-21, 26-27, 31-41. In my opinion, also, the last statement seems to be correct, as the other shlokas treat only of Prayogas (applications of Mantras) for worldly purposes.[36] Only a few of these Prayogas are recognized by all the commentators; while the rest are passed over as being entirely Karmic.

"As has been remarked already, 'Ānanda-Laharī' is but an enlargement of the work called Subhagodaya by Gaudapāda, who is the Guru of the author's Guru. That work gives only the main points, without any of the characteristic admixture of illustrations, etc., above noticed.

"Of all the commentaries on 'Ānanda-Laharī' Lakshmīdhara's seems to be the most recent; yet in spite of this it is the most popular, and with reason, too. Other commentaries advocate this or that aspect of the various philosophical schools; but Lakshmīdhara collates some of the views of others, and records them side by side with his own. His commentary is in this way the most elaborate. He sides with no party;[37] his views are broad and liberal. All schools of philosophers are represented in his commentaries. Lakshmīdhara has also commented on many other works on Mantrashāstra, and is consequently of much high repute. So his commentaries are as valuable to both 'Ānanda-Laharī' and 'Saundarya-Laharī' as Sāyana's are to the Vedas.

"Lakshmīdhara seems to have been an inhabitant of Southern India; the observances and customs he describes all point to this conclusion; the illustrations he adduces smack invariably of the South, and even to this day his views are more followed in the South than in the North. He has also written an elaborate commentary on Gaudapāda's Subhagodaya. The references to that in the commentary to this work, and the commentator's apology here and there for repeating what he has written on the former occasion, lead to the inference that the author had for his life-work the commentary on the original book.

---

[36] Thus, vv. 13, 18, 19 are said to treat of Madana-prayoga—that is, application for the third purushārtha or Kāma (desire).

[37] He seems to be very adverse to the Kaula School, and if his views are accurately reproduced by the Pandit he is not always correct as to their teaching.—A. A.

"Achyutānanda's commentaries are in Bengali characters, and are followed as authority in Bengal even to this day.[38] Various commentaries are followed in various places, but few have risen to be universally accepted.

"There are only three or four works treating of Prayoga (application); I have had access to all of them. But here I have followed only one of them, as being the most prominent and important. It comes from an ancient family in Conjeeveram. It contains 100 slokas. The Yantras (figures) for the Mantras contained in the shlokas, the different postures of the worshipper, and similar prescriptions, are clearly described in it to the minutest detail.

"There seems to be some mystical connection between each shloka and its Bijākshara.[39] But it is not intelligible, nor has any of the Prayoga Kartas[40] explained the same.

"The following is a list of commentaries written upon 'Ānanda-Laharī'; some of them include 'Saundarya-Laharī' also:

"1. 'Manoramā,' a Commentary. 2. A Commentary by Appaya Dīkshita (Tanjore Palace Library). 3. 'Vishnupakshī.' Perhaps this may be the same as No. 14 given below. 4. By Kavirājasharman—about 3,000 granthas (Deccan College Library). 5. 'Manjubhūshanī,' by Krishnāchārya, the son of Vallabhāchārya—shlokas about 1,700. He says in his Introduction that Shrī Shankarāchārya praised the Brahmashakti called Kundalinī when he was meditating on the banks of the Ganges. He gives the purport of this work in his first shloka: 'I praise constantly the Kundalinī, who creates innumerable worlds continuously, though She is like a filament of the lotus, and who resides at the root of the tree (Mūlādhāra) to be roused and led (to Sahasrāra).' This is popular in the Bengal Presidency. 6. Another Commentary, called 'Saubhāgyavardhanī,' by Kaivalyāsharma. The Adyar Library has a copy of it. This is popular throughout India, so we can get as many MSS. of the same as we require from different places. It contains about 2,000 granthas. 7. By Keshavabhatta. 8. 'Tattvadīpikā,' by Gangahari, a small commentary based on Tantrashāstra. 9. By Gangādhara. 10. By Gopīramanatarka-pravachana—granthas about 1,400. Seems to be of recent origin. 11. Gaurīkāntasārvabhaumabhattāchārya—granthas about 1,300. Of recent origin. 12. By Jagadīsha. 13. By Jagannātha Panchānana. 14. By Narasimha—granthas 1,500. The chief peculiarity of this commentary is that it explains the text in two different ways, each shloka being applicable to Devī and Vishnu at the same time. Though some commentators have given different meanings to some of the verses, yet

[38] I have followed this commentary also in my "Wave of Bliss."—A. A.

[39] Bīja or root-mantra.—A. A.

[40] Those writers who deal with the practical application.—A. A.

all of them apply to the different aspects of Devī alone, and not to the different Devatās. 15. 'Bhāvārthadīpa,' by Brahmānanda[41]—granthas about 1,700. 16. By Mallabhatta. 17. By Mahādevavidyāvāgīsha. 18. By Mādhavavaidya (Deccan College Library). 19. By Rāmachandra—granthas about 3,000 (Deccan College Library). 20. By Rāmanandatīrtha. 21. Lakshmīdhara's; which is well known to the public, and needs no comment. This has been brought out excellently in Deva Nāgara type by the Mysore Government lately. 22. By Vīshvambhara. 23. By Shrīkanthabhatta. 24. By Rāma Sūri. 25. By Dindima (Adyar Library). 26. By Rāmachandra Misra—granthas about 1,000 (Deccan College Library). 27. By Achyutānanda (printed in Bengali characters). 28. Sadāshiva (Government Oriental Library, Madras). 29. Another nameless Commentary (Government Oriental Library, Madras). 30. By Shrīrangadāsa. 31. By Govinda Tarkavāgīsha Bhattāchārya—granthas 600. He seems to give the Yantra also for each verse. Further, he says that the god Mahādeva specially incarnated as Shangkarāchārya to promulgate the science of Shrīvidyā. 32. Sudhāvidyotinī, by the son of Pravarasena. This commentator says that the author of this famous hymn was his father, Pravarasena, Prince of the Dramidas. He tells us a story in connection with Pravarasena's birth which is very peculiar. As he was born in an inauspicious hour, Dramida, the father of Pravarasena, in consultation with his wise Minister, by name Suka, threw him out in the forest, lest he (the father) should lose his kingdom. . . . The child praised Devī by this hymn, and, pleased with it, the Devī fostered and took care of him in the forest. The story ends by saying that the boy returned to his father's dominion and became King. By his command, his son, the present commentator, wrote Sudhāvidyotinī, after being fully initiated into this mystic Shāstra, Shrīvidyā. The account, however, appears to be rather fantastic. This MS. I got from South Malabar with much difficulty. It gives the esoteric meaning of the verses in 'Ānanda-Laharī,' and seems to be a valuable relic of occult literature. 33. The book of Yantras with Prayoga. This is very rare and important.

"Besides the above commentaries, we do not know how many more commentaries there are upon this hymn."

The celebrity of "Ānandalaharī" and the great number of commentaries upon it are proof of the widespread and authoritative character of the Yoga here described.

To conclude with the words of the Commentator on the Trishatī: "It is *well known in Yoga-Shāstras* that nectar (Amrita) is in the head of all breathing creatures (Prānī), and that on Kundalī going there by the

[41] This is the celebrated Bengali Paramahangsa guru of Pūrnānanda Svāmī, author of the Shatchakranirupana. Brahmānanda was author of the celebrated Shāktānanda taranginī.—A. A.

Yoga-path which is moistened by the current of that nectar Yogins become like Īshvara."[42]

The Chakras, however, mentioned are not always those of the body above stated, as would appear from the following account, which, it will be observed, is peculiar, and which is taken from the Shatchakra Upanishad of the Atharvaveda.[43] Apparently reference is here made to cosmic centers in the worship of the Vishnu Avatāra called Nrisingha.

"Om. The Devas, coming to Satyaloka, thus spoke to Prajāpati, saying, 'Tell us of the Nārasingha[44] Chakra' (to which he replied). There are six Nārasingha Chakras. The first and second have each four spokes; the third, five; the fourth, six; the fifth, seven; and the sixth, eight spokes. These six are the Nārasingha Chakras. Now, what are their names (that is what you ask). They are Āchakra,[45] Suchakra,[46] Mahāchakra,[47] Sakalaloka-rakshanachakra,[48] Dyuchakra,[49] Asurāntaka-chakra.[50] These are their respective names, [1]

"Now, what are the three circles (Balaya)? These are inner, middle, and outer.[51] The first is Bīja;[52] the second, Nārasingha-gāyatrī;[53] and the third, or outer, is Mantra. Now, what is the inner circle? There are six such (for each Chakra has one); these are the Nārasingha, Mahālākshmya, Sārasvata, Kāmadeva, Pranava, Krodhadaivata (Bījas), respectively.[54] These are the six interior circles of the six Nārasingha Chakras. [2]

"Now, what is the middle circle? There are six such. To each of these belong Nārasinghāya, Vidmahe, Vajranakhāya, Dhīmahi, Tannah, Singhahprachodayāt, respectively.[55] These are the six circles of the six

---

[42] Sarvveshāng prāninārng shirasi amritam asti iti yogamārgena kundalinīgamane tatratya tatpravāhāplutena yoginām Īshvarasāmyam jāyate iti yogashāstreshu prasiddham (Comm. v. 1).

[43] Bibliotheca Indica, ed. Asiatic Society (1871). The notes are from the Commentary of Nārāyana.

[44] The man-lion incarnation of Vishnu.

[45] Ānandātmaka; in the self of Ānanda (bliss).

[46] Good, perfect.

[47] Lustrous (Tejomaya).

[48] The Chakra which by the Shaktis of Jnāna and Kriyā protects all regions (Loka).

[49] The Chakra of the path reached by Yoga.

[50] The Chakra which is the death of all Asuras, or liars.

[51] That is, each Chakra has three divisions—inner, middle, and outer; or Bīja, Nārasingha Gāyatrī, Mantra.

[52] The root mantra, which in this case are those given in the next note but one.

[53] That is, the Mantra; Nārasinghāya vidmahe vajranakhāya dhīmahi tanna*h* singha*h* prachodayāt. (May we contemplate on Narasingha, may we meditate on his Vajra-like claws. May that Man-lion direct us.)

[54] That is, the following Bījas: Kshaung (in Āchakra); Shrīng, His Shakti (in Suchakra); Aing (in Mahāchakra); Klīng (in Sakalalokara*kshan*a chakra); Om (in Dyuchakra); and Hūng (in Asurāntakachakra).

[55] That is, to each of them is assigned the several parts of the Nārasingha-gāyatrī above mentioned.

Nārasingha Chakras. Now, what are the six outer circles? The first is Ānandātmā or Āchakra; the second is Priyātmā or Suchakra; the third is Jyotirātmā or Mahāchakra; the fourth is Māyātmā or Sakala-loka-rakshana Chakra; the fifth is Yogātmā or Dyuchakra; and the sixth is Samāptātmā or Asurāntakachakra. These are the six outer circles of the six Nārasingha Chakras.[56] [3]

"Now, where should these be placed?[57] Let the first be placed in the heart;[58] the second in the head;[59] the third at the site of the crown-lock[60] (Shikhāyām); the fourth all over the body;[61] the fifth in all the eyes[62] (Sarveshu netreshu); and the sixth in all the regions[63] (Sarveshu desheshu). [4]

"He who does Nyāsa of these Nārasingha Chakras on two limbs becomes skilled in Anushtubh,[64] attains the favor of Lord Nrisingha, success in all regions and amongst all beings, and (at the end) liberation (Kaivalya). Therefore should this Nyāsa be done. This Nyāsa purifies. By this one is made perfect in worship, is pious, and pleases Nārasingha. By the omission thereof, on the other hand, the favor of Nrisingha is not gained nor is strength, worship, nor piety generated. [5]

"He who reads this becomes versed in all Vedas, gains capacity to officiate as priest at all sacrifices, becomes like one who has bathed in all places of pilgrimage, an adept in all Mantras, and pure both within and without. He becomes the destroyer of all Rākshasas, Bhūtas, Pishāchas, Shākinīs, Pretas, and Vetālas.[65] He becomes freed of all fear; therefore should it not be spoken of to an unbeliever."[66] [6]

Notwithstanding the universal acceptance of this Yoga, it has not escaped some modern criticism. The following passage in inverted commas is a summary[67] of that passed by an English-educated Hindu,[68]

---

[56] The Ātmā as bliss, love, light or energy, Māyā, Yoga, and the concluding Chakra which is the destruction of all Asuras.

[57] That is, how should Nyāsa be done? This is explained in the text and following notes where the Nyāsa is given.

[58] Kshaung Nārasinghāya āchakrāya ānandātmane svāhā hridayāya nama*h*.

[59] Shrīng vidmahe suchakrāya priyātmane svāhā shirase svāhā.

[60] Aing vajranakhāya mahāchakrāya jyotirātmane svāhā shikhāyai vas*hat*.

[61] Klīng dhīmahi sakala-loka-rakshana-chakrāya māyātmane svāhā kavachāya hūng.

[62] Ong tanno dyuchakrāya yogātmane svāhā netratrayāya vaushat.

[63] Haung nrisinghah prachodayāt asurāntaka-chakrāya satyātmane svāhā astrāya phat.

[64] That is, he becomes capable of speech—a poet. He knows the beginning and end of all things and able to explain all things.

[65] Various forms of terrifying and malignant spirits.

[66] That is, not to one who is not competent (Adhikārī) to receive this knowledge. Here ends the Ātharva*n*īya S*hat*chakropani*sh*at.

[67] If my summary, taken from the Bengalī, points the pious acerbities of the original the critic would, I am sure, not complain.

formerly a lawyer and now a Guru, from one of whose disciples I received it. It was elicited by the gift of the Sanskrit text of the works here translated:

"Yoga as a means to liberation is attained by entry through the doors of Jnāna (Knowledge) and Karma (Action). Yoga is doubtless bliss, for it is the union of the Jīvātmā with the Brahman who is Bliss (Ānanda). But there are various forms of Bliss. There is, for instance, physical bliss, gross or subtle as it may be. It is a mistake to suppose that because a method of Yoga procures bliss it therefore secures liberation. In order that we be liberated we must secure that particular Bliss which is the Brahman. Some centuries ago, however, a band of Atheists (*i.e.*, the Buddhists) discovered the doctrine of the Void (Shūnyavāda), and by a false display of a new kind of Nirvāna Mukti locked up these two doors which gave entry to liberation. To-day these doors are secured by three padlocks. The first is the doctrine that by faith one attains Krishna, but where there is argument (Tarka) He is far away. The second is the error of the Brahmos, who in Western fashion think that they can control the formless, changeless Brahman by shutting their eyes in church and repeating that He is the merciful, loving Father who is ever occupied with our good, and that if He be flattered He will be pleased; for worship (Upāsanā) is flattery. The third is the opinion of those to whom all religious acts are nothing but superstition; to whom self-interest is the only good, and whose pleasure it is to throw dust into the eyes of others and secure the praise of those whom they have thus blinded. Vishnu, in order to cause the disappearance of the Vedas in the Kali age, manifested as the atheist Buddha, and allowed various false doctrines, such as that of the Arhatas, to be proclaimed. Rudra was affected by the sin of destroying the head of Brahmā. Then he began to dance, and a number of Uchchhishta (or low maglinant) Rudras whose deeds are never good issued from His body. Vishnu and Shiva asked each other, 'Can we do these people any good?' Their partial manifestations then promulgated Shāstras opposed to the Vedas, fitted for the atheistic bent of their minds, that they might haply thereby rise through them to higher things. God fools the wicked with such Scriptures. We must now, however, discriminate between Shāstras. It is not because it is said in Sanskrit 'Shiva says' (Shiva uvācha) that we should accept all which follows this announcement. All that is opposed to Veda and Smriti must be rejected. Of the enemies of the Vedas[69] for whom such

[68] It is always important to record such a fact, for it generally influences the outlook on things. In some cases the mind is so Westernized that it is unable to correctly appreciate ancient Indian ideas.

[69] This no Tantrik would admit. He would say that it is ignorance (Avidyā) which sees any differences between Veda and Āgama. The critic re-echoes some Western criticisms.

Shāstras were designed, some became Vaishnavas, and other Shaivas. One of such Scriptures was the Tantra with a materialistic Yoga system called Shatchakra-Sādhana, which is nothing but a trickery on the part of the professional Gurus, who have not hesitated also to promulgate forged scriptures. 'The very mention of Tantrik Shāstra fills us with shame.' The Shatchakra Sādhana is a mere obstruction to spiritual advancement. The bliss which is said to be attained by leading Kundalī to the Sahasrāra is not denied, since it is affirmed by those who say they have experienced it. But this Bliss (Ānanda) is merely a momentary superior kind of physical Bliss which disappears with the body, and not the Bliss which is Brahman and liberation. Moksha is not to be got by entering the Sahasrāra, but in leaving it by piercing the Brahmarandhra and becoming bodiless.[70]

"The Tantrik seeks to remain in the body, and thus to obtain liberation cheaply, just as the Brahmos and Members of the Ārya Samāja have become Brahmajnānīs (knowers of the Brahman) at a cheap price. Nectar, too, is cheap with the Tantriks. But what is cheap is always worthless, and this shows itself when one attempts to earn some fruit from one's endeavors. 'And yet all men are attracted when they hear of Shatchakra.' 'Many are so steeped in Tantrik faith that they can find nothing wrong with its Shāstras.' And the Hindu nowadays has been put in such a maze by his Tantrik Gurus that he does not know what he wants. For centuries he has been accustomed to the Tantrik Dharma,[71] and his eyes are therefore not clear enough to see that it is as truly unacceptable to a Hindu as it is to a Mussalman. In fact, these persons (for whose benefit the Guru makes these remarks) are full of Mlechchhatā,[72] though, after all, it must be admitted to be some advance for such a creature as a Mlechha to adhere even to Tantrik doctrine. For bad as it is it is better than nothing at all. All the same, the Gurus delude them with their fascinating talk about Shatchakra. Like a lot of the present-day advertisers, they offer to show their so-called 'Lotuses' to those who will join them. Men are sent to collect people to bring them to a Dīkshāguru (initiator). In this respect

---

[70] It is true that complete Mukti or Kaivalya is bodiless (Videha). But there is a Mukti in which the Yogī retains his body (Jīvanmukti). In truth, there is no "leaving," for Ātmā, as Shangkara says, does not come and go.

[71] This, at any rate, attests its wide pervasiveness.

[72] This is a contemptuous term which has descended from the days when the stranger was looked on as an object of enmity or contempt. Just as the Greeks and Chinese called anyone not a Greek or a Chinese a "barbarian," so Hindus of the Exoteric School call all non-Hindus, whether aboriginal tribes or cultivated foreigners, Mlechhas. Mlechhatā is the state of being a Mlechha. It is to the credit of the Shākta Tantra that it does not encourage such narrow ideas.

the Tantriks act just like coolie recruiters for the tea-gardens.[73] The Tantrik says there are really 'Lotuses' there; but if the Lotuses are really there, why are we not told how we may see them?[74] And there also are supposed to be Devatās, Dākinīs, Yoginīs, 'all ready at every moment for inspection.'[75] And, then, how material it all is! They speak of a Parashiva above Shiva, as if there was more than one Brahman. And, then, the nectar is said to be of the color of lac. Well, if so, it is a gross (Sthūla) and perceptible thing; and as a doctor can then squeeze it out there is no need for a Guru.[76] In short, the Tantrik Shatchakra is nothing but 'a sweet in the hands of a child.' A child who is wayward is given a sweet to keep him quiet. But if he has sense enough to know that the sweet is given to distract him, he throws it away, and finds the key to the locked doors of Yoga, called Karma and Jnāna. This process of Yoga was expelled from Hindu society centuries ago. For nearly 2,500 years ago Shangkara,[77] when destroying atheism, exterminated also Shatchakrayoga. (When Shangkara disputed with the Kāpālika Krakacha, the latter invoked to his aid the fierce form of Shiva called Bhairava. But on Shangkara's worshipping the God, the latter said to Krakacha, 'Thy time has come,' and absorbed His devotee into Himself.)[78] Shangkara then showed the worthlessness of the Tantras. They are again to-day attempting to enter Hindu society, and must be again destroyed."

The writer of the note thus summarized omitted to notice that the Chakras are mentioned in the Upanishads, but endeavored to meet the fact that they are also described in the Purānas by the allegation that the Pauranik Chakras are in conformity with the Vedas, whereas the Tantrik Chakras are not. It is admitted that in the Shiva Purāna there is an account of the six centers, but it is said that they are not there alleged to actually exist, nor is anything mentioned of any Sādhanā in connection with them. They are, it is contended, to be imagined only for the purpose of worship. In external worship Devas and Devīs are worshipped in similar Lotuses. The Purānas, in fact, according to this view, convert what is external worship into internal worship. If, according to the Purāna, one worships an interior lotus, it is not to be supposed that there is anything there. One is worshipping merely a

---

[73] These wander about India persuading the villagers to go and work on the tea-gardens, to which they are then conveyed by means which, to say the least, are not always admirable.

[74] The books and the Gurus claim to do so.

[75] It is not a peep-show open to any. Only those see who have mastered the great difficulties in this path.

[76] These observations display misunderstanding of the subject dealt with. I deal later with this class of criticism. I limit my present observations to the historical origins of this Yoga.

[77] This is the Indian tradition as to the philosopher's date.

[78] The parenthesis is mine. See also Mādhava's Shangkaravijaya, Ch. XV.

figment of one's imagination, though it is curious to note that it is said that this figment secures certain advantages to the worshipper, and the latter must commence, according to this critic, with the Chakra which he is qualified to worship. It is not obvious how any question of such competency arises when each of the Chakras is imagined only. Attention is drawn to the fact that in the Linga Purāna there is nothing about the rousing of Kundalī, the piercing of the six centers, the drinking of nectar, and so forth. The Purāna merely says, "Meditate on Shiva and Devī in the different lotuses." There is, it is thus contended, a radical difference between the two systems. "In the Pauranik description of the Chakras everything is stated clearly; but with the Tantriks all is mystery, or else how indeed, except by such mystification, could they dishonestly carry on their profession as Gurus?"

Buddhists may dispute this critic's understanding of their Shūnyavāda, as Tantriks will contest his account of the origin of their Shāstra. The Historian will call in question the statement that Shangkara[79] abolished the Tantra. For, according to the Shangkaravijaya, his action was not to abolish any of the sects existing at his time, but to reform and establish bonds of unity between them, and to induce them all through their differing methods to follow a common ideal. Thus, even though Krakacha was absorbed into his God, the extreme Tantrik sect of Kāpālikas which he represented is said to have continued to exist with Shangkara's approval, though possibly in a modified form, under its leader Vatukanātha. The Brahmos, Āryasamāj, Vaishnavas, and Shaivas, may resent this critic's remarks so far as they touch themselves. I am not here concerned with this religious faction, but will limit the following observations in reply to the subject in hand:

The criticism, notwithstanding its "pious" acerbity against forms of doctrine of which the writer disapproved, contains some just observations. I am not here concerned to establish the reality or value of this Yoga method, nor is proof on either of these points available except through actual experiment and experience. *De experientia non est disputandum.* From a doctrinal and historical point of view, however, it seems that this critic did not have a sufficient knowledge[80] of the subject which he has thus so vigorously condemned, or of the wide acceptance which this Yoga has received in India. It is true that Karma with Jnāna are means for the attainment of Moksha. These and Bhakti (devotion) which may partake of the character of the first or the

---

[79] See *ante*, p. 22.

[80] An English education, such as the Author of this criticism received, not infrequently has the effect of divorcing those thus educated, not only from a knowledge of Indian Shāstra, but from the possibility of understanding it.

second, according to the nature of its display,[81] are all contained in the eight processes of Yoga. Thus, they include Tapas, a form of Karma yoga,[82] and Dhyāna, a process of Jnāna yoga. As will be later pointed out, the "eight-limbed" yoga (Ashtāngayoga) includes Hatha processes, such as Āsana and Prānāyāma. What Hathayogīs have done is to develop the physical or Hatha processes and aspect. The true view of Hathavidyā recognizes that it is an *auxiliary* of Jnāna whereby Moksha is obtained. It is also obviously true that all Bliss is not Moksha. Ānanda (Bliss) of a kind may be secured through drink or drugs, but no one supposes that this is liberating Bliss. Similarly, Hathayoga processes may secure various forms of gross or subtle bodily Bliss which are not The Bliss. There is, however, a misunderstanding of the system here described when it is described as merely materialistic. It has, like other forms of Yoga, a material side or Hatha aspect, since man is gross, subtle, and spiritual; but it has a Jnāna aspect also. As the Jīva is both material and spiritual, discipline and progress in both the aspects is needed. Kundalī is aroused by Mantra, which is Consciousness (Chaitanya) embodied in sound. "It is he whose being is immersed in the Brahman," who arouses the Devī Kundalī by the Mantra Hūngkāra (v. 50). The Devī is Herself Shuddha Sattva[83] (v. 51). "The wise and excellent Yogī, wrapt in Samādhi and devoted to the Lotus Feet of his Guru, should lead Kulakundalī along with Jīva to Her Lord the Parashiva in the abode of liberation within the pure Lotus, and meditate upon Her who grants all desires as the Chaitanyarūpā Bhagavatī (that is, the Devī whose substance is Consciousness itself); and as he leads Kulakundalī he should make all things absorb in Her." Meditation is made on every center in which She operates. In the Ājnā center Manas can only unite with and be absorbed into Kundalī by becoming one with the Jnānashakti which She is, for She is all Shaktis. The Layayoga is therefore a combination of Karma and Jnāna. The former mediately and the latter directly achieves Moksha. In the Ājnā is Manas and Om, and on this the Sādhaka meditates (v. 33). The Sādhaka's Ātmā must be transformed into a meditation on this lotus (v. 34). His Ātmā is the Dhyāna of Om, which is the inner Ātmā of those whose Buddhi is pure. He realizes that he and the Brahman are one, and that Brahman is alone real (Sat) and all else unreal (Asat). He thus becomes an Advaitavādī, or one who realizes the identity of the

---

[81] Thus, the offering of flowers and the like to the Divinity partakes of the nature of Karma; whilst Bhakti in its transcendental aspect, in which by love of the Lord the devotee is merged in Him, is a form of Samādhi.

[82] When, however, we deal with what are called the three Kāndas—viz., Karma, Upāsanā, and Jnāna—Tapas and the like practices form part of Upāsanā Kānda. The above definition is for the purposes of Yoga classification only.

[83] Sattva, Atisattva, Paramasattva, Shuddhasattva, and Vishuddhasattva, are five different forms of Chaitanya.

individual and universal Self (*ib.*). The mind (Chetas) by repeated practice (Abhyāsa) is here dissolved, and such practice is mental operation itself (v. 36). For the Yogī meditating on the Mantra whereby he realizes the unity of Prāna and Manas closes the "house which hangs without support." That is, he disengages the Manas from all contact with the objective world (v. 36), in order to attain the Unmanî Avasthā. Here is Paramashiva. The Tantrik does not suppose that there are several Shivas in the sense of several distinct Deities. The Brahman is one. Rudra, Shiva, Paramashiva, and so forth, are but names for different manifestations of the One. When it is said that any Devatā is in any Chakra, it is meant that that is the seat of the operation of the Brahman, which operation in its Daiva aspect is known as Devatā. As these operations vary, so do the Devatās. The Hangsah of the Sahasrāra contains in Himself all Devatās (v. 44). It is here in the Ājnā that the Yogī places at the time of death his Prāna and enters the supreme Purusha, "who was before the three worlds, and who is known by the Vedānta" (v. 38). It is true that this action, like others, is accompanied by Hatha processes. But these are associated with meditation. This meditation unites Kundalī and Jīvātmā with the Bindu which is Shiva and Shakti (Shivashaktimaya), and the Yogī after such union, piercing the Brahmarandhra, is freed from the body at death and becomes one with Brahman (*ib.*). The secondary causal body (Kāranāvāntara Sharīra) above Ājnā and below Sahasrāra is to be seen only through meditation (v. 39), when perfection has been obtained in Yoga practice. V. 40 refers to Samādhì Yoga.

Passing to the Sahasrāra, it is said, "well concealed and attainable only by great effort, is that subtle 'Void' (Shūnya) which is the chief root of liberation" (v. 42). In Paramashiva are united two forms of Bliss (v. 42)—namely, Rasa or Paramānanda Rasa (that is, the bliss of Moksha) and Virasa (or the bliss which is the product of the union of Shiva and Shakti). It is from the latter union that there arise the universe and the nectar which floods the lesser world (Kshudrabrahmānda), or the body. The ascetic (Yati) of pure mind is instructed in the knowledge by which he realizes the unity of the Jīvātmā and Paramātmā (v. 43). It is "that most excellent of men who has controlled his mind (Niyata-nìja-chitta)—that is, concentrated the inner faculties (Antahkarana) on the Sahasrāra, and has known it—who is freed from rebirth," and thus attains Moksha (v. 45). He becomes Jīvanmukta, remaining only so long in the body as is necessary to work out the Karma, the activity of which has already commenced—just as a revolving wheel will yet run a little time after the cause of its revolving has ceased. It is the Bhagavatī Nirvāna-Kalā which grants divine liberating knowledge—that is, Tattvajnāna, or knowledge of the Brahman (v. 47). Within Her is Nityānanda, which is "pure Consciousness itself" (v. 49), and "is attainable only by Yogīs through pure Jnāna" (*ib.*). It is this Jnāna which secures liberation (*ib.*). The Māyā Tantra says: "Those who are learned in Yoga say that it is the unity of Jīva and Ātmā (in Samādhi). According to the experience of others, it is the knowledge (Jnāna) of the identity of Shiva and Ātmā. The Āgamavādīs say that knowledge (Jnāna) of Shakti is Yoga. Other wise men say that the knowledge (Jnāna) of the Purāna Purusha is Yoga; and others again, the Prakritivādīs, declare that the knowledge of the union of Shiva and Shakti is Yoga" (v. 57). "The Devī, by dissolving Kundalinī in the Parabindu, effects the liberation of some Sādhakas through their meditation upon the identity of Shiva and Ātmā in the Bindu. She does so in the case of others by a similar process and by meditation (Chintana) on Shakti. In other cases this is done by concentration of thought on the Paramapurusha, and in others cases by the meditation of the Sādhaka on the union of Shiva and Shakti" (*ib.*). In fact, the worshipper of any particular Devatā should realize that he is one with the object of his worship. In Pranava worship, for instance, the worshipper realizes his identity with the Ongkāra. In other forms of worship he realizes his identity with Kundalinī, who is embodied by the different Mantras worshipped by different worshippers. In short, Jnāna is Kriyājnāna and Svarūpajnāna. The latter is direct spiritual experience. The former are the meditative processes leading to it. There is here Kriyājnāna, and when Kundalinī unites with Shiva She gives Jnāna (Svarūpa), for Her nature (Svarūpa), as also His, is that.

After union with Shiva, Kundalī makes Her return journey. After She has repeatedly[84] gone to him, She makes a journey from which, at the will of the Yogī, there is no return. Then the Sādhaka is Jīvanmukta. His body is preserved until such time as the active Karma is exhausted, when he can achieve bodiless (Videha) or Kaivalya Mukti (supreme liberation). "The revered Lord Preceptor"—that is, Shangkarāchāryya—in his celebrated Ānanda-Laharī thus hymns Her return (v. 53):

"Kuharini, Thou sprinklest all things with the stream of nectar which flows from the tips of Thy two feet; and as Thou returneth to Thine own place, Thou vivifieth and maketh visible all things that were aforetime invisible; and on reaching Thy abode Thou resumeth Thy snake-like coil and sleepeth." That is, as Her passage upward was Layakrama (dissolution of the Tattvas), so Her return is Srishtikrama (re-creation of the Tattvas). V. 54 says that the Yogī who has practiced Yama and Niyama and the like (that is, the other processes of Ashtāngayoga, including Dhyāna with its resulting Samādhi), and whose mind has been thus controlled, is never again reborn. Gladdened by the constant realization of the Brahman, he is at peace.

---

[84] This is necessary in order that the aptitude be attained. By repetition the act becomes natural, and its result in the end becomes permanent.

Whether the method above described be or be not effectual or desirable, it must be obvious upon a perusal of the text, which gives an explanation of it, that the Yoga which the author affirms to be the cause of liberation is not merely material, but that it is the arousing of the static vital force (Jīvashakti) and world consciousness (Jagachchaitanya) which makes man what he is. The Yogī thus does claim to secure the Bliss of liberation by making entry thereto through the doors of Karma and Jnānayoga.

A Brahmo Author[85] who is so little favorable to the Tantra as to describe the difference between it and the Veda as being "as great as that which exists between the Netherworld (Pātāla) and Heaven (Svarga)"[86] does not deny the efficiency of the Tantrik Shatchakra Sādhanā, but contrasts it with the Vaidika-Gāyatrī-Sādhanā in an account of the two methods which I here summarize in inverted commas.

"The Chakras (the existence of which is not disputed) are placed where the nerves and muscles unite.[87] The Ājnā is the place of the Command. This manifests in the operation of Buddhi. If the command is followed, the Sādhaka becomes pure of disposition (Bhāva) and speech. Speech displays itself in the throat, the region of the Vishuddha. The next lower Chakra is called Anāhata because of its connection with Nāda, which is self-produced in the heart. The Vāyu in Anāhata is Prānashakti. Here when free from sin one can see the Ātmā. Here the Yogī realizes 'I am He.' Fire is at the navel. The seat of desire is at the root of the Svādhishthāna. In the lowest lotus the Mūlādhāra are the three Shaktis of Jīva—namely, Ichchhā, Kriyā, and Jnāna—in an unconscious unenlivened state. The Sādhaka by the aid of the Parātmā as fire (Agni) and air (Vāyu)[88] awakens these three forces (Shaktis), and ultimately by the grace of the Parātmā he is united with the Turīya Brahman."

"In days of old Sādhanā commenced at the Mūlādhāra Chakra; that

---

[85] Gāyatrīmūlaka Shatchakrer vyākhyāna O Sādhanā (Mangala Ganga Mission Press).

[86] The unorthodox author cited, quoting the saying that "to attain Siddhi (fruition) in Shruti (study and practice of ordinances of the Vedas) the Brāhmana should follow the Tantra," asks, in conformity with his views on the latter Shāstra, "How can those who are divorced from Veda get Siddhi in Shruti?" This echoes a common reproach, that the Tantra is opposed to the Vedas which the Shāstra itself denies. The Kulārnava Tantra speaks of it, on the contrary, as Vedātmaka. Of course it is one question to claim to be based on Veda and another whether a particular Shāstra is in fact in accordance with it. On this the Indian schools dispute, just as the Christian sects differ as to the Bible which all claim as their basis.

[87] This definition is inaccurate. As explained later, the physical ganglia are merely gross correspondences of the subtle vital Chakras which inform them.

[88] The Author here refers to the processes subsequently described, whereby air is indrawn and the internal fires are set ablaze to rouse the sleeping Serpent. The Parātmā is the Supreme Ātmā.

is, those who were not Sādhakas of the Gāyatrī-Mantra commenced from below at the lowest center. There was a good reason for this, for thereby the senses (Indriya) were controlled. Without such control purity of disposition (Bhāva) cannot be attained. If such purity be not gained, then the mind (Chitta) cannot find its place in the heart; and if the Chitta be not in the heart there can be no union with the Parātmā. The first thing, therefore, which a Sādhaka has to do is to control the senses. Those who achieved this without fixing their minds on the Lord (Īshvara)[89] had to go through many difficult and painful practices (such as the Mudrās, Bandhas, etc., mentioned later) which were necessary for the control of the Indriyas and of the action of the Gunas. All this is unnecessary in the Gāyatrī Sādhanā or method. It is true that the senses should be controlled in the three lower centers (Chakras)—that is, cupidity (Lobha) in the Mūlādhāra, lust (Kāma) in the Svādhishthāna at the root of the genitals, and anger (Krodha) at the navel. These three passions are the chief to set the senses in motion, and are the main doors to Hell. The way, however, in which control should be effected is to place the Chitta (mind) on Sattā (existence) of Paramātmā in these Chakras. The Chitta should be taken to each of these three lowest centers and controlled, whereby these passions which have their respective places at those centers are controlled. Whenever, therefore, the senses (Indriya) get out of control, fix the Chitta (mind) on the Paramātmā in the particular Chakra."

[To give the above an English turn of thought: if, say, anger is to be controlled, carry the mind to the navel, and there meditate upon the existence of the Supreme One (Paramātmā) in this center, not merely as the Supreme without the body and within the body, but as embodied in that particular part of it; for that is Its manifestation. The result is that the passionate activity of this center is subdued; for its functioning is attuned to the state of the Ātmā which informs it, and both the body and mind attain the peace of the Ātmā on which the self is centered.[90]]

"Having thus controlled the senses, the Gāyatrī Sādhanā commences, not at the lowest, but at the highest, of the six centers—namely, the Ājnā between the eyebrows. There is no necessity for the difficult and painful process of piercing the Chakras from below.[91] Fix the mind on the Lord (Īshvara) in the highest center. For the ether (Ākāsha) there is the existence (Sattā) of the Supreme Ātmā. There and in the two lower centers (Vishuddha and Anāhata) enjoyment is had with Īshvara. The union between Jīva and Prakriti is called Honey

[89] This observation suggests a line of thought which is of value. Some pursue the path of devotion (Bhakti), but what of those who have it not or in less degree?

[90] The paragraph in brackets is mine.—A. A.

[91] This observation shows a misunderstanding of the specific character of the Yoga. If it is desired to rouse Kundalī, then operation must commence at the lowest center. There are, however, other forms of Yoga in which Kundalī is not aroused.—A. A.

(Madhu) in the Upanishads. By Sādhanā of the Ājnā center (Chakra) purity of being (Bhāvashuddhi) is attained, and purity of speech follows on the attainment of such Bhāva. Yoga with the Supreme Devatā who is all-knowing is had here. He who is freed from all disturbing conditions of body and mind reaches the state which is beyond the Gunas (Gunātīta), which is that of the Supreme Brahman."

We may conclude these two criticisms with the true Indian saying somewhat inconsistently quoted in the first: "To dispute the religion (Dharma) of another is the mark of a narrow mind. O Lord! O Great Magician! with whatsoever faith or feeling we call on Thee Thou art pleased."

Whatsoever difference there has been, or may be, as to forms and methods, whether in Upāsanā or Yoga, yet all Indian worshippers of the ancient type seek a common end in unity with Light of Consciousness, which is beyond the regions of Sun, Moon, and Fire.

Recently some attention has been given to the subject in Western literature of an occult kind. Generally its authors and others have purported to give what they understood to be the Hindu theory of the matter, but with considerable inaccuracies. These are not limited to works of the character mentioned. Thus, to take but two instances of these respective classes, we find in a well-known Sanskrit dictionary[92] that the Chakras are defined to be "circles or depressions (*sic*) of the body for mystical or chiromantic purposes," and their location has in almost every particular been wrongly given. The Mūlādhāra is inaccurately described as being "above the pubis." Nor is the Svādhishthāna the umbilical region. Anāhata is not the root of the nose, but is the spinal center in the region of the heart; Vishuddha is not "the hollow between the frontal sinuses," but is the spinal center in the region of the throat. Ājnā is not the fontanelle or union of the coronal and sagittal sutures, which are said to be the Brahmarandhra,[93] but is in the position allotted to the third eye, or Jnānachakshu. Others, avoiding such gross errors, are not free from lesser inaccuracies. Thus, an author who, I am informed, had considerable knowledge of things occult, speaks of the Sushumnā as a "force" which "cannot be energized until Idā and Pinggalā have preceded it," which "passes to the accompaniment of violent shock through each section of the spinal marrow," and which on the awakening of the sacral plexus passes along the spinal cord and impinges on the brain, with the result that the neophyte finds "himself to be an unembodied soul alone in the black abyss of empty space, struggling against dread and terror unutterable." He also writes that the "current" of Kundalinī is called Nādī; that the

---

[92] Professor Monier Williams, Sanskrit Dictionary, *sub voc.* "Chakra."

[93] A term which is also employed to denote the Brahmanādī, in that the latter is the passage whereby the Brahmarandhra in the cerebrum is attained.

Sushumnā extends as a nerve to the Brahmarandhra; that the Tattvas are seven in number; and other matters which are inaccurate. The Sushumnā is not a "force,"[94] and does not pass and impinge upon anything, but is the outer of the three Nādīs, which form the conduit for the force which is the arousing of the Devī called Kundalinī, which force is not itself a Nādī, but passes through the innermost, or Chitrinī Nādī, which terminates at the twelve-petalled lotus below the Sahasrāra, from which ascent is made to the Brahmarandhra. It would be easy to point out other mistakes in writers who have referred to the subject. It will be more profitable if I make as correct a statement as my knowledge admits of this mode of Yoga. But I desire to add that some modern Indian writers have also helped to diffuse erroneous notions about the Chakras by describing them from what is merely a materialistic or physiological standpoint. To do so is not merely to misrepresent the case, but to give it away; for physiology does not know the Chakras as they exist in themselves—that is, as centers of consciousness—and of its activity as Prānavāyu Sūkshma or subtle vital force; though it does deal with the gross body which is related to them. Those who appeal to physiology only are like to return non-suited.

We may here notice the account of a well-known "Theosophical" author[95] regarding what he calls the "Force centers" and the "Serpent Fire," of which he writes that he has had personal experience. Though Mr. Leadbeater also refers to the Yoga Shāstra, it may perhaps exclude error if we here point out that his account does not profess to be a representation of the teaching of the Indian Yogīs (whose competence for their own Yoga the author somewhat disparages), but that it is the Author's own original explanation (fortified, as he conceives, by certain portions of Indian teaching) of the personal experience which (he writes) he himself has had. This experience appears to consist in the conscious arousing of the "Serpent Fire," with the enhanced "astral" and mental vision which he believes has shown him what he tells us. The centers, or Chakras, of the human body are by Mr. Leadbeater described to be vortices of "etheric" matter[96] into which rush from the "astral"[97] world, and at right angles to the plane of the whirling disc, the sevenfold force of the Logos bringing "divine life" into the physical body. Though all these seven forces operate on all the centers, in each of them one form of the force is greatly predominant. These inrushing forces are alleged to set up on the surface of the "etheric double"[95] secondary forces at right angles to themselves. The primary force on

---

[94] Except in the sense that everything is a manifestation of power.

[95] "The Inner Life," by C. W. Leadbeater, pp. 443-478, First Series.

[96] The petals of the lotus are Prānashaktī manifested by Prānavāyu. Each lotus is a center of a different form of "matter" (Bhūta) there predominant.—A. A.

[97] This is a Western term.—A. A.

entrance into the vortex radiates again in straight lines, but at right angles. The number of these radiations of the primal force is said to determine the number of "petals"[94] (as the Hindus call them) which the "Lotus" or vortex exhibits. The secondary force rushing round the vortex produces the appearance of the petals of a flower, or, "perhaps more accurately, saucers or shallow vases of wavy iridescent glass." In this way—that is, by the supposition of an etheric vortex subject to an incoming force of the Logos—both the "Lotuses" described in the Hindu books and the number of their petals is accounted for by the author, who substitutes for the Svādhishthāna center a six-petalled lotus at the spleen,[98] and corrects the number of petals of the lotus in the head, which he says is not a thousand, as the books of this Yoga say, "but exactly 960."[99] The "etheric" center which keeps alive the physical vehicle is said to correspond with an "astral" center of four dimensions, but between them is a closely woven sheath or web composed of a single compressed layer of physical atoms, which prevents a premature opening up of communication between the planes. There is a way, it is said, in which these may be properly opened or developed so as to bring more through this channel from the higher planes than ordinarily passes thereby. Each of these "astral" centers has certain functions: At the navel, a simple power of feeling; at the spleen, "conscious travel" in the astral body; at the heart, "a power to comprehend and sympathize with the vibrations of other astral entities"; at the throat, power of hearing on the astral plane; between the eyebrows, "astral sight"; at the "top of the head," perfection of all faculties of the astral life.[100] These centers are therefore said to take the place to some extent of sense organs for the astral body. In the first center, "at the base of the spine," is the "serpent fire," or Kundalinī, which exists in seven layers or seven degrees of force.[101] This is the manifestation in etheric matter, on the physical plane, of one of the great world forces, one of the powers of the Logos of which vitality and electricity are examples. It is not, it is said, the same as Prāna, or vitality.[102] The "etheric centers" when fully aroused by the "Serpent Fire" bring down, it is alleged, into physical consciousness whatever may be the quality inherent in the astral center which corresponds to it. When vivified by the "Serpent Fire" they become gates of connection between the physical and "astral" bodies.

---

[98] Not mentioned in the account here given.—A. A.

[99] So little attention seems to be given to exactitude in this matter that one of the letters is dropped in order to make 1,000 petals—that is, 50 × 20. "Thousand" is, I think, here only symbolic of magnitude.—A. A.

[100] Certain Siddhis are said to be gained at each center. But the top of the head is far beyond the "astral" life. There Samādhi, or union with the Supreme Consciousness, is had.—A. A.

[101] Parashabda has seven aspects from Kundalī to Bindu.—A. A.

[102] Kundalī is Shabdabrahman or the "Logos" in bodies, and is in Her own form (Svarūpa) Consciousness, and is all Powers (Sarva shaktimaya).—A. A.

When the astral awakening of these centers first took place, this was not known to the physical consciousness. But the sense body can now "be brought to share all these advantages by repeating that process of awakening with the etheric centers." This is done by the arousing through will-force of the "Serpent Fire," which exists clothed in "etheric matter in the physical plane, and sleeps[103] in the corresponding etheric center—that at the base of the spine." When this is done it vivifies the higher centers, with the effect that it brings into the physical consciousness the powers which were aroused by the development of their corresponding astral centers. In short, one begins to live on the astral plane, which is not altogether an advantage, were it not that entry into the heaven world is said to be achieved at the close of life on this plane.[104] Thus, at the second center one is conscious in the physical body "of all kinds of astral influences, vaguely feeling that some of them are friendly and some hostile without in the least knowing why." At the third center one is enabled to remember "only partially" vague astral journeys, with sometimes half-remembrance of a blissful sensation of flying through the air. At the fourth center man is instinctly aware of the joys and sorrows of others, sometimes reproducing in himself their physical aches and pains. At the arousing of the fifth center he hears voices "which make all kinds of suggestions to him." Sometimes he hears music "or other less pleasant sounds."[105] Full development secures clairaudience in the "astral" plane. The arousing of the sixth center secures results which are at first of a trivial character, such as "half seeing landscapes and clouds of color," but subsequently amount to clairvoyance. Here it is said there is a power of magnification by means of an "etheric" flexible tube which resembles "the microscopic snake on the headdress of the Pharaohs." The power to expand or control the eye of this "microscopic snake" is stated to be the meaning of the statement, in ancient books, of the capacity to make oneself large or small at will.[106] When the pituitary body is brought into working order, it forms a link with the astral vehicle, and when the Fire reaches the sixth center, and fully vivifies it, the voice of the "Master" (which in this case means the higher self in its various stages) is heard.[107] The awakening of the seventh center enables one to leave the body in full consciousness. "When the fire has thus passed through all these centers in a certain order (which varies for different types of

---

[103] Kundalī is called the serpent (Bhujangī). She sleeps in the Mūlādhāra. As to what she is, see last note.

[104] The end of Kundalī Yoga is beyond all Heaven worlds.

[105] According to the text translated, the sound of the Shabda Brahman is heard at the Anāhata, or fourth center.—A. A.

[106] There is no mention of such a "snake." The Siddhis animā, etc., do not depend on it. It is consciousness which identifies itself with the small or the great.—A. A.

[107] As the text here translated says, the Ājnā is so called because here is received the command of the Guru from above.—A. A.

people), the consciousness becomes continuous up to the entry into the heaven world[108] at the end of the life on the astral plane."

As has been seen from the account hereinbefore given, there are some resemblances between this account and the teaching of the Yoga Shāstra, with which in a general way the author cited appears to have some acquaintance, and which may have suggested to him some features of his account. There are firstly seven centers, which with one exception correspond with the Chakras described. The author says that there are three other lower centers, but that concentration on them is full of danger. What these are is not stated. There is no center lower, that I am aware of, than the Mūlādhāra, and the only center near to it which is excluded, in the above-mentioned account, is the Apas Tattva center, or Svādhishthāna. Next there is the Force "the Serpent Fire," which the Hindus call Kundalinī, in the lowest center, the Mūlādhāra. Lastly, the effect of the rousing of this force, which is accomplished by will power (Yogabala), is said to exalt the physical consciousness through the ascending planes to the "heaven world." To use the Hindu expression, the object and aim of Shatchakrabheda is Yoga. This is ultimately union with the Paramātmā; but it is obvious that, as the body in its natural state is already, though unconsciously, in Yoga, otherwise it would not exist, each conscious step upwards is Yoga, and there are many stages of such before complete or Kaivalya Mukti is attained. This and, indeed, many of the preceding stages are far beyond the "heaven world" of which the author speaks. Yogīs are not concerned with the "heaven world," but seek to surpass it; otherwise they are not Yogīs at all. What, according to this theory, manifested force apparently does is this: it enhances the mental and moral qualities of the self operator as they existed at the time of its discovery. But if this be so, such enhancement may be as little desirable as the original state. Apart from the necessity for the possession of health and strength, the thought, will, and morality, which it is proposed to subject to its influence must be first purified and strengthened before they are intensified by the vivifying influence of the aroused force. Further, as I have elsewhere pointed out,[109] the Yogīs say that the piercing of the Brahmagranthi sometimes involves considerable pain, physical disorder, and even disease, as is not unlikely to follow from concentration on such a center as the navel (Nābhipadma).

To use Hindu terms, the Sādhaka must be competent (Adhikārī), a matter to be determined by his Guru, from whom alone the actual method of Yoga can be learned. The incidental dangers, however, stated by Mr. Leadbeater go beyond any mentioned to me by Indians themselves, who seems to be in general unaware of the subject of

---

[108] See note 104, *ante*.

[109] In my edition of Mahānirvāna Tantra, CXXIV.

"phallic sorcery," to which reference is made by Mr. Leadbeater, who speaks of Schools of (apparently Western) "Black Magic" which are said to use Kundalinī for the purpose of stimulating the sexual center.[110] It is possible that perverse or misguided concentration on sexual and connected centers may have the effect alluded to. I have, however, never heard Indians refer to this matter, probably because, by reason of the antecedent discipline required of those who would undertake this Yoga, the nature of their practice, and the aim they have in view, such a possibility does not come under consideration. The Indian who practices this or any other kind of spiritual Yoga ordinarily does so not on account of a curious interest in occultism or with a desire to gain "astral" or similar experiences.[111] His attitude in this as in all other matters is essentially a religious one, based on a firm faith in Brahman (Sthiranishthā), and inspired by a desire for union with It which is liberation. What is competency for Tantra (Tantrashāstrādhikāra) is described in the second chapter of the Gandharva Tantra as follows: The aspirant must be intelligent (Daksha), with senses controlled (Jitendriyah), abstaining from injury to all beings (Sarvahingsāvinirmuktah), ever doing good to all (Sarvaprānihite ratah), pure (Shuchi); a believer in Veda (Āstika), whose faith and refuge is in Brahman (Brahmishthah, Brahmavādī, Brāhmī, Brahmaparāyana), and who is a non-dualist (Dvaitahīna). "Such a one is competent in this Scripture, otherwise he is no Sādhaka" (So'smin Shāstredhikārīsyāt tadanyatra na sādhakah). With such an attitude it is possible that, as pointed out by an Indian writer (p. 28 *ante*), concentration on the lower centers associated with the passions may, so far from rousing, quiet them. It is quite possible, on the other hand, that another attitude, practice, and purpose, may produce another result. To speak, however, of concentration on the sexual center is itself misleading, for the Chakras are not in the gross body, and concentration is done upon the subtle center, with its presiding consciousness, even though such centers may have ultimate relation with gross physical function. Doubtless, also, there is a relationship and correspondence between the Shaktis of the mental and sexual centers, and the force of the latter, if directed upwards, extraordinarily heightens all mental and physical functioning. In fact, those who are "centered" know how to make all their forces converge upon the object of their will, and train

---

[110] Another author says: "The mere dabbler in the pseudo-occult will only degrade his intellect with the puerilities of psychism, become the prey of the evil influence of the phantasmal world, or ruin his soul by the foul practices of phallic sorcery—as thousands of misguided people are doing even in this age" ("The Apocalypse Unsealed," p. 62). Is this so?

[111] Those who do practice magic of the kind mentioned have recourse to the Prayoga, which leads to Nāyikā Siddhi, whereby commerce is had with female spirits. The process in this work described is one upon the path of liberation, and has nothing to do with sexual black magic.

and then use all such forces and neglect none. The experienced followers of this method, however, as I have stated, allow that this method is liable to be accompanied by certain inconveniences or dangers, and it is therefore considered inadvisable except for the fully competent (Adhikārī).

There are, on the other hand, many substantial points of difference between the account which has been summarized and the theory which underlies the form of Yoga with which this work deals. The terminology and classification adopted by that account may be termed "Theosophical;"[112] and though it may be possible for those who are familiar both with this and the Indian terminology to establish points of correspondence between the two systems, it must by no means be assumed that the connotation even in such cases is always exactly the same. For though "Theosophical" teaching is largely inspired by Indian ideas, the meaning which it attributes to the Indian terms which it employs is not always that given to these terms by Indians themselves. This is sometimes confusing and misleading, a result which would have been avoided had the writers of this school adopted in all cases their own nomenclature and definitions.[113] Though for the visualization of our conceptions the term "planes" is a convenient one, and I here employ it, the division by "principles" more nearly adumbrates the truth. It is not easy to correlate with complete accuracy the Indian and Theosophical theories as to man's principles. It has, however, been stated[114] that the physical body has two divisions, the "dense" and "etheric" body; that these correspond to the Annamaya and Prānamayakoshas, and that the "astral" body corresponds to the Kāmik side of the Manomayakosha. Assuming for argument the alleged correspondence, then the "etheric centers" or Chakra of Mr. Leadbeater's account appear to be centers of energy of the Prāna vāyu. The lotuses are also this and centers of the universal consciousness. Kundalinī is the static form of the creative energy in bodies which is the source of all energies, including Prāna. According to Mr. Leadbeater's theory, Kundalinī is some force which is distinct from

[112] I am aware that the Theosophical Society has no official doctrine. What I call "Theosophical" are the theories put forward by its leading exponents and largely accepted by its members. I put the word in inverted commas to denote doctrine so taught and held by this Society, with which doctrines Theosophy in its general sense is not necessarily wholly identified.

[113] Thus, the Theosophical Sanskritist Srīsha Chandra Vasu, in his "Introduction to Yoga Philosophy," calls the Linga Sharīra "the etherial duplicate" (p. 35). According to the ordinary Indian use of that term this is not so, for the Linga Sharīra is the subtle body—that is, the Antahkarana and Indriyas—vehicled by the Tanmātras, or, according to another account, the five Prānas. Elsewhere (p. 51) it is called the "Astral" body, and some statements are made as to the Chakras which are not in accordance with the texts with which I am acquainted.

[114] "Ancient Wisdom," p. 176, by Mrs. A. Besant.

Prāna, understanding this term to mean vitality or the life principle, which on entrance into the body shows itself in various manifestations of life which are the minor Prānas, of which inspiration is called by the general name of the force itself (Prāna). Verses 10 and 11 say of Kundalinī: "It is She who maintains all the beings (that is, Jīva-jīvātman) of the world by means of inspiration and expiration." She is thus the Prāna Devatā, but, as She is (Comm., vv. 10 and 11) Srishti-sthitilayātmikā, *all* forces therefore are in Her. She is, in fact, the Shabdabrahman or "Logos" in bodies. The theory discussed appears to diverge from that of the Yogīs when we consider the nature of the Chakras and the question of their vivification. According to Mr. Leadbeater's account, the Chakras are all vortices of "etheric matter," apparently of the same kind and subject to the same external influence of the inrushing sevenfold force of the "Logos," but differing in this, that in each of the Chakras one or other of their sevenfold forces is predominant. Again, if, as has been stated, the astral body corresponds with the Manomayakosha, then the vivification of the Chakras appears to be, according to Mr. Leadbeater, a rousing of the Kāmik side of the mental sheath. According to the Hindu doctrine, these Chakras are differing centers of consciousness, vitality, and Tāttvik energy. Each of the five lower Chakras is the center of energy of a gross Tattva—that is, of that form of Tattvik activity or Tanmātra which manifests the Mahābhūta or sensible matter. The sixth is the center of the subtle mental Tattva, and the Sahasrāra is not called a Chakra at all. Nor, as stated, is the splenic center included among the six Chakras which are dealt with in this account.

In the Indian system the total number of the petals corresponds with the number of the letters of the Sanskrit Alphabet; and the number of the petals of any specific lotus is determined by the disposition of the Nādīs around it. These petals, further, bear subtle sound-powers, and are fifty in number, as are the letters of the Sanskrit Alphabet, which as representing all words and language is that by which all the ideation which creates the world manifests itself.

This work also describes certain things which are gained by contemplation on each of the Chakras. Some of them are of a general character, such as long life, freedom from desire and sin, control of the senses, knowledge, power of speech, and fame. Some of these and other qualities are results common to concentration on more than one Chakra. Others are stated in connection with the contemplation upon one center only. But all such statements seem to be made, not with the intention of accurately recording the specific result, if any, which follows upon concentration upon a particular center, but by way of praise for increased self-control, or Stuti-vāda; as where it is said in v. 21 that contemplation on the Nābhi-padma gains for the Yogī power to destroy and create the world.

It is also said that mastery of the centers may produce various Siddhis or powers in respect of the predominating elements there. And this is, in fact, alleged.[115] Pandit Ananta Shāstrī says:[116] "We can meet with several persons every day elbowing us in the streets or bazaars who in all sincerity attempted to reach the highest plane of bliss, but fell victims on the way to the illusions of the psychic world, and stopped at one or the other of the six Chakras. They are of varying degrees of attainment, and are seen to possess some power which is not found even in the best intellectual of the ordinary run of mankind. That this school of practical psychology was working very well in India at one time is evident from these living instances (not to speak of the numberless treatises on the subject) of men roaming about in all parts of the country." The mere rousing of the Serpent power does not, from the spiritual Yoga standpoint, amount to much. Nothing, however, of real moment, from the higher Yogīs' point of view, is achieved until the Ājnā Chakra is reached. Here, again, it is said that the Sādhaka whose Ātmā is nothing but a meditation on this lotus "becomes the creator, preserver, and destroyer, of the three worlds"; and yet, as the commentator points out (v. 34), "This is but the highest Prashangsā-vāda or Stutivāda—that is, compliment—which in Sanskrit literature is as often void of reality as it is in our ordinary life. Though much is here gained, it is not until the Tattvas of this center are also absorbed, and complete knowledge[117] of the Sahasrāra is gained, that the Yogī attains that which is both his aim and the motive of his labor, cessation from rebirth which follows on the control and concentration of the Chitta on the Shivasthānam, the Abode of Bliss. It is not to be supposed that simply because the Serpent Fire has been aroused that one has thereby become a Yogī or achieved the end of Yoga. There are other points of difference which the reader will discover for himself, but into which I do not enter, as my object in comparing the two accounts has been to establish a general contrast between this modern account and that of the Indian schools. I may, however, add that the differences are not only as to details. The style of thought differs in a way not easy shortly to describe, but which will be quickly recognized by those who have some familiarity with the Indian Scriptures and mode of thought. The latter is ever disposed to interpret all processes and their results from a subjective or idealistic standpoint, though for the purposes of Sādhana the objective aspect is not ignored. The Indian theory is highly

---

[115] See Yogatattva Upanishad, where contemplation on the earth center secures mastery over earth, etc. At the same time it points out that these "powers" are obstacles to liberation.

[116] Ānandalaharī, p. 35.

[117] This, it is obvious, comes only after long effort, and following on less complete experiences and results. According to Indian notions, success (Siddhi) in Yoga is the fruit of experiences of many preceding lives.

philosophical. Thus, to take but one instance, whilst Mr. Leadbeater attributes the power of becoming large or small at will (Animā and Mahimā Siddhi) to a flexible tube or "microscopic snake" in the forehead, the Hindu says that all powers (Siddhi) are the attribute (Aishvaryya) of the Lord Ishvara, or creative consciousness, and that in the degree that the Jīva realizes that consciousness[118] he shares the powers inherent in the degree of his attainment.

That which is the general characteristic of the Indian systems, and that which constitutes their real profundity, is the paramount importance attached to consciousness and its states. It is these states which create, sustain, and destroy, the worlds. Brahmā, Vishnu, and Shiva, are the names for functions of the one Universal Consciousness operating in ourselves. And whatever be the means employed, it is the transformation of the "lower" into "higher" states of consciousness which is the process and fruit of Yoga and the cause of all its experiences. In this and other matters, however, we must distinguish both practice and experience from theory. A similar experience may possibly be gained by various modes of practice, and an experience may be in fact a true one, though the theory which may be given to account for it is incorrect.

The following sections will enable the reader to pursue the comparison for himself.

As regards practice, I am told that Kundalinī cannot be roused except in the Mūlādhāra and by the means here indicated, though this may take place by accident when by chance a person has hit upon the necessary positions and conditions, but not otherwise. Thus the story is told of a man being found whose body was as cold as a corpse, though the top of the head was slightly warm. (This is the state in Kundalī Yoga Samādhi.) He was massaged with ghee (clarified butter), when the head got gradually warmer. The warmth descended to the neck, when the whole body regained its heat with a rush. The man came to consciousness, and then told the story of his condition. He said he had been going through some antics, imitating the posture of a Yogī, when suddenly "sleep" had come over him. It was surmised that his breath must have stopped, and that, being in the right position and conditions, he had unwittingly roused Kundalī, who had ascended to Her cerebral center. Not, however, being a Yogī, he could not bring her down again. This, further, can only be done when the Nādīs (*v. post*) are pure. I told the Pandit (who gave me this story), who was learned in this Yoga, and whose brother practiced it, of the case of a European friend of mine who was not acquainted with the Yoga processes here described, though he had read something about Kundalī in translations of Sanskrit

[118] As this is by the Devī's grace, She is called "the giver of the eight Siddhis" (Īshitvādyāshtasiddhidā). See Trishatī, II. 47. She gives aishvaryya.

works, and who, nevertheless, believed he had roused Kundalī by meditative processes alone. In fact, as he wrote me, it was useless for him as a European to go into the minutia of Eastern Yoga. He, however, saw Idā and Pinggalā (*v. post*), and the "central fire" with a trembling aura of rosy light, and blue or azure light, and a white fire which rose up into the brain and flamed out in a winged radiance on either side of the head. Fire was seen flashing from center to center with such rapidity that he could see little of the vision, and movements of forces were seen in the bodies of others. The radiance or aura round Idā was seen as moonlike—that is, palest azure—and Pinggalā red or rather pale rosy opalescence. Kundalī appeared in vision as of intense golden-like white fire rather curled spirally. Taking the centers, Sushumnā, Idā, and Pinggalā, to be symbolized by the Caduceus of Mercury,[119] the little ball at the top of the rod was identified with the Sahasrāra or pineal gland,[120] and the wings as the flaming of auras on each side of the center when the fire strikes it. One night, being abnormally free from the infection of bodily desires, he felt the serpent uncoil, and it ran up, and he was "in a fountain of fire," and felt, as he said, "the flames spreading wing-wise about my head, and there was a musical clashing as of cymbals, whilst some of these flames, like emanations, seemed to expand and meet like gathered wings over my head. I felt a rocking motion. I really felt frightened, as the Power seemed something which could consume me." My friend wrote me that in his agitation he forgot to fix his mind on the Supreme, and so missed a divine adventure. Perhaps it was on this account that he said he did not regard the awakening of this power as a very high spiritual experience or on a level with other states of consciousness he experienced. The experience, however, convinced him that there was a real science and magic in the Indian books which treat of occult physiology.

The Pandit's observations on this experience were as follows: If the breath is stopped and the mind is carried downwards heat is felt. It is possible to "see" Kundalinī with the mental eye, and in this way to experience Her without actually arousing Her and bringing Her up, which can only be effected by the Yoga methods prescribed. Kundalinī may have thus been seen as Light in the basal center (Mūlādhāra). It was the Buddhi (*v. post*) which perceived Her, but as the experiencer had not been taught the practice he got confused. There is one simple test whether the Shakti is actually aroused. When she leaves a particular center the part so left becomes as cold and apparently lifeless

[119] In which the rod is the central channel (Sushumnā), which is interlaced by the Idā and Pinggalā sympathetics, the points of section being at the centers. The two wings at the top are the two lobes or petals of the Ājnā Chakra.

[120] Here I differ. The Sahasrāra is at the top of the skull or upper brain. The pineal gland is much lower in the region of the Ājnā Chakra.

as a corpse. The progress upwards may thus be externally verified by others. When the Shakti (Power) has reached the upper brain (Sahasrāra) the whole body is cold and corpse-like, except the top of the skull, where some warmth is felt, this being the place where the static and kinetic aspects of Consciousness unite.

The present work is issued, not with the object of establishing the truth or expediency of the principles and methods of this form of Yoga (a matter which each will determine for himself), but as a first endeavor to supply, more particularly for those interested in occultism and mysticism, a fuller, more accurate, and rational presentation of the subject.

An understanding of the recondite matters in the treatise here translated is, however, only possible if we first shortly summarize some of the philosophical and religious doctrines which underlie this work, and a knowledge of which in his reader is assumed by its author.

The following sections, therefore, of this Introduction will deal firstly with the concepts of Consciousness[121] and Unconsciousness, and their association in the Embodied Spirit or Jīvātmā. Nextly the kinetic aspect of Spirit, or Shakti, is considered; its creative ideation and manifestation in the evolved macrocosm and in the human body or microcosm (Kshudrabrahmānda), which is a replica on small scale of the greater world. After an account of the Logos and the letters of speech, I conclude with the method of involution, or Yoga. The latter will not be understood unless the subject of the preceding sections has been mastered.

It is necessary to explain and understand the theory of world evolution even in the practical matters with which this work is concerned. For as the Commentator says in v. 39, when dealing with the practice of Yoga, the rule is that things dissolve into that from which they originate, and the Yoga process here described is such dissolution (Laya). This return or dissolution process (Nivritti) in Yoga will not be understood unless the forward or creative (Pravritti) process is understood. Similar considerations apply to other matters here dealt with.

II. Consciousness and Its Power (Shiva-Shakti)

The bases of this Yoga are of a highly metaphysical and scientific character. For its understanding there is required a full acquaintance with Indian philosophy, religious doctrine, and ritual in general, and in particular with that presentment of these three matters which is given in

---

[121] For the meaning of this term as here used, see my "Shakti anp Shākta."

the Shākta and Monistic (Advaita)[122] Shaiva Tantras. It would need more than a bulky volume to describe and explain in any detail the nature and meaning of this Yoga, and the bases on which it rests. I must therefore assume in the reader either this general knowledge or a desire to acquire it, and confine myself to such an exposition of general principles and leading facts as will supply the key by which the doors leading to a theoretical knowledge of the subject may be opened by those desirous of passing through and beyond them, and as will thus facilitate the understanding of the difficult texts here translated. For on the practical side I can merely reproduce the directions given in the books, together with such explanations of them as I have received orally. Those who wish to go farther, and to put into actual process this Yoga, must learn directly of a Guru who has himself been through it (Siddha). His experience alone will say whether the aspirant is capable of success. It is said that of those who attempt it one out of a thousand may have success. If the latter enters upon the path, the Guru alone can save him from attendant risks, molding and guiding the practice as he will according to the particular capacities and needs of his disciples. Whilst, therefore, on this heading it is possible to explain some general principles, their application is dependent on the circumstances of each particular case.

Veda says: "All this (that is, the manifold world) is (the one) Brahman" (Sarvvam khalvidam Brahma).[123] How the many can be the one[124] is variously explained by the different schools. The interpretation here given is that of the grand doctrine underlying and

---

[122] Kulārnava Tantra speaks of that "Monism of which Shiva speaks" (Advaitantu Shivenoktam, I. 108). See also Mahānirvāna Tantra, Ch. II., vv. 33-44, III. 33-35, 50-64; Prapanchasāra Tantra, II., XIX., XXIX. Prapanchasāra Tantra, Ch. XIX.; for the identity of Jīvātmā and Paramātmā is liberation (Mukti), which the Vedāntasāra defines to be Jīvabrahmanor aikyam. See Mahānirvāna Tantra, where they are given (VIII. 264, 265, V. 105). See also Prapanchasāra Tantra, II., where Hrīng is identified with Kundalī and Hangsah, and then with "So' hang." See also *ib.*, Ch. XXIV.: "That which is subtle I am" (Yah Sūkshmah So' hang); and Jnānārnava Tantra, XXI. 10. As to Brahmāsmi, see Kulārnava Tantra, IX. 32, and *ib.*, 41: So' ham bhāvena pūjayet. The Shākta disciple (Sādhaka) should not be a dualist. Mahārudrayāmala, I. Khanda, Ch. 15; II. Khanda, Ch. 2, Similarly, the Gandharva Tantra, Ch. 2, says that he must be devoid of dualism (Dvaitahīna). See Prānatoshinī, 108. In fact, that particular form of worship which has earned the Kaula Tantras their ill-name is a practical application of Advaitavāda. Kaulāchāra is said to properly follow a full knowledge of Vedāntik doctrine. As the Shatchakra-nirūpana here translated says, the Jīvātmā or embodied spirit is the same as the Paramātmā or supreme spirit, and knowledge of this is the root of all wisdom (Mūlavidyā).

[123] This, as the Mahānirvāna Tantra says (VII. 98), is the end and aim of Tāntrika Kulāchāra, the realization of which saying the Prapanchasāra Tantra calls the fifth or supreme state (Ch. XIX., Vol. III., "Tantrik Texts").

[124] Thus it is said of Devī that She is in the form of one and many (Ekānekāksharākritih). Ekam = ekam ajnānam or Māyā. Anekāni = the several ajnānas—that is, Avidyā. She is both as Upādhi of Īshvara and Jīva (Trishatī, II. 23).

contained in the Shākta Tantras or Āgamas. In the first place, what is the one Reality which appears as many? What is the nature of Brahman as it is in itself (Svarūpa)? The answer is Sat-Chit-Ānanda—that is, being-feeling-consciousness-bliss. Consciousness or feeling, as such (Chit, or Chaitanya, or Samvit), is identical with being as such. Though in ordinary experience the two are essentially bound up together, they still seem to diverge from each other. Man by his constitution inveterately believes in an objective existence beyond and independent of himself. And this is so as long as, being embodied spirit (Jīvātmā), his consciousness is veiled by Māyā. But in the ultimate basis of experience, which is the Supreme Spirit (Paramātmā), the divergence has gone, for in it lie in undifferentiated mass experiencer, experience, and the experienced. When, however, we speak of Chit as feeling-consciousness we must remember that what we know and observe as such is only a limited changing manifestation of Chit, which is in itself the infinite changeless principle which is the background of all experience. This being-consciousness is absolute bliss (Ānanda), which is defined as "resting in the self" (Svarūpa-vishrānti). It is bliss because, being the infinite all (Pūrna), it can be in want of nothing. This blissful consciousness is the ultimate and real nature or Svarūpa, as it is called, of the one reality, the own form or the *propria forma* of the scholastics. Svarūpa is the nature of anything as it is in itself, as distinguished from what it may appear to be. This supreme consciousness is the Supreme Shiva (Parashiva). It never changes, but eternally endures the same throughout all change.

But if this be so, how is it that everything we see is associated with apparent unconsciousness? Our mind is evidently not a pure, but a limited consciousness. What limits it must be something either in itself unconscious or, if conscious, capable of producing the appearance of unconsciousness.[125] In the phenomenal world there is nothing absolutely conscious nor absolutely unconscious. Consciousness and unconsciousness are always intermingled. Some things, however, appear to be more conscious, and some more unconscious than others. This is due to the fact that Chit, which is never absent in anything, yet manifests itself in various ways and degrees. The degree of this manifestation is determined by the nature and development of the body in which it is enshrined. Spirit remains the same; the body changes. The manifestation of consciousness is more or less limited as ascent is made from the mineral to man. In the mineral world Chit manifests as the lowest form of sentiency evidenced by reflex response to stimuli, and that physical consciousness which is called in the West atomic memory. The sentiency of plants is more developed, though it is, as

[125] The alternative is given to meet the differing views of Māyāvāda and Shaktivāda.

Chakrapāni says, in the Bhānumatī a dormant consciousness. This is further manifested in those micro-organisms which are intermediate stages between the vegetable and animal worlds, and have a psychic life of their own. In the animal world consciousness becomes more centralized and complex, reaching its fullest development in man, who possesses all the psychic functions, such as cognition, perception, feeling, and will. Behind all these particular changing forms of sentiency or consciousness is the one formless, changeless Chit as it is in itself (Svarūpa), and as distinguished from the particular forms of its manifestation.

As Chit throughout all these stages of life remains the same it is not really developed. The appearance of development is due to the fact that is now more and now less veiled by mind and matter. It is this veiling and projection by the cosmic consciousness (Shakti) which creates the world. What is it, then, which veils consciousness and projects the world-show?

The answer is Shakti as Māyā. Is Shakti the same as or different from Shiva or Chit? It must be the same, for otherwise all could not be one Brahman. But if it is the same it must be also Chit or Consciousness. Therefore it is Sachchidānandamayī[126] and Chidrūpinī.[127]

And yet there is, at least in appearance, some distinction. Shakti, which comes from the root *Shak*, "to have power," "to be able," means power. As She is one with Shiva, She as such power is the power of Shiva or Consciousness. There is no difference between Shiva as the possessor of power (Shaktimān) and power itself. The power of consciousness is consciousness in its active aspect. Whilst, therefore, both Shiva and Shakti are consciousness, the former is the changeless static aspect of consciousness, and Shakti is the kinetic active aspect of the same consciousness. The particular power whereby the dualistic world is brought into being is Māyā-Shakti, which is both a veiling (Āvarana) and projecting (Vikshepa) Shakti. Consciousness veils itself to itself, and projects from the store of its previous experiences (Sangskāra) the notion of a world in which it suffers and enjoys. The universe is thus the creative imagination (Srishtikalpanā, as it is called) of the Supreme World-thinker (Īshvara). Māyā is that power by which things are "measured"—that is, formed and made known (Mīyate anena iti māyā). It is the sense of difference (Bhedabuddhi), or that which makes man see the world, and all things and persons therein, as different from himself, when in truth he and it and they are the one self.

---

[126] That is, its substance is Sat, Chit, Ānanda. The suffixes Mayī and Rūpinī indicate a subtle distinction—namely, that She is Chit, and yet by appearance something different from it.

[127] In the form or nature of Chit. As the Kubjikā Tantra says, the Paramā Kalā is both Chit (Chidrūpā) and Nāda (Nādarūpā).

It is that which establishes a dichotomy in what would otherwise be a unitary experience, and is the cause of the dualism inherent in all phenomenal experience. Shakti veils consciousness by negating in various degrees Herself as consciousness.

Before the manifestation of the universe, Being-Consciousness-Bliss alone was—that is, Shiva-Shakti as Chit and Chidrūpinī respectively. Consciousness not exercising its power, Consciousness alone changelessly was. In this the quiescent state of the Ātmā or Self, Shakti being latent, is one with it. The Devī in the Kulachūdāmani Nigama[128] says: "I, though Prakriti, lie hidden in Consciousness-Bliss." Rāghava Bhatta says:[129] "She who is eternal (Anādirūpā) existed in a subtle state, as it were Consciousness, during the great dissolution."

This is Parashiva, who in the scheme of the thirty-six Tattvas is known as Parāsamvit. This is the perfect experience and perfect universe. By this latter term is not meant any heaven in the sense of a perfected world of forms. The perfect universe is Shakti herself in Her own nature as consciousness experienced by Shiva as consciousness. As the Upanishad says, "The self knows and loves the self." It is this love which is bliss or "resting in the self," for, as it is elsewhere said, "Supreme love is bliss" (Niratishaya-premāspadatvamānandatvam). If, however, there be one Changeless Consciousness there is no manifestation. If, again, we assume some other than Consciousness as cause of the universe, then the Monistic (Advaita) truth is destroyed, as in the dualistic Sāngkhya, which assumes, in addition to and independent of the Purusha consciousness, the Prakritiun consciousness as the material cause (Upādānakārana) of the world. All Indian Monism, therefore, posits a dual aspect of the single consciousness—one the transcendental changeless aspect (Parāsamvit),[130] and the other the creative changing aspect, which is called Shiva-Shakti Tattva.[131] In Parāsamvit the "I" (Aham) and the "This" (Îdam), or universe of objects, are indistinguishably mingled in the supreme unitary experience.[132] In Shiva-Shakti Tattva Shakti, which is the negative aspect of the former, Her function being negation (Nishedha-vyapāra-

---

[128] Ahang prakritirūpā chet chidānanda-parāyanā (Ch. I., vv. 16-24, Vol. IV., "Tantrik Texts").

[129] Yā anādirūpā chaitanyādhyāsena mahāpralaye sūkshmā sthitā (Comm. on Shāradā Tilaka, Ch. I.)—that is, the Adhyāsa or attribution is given from the world aspect. Transcendentally She is then in her own nature (Svarūpa).

[130] This is Paramashiva, or Nirguna (attributeless), or Nishkala (partless), Shiva, or Parabrahman.

[131] This is Saguna (with attribute), or Sakala (with parts), Shiva, or Shabdabrahman (Brahman as the source of "sound," *v. post*).

[132] As the Yoginīhridaya Tantra says: The Parā Devī is Prakāshavimarshasāmarasyarūpinī. This is the Nirvikalpa-jnāna state in which there is no distinction of "This" and "That" of "I" and "This." In Vikalpa-jnāna there is subject and object.

rūpā Shaktih), negates herself as the Îdam of experience, leaving the Shiva consciousness as a mere "I," "not looking towards another" (Ananyonmukhah aham pratyayah). This is a state of mere subjective illumination (Prakāsha mātra)[133] to which Shakti, who is called Vimarsha,[134] again presents Herself, but now with a distinction of "I" and "This" as yet held together as part of one self.

At this point, the first incipient stage of dualism, there is the first emanation of consciousness, known as Sadāshiva or Sadākhya Tattva, which is followed by the second or Īshvara Tattva, the Lord. Some worship predominantly the masculine or right side of the conjoint male and female figure (Ardhanārīshvara). Some, the Shāktas, predominantly worship the left, and call Her Mother, for She is the great Mother (Magna Mater), the Mahādevī who conceives, bears, and nourishes the universe sprung from Her womb (Yoni). This is so because She is the active aspect[135] of consciousness, imagining (Srishtikalpanā)[136] the world to be, according to the impressions (Sangskāra) derived from enjoyment and suffering in former worlds. It is natural to worship Her as Mother. The first Mantra into which all men are initiated is the word Mā (Mother). It is their first word and generally their last. The father is a mere helper (Sahakāri-mātra) of the Mother.[137] The whole world of the five elements also springs from the Active Consciousness or Shakti, and is Her manifestation (Pūrna vikāsha). Therefore men worship the Mother,[138] than whom is none

---

[133] Paramashiva has two effects—Prakāsha and Vimarsha, or Kāmeshvara and Kāmeshvarī or Paralinga. Prakāsha = asphutasphutikara, or manifestation of what is not manifest.

[134] This word comes from the root *mrish* = to touch, to affect. The Kulārnavā Samhitā defines it as hridayangamībhāva, or "the state or feeling of going into the heart." Vimarshinī Shakti = drāvanam. She is melted or transformed into the world.

[135] The quiescent Shiva aspect is by its definition inert. It is because of this that the Devī is in Tantra symbolically represented as being above the body of Shiva, who lies under Her like a corpse (Shava). As the Kubjikā Tantra, Ch. I., states, it is not Brahmā, Vishnu, and Rudra, who create, maintain, and destroy, but their Shaktis, Brahmānī, Vaishnavī, Rudrānī. See Prānatoshinī, 9. Activity is the nature of Prakriti (Sāngkhya Pravachana Sūtra, III. 66). For the same reason the female form is represented in union with but above (Viparīta) the male. When the Devī stands above Shiva, the symbolism also denotes (particularly in the case of Kālī) the liberating aspect of the Mother. See "Principles of Tantra," I. 323.

[136] The world is called an imagination (Kalpanā), for it is creative ideation. As the Yoginīhridaya Tantra says, "the picture of the world is designed by Her own will" (Svechchhāvishvamayollekhakhachitam), "seeing which Bhagavān was very pleased."

[137] The Supreme Father gives His illumination (Prakāsha). She, the Vimarshashakti, creates, but not alone. (Vimarshashaktih prakāshātmanā paramashivena sāmarasya-vishvam srijati na tu kevalā—Yoginīhridaya.)

[138] In Mātri-bhāva, according to the Sanskrit term. Philosophically also this is sound, for all that we can know (outside ecstasy or Samādhi) is the Mother in Her form as the world. The Supreme Shakti, who is not different from Shiva (Parāshaktishivābhinnā), is embodied in every order of thing (sarvakramasharīrinī—Yoginīhridaya).

more tender,[139] saluting Her smiling beauty as the Rosy Tripurasundarī, the source of the universe, and Her awe-inspiring grandeur as Kālī, who takes it back into Herself.

In the Mantra side of the Tantra Shāstra, dealing with Mantra and its origin, these two Tattvas emanating from Shakti are known as Nāda and Bindu. Parashiva and Parāshakti are motionless (Nihspanda) and soundless (Nihshabda).

Nāda is the first produced movement in the ideating cosmic consciousness leading up to the Sound-Brahman (Shabdabrahman), whence all ideas, the language in which they are expressed (Shabda), and the objects (Artha) which they denote, are derived.

Bindu literally means a point and the dot (Anusvāra), which denotes in Sanskrit the nasal breathing (°). It is in the Chandrabindu nasal breathing placed above Nāda (ँ). In its technical Mantra sense it denotes that state of active consciousness or Shakti in which the "I" or illuminating aspect of consciousness identifies itself with the total "This" as the yet dualistically unmanifest state of the universe.[140] It subjectifies the "This," thereby becoming a point (Bindu) of consciousness with it. When consciousness apprehends an object as different from itself it sees that object as extended in space. But when that object is completely subjectified (such as to ourselves our own mind) it is experienced as an unextended point. This is the universe experience of the Lord experiencer as Bindu.[141]

Where does the universe go at dissolution? It is withdrawn into that Shakti which projected it. It collapses, so to speak, into a mathematical point without any magnitude whatever.[142] This is the Shivabindu, which again is withdrawn into the Shiva-Shakti-Tattva which produced it. It is conceived that round the Shiva Bindu there is coiled Shakti, just as in the earth center called Mūlādhāra Chakra in the human body a serpent clings round the self-produced Phallus (Svayambhulinga). This coiled Shakti may be conceived as a mathematical line, also without magnitude, which, being everywhere in contact with the point round which it is coiled, is compressed together with it, and forms therefore also one and the same point. There is one indivisible unity of dual aspect which is figured also in the Tantras[143] as

---

[139] It is said that "there is nothing more tender than Prakriti," who serves Purusha in every way, finally giving Mukti by retiring from Him.

[140] For until the operation of Māyā at a later stage the "This" is still experienced as part of the "It." Therefore there is no manifestion or dualism.

[141] For the same reason Shakti is then said to be Ghanībhūtā, which is literally massive or condensed. It is that state of gathered-up power which immediately precedes the burgeoning forth (Sphurana) of the universe.

[142] The imagery, like all of its kind, is necessarily imperfect; for such a point, though it has no magnitude, is assumed to have a position. Here there is none, for we are in spacelessness.

[143] See the Commentary, *post.*

a grain of gram (Chanaka), which has two seeds so closely joined as to look as one surrounded by an outer sheath.[144]

To revert to the former simile, the Shakti coiled round Shiva, making one point (Bindu) with it, is Kundalinī Shakti. This word comes from the adjective Kundalī or "coiled." She is spoken of as coiled because She is likened to a serpent (Bhujanggī), which, when resting and sleeping, lies coiled; and because the nature of Her power is spiraline, manifesting itself as such in the worlds—the spheroids or "eggs of Brahmā" (Brahmānda), and in their circular or revolving orbits and in other ways. Thus the Tantras speak of the development of the straight line (Rijurekhā) from the point which, when it has gone its length as a point, is turned (Vakrarekhā angkushākāra) by the force of the spiraline sack of Māyā in which it works so as to form a figure of two dimensions, which again is turned upon itself, ascending as a straight line into the plane of the third dimension, thus forming the triangular or pyramidal figure called Shringātaka.[145] In other words, this Kundalī Shakti is that which, when it moves to manifest itself, appears as the universe. To say that it is "coiled" is to say that it is *at rest*—that is, in the form of *static potential energy*. This Shakti coiled round the Supreme Shiva is called Mahākundalī ("The great coiled power"), to distinguish it from the same power which exists in individual bodies, and which is called Kundalī or Kundalinī.[146] It is with and through the last power that this Yoga is affected. When it is accomplished the individual Shakti (Kundalī) is united with the great cosmic Shakti (Mahā-kundalī), and She with Shiva, with whom in truth She is one. Kundalinī is an aspect of the eternal Brahman (Brahmarūpā Sanātanī) and is both Nirgunā and Sagunā. In Her Nirguna aspect She is pure consciousness (Chaitanyarūpinī) and bliss itself (Ānandarūpinī, and in creation Brahmānandaprakāshinī). As Sagunā She it is by whose power all creatures are displayed (Sarvabhūtaprakāshinī).[147] Kundalī Shakti in individual bodies is *power at rest*, or the *static center* round which every form of existence as moving power revolves. In the universe there is always in and behind every form of activity a static background. This is one of the profound truths of the Shākta Tantras, which, as later explained, is borne out by recent discoveries of modern science. The one consciousness is polarized into static and kinetic aspects of conscious energy for the purpose of creation. This Yoga is

---

[144] The two seeds are Shiva and Shakti, and the sheath is Māyā. When they come apart there is creation. Again the imagery is faulty, in that there are two seeds, but Shiva and Shakti are the One with dual aspect.

[145] The shape of the Singara water-nut, which grows in the lakes of Kashmir. Here I may observe that Yantras, though drawn on the flat, must be conceived of in the solid mass. The flat drawing is a mere suggestion of the three dimensional figure which the Yantra is.

[146] Because She is thus bent the Devī is called Kubjikā (hunchback).

[147] Kubjikā Tantra, Ch. I., Prānatoshinī, p. 8.

the resolution of this duality into unity again.

The Indian Scriptures say, in the words of Herbert Spencer in his "First Principles," that the universe is an unfoldment (Srishti) from the homogeneous (Mūlaprakriti) to the heterogeneous (Vikriti), and back to the homogeneous again (Pralaya or dissolution). There are thus alternate states of evolution and dissolution, manifestation taking place after a period of rest. So also Professor Huxley, in his "Evolution and Ethics," speaks of the manifestation of cosmic energy (Māyā Shakti) alternating between phases of potentiality (Pralaya) and phases of explication (Srishti). "It may be," he says, "as Kant suggests, every cosmic magma predestined to evolve into a new world has been the no less predestined end of a vanished predecessor." This the Indian Shāstra affirms in its doctrine that there is no such thing as an absolutely first creation, the present universe being but one of a series of worlds which are past and are yet to be.

At the time of dissolution (Pralaya) there is in consciousness as Mahākundalī, though undistinguishable from its general mass, the potentiality or seed of the universe to be. Māyā potentially exists as Mahākundalī, who is Herself one with Consciousness or Shiva. This Māyā contains, and is in fact constituted by, the collective Sangskāra or Vāsanā—that is, the mental impressions produced by Karma accomplished in previously existing worlds. These constitute the mass of the potential ignorance (Avidyā) by which Consciousness veils itself. They were produced by desire for worldly enjoyment, and themselves produce such desire. The worlds exist because they in their totality will to exist. Each individual exists because his will desires worldly life. This seed is therefore the collective or cosmic will towards manifested life—that is, the life of form and enjoyment. At the end of the period of rest, which is dissolution, this seed ripens in Consciousness. Consciousness has thus a twin aspect: its liberation (Mukti) or formless aspect, in which it *is* as mere Consciousness-Bliss; and a universe or form aspect, in which it *becomes* the worlds of enjoyment (Bhukti). One of the cardinal principles of the Shākta Tantra is to secure by its Sādhanā both liberation (Mukti) and enjoyment (Bhukti).[148] This is possible by the identification of the self when in enjoyment with the soul of the world. When this seed ripens Shiva is said to put forth His Shakti. As this Shakti is Himself, it is He in his Shiva-Shakti aspect who comes forth (Prasarati) and endows Himself with all the forms of worldly life. In the pure, perfect, formless Consciousness there springs up the desire to manifest in the world of forms—the desire for enjoyment of and as form. This takes place as a

---

[148] Bhogena moksham āpnoti bhogena kulasādhanam
Tasmāt yatnāt bhogayukto bhavet vīravarah sudhīh.
(Kulārnava Sanghitā, v. 219.)

limited stress in the unlimited unmoving surface of pure Consciousness, which is Nishkala Shiva, but without affecting the latter. There is thus change in changelessness and changelessness in change. Shiva in His transcendent aspect does not change, but Shiva (Sakala) in His immanent aspect as Shakti does. As creative will arises Shakti thrills as Nāda,[149] and assumes the form of Bindu, which is Īshvara Tattva, whence all the worlds derive. It is for their creation that Kundalī uncoils. When Karma ripens, the Devī, in the words of the Nigama,[150] "becomes desirous of creation, and covers Herself with Her own Māyā." Again, "the Devī, joyful in the mad delight of Her union with the Supreme Akula,[151] becomes Vikārinī"[152]—that is, the Vikāras or Tattvas of mind and matter which constitute the universe appear.

The Shāstras have dealt with the stages of creation in great detail both from the subjective and objective viewpoints as changes in the limited consciousness or as movement (Spanda), form, "sound" (Shabda). Both Shaivas and Shāktas equally accept the thirty-six categories or Tattvas, the Kalās, the Shaktis Unmanī, and the rest in the Tattvas, the Shadadhvā, the Mantra concepts of Nāda, Bindu, Kāmakalā, and so forth.[153] Authors of the Northern Shaiva school, of which a leading Shāstra is the Mālinīvijaya Tantra, have described with great profundity these Tattvas. General conclusions only are, however, here summarized. These thirty-six Tattvas are in the Tantras divided into three groups, called Ātmā. Vidyā, and Shiva Tattvas. The first group includes all the Tattvas, from the lowest Prithivi ("earth") to Prakriti, which are known as the impure categories (Ashuddhatattva); the second includes Māyā, the Kanchuka,[154] and Purusha, called the pure-impure categories (Shuddhaashuddha Tattva); and the third includes the five highest Tattvas, called the pure Tattvas (Shuddha Tattva), from Shiva Tattva to Shuddhavidyā. As already stated, the supreme changeless state (Parāsamvit)[155] is a unitary experience in which the "I" and "This" coalesce into a unity in which neither are

---

[149] Literally "sound," that initial activity which is the first source of that Shabda (sound) which is the word to which corresponds the Artha or object.

[150] Kulachūdāmani, Vol. IV., "Tantrik Texts," Ch. I., vv. 16-24.

[151] Akula is a Tantrik name for Shiva, Shakti being called Kula, which is Mātri, Māna, Meya. In the Yoginīhridaya Tantra it is said (Ch. I.): Kulam meyamānamātrilakshanam kaulastat samashtih. These three are Knower, Knowing, Known, for that is consciousness as Shakti.

[152] Kulachūdāmani, Vol. IV., "Tantrik Texts," Ch. I., vv. 16-24.

[153] See as to these terms the author's "Studies in the Mantrashāstra."

[154] Forms of Shakti whereby the natural perfections of Consciousness are limited. Thus, from all-knowing it becomes little-knowing; from being almighty, it becomes a little doer, etc.

The term Samkocha (contraction) expresses the same idea. The Devī is Samkuchadrūpā through Mātri, Māna, Meya, and therefore so also is Shiva as jīva (tathā shivo, pi samkuchadrūpa).—Yoginīhridaya Tantra.

[155] This is not counted as a Tattva.

perceived as such.

In the kinetic or Shakti aspect, as presented by the pure categories, experience recognizes an "I" and "This," but the latter is regarded, not as something opposed to and outside the "I," but as part of a one self which has two sides—an "I" (Aham) and "This" (Idam). The emphasis varies from insistence on the "I" to insistence on the "This," and then to equality of emphasis on the "I" and "This as a preparation for the dichotomy in consciousness which follows.

The pure-impure categories are intermediate between the pure and the impure. The essential characteristic of experience constituted by the impure categories is its dualism effected through Māyā—and its limitations—the result of the operation of the Kanchukas. Here the "This" is not seen as part of the self, but as opposed to and without it as an object seen outside. Each consciousness thus became mutually exclusive the one of the other. The states thus described are threefold: a transcendent mingled "I" and "This," in which these elements of experience are as such not perceived; a pure form of experience intermediate between the first and last, in which both the "I" and the "This" are experienced as part of the one self; and, thirdly, the state of manifestation proper, when there is a complete cleavage between the "I" and the "This," in which an outer object is presented to the consciousness of a knower. This last stage is itself twofold. In the first the Purusha experiences a homogeneous universe, though different from himself as Prakriti; in the second Prakriti is split up into its effects (Vikriti), which are mind and matter, and the multitudinous beings of the universe which these compose. Shakti as Prakriti first evolves mind (Buddhi, Ahangkāra, Manas) and senses (Indriya), and then sensible matter (Bhūta) of fivefold form ("ether," "air," "fire," "water," "earth")[156] derived from the supersensible generals of the sense particulars called Tanmātra. When Shakti has entered the last and grossest Tattva ("earth")—that is, solid matter—there is nothing further for Her to do. Her creative activity then ceases, and *She rests.* She rests in Her last emanation, the "earth" principle. She is again coiled and sleeps. She is now Kundalī Shakti, whose abode in the human body is the earth center or Mūlādhāra Chakra. As in the supreme state She lay coiled as the Mahākundalī round the Supreme Shiva, so here She coils round the Svayambhu Lingga in the Mūlādhāra.

The Mantra evolution is set forth with great clarity in the Shāradā Tilaka, wherein it is said that from the Sakala Shiva (Shiva Tattva), who is Sat-Chit-Ānanda, issued Shakti (Shakti Tattva); from the latter

---

[156] These terms have not the ordinary English meaning, but denote the ethereal, gaseous, igneous, liquid, and solid states of matter. In worship (Pūjā) they are symbolized by the following ingredients (Upachāra): Pushpa (flower), ether; Dhūpa (incense), air; Dīpa (agni), fire; Naivedya (food offering), water; Chandana (sandal), earth.

Nāda (Sadākhya Tattva); and from Nāda evolved Bindu (Īshvara Tattva),[157] which, to distinguish it from the Bindu which follows, is called the Supreme Bindu (Para-Bindu). Nāda and Bindu are, like all else, aspects of Shakti, being those states of Her which are the proper conditions for (Upayogāvasthā) and in which She is prone to (Uchchhanāvasthā) creation. In those Tattvas the germ of action (Kriyā Shakti) sprouts towards its full manifestation.

The Tantras, in so far as they are Mantra Shāstras, are concerned with Shabda or "sound," a term later explained. Mantra is manifested Shabda. Nāda, which also literally means sound, is the first of the produced intermediate causal bodies of Shabda. Bindu, which has previously been explained, is described as the state of the letter Ma before manifestation, consisting of the Shiva-Shakti Tattva enveloped by Māyā or Parama Kundalī. It implies both the void (Shūnya)—that is, the Brahman state (Brahmapada)—in the empty space within the circle of the Bindu; as also the Gunas which are implicitly contained in it, since it is in indissoluble union with Shakti, in whom the Gunas or factors constituting the material source of all things are contained.[158] The Parabindu is called the Ghanāvasthā state of Shakti. It is Chidghana or massive consciousness—that is, Chit associated with undifferentiated (that is, Chidrūpinī) Shakti, in which lie potentially in a mass (Ghana), though undistinguishable the one from the other, all the worlds and beings to be created. This is Parama Shiva, in whom are all the Devatās. It is this Bindu who is the Lord (Īshvara) whom some Pauranikas call Mahāvishnu and others the Brahmapurusha.[159] As the Commentator says, it does not matter what He is called. He is the Lord (Īshvara) who is worshipped in secret by all Devas,[160] and is pointed to in different phases of the Chandrabindu, or Nāda, Bindu, Shakti, and Shānta of the Om and other Bīja Mantras. Its abode is Satyaloka, which within the human body exists in the pericarp of the thousand-petalled lotus (Sahasrāra) in the highest cerebral center. The Shāradā[161] then says that this Parabindu, whose substance is Supreme Shakti, divides itself into three—that is, appears under a threefold aspect. There are thus three Bindus, the first of which is called Bindu,[162] and the others Nāda and Bīja. Bindu is in the nature of Shiva and Bīja of Shakti. Nāda is Shiva-Shakti—that is, their mutual relation or interaction (Mithah

---

157 Sachchidānanda-vibhavāt sakalāt parameshvarāt
Āsīchchhaktistato nādo, nādād bindu-samudbhavah

(Ch. I.).

158 See vv. 4, 37-49, S.N., *post*; Todala Tantra, Ch. VI.; and Kangkālamālinī Tantra, cited in v. 43.

159 S.N., v. 49.

160 *Ib.*, v. 41.

161 Ch. I.

162 Kāryya, or produced Bindu, to distinguish it from the causal (Kārana) Bindu or Parabindu.

samavāyah)[163] or Yoga (union), as the Prayogasāra calls it.[164] The threefold Bindu (Tribindu) is supreme (Para), subtle (Sūkshma), and gross (Sthūla).[165] Nāda is thus the union of these two in creation. As the text says (v. 40), it is by this division of Shiva and Shakti that there arises creative ideation (Srishti-Kalpanā). The causal Bindu is from the Shakti aspect undifferentiated Shakti (Abhedarūpā Shakti) with all powers (Sarvashaktimaya); from the Prakriti aspect Trigunamayī Mūlaprakriti; from the Devatā aspect the unmanifest (Avyakta); from the Devī aspect Shāntā. The three Bindus separately indicate the operations of the three powers of will (Ichchhā), knowledge (Jnāna), and action (Kriyā), and the three Gunas (Rajas, Sattva, Tamas); also the manifestation of the three Devīs (Vāmā, Jyeshthā, Raudrī) and the three Devatās (Brahmā, Vishnu, Rudra) who spring from them.[166] It is said in

---

[163] Parashaktimayah sākshāt tridhāsau bhidyate punah
Bindurnādo bījam iti tasya bhedāh samīritāh
Binduhshivātmako bījang shaktirnādastayormithah
Samavāyah samākhyātah sarvvāgamavishāradaih (Ch. I.).

The first word of the third line reads better as Binduhshivātmako than as Bindurnādatmako, as in some MSS., such as in that from which I quoted in Introduction to the Mahānirvāna. The Commentary to v. 40, *post*, also speaks of Bindu as being Nādātmaka, but explains that that means Shivātmaka. See also to same effect Kriyāsāra.

[164] See Rāghava Bhatta's Comm. on Ch. I. v. 8 of Shāradā.
Nirgunah sagunashcheti shivo jneyah sanātanah
Nirgunāchchaiva sangjātā bindavastraya eva cha
Brahmavindurvishnubindū rudrabindur maheshvari.

The verse as cited in Prānatoshinī (p. 13) reads in second line Nirgunāshchaiva; but this must be a mistake for Nirgunāchchhaiva, for the Bindus themselves are not nirguna, but spring from it.

[165] Asmāchcha kāranavindohsakāshāt kramena kāryyabindustato nādastato bījamiti trayam utpannam tadidang parasūkshmasthūlapadaih kathyate (Lalitā-Sahasranāma, Comm.).

These represent the Chit, Chidachit, Achit aspects of nature. Chidangshah chidachinmishrah achidangshashcha teshāng rūpāni (Bhāskararāya; Comm. Lalitā). Kālena bhidyamānastu sa bindurbhavati tridhā, Sthūlasūkshmaparatvena tasya traividhyamishyate. Sa bindunādabījatvabhedena cha nigadyate (Pra. sāra I. 42). Ete cha Kāranabindvādayashchatvāra ādhidaivatamavyakteshvarahiranyagarbhavirātsvarūpāh shāntāvāmājyesthāraudrīrūpā ambikechchhājnānakriyārūpāshcha (*ib.*). Ādhibhūtantukāmarūpapūrnagirijālandharaudhyānapītharūpāh. Pītharūpā iti tu nityāhridaye spashtam (*ib.*). Citing Rahasyāgama.

[166] Ichchhā, Rajas, Vāmā, Brahmā, Pashyantīshabda,
Jnāna, Sattva, Jyeshthā, Vishnu, Madhyamāshabda,
Kriyā, Tamas, Raudrī, Rudra, Vaikharīshabda.

See Comm. 22, Shloka Kāmakalāvilāsa, Sangketa 1, Yoginīhridaya Tantra, and Saubhāgya Sudhodaya, cited in Sangketa 2 of the last Tantra. As the Rudra Yāmala says (II. 22), the three Devas are aspects of the One.

Ekā mūrtistrayo devā brahmavishnumaheshvarāh
Mama vigrahasangkliptā srijatyavati hanticha.

the Prayogasāra and Shāradā that Raudrī issued from Bindu, Jyesthā from Nāda, and Vāmā from Bīja. From these came Rudra, Vishnu, Brahmā, which are in the nature of Jnāna, Kriyā, Ichchhā, and Moon, Sun, and Fire.[167] The three Bindus are known as Sun (Ravi), Moon (Chandra), and Fire (Agni), terms constantly appearing in the works here translated.

In Sun there are Fire and Moon.[168] It is known as Mishra Bindu, and in the form of such is not different from Paramashiva, and is Kāmakalā.[169] Kāmakalā is the triangle of divine desire formed by the three Bindus—that is, their collectivity (Samashtirūpā).[170] This Kāmakalā is the root (Mūla) of all Mantra. Moon (Soma, Chandra) is Shiva Bindu, and white (Sita Bindu); Fire (Agni) is Shaktibindu, and red (Shonabindu); Sun is a mixture of the two. Fire, Moon, and Sun are the Ichchhā, Jnāna, Kriyā Shaktis (will, knowledge, action) manifesting in the Mūlādhāra (head and heart). On the material plane the white Bindu assumes the form of semen (Shukra), and the red Bindu of menstrual fluid (Rajasphala, Shonita). Mahābindu is the state before the manifestation of Prakriti.[171] All three Bindus—that is, the Kāmakalā—are Shakti, though one may indicate predominantly the Shiva, the other the Shakti aspect. Sometimes Mishra Bindu is called Shakti Tattva, to denote the supremacy of Shakti, and sometimes Shiva Tattva, to denote the supremacy of the possessor of power (Shaktimān). It is of coupled form (Yāmalarūpa). There is no Shiva without Shakti, nor Shakti without Shiva.[172] To separate[173] them is as impossible as to separate the

---

But see next note.

[167] Cited in Prānatoshinī, p. 8:

Raudrībindostato nādāt jyeshthā bījādajāyata
Vāmā tābhyah samutpannāh rudra-brahma-ramādipāh
Te jnānechchhā-kriyātmāno vahnīndvarka-svarūpinah.
Ichchhā kriyā tathā jnānang gaurī brāhmītu vaishnavī
Tridhā shaktih sthitā yatra tatparang jyotiromiti.

As the author of the Prānatoshinī (p. 9) says, the names are not to be read in the order of words (Pratishabdam), otherwise Jnāna would be associated with Vaishnavī, but according to the facts (Yathā sambhavam) as stated in the text. According to this account it would seem that Jnāna Sattva and Kriyā Tamas in note 1 should be transposed.

[168] It is Agnīshomamayah. See Tīkā, vv. 6, 7, of Kāmakalāvilāsa.

[169] That is, Kāmayukta Kalā, creative will with Kalā (here its manifestation).

Mahābindu = Paramashiva = Mishrabindu = Ravi = Kāmakalā.
Ravi-paramashivābhinnā mishrabindurūpā Kāmakalā.

[170] As Ravi or Sūrya Bindu (Sun) is in the form of Parashiva, and in it are the other two Bindus, it is the Samashtirūpa of them, and is thus called Kāmakalā.

[171] This, which is O, becomes 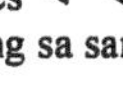—that is, Chandra, Ravi, and Ra (fire).

[172] Tayoryad yāmalang rūpang sa sanghatta iti smritah

moving wind from the steadfast ether in which it blows. In the one Shiva-Shakti there is a union (Maithuna),[174] the thrill of which is Nāda, whence Mahābindu is born, which itself becomes threefold (Tribindu), which is Kāmakalā.[175] It is said in the Shāradā-Tilaka that on the "bursting" or differentiation of the Supreme Bindu there was unmanifested "sound" (Shabda).[176] This manifested Shabda is through action (Kriyā Shakti) the source of the manifested Shabda and Artha described later.[177] The Brahman as the source of language (Shabda) and ideas on one hand, and the objects (Artha) they denote on the other, is called Shabdabrahman, or the Logos.[178] From this differentiating Bindu in the form of Prakriti are evolved the Tattvas of mind and matter in all their various forms, as also the Lords of the Tattvas (Tattvesha)—that is, their directing intelligences—Shambhu,[179] the presiding Devatā over

---

Ānandashaktih saivoktā yato vishvang visrijyati
Na Shivah Shaktirahito na Shaktih Shivavarjitā.

(Tantrāloka-Āhnika, 3.)

The coupled form of these two (Shivā-Shakti) is called junction. That is called the blissful Shakti from which creation arises. There is no Shiva without Shakti, nor Shakti without Shiva.

[173] *Ib.*, 3 Ahn.

[174] On the physical plane this word denotes sexual union.

[175] In the Shrīchakra this is in the region of Baindava Chakra, the highest, followed by the triangular Chakra, which is Kāmeshvarī, Bhagamālinī, and Vajreshvarī. See further as to Kāmakalā, *post*.

[176] Bhidyamānāt parādvindoravyaktātmaravo' bhavat
Shabdabrahmeti tang prāhuh sarvvāgamavishāradāh.

(Shāradā Tilaka, Ch. I.)

See Introduction to my Mahānirvāna Tantra, p. XXII. It will be observed that in this verse the first Bindu is called Para, and to make this clear the author of the Prānatoshini adds the following note:

Parādvindorityanena shaktyavasthārupo yah prathamo bindustasmāt (By Parabindu is meant the first Bindu, which is a state of Shakti).

[177] See Rāghava Bhatta, Comm. v. 12, Shāradā, and the same.

Kriyāshaktipradhānāyāh shabdashabdārthakāranam
Prakriterbindurupinyāh shabdabrahmā bhavat param.

[178] It is said in the Prānatoshinī, p. 22, that Shambhu is the "associate of time" (Kālabandhu), because Kāla in the form of Nāda assists in giving birth to Him and the other Devatās.

As the Kulārnava Tantra (Khanda 5, Ullāsa I.) says, the one Brahman has twofold aspect as Paramabrahman (transcendent) and Shabdabrahman (immanent). Shabdabrahmaparambrahmabhedena brahmanor dvaividhyam uktam. And see also Shrīmad Bhāgavata, 6 Khanda, 16 Ch. Tena shabdārtharūpavishishtasya shabdabrahmatvam avadhāritam (Prānatoshini, 13).

[179] Atha bindvātmanah shambhoh kālabandhoh kalātmanah
Ajāyata jagat-sākshī sarvvavyāpī sadāshivah
Sadāshivāt bhaved Īsha stato Rudrasamudbhavah
Tato Vishnu stato Brahmā teshām evam samudbhavah.

(Ch. I., vv. 15, 16.)

the Ājnā Chakra, the center of the mental faculties; and Sadāshiva, Īsha, Rudra, Vishnu, Brahmā, the Devatās of the five forms of matter, concluding with Prithivī ("earth") in the Mūlādhāra center, wherein the creative Shakti, having finished Her work, again rests, and is called Kundalinī.

Just as the atom consists of a static center round which moving forces revolve, so in the human body Kundalī in the earth Chakra is the static center (Kendra) round which She in kinetic aspect as the forces of the body works. The whole body as Shakti is in ceaseless movement. Kundalī Shakti is the immobile support of all these operations. When She is aroused and Herself moves upwards, She withdraws with and into Herself these moving Shaktis, and then unites with Shiva in the Sahasrāra lotus. The process upward (evolution) is the reverse of the involution above described.

Before proceeding to a description of the Chakras it is, firstly, necessary to describe more fully the constituents of the body—that is, the Tattvas—mentioned, extending from Prakriti to Prithivī. It is of these Tattvas that the Chakras are centers. Secondly, an explanation is required of the doctrine of "sound" (Shabda), which exists in the body in the three inner states (Parā, Pashyantī, Madhyamā), and is expressed in uttered speech (Vaikharī) This will help the reader to an understanding of the meaning of Mantra or manifested Shabda, and of the "Garland of Letters" which is distributed throughout the six bodily centers.

III. Embodied Consciousness (Jīvātmā)

The transcendental consciousness is called the Supreme Ātmā. The consciousness which is either in fact embodied or liable to be embodied is the Jīvātmā. These are but names for differing aspects of the same Self or Ātmā. In the first case consciousness is liberated from, and in the second it is with, form. As Consciousness is in itself formless, form is derivable from its power (Shakti). This power evolves itself into Prakriti Shakti—that is, the immediate source and the constituent of mind and matter. The corresponding consciousness aspect of the same power is called Purusha. This term is sometimes applied to the Supreme, as in the name Brahmapurusha.[180] Here is meant a limited consciousness—limited by the associated Prakriti and Her products of mind and matter. In this sense the term Purusha does not mean merely a

---

Here they are mentioned in connection with the form creation (Arthasrishti). The Prānatoshinī says: Atra Arthasrishtau punah rudrādīnāmutpattistu artharūpena. Pūrvvamteshām utpattih shabdarūpena, ato na paunaruktyam iti kalāmāyā tadātmanastadutpannatvāt.

[180] So it is said Purushāt na parang kinchit sā kāshthā sā pārāgatih.

human being, or indeed any animal, but all beings and things which are centers of expressed or hidden consciousness. In this sense an atom of sand is a Purusha—that is, a consciousness identifying itself with that particular form of solid matter faintly showing its existence in atomic memory and in its response to stimuli. For with that with which we identify ourselves, that we become. This is from the philosophical aspect. More popularly by Purusha, as by Jīva, is meant sentient being with body and senses—that is, organic life.[181] Man is a microcosm (Kshudrabrahmānda).[182] The world is the macrocosm (Brahmānda). There are numberless worlds and universes, each of which is governed by its own Lords, though there is but one great Mother of all whom these Lords themselves worship, placing on their heads the dust of Her feet. In everything there is all that is in anything else. There is thus nothing in the universe which is not in the human body. There is no need to throw one's eyes into the heavens to find God. He is within, being known as the "Ruler within" (Antaryāmin) or "Inner self" (Antarātmā).[183] All else is His power as mind and matter. Whatever of mind or matter exists in the universe exists in some form or manner in the human body. So it is said in the Vishvasāra Tantra: "What is here is there. What is not here is nowhere."[184] In the body there are the Supreme Shiva-Shakti who pervade all things. In the body is Prakriti Shakti and all Her products. In fact, the body is a vast magazine of power (Shakti). The object of the Tantric rituals is to raise these various forms of power to their full expression. This is the work of Sādhanā. The Tantras say that it is in the power of man to accomplish all he wishes if he centers his will thereon. And this must be so, for man is in his essence one with the Supreme Lord (Īshvara), and the more he manifests spirit the greater is he endowed with its powers. The center and root of all his powers is Kundalī Shakti. The center in which the quiescent consciousness is realized is the upper brain or Sahasrāra, whence in the case of the Yogī the Prāna escapes through the

---

181 Dehendriyādiyuktah chetano jīvah. The Kulārnava Tantra, I. 7-9, describes the Jīvas as parts of Shiva enveloped in Māyā (which gives them the false notion of separation from Him), like sparks issuing from fire—an old Vedantic idea. As, however, Jīva in Vedānta is really Brahman (jīvo brahmaiva nāparah) there is in reality no independent category called Jīva (Nahi jīvonāma kashchit svatantrah padārthah). Ātmā is called Jīva when with upādhi—that is, body, etc. Philosophically, all Ātmā with upādhi (attribute) is Jīva.

182 "Little egg (spheroid) of Brahmā."

183 The Jnānārnava Tantra (XXI. 10) says that "antah" means secret and subtle, for the Ātmā fine like an atom is within everything. This is the bird Hangsah which disports in the lake of ignorance. On dissolution, when it is Sanghārarūpī, Ātmā is revealed. The Mother is the Antaryāmin of the Devatās also, such as the five Shivas, Brahmā, etc.; for She is Parabrahmānandarūpā, Prakāsharūpā, Sadrūpā, and Chidrūpā, and thus directs them (Trishatī, II. 47).

184 Yadihāsti tadanyatra yannehāsti natat kvachit—an Indian version of the Hermetic maxim, "As above, so below."

Brahmarandhra at death. (See Plate VIII.) The mind and body are constituted of the products of Prakriti. Both having the same origin, each, whether mind or matter, are "material" things—that is, they are of the nature of forces,[185] and limited instruments through which Consciousness functions, and thus, though itself unlimited, appears to be limited. The light in a lantern is unaffected, but its manifestation to those without is affected by the material through which the light shines. Prakriti is not scientific matter. The latter is only its grossest product, and has no lasting existence. Prakriti is the ultimate "material" or substantive cause of both mind and matter, and the whole universe which they compose. It is the mysterious fructescent womb (Yoni) whence all is born.[186] What She is in Herself cannot be realized. She is only known by Her effects.[187] Mūla Prakriti is the noumenal cause of the phenomenal world from which creation arises.[188] Ultimately, as it is in itself (Svarūpa), Prakriti Shakti, like all else, is Consciousness.[189] Consciousness, however, assumes the form of Prakriti—that is, creative power—when evolving the universe. That form consists of the Gunas or modes of this natural principle which are called Sattva, Rajas, Tamas.[190] The general action of Shakti is to veil consciousness.

[185] So Herbert Spencer holds, in conformity with Indian doctrine, that the universe, whether physical or psychical, is a play of force which in the case of matter we as the self or mind experience as object.

[186] The word has been said to be derived from *Kri* and the affix *Ktin*, which is added to express *bhāva*, or the abstract idea, and sometimes the Karma, or object of the action, corresponding with the Greek affix sis. *Ktin* inflected in the nominative becomes *tis*. Prakritis therefore has been said to correspond with *φύσις* (nature) of the Greeks (Banerjee, "Dialogues on Hindu Philosophy," 24). It is also called Pradhāna. Pra + dhā + anat = Pradhatte sarvvam ātmani, or that which contains all things in itself; the source and receptacle of all matter and form. Pradhāna also literally means "chief" (substance), for according to Sāngkhya it is the real creator.

[187] See the splendid Hymn to Prakriti in Prapanchasāra Tantra, Vol. III., "Tantrik Texts." What can be seen by the eyes can be defined, but not She. "It cannot be seen by the eyes." Kena Up., 1-6: "Yat chakshushā na pashyati." She is beyond the senses. Hence the Trishatī addresses the Devī (II. 44) as idrigityavinirdeshyā (who is not to be particularly pointed out as being this or that). See Shāradā Tilaka, Vāmakeshvara, and Vishvasāra Tantras, cited in Prānatoshinī, p. 24. She is ineffable and inconceivable: with form (Vikriti), yet Herself (Mūlaprakriti) formless. Mahānirvāna Tantra, IV. 33-35. Thus Sāyana (Rig Veda, X. 129, 2) says that, whilst Māyā is Anirvāchyā (indefinable), since it is neither Sat nor Asat, Chit is definable as Sat.

[188] Kriteh prārambho yasyāh. That is, by which creation (Srishti) maintenance (Sthiti), and dissolution (Laya) are done (Prakriyate kāryyādikam anayā).

[189] See Sadānanda's Comm. on 4th Mantra of Īsha Up. "The changeless Brahman which is consciousness appears in creation as Māyā which is Brahman (Brahmamayī) consciousness (Chidrūpinī), holding in Herself unbeginning (anādi) Karmik tendencies (Karmasangskāra) in the form of the three Gunas. Hence She is Gunamayī despite being Chinmayī. And as there is no second principle these Gunas are Chit Shakti."

[190] The three Gunas *are* Prakriti. The Devī, as in the form of Prakriti, is called Trigunātmikā (who is composed of the three Gunas). All nature which issues from Her, the Great Cause (Mahākāranasvarūpā), is also composed of the same Gunas in different states of relation.

Prakriti, in fact, like the *materia prima* of the Thomistic philosophy, is a *finitising* principle. To all seeming, it finitises and makes form in the infinite formless Consciousness.[191] So do all the Gunas. But one does it less and another more. The first is Sattvaguna, the function of which, relative to the other Gunas, is to reveal consciousness. The greater the presence or power of Sattvaguna, the greater the approach to the condition of pure consciousness. Similarly, the function of Tamas Guna is to suppress or veil consciousness. The function of Rajasguna is to make active—that is, it works on Tamas to suppress Sattva, or on Sattva to suppress Tamas.[192] The object and the effect of evolution, as it is of all Sādhanā, is to develop Sattvaguna. The Gunas always coexist in everything, but variously predominate. The lower descent is made in the scale of nature the more Tamasguna prevails, as in so-called "brute substance," which has been supposed to be altogether inert. The higher ascent is made the more Sattva prevails. The truly Sāttvik man is a divine man, his temperament being called in the Tantra Divyabhāva.[193] From pure Sattva passage is made to Sat, which is Chit or pure Consciousness, by the Siddhayogī, who is identified with Pure Spirit.

Prakriti exists in two states, in one of which (so far as any effect is concerned)[194] She is quiescent. The Gunas are then in stable equilibrium, and not affecting one another. There is no manifestation. This is the unmanifest (Avyakta), the potentiality of natural power (*natura naturans*).[195] When, however, owing to the ripening of Karma, the time for creation takes place, there is a stirring of the Gunas (Gunakshobha) and an initial vibration (Spandana), known in the Tantras as Cosmic Sound (Shabdabrahman). The Gunas affect one another, and the universe made of these three Gunas is created. The products of Prakriti thus evolved are called Vikāra or Vikriti.[196] Vikriti

---

[191] See an article of mine in the *Indian Philosophical Review*, "Shakti and Māyā."

[192] In the words of Professor P. Mukhyopadhyaya, dealing with the matter monistically, these are the three elements of the Life-Stress on the surface of pure Consciousness—namely, presentation (Sattva), movement (Rajas), and veiling (Tamas), which are the three elements of creative evolution ("The Patent Wonder," p. 19).

[193] Those in whom Rajas Guna is predominant, and who work that Guna to suppress Tamas, are Vīra (hero), and the man in whom the Tamasguna prevails is a Pashu (animal).

[194] The three gunas are essentially changeful. Nāparinamyakshanamapyavatishthante gunāh (the gunas do not remain for a moment without movement). Vāchaspati Misra; Sāngkhya-Tattva-Kaumudī, 16th Kārikā. The movement is twofold: (*a*) Sarūpaparināma or Sadrisha parināma in dissolution, and (*b*) Virūpaparināma in creation.

[195] This is, in fact, the definition of Prakriti as opposed to Vikriti: Sattvarajastamasāng sāmyāvasthā prakritih. Sāngkhya Kaumudi Kārikā 3: Sāngkhya Pravachana, I. 61.

[196] Vikāra or Vikriti is something which is really changed, as curd from milk. The former is a Vikriti of the latter. Vivartta is apparent but unreal change, such as the appearance of what was and is a rope as a snake. The Vedāntasāra thus musically defines the two terms:

is manifest (Vyakta) Prakriti (*natura naturata*). In the infinite and formless Prakriti there appears a strain or stress appearing as form. On the relaxation of this strain in dissolution forms disappear in formless Prakriti, who as power (Shakti) re-enters the Brahman-Consciousness. These Vikritis are the Tattvas issuing from Prakriti,[197] the Avidyā Shakti—namely, the different categories of mind, senses, and matter.

The bodies are threefold: causal (Kāranasharīra, or Parasharīra, as the Shaivas call it), subtle (Sūkshmasharīra), and gross (Sthūlasharīra). These bodies in which the Ātmā is enshrined are evolved from Prakriti Shakti, and are constituted of its various productions. They form the tabernacle of the Spirit (Ātmā), which as the Lord is "in all beings, and who from within all beings controls them."[198] The body of the Lord (Īshvara) is pure Sattvaguna (Shuddhasattvagunapradhāna).[199] This is the aggregate Prakriti or Māyā of Him or Her as the Creator-Creatrix of all things. Jīva, as the Kulārnava Tantra[200] says, is bound by the bonds (Pāsha); Sadāshiva is free of them.[201] The former is Pashu, and the latter Pashupati, or Lord of Pashus (Jīvas). That is, Ishvarī[202] is not affected by Her own Māyā. She is all-seeing, all-knowing, all-powerful. Īshvara thus rules Māyā. Jīva is ruled by it. The body of the Mother and Her child the Jīva are not, thus, the same. For the latter is a limited consciousness subject to error, and governed by that Māyāshakti of Hers which makes the world seem to be different from what it in its essence is. The body of Jīva is therefore known as the individual Prakriti or Avidyā, in which there is impure Sattva, and Rajas and Tamas (Malinasattvagunapradhāna). But in the Mother are all

---

Satattvato nyathāprathā vikāra ityudīritah
Atattvato nyathāprathā vivarta ityudīritah.

V. 40 of the Shatchakra speaks of Vikriti as a reflection (Pratibimba) of Prakriti. It is Prakriti modified.

197 As already explained, there are Tattvas which precede the Purusha-Prakriti Tattvas. Etymologically Tattva is an abstract derivation from the pronoun "Tat" (That), or Thatness, and may, it has been pointed out, be compared with the Hæcceitas of Duns Scotus. The Tattva in a general sense is Truth or Brahman. But in the Sānkhya it has a technical sense, being employed as a concrete term to denote the eight "producers," the sixteen "productions," and the twenty-fifth Tattva or Purusha.

198 Yah sarveshu bhuteshu tishthan; yah sarvāni bhutāni antaro yamayati (Brīh. Up., iii. 7, 15). The Jīva is thus Chaitanyarūpa with the Upādhi ajnāna and its effects, mind and body, and which is Abhimānin, or attributor to itself, of the waking, etc., states.

199 Shangkara's Bhāshya, II. 3-45. The Jīva is Chaitanya distinguished by Upādhi. The latter term means distinguishing property, attribute, body, etc., and here body (Deha) senses (Indriya) mind (Manas, Buddhi), etc. (*ib.* I. 2-6).

200 1 Khan da 5.

201 Pāshabaddho bhavejjīvah pāshamuktah sadāshivah (Kulārnava Tantra, IX. 48), upon which the author of the Prānatoshinī, who cites this passage, says: "Thus the identity of Shiva and Jīva is shown" (iti shivajīvayoraikyam uktam).

202 Feminine of Īshvara. Some worship Shiva, some Devī. Both are one.

creatures. And so in the Trishatī[203] the Devī is called "in the form of one and many letters" (Ēkānekākksharākritih). As Ekā She is the Ajnāna which is pure Sattva and attribute (Upādhi) of Īshvara; as Anekā She is Upādhi or vehicle of Jīva. Whilst Īshvara is one, Jīvas are many, according to the diversity in the nature of the individual Prakriti caused by the appearance of Rajas and Tamas in it in differing proportions. The Ātmā appears as Jīva in the various forms of the vegetable, animal, and human worlds.

The first or *causal body* of any particular Jīva, therefore, is that Prakriti (Avidyā Shakti) which is the cause of the subtle and gross bodies of this Jīva which are evolved from it. This body lasts until liberation, when the Jīvātmā ceases to be such and is the Paramātmā or bodiless Spirit (Videha Mukti). The Jīva exists in this body during *dreamless sleep* (Sushupti).

The second and third bodies are the differentiations through evolution of the causal body, from which first proceeds the subtle body, and from the latter is produced the gross body.

The *subtle body*, which is also called Linga Sharīra or Puryashtaka, is constituted of the first evolutes (Vikriti) from the causal Prakritic body—namely, the Mind (Antahkarana), the internal instrument, together with the external instruments (Bāhyakarana), or the Senses (Indriya), and their supersensible objects (Tanmātra). The third or gross body is the body of "matter" which is the gross particular object of the senses[204] derived from the supersensibles.

Shortly, this subtle body may be described as the mental body, as that which succeeds is called the gross body, of matter. Mind, which is called the "working within" or "internal instrument" (Antahkarana), is one only, but is given different names to denote the diversity of its functions.[205] The Sāngkhya thus speaks of Buddhi, Ahangkāra, Manas, to which the Vedānta adds Chitta, being different aspects or attributes (Dharma) of mind as displayed in the psychical processes by which the Jīva knows, feels, and wills.

These may be considered from the point of view of evolution—that is, according to the sequence in which the limited experience of the Jīva is evolved—or from that in which they are regarded after creation, when the experience of concrete sense objects has been had. According to the former aspect, Buddhi or Mahat Tattva is the state of mere presentation; consciousness of being only, without thought of "I" (Ahangkāra), and unaffected by sensations of particular objects (Manas and Indriyas). It is thus the impersonal Jīva Consciousness, a state of impersonal experience which, at least in some of its aspects, may be

---

203 Comm. by Shangkara on v. 23.

204 The definition of a Bhūta (sensible matter) is that which can be seen by the outer organ, such as the eye, ear, etc.

205 Sângkhya Pravachana Sūtra, II. 16.

that which is spoken of as the subliminal consciousness.[206] Ahangkāra, of which Buddhi is the basis, is the personal consciousness which realizes itself as a particular "I," the experiencer. The Jīva, in the order of creation, first experiences in a vague general way without consciousness of the self, like the experience which is had immediately on waking after sleep. It then refers this experience to the limited self, and has the consciousness "lam So-and-so."

Manas is the desire which follows on such experience, and the senses and their objects are the means whereby that enjoyment is had which is the end of all will to life. Whilst, however, in the order of evolution Buddhi is the first principle, in the actual working of the Antahkarana after creation has taken place it comes last.

It is more convenient, therefore, to commence with the sense-objects and the sensations they evoke. Matter as the objective cause of perception is not in its character as such under the cognizance of the senses. All that can be predicated of it is its effect upon these senses, which is realized by the instrumentality of mind in its capacity as Manas. The experiencer is affected in five different ways, giving rise in him to the sensations of hearing, touch and feel,[207] color and form[208] and sight, taste, and smell.[209] But sensible perception exists only in respect of particular objects. Thus, sound as the gross object of the sense (Indriya) of hearing is either high, low, harsh, sweet, and so forth. Sound is thus perceived in its variations only. But there exist also general elements of the particulars of sense perception. That general ideas may be formed of particular sense objects indicates, it is said,[210] their existence in some parts of the Jīva's nature as facts of experience; otherwise the generals could not be formed from the particulars given by the senses as the physical facts of experience. There is therefore an abstract quality by which sensible matter (Mahābhūta) is perceived. This abstract quality is called a Tanmātra, which means the "mere thatness," or abstract quality, of an object. Thus, the Tanmātra of sound (Shabdatanmātra) is not any particular sensible form of it, but the "thatness" of sound—that is, sound *as such* apart from any of its particular variations stated. The Tanmātras have, therefore, aptly been

---

[206] As suggested by Jagadisha Chatterji in "Kashmir Shaivaism," p. 101, n.

[207] See note 213, *post.*

[208] Rūpa is primarily color. By means of color form is perceived, for a perfectly colorless thing is not perceivable by the gross senses.

[209] The other objects of the senses are the speakable, prehensible, approachable, excitable (that which is within the genitals), and excretable. "Each sense is suited to a particular class of influences—touch to solid pressure, hearing to aerial pressure, taste to liquid, light to luminous rays" (Bains, "Mind and Body," p. 22. 1892).

See Sāngkhya Pravachana Sūtra, II. 26-28, 40; Sāngkhya Tattva Kaumudī, 27 Kārikā.

[210] See for this in greater detail "Kashmir Shaivaism," 125.

called the "generals of the sense particulars"[211]—that is, the general elements of sense perception. These necessarily come into existence when the senses (Indriya) are produced; for a sense necessitates something which can be the object of sensation. These Sūkshma (subtle) Bhūta, as they are also called, are not ordinarily themselves perceived, for they are supersensible (Atīndriya). Their existence is only mediately perceived through the gross particular objects of which they are the generals, and which proceed from them. They can be the objects of immediate (Pratyaksha) perception only to Yogīs.[212] They are, like the gross sense objects derived from them, five in number—namely, sound as such (Shabdatanmātra), touch and feel as such[213] (Sparshatanmātra), color and form as such (Rūpatanmātra), flavor as such (Rasatanmātra), and odor as such (Gandhatanmātra). Each of these evolves from that which precedes it.[214]

Sensations aroused by sense objects are experienced by means of the outer instruments (Bāhyakarana) of the Lord of the body, or senses (Indriya), which are the gateways through which the Jīva receives worldly experience. These are ten in number, and are of two classes: viz., the five organs of sensation or perception (Jnanendriya), or ear (hearing), skin (feeling by touch), eye (sight), tongue (taste), and nose (smell); and the five organs of action (Karmendriya), which are the reactive response which the self makes to sensation—namely, mouth, hands, legs, anus, and genitals, whereby sneaking, grasping, walking, excretion, and procreation, are performed, and through which effect is given to the Jīva's desires. These are afferent and efferent impulses respectively.

The Indriya, or sense, is not the physical organ, but the faculty of mind operating through that organ as its instrument. The outward sense organs are the usual means whereby on the physical plane the functions of hearing and so forth are accomplished. But, as they are mere instruments and their power is derived from the mind, a Yogī may accomplish by the mind only all that may be done by means of these physical organs without the use of the latter.

With reference to their physical manifestations, but not as they are in themselves, the classes into which the Indriyas are divided may be described as the sensory and motor nervous systems. As the Indriyas are not the physical organs, such as ear, eye, and so forth, but faculties of the Jīva desiring to know and act by their aid, the Yogī claims to accomplish without the use of the latter all that is ordinarily done by

---

211 See note 210.

212 So it is said Tāni vastūni tanmātrādīni pratyaksha-vishayāni (that is, to Yogīs).

213 Whereby the thermal quality of things is perceived.

214 In a general way the last four correspond with the Vaisheshika Paramānus. There are differences, however. Thus, the latter are eternal (Nitya) and do not proceed from one another.

their means. So a hypnotized subject can perceive things, even when no use of the special physical organs ordinarily necessary for the purpose is made.[215] The fact of there being a variety of actions does not necessarily involve the same number of Indriyas. An act of "going" done by means of the hand (as by a cripple) is to be regarded really as an operation of the Indriya of feet (Padendriya), even though the hand is the seat of the Indriya for handling.[216] By the instrumentality of these Indriyas things are perceived and action is taken with reference to them. The Indriyas are not, however, sufficient in themselves for this purpose. In the first place, unless attention co-operates there is no sensation (Ālochana) at all. To be "absent-minded" is not to know what is happening.[217] Attention must therefore co-operate with the senses before the latter can "give" the experiencer anything at all.[218] Nextly, at one and the same moment the experiencer is subject to receive a countless number of sensations which come to and press upon him from all sides. If any of these is to be brought into the field of consciousness, it must be selected to the exclusion of others. The process of experience is the selection of a special section from out of a general whole, and then being engaged on it, so as to make it one's own, either as a particular object of thought or a particular field of operation.[219] Lastly, as Western psychology holds, the senses give not a completed whole, but a manifold—the manifold of sense. These "points of sensation" must be gathered together and made into a whole. These three functions of attention, selection, and synthesizing the discrete manifold of the senses, are those belonging to that aspect of the mental body, the internal agent (Antahkarana), called Manas.[220] Just as Manas is necessary to the senses (Indriya), the latter are necessary for Manas. For the latter is the seat of desire, and cannot exist by itself. It is the desire to perceive or act, and therefore exists in association with the Indriyas.

Manas is thus the leading Indriya, of which the senses are powers. For without the aid and attention of Manas the other Indriyas are incapable of performing their respective offices; and as these Indriyas are those of perception and action, Manas, which co-operates with both,

---

215 See "Kashmir Shaivaism," by J. C. Chatterji, p. 120. Thus Professor Lombroso records the case of a woman who, being blind, read with the tip of her ear, tasted with her knees, and smelt with her toes.

216 Tantrasāra Āhnika, 8.

217 See "Kashmir Shaivaism," p. 112.

218 So in the Brihadāranyaka Upanishad, I. 3-27, it is said: "My Manas (mind) was diverted elsewhere. Therefore I did not hear."

219 So, in the Text here translated *post*, Manas is spoken of as a doorkeeper who lets some enter, and keeps others outside.

220 See "Kashmir Shaivaism," 94-114. This is the Sāngkhyan and Vedāntic definition. According to the Vaisheshika, Manas is that which gives knowledge of pleasure, pain, and Jivātmā (I am So-and-so).

is said to partake of the character of both cognition and action.

Manas, through association with the eye or other sense, becomes manifold, being particularized or differentiated by its co-operation with that particular instrument, which cannot fulfill its functions except in conjunction with Manas.

Its function is said to be Sangkalpa-Vikalpa. That is, selection and rejection from the material provided by the Jnānendriya. When, after having been brought into contact with the sense objects, it selects the sensation which is to be presented to the other faculties of the mind, there is Sangkalpa. The activity of Manas, however, is itself neither intelligent result nor moving feelings of pleasure or pain. It has not an independent power to reveal itself to the experiencer. Before things can be so revealed and realized as objects of perception, they must be made subject to the operation of Ahangkāra and Buddhi, without whose intelligent light they would be dark forms unseen and unknown by the experiencer, and the efforts of Manas but blind gropings in the dark. Nor can the images built up by Manas affect of themselves the experiencer so as to move him in any way until and unless the experiencer identifies himself with them by Ahangkāra—that is, by making them his own in feeling and experience. Manas, being thus an experience of activity in the dark, unseen and unrevealed by the light of Buddhi, and not moving the experiencer until he identifies himself with it in feeling, is one in which the dark veiling quality (Tamasguna) of Shakti Prakriti is the most manifest.[221] This Guna also prevails in the Indriyas and the subtle objects of their operation (Tanmātra).

Ahangkāra the "I-maker" is self-arrogation[222]—that is, the realization of oneself as the personal "I" or self-consciousness of worldly experience, in which the Jīva thinks of himself as a particular person who is in relation with the objects of his experience. It is the power of self-arrogation whereby all that constitutes man is welded into one Ego, and the percept or concept is referred to that particular thinking subject and becomes part of its experience. When, therefore, a sensation is perceived by Manas and determined by Buddhi, Ahangkāra says: "It is I who perceive it."

This is the "I" of phenomenal consciousness as distinguished from "this" the known. Buddhi functions with its support.[223] Buddhi considered with relation to the other faculties of experience is that aspect of the Antahkarana which determines (Adhyavasāyātmikā

---

[221] See "Kashmir Shaivaism," p. 116, where the author cites the dictum of Kant that perceptions (Anschauung) without conceptions are blind.

[222] Abhimāna. Abhimāno'hangkārah. See Sāngkhya Tattva Kaumudi, 24 Kārikā, and Bk. II., Sutra 16, Sāngkhya Pravachana Sutra.

[223] Tang ahangkâram upajīvya hi buddhiradhyavasyati (Sāngkhya Tattva Kaumudī, *supra*).

buddhi*h*).[224] "A man is said to determine (Adhyavasyati) who, having perceived (Manas), and thought, 'I am concerned in this matter' (Ahangkāra), and thus having self-arrogated, comes to the determination, 'This must be done by me' (Kartavyam etat mayā)."[225] "Must be done" here does not refer to exterior action only, but to mental action (Mānasīkriyā) also, such as any determination by way of the forming of concepts and percepts ("It is so") and resolutions ("It must be done"). Buddhi pervades all effects whatever other than itself. It is the principal Tattva because it pervades all the instruments (Indriya), is the receptacle of all the Sangskāras or Karmic tendencies, and is in Sāngkhya the seat of memory.[226] It is the thinking principle which forms concepts or general ideas acting through the instrumentality of Ahangkāra, Manas, and the Indriyas. In the operations of the senses Manas is the principal; in the operation of Manas Ahangkāra is the principal; and in the operation of Ahangkāra Buddhi is the principal. With the instrumentality of all of these Buddhi acts, modifications taking place in Buddhi through the instrumentality of the sense functions.[227] It is Buddhi which is the basis of all cognition, sensation, and resolves, and makes over objects to Purusha—that is, consciousness. And so it is said that Buddhi, whose characteristic is determination, is the charioteer; Manas, whose characteristic is Sangkalpavikalpa, is the reins; and the Senses are the horses. Jīva is the Enjoyer (Bhoktā)—that is, Ātmā conjoined with body, senses, Manas, and Buddhi.[228] In Buddhi Sattvaguna predominates; in Ahangkāra, Rajas; in Manas and the Indriyas and their objects, Tamas.

Chitta[229] in its special sense is that faculty (Vritti) by which the mind first recalls to memory (Smaranam) that of which there has been previously Anubhava or Pratyaksha Jnāna—that is, immediate cognition. This Smaranam exists only to the extent of actual Anubhava. For remembrance is the equivalent of, and neither more than less than, what has been previously known;[230] remembrance being the calling up of that. Chinta, again, is that faculty whereby the current of thought

---

[224] Sāngkhya Pravachana, II. 13. The Sūtra has Adhyavasāyo buddhih; but, as the Commentator points out, Buddhi is not to be identified with its functions. Buddhi is thus called Nishchayakārini.

[225] Sāngkhya Tattva Kaumudī, 23rd Kārikā: Sarvvo vyavaharttā ālochya mattvā aham atrādhikrita ityabhimatya kartavyam etat mayā iti adhyavasyati.

[226] Sāngkhya Pravachana, II. 40-44.

[227] Sāngkhya Pravachana, II. 45, 39.

[228] Shangkara's Commentary on Kathopanishad, 3rd Valli, 4th Mantra: Ātmendriyamanoyuktang bhoktetyāhurmanīshinah; and see Sāngkhya Pravachana, II. 47.

[229] Chetati anena iti chittam.

[230] So the Pātanjala Sūtra says: Anubhūtavishayāsampramoshah smritih (Nothing is taken away from the object perceived).

dwells, thinks, and contemplates upon (Chinta)[231] the subject so recalled by Smaranam, and previously known and determined by Buddhi. For such meditation (Dhyāna) is done through the recall and fixing the mind upon past percepts and concepts. According to Vedānta, Buddhi determines but once only, and the further recall and thought upon the mental object so determined is the faculty of the separate mental category called Chitta. Sāngkhya, on the principle of economy of categories, regards Smaranam and Chintā to be functions of Buddhi.[232] In the works here translated and elsewhere Chitta is, however, currently used as a general term for the working mind—that is, as a synonym for the Antahkarana.[233]

To sum up the functions of the subtle body: the sense-objects (Bhūta, derived from Tanmātra) affect the senses (Indriya) and are perceived by Manas, are referred to the self by Ahangkāra, and are determined by Buddhi. The latter in its turn is illumined by the light of consciousness (Chit), which is the Purusha; all the Principles (Tattva) up to and including Buddhi being modifications of apparently unconscious Prakriti. Thus all the Tattvas work for the enjoyment of the Self, or Purusha. They are not to be regarded as things existing independently by themselves, but as endowments of the Spirit (Ātmā). They do not work arbitrarily as they will, but represent an organized co-operative effort in the service of the Enjoyer, the Experiencer, or Purusha.

The subtle body is thus composed of what are called the "17," viz., Buddhi (in which Ahangkāra is included), Manas, the ten senses (Indriya), and the five Tanmātra. No special mention is made of Prāna by the Sāngkhya, by which it is regarded as a modification of the Antahkarana, and as such is implicitly included. The Māyāvādins insert the Prāna pentad instead of the Tanmātra.[234]

The Jīva lives in his subtle or mental body alone when in the *dreaming* (Svapna) state. For the outside world of objects (Mahābhūta) is then shut out, and the consciousness wanders in the world of ideas. The subtle body or soul is imperishable until liberation is attained, when the Jīvātmā, or seemingly conditioned consciousness, ceases to be such, and is the Supreme Consciousness or Paramātmā Nirguna Shiva. The subtle body thus survives the dissolution of the gross body of matter, from which it goes forth (utkraman), and reincarnates[235] until

[231] Anusandhānātmikā antahkarana-vrittih iti vedāntah (It is the faculty of the Antahkarana which investigates in the Vedānta).

[232] Sāngkhyashāstrecha chintāvrittikasya chittasya buddhvāvevāntarbhāvah (In the Sāngkhya Shāstra, Chitta, the function of which is Chintā, is included in Buddhi, I. 64).

[233] Chittam antahkarana sāmānyam (Chitta is the Antahkarana in general): Sāngkhya Pravachana Bhāshya.

[234] Sāngkhya Pravachana Sūtra, III. 9.

[235] This is transmigration or pretyabhāva, which means "the arising again" (and again)—punarutpattih pretyabhāvah, as Gautama says. Pretya = having died, and Bhāva

liberation (Mukti). The Lingasharīra is not all-pervading (Vibhu), for in that case it would be eternal (Nitya), and could not act (Kriyā). But it moves and goes (gati). Since it is not Vibhu, it must be limited (parichinna) and of atomic dimension (anuparimānam). It is indirectly dependent on food. For though the material body is the food-body (annamaya), mind is dependent on it when associated with the gross body. Mind in the subtle body bears the Sangskāras which are the result of past actions. This subtle body is the cause of the third or gross body.

The whole process of evolution is due to the presence of the will to life and enjoyment, which is a result of Vāsanā, or world-desire, carried from life to life in the Sangskāras, or impressions made on the subtle body by Karma, which is guided by Īshvara. In its reaching forth to the world, the Self is not only endowed with the faculties of the subtle body, but with the gross objects of enjoyment on which those faculties feed. There therefore comes into being, as a projection of the Power (Shakti) of Consciousness, the *gross body* of matter called Sthūla Sharīra.

The word Sharīra comes from the root "Shri," to decay; for the gross body is at every moment undergoing molecular birth and death until Prāna, or vitality, leaves, the organism, which as such is dissolved. The soul (Jīvātmā) is, when it leaves the body, no longer concerned therewith. There is no such thing as the resurrection of the body. It returns to dust, and the Jīva when it reincarnates does so in a new body, which is nevertheless, like the last, suited to give effect to its Karma.

The Sthūla Sharīra, with its three Doshas, six Koshas, seven Dhatus, ten Fires, and so forth,[236] is the perishable body composed of compounds of five forms of gross sensible matter (Mahābhūta), which is ever decaying, and is at the end dissolved into its constituents at death.[237] This is the Vedāntik body of food (Annamaya Kosha), so called because it is maintained by food which is converted into chyle (Rasa), blood, and the other material components of the gross organism. The Jīva lives in this body when in the *waking* (Jāgrat) state.

The human, physical, or gross body is, according to Western science, composed of certain compounds, of which the chief are water, gelatin, fat, phosphate of lime, albumen, and fibrin, and of these water constitutes some two-thirds of the total weight. These substances are composed of simpler non-metallic and metallic elements, of which the chief are oxygen (to the extent of about two-thirds), hydrogen, carbon,

---

= "the becoming (born into the world) again." "Again" implies habitualness: birth, then death, then birth, and so on, until final emancipation, which is Moksha, or Apavarga (release), as the Nyāya calls it.

[236] See Introduction to my edition of Prapanchasāra Tantra, Vol. III., "Tantrik Texts."

[237] Decay and death are two of the six Ūrmis which, with hunger and thirst, grief and ignorance, are characteristics of the body (Dehadharma): Prapanchasāra Tantra, II.

nitrogen, calcium, and phosphorus. Again, to go one step farther back, though the alleged indestructibility of the elements and their atoms is still said by some to present the character of a "practical truth," well-known recent experiments go to re-establish the ancient hypothesis of a single primordial substance to which these various forms of matter may be reduced, with the resultant of the possible and hitherto derided transmutation of one element into another; since each is but one of the plural manifestations of the same underlying unity.

Recent scientific research has shown that this original substance cannot be scientific "matter"—that is, that which has mass, weight, and inertia. Matter has been dematerialized and reduced, according to current hypotheses, to something which differs profoundly from "matter" as known by the senses. This ultimate substance is stated to be Ether in a state of motion. The present scientific hypothesis would appear to be as follows: There is no such thing as scientific "Matter." If there seems to be such, this is due to the action of Shakti as Māyā. The ultimate and simplest physical factor from which the universe has arisen is motion of and in a substance called "ether," which is not scientific "matter." The motions of this substance give rise from the realistic point of view to the notion of "matter." Matter is thus at base one, notwithstanding the diversity of its forms. Its ultimate element is on the final analysis of one kind, and the differences in the various kinds of matter depend on the various movements of the ultimate particle and its succeeding combinations. Given such unity of base, it is possible that one form of matter may pass into another.

The Indian theory here described agrees with the Western speculations to which we have referred, that what the latter calls "scientific matter" does not really—that is, permanently—exist, but says that there are certain motions or forces (five in number) which produce the appearance of "matter," and which are ultimately reducible to ether (Ākāsha). Ākāsha, however, and scientific "ether" are not in all respects the same. The latter is an ultimate physical substance, not "matter," having vibratory movements and affording the medium for the transmission of light. Ākāsha is one of the gross forces into which the Primordial Power (Prakriti Shakti) differentiates itself. Objectively considered it is a vibration[238] which produces the psychical experience of space in which the other forces are observed to be operating. Lastly, Ākāsha is not an ultimate, but is itself derived from the supersensible Tanmātra, with its quality (Guna) whereby Ākāsha affects the senses;

---

[238] It is Spandanashīla (vibratory), according to Sāngkhya; for the products share the character of the original vibrating Prakriti, and these products are not, like Prakriti itself, all-pervading (Vibhu). The Vaisheshika Sūtrakāra regards it as a motionless, colorless (Nirūpa) continuum (Sarvvavyāpī). It is not an effect and is Vibhu, therefore it cannot vibrate (Gatikriyā). The Commentators argue that, as it is a Dravya, or thing, it must possess the general quality (Dharma) of Dravya or Kriyā—that is, action.

and this Tanmatra is itself derived from the mental I-making principle (Ahangkāra), or personal consciousness produced from the super-personal Jīva-consciousness as such (Buddhi), emanating from the root-energy, or Prakriti, the cause and basis of all forms of "material" force or substance. At the back of "matter" there is mind, and at the back of mind the creative energy (Shakti) of the Supreme who is the cause of the universe and Consciousness itself.

Matter affects the Jīva in five different ways, giving rise in him to the sensations of smell, taste, sight, touch and feel, and hearing.

As already explained, the Tanmātra are supersensible, being abstract qualities, whilst the senses perceive their variations in particular objects only. These sense-particulars are produced from the generals.

From the Shabda Tanmātra and from the combinations of the latter with the other Tanmātras are produced the gross Bhūtas (Mahābhūta), which as things of physical magnitude perceivable by the senses approach the Western definition of discrete sensible "matter." These five Mahābhūta are Ākāsha (Ether), Vāyu (Air), Tejas (Fire), Apas (Water), and Prithivi (Earth). Their development takes place from the Tanmātra, from one unit of that which is known in sensible matter as mass (Tamas), charged with energy (Rajas) by the gradual accretion of mass and redistribution of energy. The result of this is that each Bhūta is more gross than that which precedes it until "Earth" is reached. These five Bhūtas have no connection with the English "elements" so called, nor, indeed, are they elements at all, being derived from the Tanmātra. Dynamically and objectively considered they are (proceeding from Ākāsha) said to be five forms of motion, into which Prakriti differentiates itself: viz., non-obstructive, all-directed motion radiating lines of force in all directions, symbolized as the "Hairs of Shiva,"[239] affording the space (Ākāsha) in which the other forces operate; transverse motion[240] and locomotion in space (Vāyu); upward motion giving rise to expansion (Tejas); downward motion giving rise to contraction (Apas); and that motion which produces cohesion, its characteristic of obstruction being the opposite of the non-obstructive ether in which it exists and from which it and the other Tattvas spring. The first is sensed by hearing through its quality (Guna) of sound (Shabda);[241] the second by touch through resistance and feeling;[242] the

[239] "Kashmir Shaivaism," p. 132, where it is suggested that the lines of the magnetic field are connected with the lines of Dik (direction) as the lines of ethereal energy.

[240] Vāyu, as the Prapanchasāra Tantra says, is characterized by motion (Chalanapara). The Sanskrit root vā = to move. See Sushruta, Vol. II., p. 2, ed. Kaviraj Kunja Lala Bhishagratna.

[241] According to Western notions, it is the air which is the cause of sound. According to Indian notions, ether is the substratum of (Āshraya) of sound, and air (Vāyu) is a helper (Sahakārī) in its manifestation.

third by sight as color;[243] the fourth by taste through flavor; and the fifth by the sense of smell through its odor, which is produced by matter only in so far as it partakes of the solid state.[244]

The hard and stable obstructive "earth" is that which is smelt, tasted, seen, and touched, and which exists in space which is known by hearing—that is, the sounds in it. The smooth "water" is that which is tasted, seen, and touched, in space. "Fire" is what is seen and touched—that is, felt as temperature—in space. "Air" is what is so felt in space. And sound which is heard is that by which the existence of the "Ether" is known. These Bhūtas when compounded make up the material universe. Each thing therein being thus made of all the Bhūtas, we find in the Tantra that form, color, and sound, are related, a truth which is of deep ritual significance. Thus, each of the sounds of speech or music has a corresponding form, which have now been made visible to the eye by the Phonoscope.[245] Thus the deaf may perceive sounds by the eye, just as, by the Optophone, the blind may read by means of the ear.

In the same Shāstra various colors and figures (Mandalas) are assigned to the Tattvas to denote them. Ākāsha is represented by a transparent white circular diagram in which, according to some accounts there are dots (Chhidra), thus displaying the interstices which Ākāsha produces; for Ākāsha, which is all-pervading, intervenes between each of the Tattvas which are evolved from it.

Vāyu is denoted by a smoky grey, six-cornered diagram;[246] Tejas, red, triangular diagram; Apas, white, crescent-shaped diagram; and Prithivī, yellow, by the quadrangular diagram which as the superficial presentation of the cube well denotes the notion of solidity.

Similarly, to each Devatā also there is assigned a Yantra, or diagram, which is a suggestion of the form assumed by the evolving Prakriti or body of that particular Consciousness.

The gross body is, then, a combination of the compounds of these Mahābhūtas, derivable from the Ākāsha ("Ether") Tattva.

The Bhūtas and the Tanmātra, as parts of these compounds, pervade the body, but particular Bhūtas are said to have centers of force in particular regions. Thus the centers (Chakra) of "earth" and "water" are the two lower ones in the trunk of the body. "Fire" predominates in

---

[242] Touch is not here used in the sense of all forms of contact, for form and solidity are not yet developed, but that particular contact by which is realized the thermal quality of things.

[243] Fire is the name for that action which builds and destroys shapes.

[244] All matter in the solid state (Pārthiva) giving rise to smell is in the state of earth—*e.g.*, metals, flowers, etc.

[245] When words are spoken or sung into a small trumpet attached to the instrument, a revolving disk appears to break up into a number of patterns, which vary with the variations in sound.

[246] See as to this and the other diagrams the colored plates of the Chakras.

the central abdominal region, and "air" and "ether" in the two higher centers in the heart and throat. These five Tanmātras, five Bhūtas, and the ten senses (Indriyas) which perceive them, are known as the twenty gross Tattvas which are absorbed in Yoga in the centers of the bodily trunk. The remaining four subtle mental Tattvas (Buddhi, Ahangkāra, Manas) and Prakriti have their special center of activity in the head. Again, the Bhūtas may be specially displayed in other portions of the bodily organism. Thus, Prithivī displays itself as bone or muscle; Apas as urine and saliva; Tejas as hunger and thirst; Vāyu in grasping and walking. Fire is manifold, its great mystery being saluted by many names. So Tejas manifests both as light and heat, for, as Helmholtz says, the same object may affect the senses in different ways. The same ray of sunshine, which is called light when it falls on the eyes, is called heat when it falls on the skin. Agni manifests in the household and umbilical fires; as Kāmāgni in the Mūlādhāra center; Vadavā or submarine fire and in the "Lightning" of the Sushumnā in the spinal column.

Matter thus exists in the five states etheric,[247] aerial,[248] fiery,[249] fluid,[250] and solid.[251] Prithivī does not denote merely what is popularly called Earth. All solid (Pārthiva) odorous substance is in the Prithivī state. All substance in the fluid (Āpya) state is in the Apas state, as everything which has cohesive resistance is in that of Prithivī. This latter, therefore, is the cohesive vibration the cause of solidity of which the common earth is a gross compounded form. All matter in the aerial (Vāyava) condition is in the Vayu state. These are all primary differentiations of cosmic matter into a universe of subtly fine motion. The Tattvas regarded objectively evoke in the Indriyas smell, taste, sight, touch, and hearing.

The gross body is thus a combination of the compounds of these Mahābhūta, derivable ultimately from ether (Ākāsha), itself evolved in manner described.

The gross and subtle bodies above described are vitalized and held together as an organism by Prāna, which is evolved from the active energy (Kriyā Shakti) of the Linga Sharīra. Prāna, or the vital principle, is the special relation of the Ātmā with a certain form of matter which by this relation the Ātmā organizes and builds up as a means of having

---

[247] All-pervading (Sarvvavyāpī), though relatively so in Sāngkhya, and colorless (Nirūpa). As to vibration, *v. ante*, p. 68.

[248] With movements which are not straight (Tiryyaggamanashīla).

[249] Illuminating (Prakāsha) and heating (Tāpa).

[250] Liquid (Tarala), moving (Chalanashīla). It has the quality of Sneha, whereby things can be rolled up into a lump (Pinda), as moistened flour or earth. Some solid things become liquid for a time through heat; and others become solids, such as ice; the Jāti (species) of which is still water (Jalatva).

[251] Without hollow, dense (Ghana), firm (Dridha), combined (Sanghata), and hard (Kathina).

experience.[252] This special relation constitutes the individual Prāna in the individual body. The cosmic all-pervading Prāna is not Prāna in this gross sense, but is a name for the Brahman as the author of the individual Prāna. The individual Prāna is limited to the particular body which it vitalizes, and is a manifestation in all breathing creatures (Prānī) of the creative and sustaining activity of the Brahman, who is represented in individual bodies by the Devī Kundalinī.

All beings, whether Devatās, men, or animals, exist only so long as the Prāna is within the body. It is the life duration of all.[253] What life is has been the subject of dispute in India as elsewhere. The materialists of the Lokayata school considered life to be the result of the chemical combinations of the elements, in the same manner as the intoxicating property of spirituous liquors results from the fermentation of unintoxicating rice and molasses, or as spontaneous generation was supposed to occur under the influence of gentle warmth. This is denied by the Sāngkhya. Though Prāna and its fivefold functions are called Vāyu, life, according to this school, is not a Vāyu in the sense of a mere biomechanical force, nor any mere mechanical motion resulting from the impulsion of such Vāyu.

According to the view of this school, Prāna, or vitality, is the common function of the mind and all the senses, both sensory Jnānendriya and motor (Karmendriya), which result in the bodily motion. Just as several birds when confined in one cage cause that cage to move, by themselves moving, so the mind and senses cause the body to move while they are engaged in their respective activities. Life is, then, a resultant of the various concurrent activities of other principles or forces in the organism.

The Vedantists agree in the view that the Prāna is neither Vāyu nor its operation, but deny that it is the mere resultant of the concomitant activities of the organism, and hold that it is a separate independent principle and "material" form assumed by the universal Consciousness. Life is therefore a subtle principle pervading the whole organism which is not gross Vāyu, but is all the same a subtle kind of apparently unconscious force, since everything which is not the Ātmā or Purusha is, according to Māyāvāda Vedānta and Sāngkhya, unconscious or, in Western parlance, "material" (Jada).[254] The gross outer body is heterogeneous (Parāchchhinna) or made up of distinct or well-defined parts. On the other hand, the Prānamaya self which lies within the Annamaya self is a homogeneous undivided whole (Sādhārana) permeating the whole physical body (Sarvapindavyāpin). It is not cut

---

252 "Hindu Realism," p. 84.

253 Kaushitakī Upanishad, 3-2.

254 See Commentary on Taittirīya Upanishad, edited by Mahādeva Shāstri, and Appendix C, by Dr. Brojendra Nath Seal, to Professor B. K. Sarkar's "The Positive Background of Hindu Sociology," where some further authorities are given.

off into distinct regions (Asādhārana) as is the Pinda, or microcosmic physical body. Unlike the latter, it has no specialized organs each discharging a specific function. It is a homogeneous unity (Sādhārana) present in every part of the body, which it ensouls as its inner self. Vāyu[255] which courses through the body is the manifestation, self-begotten, the subtle, invisible, all-pervading, divine energy of eternal life. It is so called from the fact of its coursing throughout the universe. Invisible in itself, yet its operations are manifest. For it determines the birth, growth, and decay, of all animated organisms, and as such it receives the homage of all created being. As vital Vāyu it is instantaneous in action, radiating as nerve force through the organism in constant currents. In its normal condition it maintains a state of equilibrium between the different Doshas[256] and Dhātus,[256] or root principles of the body. The bodily Vāyu is divided, as are the principles called Pitta[256] and Kapha,[256] into five chief divisions according to the differences in location and function. Vāyu, known in its bodily aspect as Prāna, the universal force of vital activity, on entry into each individual is divided into tenfold functions (Vritti), of which the five chief are: Breathing, bearing the same name (Prāna) as that given to the force considered in its totality—the function whereby atmospheric air with its pervading vitality, which has been first drawn from without into the bodily system, is expired.[257]

On the physical plane Prāna manifests in the animal body as breath through inspiration (Sa), or Shakti, and expiration (Ha), or Shiva. The male principle of Prāna throws out, and the female principle draws in, in accordance with the nature of Shakti as Shabdabrahman (Kulakundalinī). Breathing is itself a Mantra, known as the Mantra which is not recited (Ajapāmantra), for it is said without volition.[258]

The divine current is Hang and Sa or the motion of Ha and Sa. This motion, which exists on all the planes of life, is for the earth plane (Bhūrloka) created and sustained by the Sun, the solar breath of which is the cause of human breath with its centrifugal and centripetal movements, the counterpart in man of the cosmic movement of the

---

[255] In the sense of Prāna. The Sanskrit root vā = to move. See Sushruta, Vol. II., p. 2, edition by Kaviraj Kunja Lala Bhishagratna.

[256] See Introduction to third volume of "Tantrik Texts," where these terms are explained. The Devatās of these Dhātu are Dākinī and the other Shaktis in the Chakras.

[257] The Vāyus have other functions than those mentioned. The matter is here stated only in a general way. See Sushruta Sanghitā, cited *ante*. Prāna is not the physical breath, which is a gross thing, but that function of vital force which exhibits itself in respiration.

[258] Thus the Niruttara Tantra (Chapter IV.) says:

> Hangkārena vahiryāti sakārena vishetpunah
> Hangseti paramangmantrang jīvo japati sarvvadā.

(By Hangkāra it goes out, and by Sakāra it comes in again. A Jīva always recites the Supreme Mantra Hangsa). See also Dhyānabindu Up.

Hangsah or Shiva-shakti Tattvas, which are the soul of the Universe. The Sun is not only the center and upholder of the solar system,[259] but the source of all available energy and of all physical life on earth. Accompanying the sunshine there proceeds from the orb a vast invisible radiation, the prerequisite of all vegetable and animal life. It is these invisible rays which, according to science, sustain the mystery of all physical life. The Sun whose body is the great luminary is in itself the Solar God, a great manifestation of the inner Spiritual Sun.[260]

Apāna, the downward "breath" which pulls against Prāna, governs the excretory functions; Samāna kindles the bodily fire and governs the processes of digestion and assimilation; Vyāna, or diffused "breathing," is present throughout the body, effecting division and diffusion, resisting disintegration, and holding the body together in all its parts; and Udāna, the ascending Vāyu, is the so-called "upward breathing." Prāna is in the heart; Apāna in the anus; Samāna in the navel; Udāna in the throat; and Vyāna pervades the whole body.[261] The five minor Vāyu are Nāga, Kūrmma, Krikara, Devadatta, and Dhananjaya, which manifest in hiccup, closing and opening the eyes, digestion,[262] yawning, and in that Vāyu "which leaves not even the corpse."[263] The functions of Prāna may be scientifically defined as follows: Appropriation (Prāna), Rejection (Apāna), Assimilation (Samāna), Distribution (Vyāna), and that vital function whereby the relation between the subtle and the gross body is maintained (Udāna). The Prāna represents the involuntary reflex action of the organism, and the Indriyas one aspect of its voluntary activity.

In the case of the individualized Prāna, or principle which vitalizes the animal organism during its earth life, it may be said, when regarded as an independent principle, to be a force more subtle than that which manifests as terrestrial matter which it vitalizes. In other words, according to this theory, the Ātmā gives life to the earth organisms through the medium of terrestrial Prāna, which is one of the manifestations of that Energy which issues from and is at base the all-pervading Ātmā, as Shakti.

Ātmā as such has no states, but in worldly parlance we speak of

---

[259] The Sun is said to hold the vast bulk of the total matter of the solar system, while it only carries about 2 per cent, of its moment of momentum.

[260] The Yoga works speak of the Moon-chit (Chichchandra). It is this spiritual moon which is shown on the cover of this book, embraced by the Serpent Kundalinī.

[261] Amritanāda Upanishad, vv. 34, 35—Anandāshrama Edition, Vol. XXIX., p. 43; Shāndilya Up., Ch. I. See also, as to Prāna, Ch. II., Prapanchasāra Tantra. It is also said that Prāna is at the tip of the nostrils (Nāsāgravarttī), and others are also said to be elsewhere. These localities denote special seats of function.

[262] Kshuddhākara; lit., "appetite-maker."

[263] As stated in Subodhini, the Commentary on Vedāntasāra, where this Vāyu is described as Poshanakāra—that is, nourishing the body.

such. So the Māndukya Upanishad[264] speaks of the four aspects (Pada) of the Brahman.

Chaitanya, or consciousness in bodies, is immanent in the individual and collective gross, subtle, and causal bodies, and as Chit transcends them. One and the same Chit pervades and transcends all things, but is given different names to mark its different aspects in the Jīva. Chit, being immutable, has itself no states; for states can only exist in the products of the changing Prakriti Shakti. From, however, the aspect of Jīva several states exist, which, though informed by the same Chit, may from this aspect be called states of consciousness.[265]

In the manifested world, Consciousness appears in three states (Avasthā):[266] waking (Jāgrat), dreaming (Svapna), and dreamless slumber (Sushupti). In the waking state the Jīva is conscious of external objects (Bahishprajna), and is the gross enjoyer of these objects through the senses (Sthūlabhuk).[267] The Jīva in this state is called Jāgarī—that is, he who takes upon himself the gross body called Vishva. Here the Jīva consciousness is in the *gross body*.

In dreaming (Svapna) the Jīva is conscious of inner objects (Antahprajna), and the enjoyer of what is subtle (Praviviktabhuk)—that is, impressions left on the mind by objects sensed in the waking state. The objects of dreams have only an external reality for the dreamer, whereas the objects perceived when awake have such reality for all who are in that state. The mind ceases to record fresh impressions, and works on that which has been registered in the waking state.

The first (Jāgrat) state is that of sense perception. Here the ego lives in a mental world of ideas, and the Jīva consciousness is in the *subtle body*. Both these states are states of duality in which multiplicity is experienced.[268]

The third state, or that of dreamless sleep (Sushupti), is defined as that which is neither waking nor dreaming, and in which the varied experiences of the two former states are merged into a simple

---

[264] This Upanishad gives an analysis of the states of Consciousness on all planes, and should be studied in connection with Gaudapāda's Kārikā on the same subject with Shangkarāchāryya's Commentary on the latter.

[265] Described in detail *post*.

[266] See Māndukya Upanishad (where these are analyzed) with Gaudapāda's Kārikā and Shangkarāchāryya's Commentary on the same.

[267] Māndukya Up., Mantra 3. Prapanchasāra Tantra: Svairindriyairyadātmā bhungte bhogān sa jāgaro bhavati (Ch. XIX., "Tantrik Texts," Vol. III.). See Īshvarapratyabhijnā: Sarvvākshagocharatvena yātu vāhyatayā sthitā (cited by Bhāskararāya in Comm. to v. 62 of Lalitā).

[268] See Māndukya Up., Mantra 4. Īshvarapratyabbijnā:
Manomātrapathedhyaksha vishayatvena vishramāt
Srishtāvabhāshabhāvānāng srishtih svapnapadang matam.
(Cited in Lalitā, *loc. cit.*).

Prapanchasāra Tantra: Sangjnārahitairapi tairasyānubhavo bhavet punah svapnah.

experience (Ekībhuta), as the variety of the day is lost in night without extinction of such variety. Consciousness is not objective (Bahishprajna) nor subjective (Antahprajna), but a simple undifferenced consciousness without an object (Prajnānaghana). In waking the Jīva consciousness is associated with mind and senses; in dreaming the senses are withdrawn; in dreamless slumber mind also is withdrawn. The Jīva called Prajna is for the time being merged in his *causal body*—that is, Prakriti inseparably associated with Consciousness—that is, with that state of Consciousness which is the seed from which the subtle and gross bodies grow. The state is one of bliss. The Jīva is not conscious of anything,[269] but on awakening preserves only the notion, "Happy I slept; I was not conscious of anything."[270] This state is accordingly that which has as its object the sense of nothingness.[271] Whilst the two former states enjoy the gross and subtle objects respectively, this is the enjoyer of bliss only (Ānandabhuk)—that is, simple bliss without an object. The Lord is always the enjoyer of bliss, but in the first two states he enjoys bliss through objects. Here he enjoys bliss itself free from both subject and object. In this way the Sushupti state approaches the Brahman consciousness. But it is not that in its purity, because it, as the other two states, are both associated with ignorance (Avidyā)—the first two with Vikriti, and the last with Prakriti. Beyond, therefore, this state there is the "fourth" (Turīya). Here the pure experience called Shuddhavidyā is acquired through Samādhi-yoga. Jīva in the Sushupti state is said to be in the causal (Kārana) body, and Jīva in the Turīya state is said to be in the great causal (Mahākārana) body.[272]

Beyond this there is a fifth state, "beyond the fourth" (Turīyātīta), which is attained through firmness in the fourth. Here the Īshvara Tattva is attained. This is the Unmesha[273] state of consciousness, of which the Sadākhya Tattva is the Nimesha.[273] Passing beyond "the spotless one attains the highest equality," and is merged in the Supreme Shiva.

The above divisions—Vishva, Taijasa, and Prajna—are those of the individual Jīva. But there is also the collective or cosmic Jīva,

---

[269] This state, when nothing is dreamt, is rarer than is generally supposed.

[270] See Pātanjala yoga-sūtra: Sukhamahamasvāpsang na kinchidavedisham iti smaranāt.

[271] Abhāvapratyayālambanā vrittirnidrā. See also Prapanchasāra Tantra: Ātmānirudyuktatayā nairākulyang bhavet sushuptirapi (Ch. XIX., Vol. III., of "Tantrik Texts").

[272] Bhāskararāya in his Comm. on Lalitā says: Ataeva sushuptidashāpannajīvopādhih kāranasharīratvena turīyadashāpannajīvopādhih mahākāranasharīratvena vyavahārah.

[273] Opening and closing of the eyes (of consciousness). The latter is the last stage before the perfect Shiva-consciousness is gained.

which is the aggregate of the individual Jīvas of each particular state.[274] In the macrocosm these collective[275] Jīvas are called Vaishvānara (corresponding to the individual Vishva body), Hiranyagarbha, and Sūtrātmā[276] (corresponding to the individual Taijasa body); and Īshvara is the name of the collective form of the Jīvas described as Prājna. Cosmically, these are the conscious Lords of the objective, subjective, and causal worlds, beyond which there is the Supreme Consciousness.

Yoga experience and liberation is attained by passing beyond the first three states of ordinary experience.

IV. The Garland of Letters (Varnamālā)

Reference is made in the Text and in this Introduction to Shabda, Varna, Mantra. It is said that the letters (Varna) of the alphabet are distributed throughout the bodily centers on the petals of the lotuses, as is shown on Plates II.-VII. In each of the lotuses there is also a seed Mantra (Bīja) of the Tattva of the center. Kundalinī is both light (Jyotirmayī) and Mantra (Mantramayī),[277] and Mantra is used in the process of rousing Her.

There is perhaps no subject in the Indian Shāstra which is less understood than Mantra and Shabda, of which it is a manifestation. The subject is so important a part of the Tantra-Shāstra that its other title is Mantra-Shāstra. Commonly Orientalists and others describe Mantra as "prayer," "formulae or worship," "mystic syllables," and so forth. These are the superficialities of those who do not know their subject. Whilst I am not aware of any work in any European language which shows a knowledge of Mantra and its science, yet there is perhaps no subject which has been so ridiculed—a not unusual attitude of ignorance. Mantra science may be well founded or not, but even in the latter case it is not the absurdity which some suppose it to be. Those who think so might except Mantras which are prayers, and the meaning of which they understand, for with prayer they are familiar. But such appreciation itself shows a lack of understanding. There is nothing

[274] Accounts vary in detail according as a greater or less number of stages of ascent are enumerated. Thus Nirvāna Tantra, cited in Comm. to v. 43 *post*, says the Paramātmā is the Devatā in the Turīya state; and Prapanchasāra Tantra (Ch. XIX.) says Jāgrat is Bīja, Svapna is Bindu, Sushupti is Nāda, Turīya is Shakti, and the Laya beyond is Shānta.

[275] The nature of the collectivity is not merely a summation of units, but a collectivity the units of which are related to one another as parts of an organized whole. Thus Hiranyagarbha is he who has the consciousness of being all the Jīvas in the dreaming state: Jīvasamashtyabhimānī Hiranyagarbhātmakah (Bhāskararāya, *op. cit.*, v. 61). He is the aggregate of these Jīvas.

[276] There is said to be this distinction between the two, that the Paramātmā manifested as the collective Antahkarana is Hiranyagarbha, and as the collective Prāna it is called Sūtrātmā. When manifest through these two vehicles without differentiation it is Antaryāmin. See Bhāskararāya, *loc. cit.*

[277] The first is the subtle, the second the gross form.

necessarily holy or prayerful about a Mantra. Mantra is a power (Mantrashakti) which lends itself impartially to any use. A man may be injured or killed by Mantra;[278] by Mantra a kind of union with the physical Shakti is by some said to be effected;[279] by Mantra in the initiation called Vedhadīkshā there is such a transference of power from the Guru to the disciple that the latter swoons under the impulse of it;[280] by Mantra the Homa fire may and, according to ideal conditions, should be lighted;[281] by Mantra man is saved, and so forth. Mantra, in short, is a power (Shakti) which is thought-movement vehicled by and expressed in speech. The root "man" means "to think."

The creative power of thought is now receiving increasing acceptance in the West. Thought-reading, thought-transference, hypnotic suggestion, magical projections (Mokshana), and shields (Grahana),[282] are becoming known and practiced, not always with good results. The doctrine is ancient in India, and underlies the practices to be found in the Tantras, some of which are kept in general concealed to prevent misuse.[283] What, however, is not understood in the West is the particular form of thought-science which is Mantravidyā. Those familiar with the Western presentment of similar subjects will more

---

[278] As in Māranam and other of the Shatkarma or abhichāra. To quote an example which I recently read in an account of an author nowise "suspect" as an Occultist, Theosophist, etc. General J. T. Harris noticed a scorpion close to the foot of a Sādhu. "Don't move," he said; "there is a scorpion by your foot." The Sadhu leaned over, and when he saw the scorpion he pointed at it with his fingers, on which the animal immediately and in the presence of the General shriveled up and died. "You seem to have some powers already," the General said; but the Sādhu simply waived the matter aside as being of no importance ("China Jim": "Incidents in the Life of a Mutiny Veteran," by Major-General J. T. Harris, p. 74. Heinemann).

[279] An extraordinary use to which it is put, I am informed by some worshippers of the Bhairava Mantra. The man projects the Mantra on to the woman, who then experiences the sensation of a physical union. The Vishnu Purāna speaks of generation by will power.

[280] As the Kulārnava Tantra says, and as may be readily understood, such a Guru is hard to get. The disciple who receives this initiation gets all the powers of his initiator. It is said that there are Gurus who can at once make their disciples fit for the highest aims.

[281] As actually happened lately in the house of a friend of a collaborator of mine. A man lit the fuel in Kushandikā Homa simply by Mantra and the Bīja of fire ("Ram") without recourse to light or match.

[282] This Sanskrit term expresses not so much a fence to which use a Kavacha is put, but the knowledge of how a man may "catch" a Mantra projected at him.

[283] In the Samhitā called Kulārnava (not the Tantra of that name) Shiva, after referring to some terrible rites with the flesh of black cats, bats, and other animals, the soiled linen of a Chandāla woman, the shroud of a corpse, and so forth, says: "Oh, Pārvati, my head and limbs tremble, my mouth is dried" (Hridayam kampate mama, gātrāni mama kampante, mukham shushyate Pārvati), adding: "One must not speak of it, one must not speak, one must speak, again and again I say it must not be spoken of" (Na vaktavyam na vaktavyam na vaktavyam punah punah).

readily understand[284] when I say that, according to the Indian doctrine here described, thought (like mind, of which it is the operation) is a power or Shakti. It is, therefore, not only as real, but in a sense more real than outer material objects, which are themselves but the projections of the creative thought of the World-thinker. The thought-movement vehicled by and expressed in speech is Mantra.[285] Mantra is the manifested Shabdabrahman.

But what is Shabda or "sound"? Here the Shākta-Tantra Shāstra follows the Mīmāngsā doctrine of Shabda, with such modifications as are necessary to adapt it to its doctrine of Shakti. Sound (Shabda), which is a quality (Guna) of ether (Ākāsha), and is sensed by hearing, is twofold—namely, lettered (Varnātmaka shabda) and unlettered, or Dhvani (Dhvanyātmaka shabda).[286] The latter is caused by the striking of two things together, and is meaningless. Shabda, on the contrary, which is Anāhata (a term applied to the Heart Lotus), is that Brahman sound which is not caused by the striking of two things together. Lettered sound is composed of sentences (Vākya), words (Pada), and letters (Varna). Such sound has a meaning.[287] Shabda manifesting as speech is said to be eternal.[288] This the Naiyāyikas deny, saying that it is transitory. A word is uttered, and it is gone. This opinion the Mīmāngsā denies, saying that the perception of lettered sound must be distinguished from lettered sound itself.[289] Perception is due to Dhvani caused by the striking of the air in contact with the vocal organs—namely, the throat, palate, and tongue. Before there is Dhvani there must be the striking of one thing against another. It is not the mere striking which is the lettered Shabda. This manifests it. The lettered sound is produced by the formation of the vocal organs in contact with air, which formation is in response to the mental movement or idea, which by the will thus seeks outward expression in audible sound.[290] It is this perception which is transitory, for the Dhavni which manifests ideas in language is such. But lettered sound, as it is in itself—that is, as the Consciousness manifesting as idea expressed in speech—is eternal. It was not produced at the moment it was perceived. It was only

---

[284] It is because the Orientalist and missionary know nothing of occultism, and regard it as superstition, that their presentment of Indian teaching is so often ignorant and absurd.

[285] The root "man," which = to think, is also the root of the Sanskrit word for man, who alone of all creation is properly a thinker.

[286] This Dhvani is the gross body of the Mantra.

[287] When the word "Ghata" is uttered, then there arises in the mind the idea of a jar.

[288] Not as audible sounds (Dhvani), but as that which finds auditory expression in audible sounds. The sensible expressions are transient. Behind them is the Eternal Logos (Shabdabrahman), whose manifestation they are.

[289] Samantu tatra darshanam ("But alike is the perception thereof").

[290] This is only one form in which letters find sensible expression. Thus writing gives visual expression, and to the blind perforated dots give tactual expression.

manifested by the Dhvani. It existed before, as it exists after, such manifestation, just as a jar in a dark room which is revealed by a flash of lightning is not then produced, nor does it cease to exist on its ceasing to be perceived through the disappearance of its manifester, the lightning. The air in contact with the voice organs reveals sound in the form of the letters of the alphabet, and their combinations in words and sentences. The letters are produced for hearing by the effort of the person desiring to speak, and become audible to the ear of others through the operation of unlettered sound or Dhvani. The latter being a manifester only, lettered Shabda is something other than its manifester.

Before describing the nature of Shabda in its different forms of development it is necessary to understand the Indian psychology of perception. At each moment the Jīva is subject to innumerable influences which from all quarters of the universe pour upon him. Only those reach his Consciousness which attract his attention, and are thus selected by his Manas. The latter attends to one or other of these sense impressions, and conveys it to the Buddhi. When an object (Artha) is presented to the mind and perceived, the latter is formed into the shape of the object perceived. This is called a mental Vritti (modification), which it is the object of Yoga to suppress. The mind as a Vritti is thus a representation of the outer object. But in so far as it is such representation the mind is as much an object as the outer one. The latter—that is, the physical object—is called the gross object (Sthūla artha), and the former or mental impression is called the subtle object (Sūkshma artha). But besides the object there is the mind which perceives it. It follows that the mind has two aspects, in one of which it is the perceiver and in the other the perceived in the form of the mental formation (Vritti) which in creation precedes its outer projection, and after the creation follows as the impression produced in the mind by the sensing of a gross physical object. The mental impression and the physical object exactly correspond, for the physical object is, in fact, but a projection of the cosmic imagination, though it has the same reality as the mind has; no more and no less. The mind is thus both cognizer (Grāhaka) and cognized (Grāhya), revealer (Prakāshaka) and revealed (Prakāshya), denoter (Vāchaka) and denoted (Vāchya). When the mind perceives an object it is transformed into the shape of that object. So the mind which thinks of the Divinity which it worships (Īshtadevatā) is at length, through continued devotion, transformed into the likeness of that Devatā. By allowing the Devatā thus to occupy the mind for long it becomes as pure as the Devatā. This is a fundamental principle of Tantrik Sādhanā or religious practice. The object perceived is called Artha, a term which comes from the root "Ri," which means to get to know, to enjoy. Artha is that which is known, and which therefore is an object of enjoyment. The mind as Artha—that is, in the form of the mental impression—is an exact reflection of the outer object or gross Artha. As the outer object is Artha, so is the interior subtle mental form which corresponds to it. That aspect of the mind which cognizes is called Shabda or Nāma (name), and that aspect in which it is its own object or cognized is called Artha or Rūpa (form). The outer physical object of which the latter is, in the individual, an impression is also Artha or Rūpa, and spoken speech is the outer Shabda. Subject and object are thus from the Mantra aspect Shabda and Artha—terms corresponding to the Vedantic Nāma and Rūpa, or concepts and concepts objectified. As the Vedānta says, the whole creation is Nāma and Rūpa. Mind is the power (Shakti), the function of which is to distinguish and identify (Bhedasangsargavritti Shakti).

Just as the body is causal, subtle, and gross, so is Shabda, of which there are four states (Bhāva), called Parā, Pashyantī, Madhyamā, and Vaikharī—terms further explained in Section V. of this Introduction. Parā sound is that which exists on the differentiation of the Mahābindu before actual manifestation. This is motionless causal Shabda in Kundalinī in the Mūlādhāra center of the body. That aspect of it in which it commences to move with a general—that is, non-particularized—motion (Sāmānya spanda) is Pashyantī, whose place is from the Mūlādhāra to the Manipūra Chakra, the next center. It is here associated with Manas. These represent the motionless and first moving Īshvara aspect of Shabda. Madhyamā sound is associated with Buddhi. It is Hiranyagarbha Shabda (Hiranyagarbharūpa) extending from Pashyantī to the heart. Both Madhyamā sound, which is the inner "naming" by the cognitive aspect of mental movement, as also its Artha or subtle (Sūkshma) object (Artha), belong to the mental or subtle body (Sūkshma or Linga sharīra). Perception is dependent on distinguishing and identification. In the perception of an object that part of the mind which identifies and distinguishes, or the cognizing part, is subtle Shabda, and that part of it which takes the shape of the object (a shape which corresponds with the outer thing) is subtle Artha. The perception of an object is thus consequent on the simultaneous functioning of the mind in its twofold aspect as Shabda and Artha, which are in indissoluble relation with one another as cognizer (Grāhaka) and cognized (Grāhya). Both belong to the subtle body. In creation Madhyamā Shabda first appeared. At that moment there was no outer Artha. Then the cosmic mind projected this inner Madhyamā Artha into the world of sensual experience, and named it in spoken speech (Vaikharī Shabda). The last or Vaikharī Shabda is uttered speech developed in the throat issuing from the mouth. This is Virāt Shabda. Vaikharī Shabda is therefore language or gross lettered sound. Its corresponding Artha is the physical or gross object which language denotes. This belongs to the gross body (Sthūla sharīra). Madhyamā Shabda is mental movement or ideation in its cognitive aspect, and Madhyamā Artha is the mental impression of the gross object. The inner thought-movement in its aspect as Shabdārtha, and considered both in its knowing aspect (Shabda) and as the subtle known object (Artha), belong to the subtle body (Sūkshma sharīra). The cause of these two is the first general movement towards particular ideation (Pashyantī) from the motionless cause, Parashabda, or Supreme Speech. Two forms of inner or hidden speech, causal and subtle, accompanying mind movement thus precede and lead up to spoken language. The inner forms of ideating movement constitute the subtle, and the uttered sound the gross, aspect of Mantra, which is the manifested Shabdabrahman.

The gross Shabda, called Vaikharī or uttered speech, and the gross Artha, or the physical object denoted by that speech, are the projection of the subtle Shabda and Artha through the initial activity of the Shabdabrahman into the world of gross sensual perception. Therefore in the gross physical world Shabda means language—that is, sentences, words, and letters, which are the expression of ideas and are Mantra. In the subtle or mental world Madhyamā Shabda is the mind which "names" in its aspect as cognizer, and Artha is the same mind in its aspect as the mental object of its cognition. It is defined to be the outer in the form of the mind. It is thus similar to the state of dreams (Svapna): as Parashabda is the causal dreamless (Sushupti) and Vaikharī the waking (Jāgrat) state. Mental Artha is a Sangskāra, an impression left on the subtle body by previous experience, which is recalled when the Jīva reawakes to world experience and recollects the experience temporarily lost in the cosmic dreamless state (Sushupti) which is dissolution (Mahāpralaya). What is it which arouses this Sangskāra? As an effect (Kārya) it must have a cause (Kāraka). This Kāraka is the Shabda or name (Nāma), subtle or gross, corresponding to that particular Artha. When the word "Ghata" is uttered this evokes in the mind the image of an object—a jar—just as the presentation of that object does. In the Hiranyagarbha state Shabda as Sangskāra worked to evoke mental images. The whole world is thus Shabda and Artha—that is, name and form (Nāma rūpa). These two are inseparably associated. There is no Shabda without Artha or Artha without Shabda. The Greek word Logos also means thought and word combined. There is thus a double line of creation, Shabda and Artha, ideas and language together with their objects. Speech, as that which is heard, or the outer manifestation of Shabda, stands for the Shabda creation. The Artha creation are the inner and outer objects seen by the mental or physical vision. From the cosmic creative standpoint the mind comes first, and from it is evolved the physical world according to the ripened Sangskāras, which led to the existence of the particular existing universe. Therefore the mental Artha precedes the physical Artha, which is an evolution in gross matter of the former. This mental state corresponds to that of dreams (Svapna) when man lives in the mental world only. After creation, which is the waking (Jāgrat) state, there is for the individual an already existing parallelism of names and objects.

Uttered speech is a manifestation of the inner naming or thought. This thought-movement is similar in men of all races. When an Englishman or an Indian thinks of an object, the image is to both the same, whether evoked by the object itself or by the utterance of its name. Perhaps for this reason a thought-reader whose cerebral center is *en rapport* with that of another may read the hidden "speech"—that is, the thought of one whose spoken speech he cannot understand. Thus, whilst the thought-movement is similar in all men, the expression of it as Vaikharī Shabda differs. According to tradition, there was once a universal language. According to the Biblical account, this was so before the confusion of tongues at the Tower of Babel. Similarly in the Rigveda a mysterious passage[291] speaks of the "three fathers and three mothers" by whose action, like that of the Elohim, "all comprehending speech" was made into that which was not so. Nor is this unlikely when we consider that difference in gross speech is due to difference of races evolved in the course of time. If the instruments by, and conditions under, which thought is revealed in speech were the same for all men, then there would be but one language. But now this is not so. Racial characteristics and physical conditions, such as the nature of the vocal organs, climate, inherited impressions, and so forth, differ. Therefore, so also does language. But for each particular man speaking any particular language the uttered name of any object is the gross expression of his inner thought-movement. It evokes that movement and again expresses it. It evokes the idea, and the idea is consciousness as mental operation. That operation can be so intensified as to be itself creative. This is Mantrachaitanya.

From the above account it will be understood that, when it is said that the "letters" are in the six bodily Chakras, it is not to be supposed that it is intended to absurdly affirm that the letters as written shapes, or as the uttered sounds which are heard by the ear, are there. The letters in this sense—that is, as gross things—are manifested only in speech and writing. This much is clear. But the precise significance of this statement is a matter of great difficulty. There is, in fact, no subject which presents more difficulties than Mantravidyā, whether considered generally or in relation to the particular matter in hand. In the first place, one must be constantly on guard against falling into a possible trap—namely, the taking of prescribed methods of realization for actualities in the common sense of that term. The former are conventional, the latter are real. Doubts on this matter are increased by some variations in the descriptive accounts. Thus in some Ganesha is the Devatā of the Mūlādhāra. In the text here translated it is Brahmā.

[291] On report of an Indian friend who has forgotten to give me the reference.

Similarly this Text gives Dākinī in the Mūlādhāra as the Devatā of the Asthi Dhātu (bony substance). When sitting in the prescribed Āsana (posture), the bones are gathered up around this Chakra, and, moreover, from it as the center of the body the bones run up and downwards. Another account, however, given to me places Devī Shākinī here.[292] Mistakes have also to be reckoned with, and can only be ascertained and rectified by a comparison of several MSS.[293] Again, four letters are said to be on the petals of the Mūlādhāra Lotus—namely, Va, Sha, *Sha*, and Sa. Why are these said to be there? Various statements have been made to me. As there are certain letters which are ascribed to each form of sensible matter (Bhūta), it seems obvious to suggest that the earth letters (Pārthiva varna) are in the earth center. But an examination on this basis does not bear the suggestion out. Next, it is said that the letters have colours, and the letters of a particular color are allocated to the lotuses of the same color. The Text does not support this theory. It has been said that certain letters derive from certain Devatā. But the letters produce the Devatā, for these are the Artha of the Mantra as Shabda. I have been also told that the letters are placed according to their seat of pronunciation (Uchchārana). But it is replied that the Mūlādhāra is the common source of this (Uchchāranasthāna) for all.[294] Again, it is said that the letters on the petals are Bījās of all activities (Kriyā) connected with the Tattva of the center, each letter undergoing variations according to the vowels.[295] All beings in Prithivī (earth) Tattva should be meditated upon in the Mūlādhāra. Here are, therefore (as we might expect), the organs of feet (Pādendriya), the action of walking (Gamanakriyā), smell (Gandha), the quality of Prithivī, the sense of smell (Ghrāna), Nivritti kalā,[296] and Brahmā (Lord of the Tattva). But we are also told that the letters Va, Sha, *Sha*, and Sa are

---

[292] This account, which may be compared with that of the text, is as follows:

Bone (Asthidhātu): Mūlādhāra chakra; Devī Shākinī.
Fat (Medadhātu): Svādhishthāna chakra; Devī Kākinī.
Flesh (Māngsadhātu): Manipūra chakra; Devī Lākinī.
Blood (Raktadhātu): Anāhata chakra; Devī Rākinī.
Skin (Tvakdhātu): Vishuddha chakra; Devī Dākinī.
Marrow (Majjādhātu): Ājnā chakra; Devī Hākinī.

In the Sahasrāra Padma are all Dhātus beginning with Shukra (semen).

[293] Thus in the text given me, from which I quote, the four letters in the Mūlādhāra are given as Va, Sha, *Sha*, and La. The latter should, according to other accounts, be undoubtedly Sa.

[294] This is true, but nevertheless there may be special seats of pronunciation for each letter or class of letters. As apparently supporting this suggestion it may be noted that the vowel sounds are placed in the throat center, and Ha and Ksha above.

[295] I am informed that the subject is dealt with in detail in the Kundalinīkalpataru, and in particular in the Adhyātmasāgara, neither of which MSS. have I yet seen.

[296] See author's "Studies in the Mantra Shāstra" (Kalās of the Shaktis). Samāna Vāyu is also located here.

the Ātmā and Bījas of the four Vedas,[297] of the four Yugas,[298] of the four oceans,[299] which are therefore called Chaturvarnātmaka, or in the self of the four letters. It is true that the four Vedas are in, and issue from, Parashabda, the seat of which is the Mūlādhāra. For Veda in its primary sense is the world as idea in the mind of the creative Brahman, portions of which have been revealed to the Rishis (seers) and embodied in the four Vedas. But why should Va be the seed of the Rigveda, Sha of the Yajurveda, and so forth? The ritual explanation, as given in the Rudrayāmala (xiv. 73, xv. 2, xvi. 1, 2), is that the petal Va is Brahmā (Rajoguna), and is the Bīja of Rik; Sha is Vishnu (Sattvaguna), and Sha, being Pundarīkātmā, is the Bīja of Yajus; *Sha* is Rudra (Tamoguna), and is the Bīja of Sāma. Sa is the Bīja of Atharva, as it is the Bīja of Shakti.[300] These four are in Parashabda in Mūlādhāra. It seems to me (so far as my studies in the Shāstra have yet carried me) that the details of the descriptions of the centers are of two kinds. There are, firstly, certain facts of objective and universal reality. Thus, for example, there are certain centers (Chakra) in the spinal column. The principle of solidity (Prithivī Tattva) is in the lowest of such centers, which as the center of the body contains the static or potential energy called Kundalī Shakti. The center as a lotus is said to have four petals, because of the formation and distribution of the Yoga-nerves[301] (Nādī) at that particular point. Solidity is denoted aptly by a cube, which is the diagram (Yantra) of that center. The consciousness of that center as Devatā is also aptly borne on an elephant, the massive solidity of which is emblematical of the solid earth principle (Prithivī). The forces which go to the making of solid matter may by the Yogī be seen as yellow. It may be that particular substances (Dhātu) of the body and particular Vritti (qualities) are connected with particular Chakras, and so forth.

There are, however, another class of details which have possibly only symbolical reality, and which are placed before the Sādhaka for the purposes of instruction and meditation only.[302] The letters as we know them—that is, as outer speech—are manifested only after passing through the throat. They cannot therefore exist as such in the Chakras. But they are said to be there. They are there, not in their gross, but in

[297] Va of Rik, Sha of Yajus, *Sha* of Sāma, and Sa of Atharva Veda.

[298] The four ages—Satya, Treta, Dvāpara, and Kali.

[299] Of sugar-cane juice, wine, ghee (Ghrita), milk.

[300] See Rudrayāmala XVII., where priority is given to Atharva as dealing with the Āchāra of Shakti. From Atharva arose Sāma, from Sāma, Yajus, and from the latter Rik.

[301] The term "nerve" is used for default of another equivalent. These Nādīs, called Yoga-Nādīs, are not, like the Nādīs of physiology, gross things, but subtle lines in which the life-force works in bodies.

[302] The Buddhist Tantras are particularly frank in pointing out that descriptions are imagined for the purposes of method only. After all, the main point is concentration and creative will, which may be attained by varying forms of practice. See the Demchog Tantra, now published as a volume of "Tantrik Texts."

their subtle and causal forms. It is these subtle forms which are called Mātrikā. But as such forms they are Shabda of and as ideating movements, or are the cause thereof. Consciousness, which is itself (Svarūpa) soundless (Nihshabda), in its supreme form (Parashabda) assumes a general undifferentiated movement (Sāmānya spanda), then a differentiated movement (Vishesha spanda), issuing in clearly articulate speech (Spashtatara spanda). The inner movement has outer correspondence in that issuing from the lips by the aid of Dhvani. This is but the Mantra way of saying that the homogeneous Consciousness moves as Shakti, and appears as subject (Shabda) and object (Artha) at first in the subtle form of mind and its contents generated by the Sangskāras, and then in the gross form of language as the expression of ideas and of physical objects (Artha), which the creative or cosmic mind projects into the world of sensual experience to be the source of impressions to the individual experiencer therein. It is true that in this sense the letters, as hidden speech or the seed of outer speech, are in the Chakras, but the allocation of particular letters to particular Chakras is a matter which, if it has a real and not merely symbolical significance, is explained in my "Shakti and Shāktā."

In each of the Chakras there is also a Bīja (seed) Mantra of each of the Tattvas therein. They are the seed of the Tattva, for the latter springs from and re-enters the former. The natural name of anything is the sound which is produced by the action of the moving forces which constitute it. He therefore, it is said, who mentally and vocally utters with creative force the natural name of anything brings into being the thing which bears that name. Thus "Ram" is the Bīja of fire in the Manipūra chakra. This Mantra "Ram" is said to be the expression in gross sound (Vaikharī Shabda) of the subtle sound produced by the activity of, and which is, the subtle "fire" force. The same explanation is given as regards "Lam" in the Mūlādhāra, and the other Bījas in the other Chakras. The mere utterance,[303] however, of "Ram" or any other Mantra is nothing but a movement of the lips. When, however, the Mantra is "awakened"[304] (Prabuddha)—that is, when there is Mantra—chaitanya (Mantra-consciousness)—then the Sādhaka can make the Mantra work. Thus in the case cited the Vaikharī Shabda, through its vehicle Dhvani, is the body of a power of consciousness which enables the Mantrin to become the Lord of Fire.[305] However this may be, in all

[303] The mind must in worship with form (Sākāra) be centered on the Deity of Worship (Ishtadevatā); and in Yoga on the light form (Jyotirmayarūpa). It is said, however, that mere repetition of a Mantra without knowing its meaning will produce *some* benefit.

[304] Thought is not then only in the outer husk, but is vitalized through its conscious center.

[305] Some attain these powers through worship (Upāsanā) of Agni Vetāla, a Devayoni; some of Agni Himself. The former process, which requires 12,000 Japa, is given in Shavaratantra. A higher state of development dispenses with all outer agents.

cases it is the creative thought which ensouls the uttered sound which works now in man's small magic, just as it first worked in the grand magical display of the World-creator. His thought was the aggregate, with creative power, of all thought. Each man is Shiva, and can attain His power to the degree of his ability to consciously realize himself as such. For various purposes the Devatās are invoked. Mantra and Devatā are one and the same. A Mantra-Devatā is Shabda and Artha, the former being the name, and the latter the Devatā whose name it is. By practice with the Mantra (Japa) the presence of the Devatā is invoked. Japa or repetition of Mantra is compared to the action of a man shaking a sleeper to wake him up. The two lips are Shiva and Shakti. Their movement is the coition (Maithuna) of the two. Shabda which issues therefom is in the nature of Bindu. The Devatā thus produced is, as it were, the "son" of the Sādhaka. It is not the Supreme Devatā (for it is actionless) who appears, but in all cases an emanation produced by the Sādhaka for his benefit only.[306] In the case of worshippers of Shiva a Boy-Shiva (Bāla Shiva) appears, who is then made strong by the nurture which the Sādhaka gives to his creation. The occultist will understand all such symbolism to mean that the Devatā is a form of the consciousness of the pure Sādhaka which the latter arouses and strengthens, and gains good thereby. It is his consciousness which becomes the boy Shiva, and which when strengthened the full-grown Divine power itself. All Mantras are in the body as forms of consciousness (Vijnāna rūpa). When the Mantra is fully practiced it enlivens the Sangskāra, and the Artha appears to the mind. Mantras are thus a form of the Sangskāra of Jīvas, the Artha of which manifest to the consciousness which is pure. The essence of all this is—concentrate and vitalize thought and will power. But for such a purpose a method is necessary—namely, language and determined varieties of practice according to the end sought. These Mantravidyā, which explains what Mantra is, also enjoins. For thought, words (gross or subtle) are necessary. Mantravidyā is the science of thought and of its expression in language.

The causal state of Shabda is called Shabdabrahman—that is, the Brahman as the cause of Shabda and Artha. The unmanifest (Avyakta) power or Shabda, which is the cause of manifested Shabda and Artha, uprises on the differentiation of the Supreme Bindu from Prakriti in the form of Bindu through the prevalence of Kriyā shakti.[307] Avyakta Rava

---

[306] If Sūryya (Sun God) be invoked, it is an emanation which comes and then goes back to the sun.

[307] See v. 12 Shāradā.

> Kriyāshaktipradhānāyāh shabdashabdārtha-kāranam
> Prakriterbindurūpinyāh shabdabrahmābhavat param.

or Shabda (unmanifest sound) is the principle of sound as such (Nāda mātra)—that is, undifferentiated sound not specialized in the form of letters, but which is, through creative activity, the cause of manifested Shabda and Artha.[308] It is the Brahman considered as all-pervading Shabda, undivided, unmanifested, whose substance is Nāda and Bindu, the proximate creative impulse in Parashiva and proximate cause of manifested Shabda and Artha.[309] It is the eternal partless Sphota[310] which is not distinguished into Shabda and Artha, but is the Power by which both exist and are known. Shabdabrahman is thus the kinetic ideating aspect of the undifferentiated Supreme Consciousness of philosophy, and the Sagunabrahma of religion. It is Chit-shakti vehicled by undifferentiated Prakriti-shakti—that is, the creative aspect of the one Brahman who is both transcendent and formless (Nirguna), and immanent and with form (Saguna).[311] As the Hathayogapradīpikā says:[312] "Whatever is heard in the form of sound is Shakti. The absorbed state (Laya) of the Tattvas (evolutes of Prakriti) is that in which no form exists.[313] So long as there is the notion of ether, so long is sound heard. The soundless is called Parabrahman or Paramātmā."[314] Shabdabrahman thus projects itself for the purpose of creation into two sets of movement—namely, firstly, the Shabda (with mental vibrations of cognition) which, passing through the vocal organs, become articulate sound; and, secondly, Artha movements denoted by Shabda in the form of all things constituting the content of mind and the objective world. These two are emanations from the same conscious activity (Shakti) which is the Word (Logos), and are in consequence

In plain English this means, in effect, that increasing activity in the Consciousness about to create (Bindu) produces that state in which it is the cause of subject and object, as mind and matter.

308 Tena shabdārtharūpa-vishishtasya shabda-brahmatvam avadhāritam (Prānatoshinī, 13).

309 See Prānatoshini, p. 10; Rāghava Bhatta, Comm. v. 12, Ch. I., Shāradā. Srishtyunmukha-paramashiva-prathamollāsamātram akhando vyakto nādabindumaya eva vyāpako brahmātmakah shabdah.

310 Sphota, which is derived from *Sphut*, to open (as a bud does), is that by which the particular meaning of words is revealed. The letters singly, and therefore also in combination, are non-significant. A word is not the thing, but that through which, when uttered, there is cognition of the thing thereby denoted. That which denotes the thing denoted is a disclosure (Sphota) other than these letters. This Sphota is eternal Shabda.

311 It is to be noted that of the five Bhūtas, Ākāsha and Vāyu belong to the formless division (Amūrtta), and the remaining three to the form division (Mūrtta). The first is sensed by hearing. Shabda is vibration for the ear as name. Agni, the head of the second division, is sensed as form (Rūpa). Artha is vibration to the eye (mental or physical) as form.

312 Ch. IV., vv. 101, 102.

313 Yatkinchinnādarūpena shruyate shaktireva sā
Yastattvānto nirākārah sa eva parameshvarah.

314 Tāvadākāshasangkalpo yāvachchhabdah pravartate
Nihshabdam tatparam brahma paramātmeti gīyate.

essentially the same. Hence the connection between the two are permanent. It is in the above sense that the universe is said to be composed of the letters. It is the fifty[315] letters of the Sanskrit alphabet which are denoted by the garland of severed human heads which the naked[316] mother, Kālī, dark like a threatening rain-cloud, wears as She stands amidst bones and carrion beasts and birds in the burning-ground on the white corpse-like (Shavarūpa) body of Shiva. For it is She who "slaughters"—that is, withdraws all speech and its objects into Herself at the time of the dissolution of all things (Mahāpralaya).[317] Shabdabrahman is the consciousness (Chaitanya) in all creatures. It assumes the form of Kundalī, and abides in the body of all breathing creatures (Prānī), manifesting itself by letters in the form of prose and verse.[318] In the sexual symbolism of the Shākta Tantras, seed (Bindu)[319] issued upon the reversed union[320] of Mahākāla and Mahākālī, which seed, ripening in the womb of Prakriti, issued as Kundalī in the form of the letters (Akshara). Kundalī as Mahāmātrikāsundarī has fifty-one coils, which are the Mātrīkās or subtle forms of the gross letters or Varna which is the Vaikharī form of the Shabda at the centers. Kundalī when with one coil is Bindu; with two, Prakriti-Purusha; with three, the three Shaktis (Ichchhā, Jnāna, Kriyā) and three Gunas (Sattva, Rajas, Tamas); with the three and a half She is then actually creative with Vikriti; with four She is the Devī Ekajatā, and so on to Shrīmātrikotpattisundarī with fifty-one coils.[321] In the body, unmanifested Parashabda is in Kundalī Shakti. That which first issues from it is in the lowest Chakra, and extends upwards through the rest as Pashyantī, Madhyamā, and Vaikhari Shabda. When Shakti first "sees"[322] She is Paramakalā[323] in the mother form (Ambikārūpā), which is supreme speech (Parāvāk) and supreme peace (Parama shāntā). She "sees" the manifested Shabda from Pashyantī to Vaikharī. The

---

[315] Sometimes given as fifty-one.

[316] She is so pictured because she is beyond Māyā (Māyātītā). She is the "Bewilderer of all" by Her Māyā, but is Herself undeceived thereby. All this Kālī symbolism will be explained in the Svarūpa-vyākhya of the "Hymn to Kālī" (Karpūrādi Stotra) which I hope to publish.

[317] The same symbolism is given in the description of the Heruka in the Buddhist Demchog Tantra.

[318] Rāghava Bhatta, Comm. Chaitanyam sarvabhūtānāng shabdabrahmeti me matam Tat prāpya kundalīrūpam prāninām dehamadhyagam Varnātmanāvirbhavati gadyapadyādi-bhedatah (Shāradā Tilaka, Ch. I.).

[319] The term Bindu also means a drop as of semen.

[320] Viparīta maithuna. Shakti is above Shiva, because She is the active and He the inert consciousness.

[321] Shaktisanggama Tantra, first Ullāsa Utpattikhanda. When with ten coils She is Dashamahāvidyā.

[322] The first movement in creation, called Īkshana ("seeing") in Veda. To see is to ideate.

[323] Parama = supreme or first. Kalā = Vimarsha-Shakti of Ātmā. She is, as such, the first cause of all the letters.

Pashyantī[324] state of Shabda is that in which Ichchhā Shakti (will) in the form of a goad[325] (Angkushākāra) is about to display the universe, then in seed (Bīja) form. This is the Shakti Vāmā.[326] Madhyamā Vāk, which is Jnāna (knowledge), and in form of a straight line (Rijurekhā), is Jyeshthā Shakti. Here there is the first assumption of form as the Mātrikā (Mātrikātvam upapannā), for here is particular motion (Vishesha Spanda). The Vaikharī state is that of Kriyā Shakti, who is the Devi Raudrī, whose form is triangular[327] and that of the universe. As the former Shakti produces the subtle letters or Mātrikā which are the Vāsanā,[328] so this last is the Shakti of the gross letters of words and their objects.[329] These letters are the garland of the Mother issuing from Her in Her form as Kundalī Shakti, and absorbed by Her in the Kundalī-yoga here described.

V. The Centers or Lotuses (Chakra, Padma)

At this stage we are in a position to pass to a consideration of the Chakras, which may shortly be described as subtle centers of operation in the body of the Shaktis of the various Tattvas or Principles which constitute the bodily Sheaths. Thus the five lower Chakra from Mūlādhāra to Vishuddha are centers of the Bhūta, or five forms of sensible matter. The Ājnā and other Chakras in the region between it and the Sahasrāra are centers of the Tattvas constituting the mental sheaths, whilst the Sahasrāra, or thousand-petalled lotus at the top of the brain, is the blissful abode of Parama Shiva-Shakti.

A description of the Chakras involves, in the first place, an account of the Western anatomy and physiology of the central and sympathetic nervous systems; secondly, an account of the Tantrik nervous system and Chakras; and, lastly, the correlation, so far as that is possible, of the two systems on the anatomical and physiological side, for the rest is in general peculiar to Tantrik occultism.

The Tantrik theory regarding the Chakras and Sahasrāra is concerned on the *physiological* side, or Bhogāyatana aspect, with the central spinal system, comprising the brain or encephalon, contained within the skull, and the spinal cord, contained within the vertebral column (Merudanda). It is to be noted that, just as there are five centers (Chakras) hereinafter described, the vertebral column itself is divided

---

[324] Pashyantī = She who "sees" (Īkshana).

[325] Here the crooked line (Vakrarekhā) comes first, and the straight second. Possibly this may be the line rising to form the triangular pyramid.

[326] So called because she "vomits forth" the universe (Vamanāt iti vāmā).

[327] Shringātaka—that is, a triangular pyramidal figure of three dimensions.

[328] That is, Sangskāra or revived impression, which is the seed of the ideating Cosmic Consciousness.

[329] Yoginīhridaya Tantra, Sangketa 1.

into five regions, which, commencing from the lowest, are the coccygeal, consisting of four imperfect vertebrae, often united together into one bone called the coccyx; the sacral region, consisting of five vertebrae united together to form a single bone, the sacrum; the lumbar region, or region of the loins, consisting of five vertebrae; the dorsal region, or region of the back, consisting of twelve vertebrae; and the cervical region, or region of the neck, consisting of seven vertebrae. As exhibited by segments, the cord shows different characteristics in different regions. Roughly speaking, these correspond to the regions which are assigned to the governing control of the Mūlādhāra, Svādhishthāna, Manipūra, Anāhata, and Vishuddha centers, or Chakras. The central system has relation with the periphery through the thirty-one spinal and twelve cranial nerves, which are both afferent and efferent or sensory and motor, arousing sensation or stimulating action. Of the cranial nerves, the last six arise from the spinal bulb (medulla), and the other six, except the olfactory and optic nerves, from the parts of the brain just in front of the bulb. Writers of the Yoga and Tantra schools use the term Nādī, by preference, for nerves. They also, it has been said, mean cranial nerves when they speak of Shiras, never using the latter for arteries, as is done in the medical literature.[330] It must, however, be noted that the Yoga Nādīs are not the ordinary material nerves, but subtler lines of direction along which the vital forces go. The spinal nerves, after their exit from the intervertebral foramina, enter into communication with the gangliated cords of the sympathetic nervous system, which lie on each side of the vertebral column. The spinal cord extends in the case of man from the upper border of the atlas, below the cerebellum, passing into the medulla, and finally opening into the fourth ventricle of the brain, and descends to the second lumbar vertebra, where it tapers to a point, called the *filum terminale*. I am told that recent microscopic investigations by Dr. Cunningham have disclosed the existence of highly sensitive grey matter in the *filum terminale* which was hitherto thought to be mere fibrous cord. This is of importance, having regard to the position assigned to the Mūlādhāra and the Serpent Power. It is continued in this for a variable distance, and there ends blindly. Within the bony covering is the cord, which is a compound of grey and white brain matter, the grey being the inner of the two, the reverse of the position in the encephalon. The cord is divided into two symmetrical halves, which are connected together by a commissure in the center of which there is a minute canal called the central spinal canal (wherein is the Brahmanādī), which is said to be the remnant of the hollow tube from

[330] Dr. Brojendranath Seal, p. 337, Appendix to Professor Benoy Kumar Sarkar's "Positive Background of Hindu Sociology." The word Dhamanī is also used for nerve. It is to be noted, however, that the present work uses Shiras for other than cranial nerves, for in v. 1 it calls Idā and Pinggalā Nādīs or Shirās.

which the cord and brain were developed.[331] This canal contains cerebro-spinal fluid. The grey matter viewed longitudinally forms a column extending through the whole length of the cord, but the width is not uniform. There are special enlargements in the lumbar and cervical regions which are due mainly to the greater amount of grey matter in these situations. But throughout the whole cord the grey matter is specially abundant at the junctions of the spinal nerves, so that a necklace arrangement is visible, which is more apparent in the lower vertebrates, corresponding to the ventral ganglionic chain of the invertebrates.[332] The white matter consists of tracts or columns of nerve fibers. At the upper border of the atlas, or first cervical vertebra, the spinal cord passes into the medulla oblongata below the cerebellum. The center canal opens into the fourth ventricle of the brain. The cerebellum is a development of the posterior wall of the hindermost of the three primary dilatations of the embryonic cerebro-spinal tube, the fourth ventricle constituting the remnant of the original cavity. Above this is the cerebrum, which with the parts below it is an enlarged and greatly modified upper part of the cerebrospinal nervous axis. The spinal cord is not merely a conductor between the periphery and the centers of sensation and volition, but is also an independent center or group of centers. There are various centers in the spinal cord which, though to a considerable extent autonomous, is connected together with the higher centers by the associating and longitudinal tracts of the spinal cord.[333] All the functions which are ascribed primarily to the spinal centers belong also to the cerebral centers. Similarly, all the "Letters" which exist distributed on the petals of the lotuses exist in the Sahasrāra. This statement, however, does not seem to refer to the collective functions of any particular Jīva, but to the fact that the Sahasrāra is the seat of the Shiva-Shakti. Parabindu is also the seat of the aggregate Jīvas and Kundalīs. For the Hangsa or Jīva, or individual Kundalī, is but an infinitesimal part of the Parabindu. It may nevertheless be the fact that the functions ascribed primarily to the lower Chakra belong also to the cerebral centers of the Jīva as contrasted with the highest Īshvara body, which is their ultimate aggregate and undifferentiated cause. The centers influence not only the muscular combinations concerned in volitional movements, but also the functions of vascular innervation, secretion, and the like, which have their proximate centers in the spinal cord. The cerebral centers are said, however, to control these functions only in relation with the manifestations of volition, feeling, and emotion; whereas the spinal centers with the subordinate sympathetic system are said to constitute

[331] See Ferrier's "Functions of the Brain."
[332] *Ib.*, 7.
[333] See Ferrier's "Functions of the Brain," p. 80.

the mechanism of unconscious adaptation, in accordance with the varying conditions of stimuli which are essential to the continued existence of the organism. The Medulla, again, is also both a path of communication between the higher centers and the periphery and an independent center regulating functions of the greatest importance in the system. It is to be noted that the nerve fibers which carry motor impulses descending from the brain to the spinal cord cross over rather suddenly from one side to the other on their way through the spinal bulb (medulla), a fact which has been noted in the Tantras in the description of the Mukta Triveni. The latter is connected by numerous afferent and efferent tracts with the cerebellum and cerebral ganglia. Above the cerebellum is the cerebrum, the activity of which is ordinarily associated with conscious volition and ideation and the origination of voluntary movements. The notion of Consciousness, which is the introspective subject-matter of psychology, must not, however, be confused with that of physiological function. There is therefore no organ of consciousness, simply because "Consciousness" is not an organic conception, and has nothing to do with the physiological conception of energy, whose inner introspective side it presents.[334] Consciousness in itself is the Ātmā. Both mind and body, of which latter the brain is a part, are imperfect or veiled expressions of Consciousness, which in the case of body is so veiled that it has the appearance of unconsciousness. The living brain is constituted of gross sensible matter (Mahābhūta) infused by Prāna. Its material has been worked up so as to constitute a suitable vehicle for the expression of consciousness in the form of mind (Antahkarana). As consciousness is not a property of the body, neither is it a mere function of the brain. The fact that mental consciousness is affected or disappears with disorder of the brain proves the necessity of the latter for the expression of *such* consciousness, and not that consciousness is inherent alone in brain or that it is the property of the same. On each side of the vertebral column there is a chain of ganglia connected with nerve fiber, called the sympathetic cord (Idā and Pinggalā), extending all the way from the base of the skull to the coccyx. This is in communication with the spinal cord. It is noteworthy that there is in the thoracic and lumbar regions a ganglion of each chain corresponding with great regularity to each spinal nerve, though in the cervical region many of them appear to be missing; and that extra large clusters of nervous structure are to be found in the region of the heart, stomach, and lungs, the regions governed by the Anāhata, Manipura, and Vishuddha, respectively, the three upper of the five Chakras hereinafter described. From the sympathetic chain on each side nerve fibers pass to the viscera of the abdomen and thorax. From these, nerves are also given off which pass

[334] Auguste Forel's "Hygiene of Nerves and Mind," 95.

back into the spinal nerves, and others which pass into some of the cranial nerves; these are thus distributed to the blood vessels of the limbs, trunk, and other parts to which the spinal or cranial nerves go. The sympathetic nerves chiefly carry impulses which govern the muscular tissue of the viscera and the muscular coat of the small arteries of the various tissues. It is through the sympathetic that the tone of the blood vessels is kept up by the action of the vaso-motor center in the spinal bulb. The sympathetic, however, derives the impulses which it distributes from the central nervous system; these do not arise in the sympathetic itself. The impulses issue from the spinal cord by the anterior roots of the spinal nerves, and pass through short branches into the sympathetic chains. The work of the sympathetic systems controls and influences the circulation, digestion, and respiration.[335]

The anatomical arrangement of the central nervous system is excessively intricate, and the events which take place in that tangle of fiber, cell, and fibril, are, on the other hand, even now almost unknown.[336] And so it has been admitted that in the description of the physiology of the central nervous system we can as yet do little more than trace the paths by which impulses *may* pass between one portion of the system and another, and from the anatomical connections deduce, with more or less probability, the nature of the physiological nexus which its parts form with each other and the rest of the body.[337] In a general way, however, there may (it is said) be reasons to suppose that there are nervous centers in the central system related in a special way to special mechanisms, sensory, secretory, or motor, and that centers, such as the alleged genito-spinal center, for a given physiological action exist in a definite portion of the spinal cord. It is the subtle aspect of such centers as expressions of consciousness (Chaitanya) embodied in various forms of Māyā Shakti which is here called Chakra. These are related through intermediate conductors with the gross organs of generation, micturition, digestion, cardiac action, and respiration in ultimate relation with the Mūlādhāra Svādhishthāna, Manipūra, Anāhata, and Vishuddha Chakras respectively, just as tracts have been assigned in the higher centers as being in special, even if not exclusive, relation with various perceptive, volitional, and ideative processes.

With this short preliminary in terms of modern Western physiology and anatomy, I pass to a description of the Chakras and Nādīs (nerves), and will then endeavor to correlate the two systems.

The conduits of Prānik force are the nerves called Nādī, which are reckoned to exist in thousands in the body. "As in the leaf of the

---

[335] See Foster and Shore's "Physiology," 206, 207.

[336] "Manual of Physiology," by G. N. Stewart, 5th edition, p. 657 (1906).

[337] "Manual of Physiology," by G. N. Stewart, 5th edition, p. 657 (1906).

Ashvattha tree (*Ficus religiosa*) there are minute fibers, so is the body permeated by Nādīs."[338] Nādī is said in v. 2 to be derived from the root *nad*, or motion. For here the Prāna moves. The Bhūtashuddhi Tantra speaks of 72,000, the Prapanchasāra Tantra of 300,000, and the Shiva Sanghitā of 350,000; but of these, whatever be their total extent, only a limited number are of importance. Some are gross Nādīs, such as the physical nerves, veins, and arteries, known to medical science. But they are not all of this gross or physical and visible character. They exist, like all else, in subtle forms, and are known as Yoga Nādīs. The latter may be described as subtle channels (Vivara) of Prānik energy. The Nādīs are, as stated, the conduits of Prāna. Through them its solar and lunar currents run. Could we see them, the body would present the appearance of those maps which delineate the various ocean currents. They are the paths along which Prānashakti goes. They therefore belong to the vital science as life-element, and not to the medical Shāstra (Vaidyashāstra). Hence the importance of the Sādhanā, which consists of the physical purification of the body and its Nādīs. Purity of body is necessary if purity of mind is to be gained in its extended Hindu sense. Purification of the Nādīs is perhaps the chief factor in the preliminary stages of this Yoga; for just as their impurity impedes the ascent of Kundalī Shakti, their purity facilitates it. This is the work of Prānāyāma (*v. post*).

Of these Nādīs, the principal are fourteen, and of these fourteen Idā, Pinggalā, and Sushumnā, are the chief. Of these three, again, Sushumnā is the greatest, and to it all others are subordinate; for by the power of Yoga (Yogabala) Prāna is made to go through it, and, passing the Chakras, leave the body through the Brahmarandhra. It is situate in the interior of the cerebro-spinal axis, the Merudanda, or spinal column, in the position assigned to its interior canal, and extends from the basic plexus, the Tāttvika center called the Mūlādhāra, to the twelve-petalled lotus in the pericarp of the Sahasrāra Padma, or thousand-petalled lotus. Within the fiery red Tāmasika Sushumnā is the lustrous Rājasika Vajrā or Vajrinī Nādī, and within the latter the pale nectar-dropping Sāttvik Chitrā or Chitrinī. The interior of the latter is called the Brahma Nādī. The first is said to be fire-like (Vahnisvarupā), the second sun-like (Sūryyasvarūpā), and the third moon-like (Chandrasvarūpā).[339] These are the threefold aspect of the Shabdabrahman. The opening at the end of the Chitrinī Nādī is called the door of Brahman (Brahmadvāra), for

---

[338] Shāndilya Up., Ch. I., where the Nādīs are given and their purification spoken of; Dhyānabindu Up.; and as to Sushumnā see Mandalabrāhmana Up., First Brāhmana.

[339] Hence She is called in the Lalitā-sahasranāma (v. 106) Mūlādhārāmbujārū*dhā*. Fire, Sun, and Moon are aspects of the differentiated Parabindu or Kāmakalā (v. *ante*).

through it the Devī Kundalī enters to ascend.[340] It is along this last-mentioned Nādī, known as the Kula Mārga and the "Royal Road," that the Shakti Kundalinī is led in the process hereafter described.

Outside this nerve are the two Nādīs, the pale Idā or Shashī (Moon) and the red Pinggalā or Mihira (Sun), which are connected with the alternate breathing from the right to the left nostril and *vice versa.* The first, which is "feminine" (Shaktirūpā) and the embodiment of nectar (Amritavigrahā), is on the left; and the second, which is "masculine," as being in the nature of Rudra (Raudrātmikā), is on the right. They both indicate Kāla, and Sushumnā devours Kāla. For on that path entry is made into timelessness. The three are also known as Gangā (Idā), Yamunā (Pinggalā), and Sarasvatī (Sushumnā), after the names of the three sacred rivers of India. The Mūlādhāra is the meeting-place of the three "rivers," and hence is called Yuktatrivenī. Proceeding from the Ādhāra lotus, they alternate from right to left and left to right, thus going round the lotuses. According to another account, their position is that of two bows on either side of the spinal cord. An Indian medical friend tells me that these are not discrepant accounts, but represent different positions according as Idā and Pinggalā exist inside or outside the spinal cord. When they reach the space between the eyebrows known as the Ājnā Chakra, they enter the Sushumnā, making a plaited knot of three called Muktatrivenī. The three "rivers," which are again united at this point, flow separately therefrom, and for this reason the Ājnā Chakra is called Muktatrivenī. After separation, the Nādī which proceeded from the right testicle goes to the left nostril, and that from the left testicle to the right nostril. It has been said that the distinction made between the heating "sun" and cooling "moon" is that which exists between the positive and negative phases of the same subject-matter, positive and negative forces being present in every form of activity. Pinggalā is thus, according to this view, the conduit of the positive solar current, and Idā of the negative lunar current. There are also, as we have seen, interior solar and lunar Nādīs in the fiery Sushumnā where the two currents meet. Similarly, there are three Nādīs which in Latāsādhanā are worshipped in the Madanāgāra—viz., Chāndrī, Saurī, Āgneyī, representing the sun, moon, and fire. These are all but microsmic instances of the vaster system of cosmic matter, every portion of which is composed of the three Gunas (Trigunātmaka) and the threefold Bindus, which are Sun, Moon, and Fire.

As regards nerve cords and fibers, cranial and spinal nerves, and the connected sympathetic nerves, Dr. Brojendranath Seal says: "With

---

[340] The sun generally represents poison, and the moon nectar (Shāndilya Up., Ch. I.). Both were obtained at the churning of the ocean, and represent the upbuilding and destructive forces of Nature.

the writers on the Yoga, all the Shirās, and such of the Dhamanīs as are not vehicles of vital current, metabolic fluid, lymph, chyle, or blood, are cranial nerves, and proceed from the heart through the spinal cord to the cranium. These cranial nerves include pairs for the larynx and the tongue, for the understanding and use of speech, for the raising and lowering of the eyelids, for weeping, for the sensations of the special senses, etc., a confused and unintelligent reproduction of Sushruta's classification. But the enumeration of the spinal nerves with the connected sympathetic chain and ganglia is a distinct improvement on the old anatomists."[341]

He then continues: "The Sushumnā is the central cord in the vertebral column (Brahmadanda or Meru). The two chains of sympathetic ganglia on the left and right are named Idā and Pinggalā respectively. The sympathetic nerves have their main connection with Sushumnā at the solar plexus (Nābhi chakra). Of the seven hundred nerve cords of the sympathetic spinal system (see Sangītaratnākara), the fourteen most important are:[342]

"1. Sushumnā, in the central channel of the spinal cord. 2. Idā, the left sympathetic chain, stretching from under the left nostril to below the left kidney in the form of a bent bow. 3. Pinggalā, the corresponding chain on the right. 4. Kuhū, the pudic nerve of the sacral plexus, to the left of the spinal cord. 5. Gāndhārī, to the back of the left sympathetic chain, supposed to stretch from below the corner of the left eye to the left leg. It was evidently supposed that some nerves of the cervical plexus came down through the spinal cord and joined on to the great sciatic nerve of the sacral plexus. 6. Hastijihvā, to the front of the left sympathetic chain, stretching from below the corner of the left eye to the great toe of the left foot, on the same supposition as before. Pathological facts were believed to point to a special nerve connection between the eyes and the toes. 7. Sarasvatī, to the right of Sushumnā, stretching up to the tongue (the hypoglossal nerves of the cervical plexus). 8. Pūshā, to the back of the right sympathetic chain, stretching from below the corner of the right eye to the abdomen (a connected chain of cervical and lumbar nerves). 9. Payasvinī, between Puṣā and Sarasvatī, auricular branch of the cervical plexus on the left. 10. Shankhinī, between Gāndhārī and Sarasvatī, auricular branch of the cervical plexus on the left. 11. Yashasvinī, to the front of the right sympathetic chain, stretching from the right thumb to the left leg (the radial nerve of the brachial plexus continued on to certain branches of the great sciatic). 12. Vārunā, the nerves of the sacral plexus, between Kuhu and Yashasvinī, ramifying over the lower trunk and limbs. 13.

---

[341] P. 340, Appendix to Professor Sarkar's "Positive Background of Hindu Sociology." The author annexes a plan which attempts to give a rough idea of the relative position of the principal nerves of the sympathetic spinal system.

[342] Some of these are referred to in the present work; see v. 1.

Visvodarā, the nerves of the lumbar plexus, between Kuhu and Hastijihvā, ramifying over the lower trunk and limbs. 14. Alambushā, the coccygeal nerves, proceeding from the sacral vertebræ to the urino-genitary organs."[343]

The Tattvas in the body pervaded by Prāna have certain special centers of predominance and influence therein, which are the Chakras (centers or circles or regions) or Padmas (lotuses) of which this work is a description.

Inside the Meru, or spinal column, are the six main centers of Tattvik operation, called Chakras or Padmas, which are the seats of Shakti, as the Sahasrāra above is the abode of Shiva.[344] These are the Mūlādhāra, Svādhishthāna, Manipūra, Anāhata, Vishuddha, and Ājnā, which *in the physical body* are said to have their correspondences in the principal nerve plexuses and organs, commencing from what is possibly the sacro-coccygeal plexus to the "space between the eyebrows," which some identify with the pineal gland, the center of the third or spiritual eye, and others with the cerebellum. The Chakras[345] themselves are, however, as explained later, centers of Consciousness (Chaitanya) as extremely subtle force (Shakti); but the gross regions which are built up by their coarsened vibrations, which are subject to their influence, and with which loosely and inaccurately they are sometimes identified, have been said to be various plexuses in the trunk of the body and the lower cerebral centers mentioned. In the portion of the body below the Mūlādhāra are the seven lower worlds, Pātāla and others, together with the Shaktis which support all in the universe.

The first center, or Mūlādhāra Chakra, which is so called from its being the root of Sushumnā where Kundalī rests,[346] is at the place of meeting of the Kanda (root of all the Nādīs) and the Sushumnā Nādī, and is in the region midway between the genitals and the anus. It is thus the center of the body for men.[347] By this and similar statements made as regards the other lotuses, it is not meant that the Chakra proper is in the region of the gross body described, but that it is *the subtle center* of that gross region, such center existing in the spinal column which forms its axis. The reader must bear this observation in mind in the descriptions of the Chakras, or an erroneous notion will be formed of

---

343 Citing Sangīta-ratnākara, Shlokas 144-156; also the Yogārnava Tantra. This account has in parts been adversely criticized by an Indian medical friend, who tells me that it is in those parts influenced too much by Western physiology.

344 Varāha Up., Ch. V.

345 See Ch. V., Varāha Up. and Dhyānabindu Up., and Ch. III., Yoga Kundalī Up.

346 Derived from Mūla (root) and Ādhāra (support).

347 Shāndilya Up., Ch. I., where also the centers for birds and other animals are given. In some Kashmir "Nādīchakra" Kundalī is represented above the position given in the Text.

them. This crimson Mūlādhāra lotus[348] is described as one of four petals, the Vrittis of which are the four forms of bliss known as Paramānanda, Sahajānanda, Yogānanda, and Vīrānanda.[349] On these four petals are the golden letters Vang (वं), Shang (शं), S*h*ang (षं), and Sang (सं).[350] Each letter in its Vaikharī form is a gross manifestation of inner or subtle Shabda. On the petals are figured the letters, which are each a Mantra, and as such a Devatā. The petals are configurations made by the position of the Nādīs at any particular center, and are in themselves Prānashakti manifested by Prānavāyu in the living body. When that Vāyu departs they cease to be manifest. Each letter is thus a particular Shabda or Shakti and a surrounding (Āvarana) Devatā of the Principal Devatā and its Shakti of the particular Chakra. As Shakti they are manifestations of Kundalī, and in their totality constitute Her Mantra body, for Kundalī is both light (Jyotirmayī) and Mantra (Mantramayī). The latter is the Sthūla aspect of which Japa is done. The former is the Sūkshma aspect which is led up to in Yoga. Their specific enumeration and allocation denote the differentiation in the body of the total Shabda. This lotus is the center of the yellow Prithivī, or "earth" Tattva, with its quadrangular Mandala, the Bīja or Mantra of which Tattva is Lang (लं).[351]

At this center is the Prithivī Tattva, the Bīja of which is "La," with Bindu or the Brahma-consciousness presiding over this center or "Lang," which is the expression in gross (Vaikharī) sound of the subtle sound made by the vibration of the forces of this center. So, again, the subtle Tejas Tattva and its Bīja Rang is in the Manipūra Chakra, and the gross fire known as Vaishvānara is in the physical belly, which the subtle center governs. This Bīja represents in terms of Mantra the Tattva regnant at this center, and its essential activity. With the symbolism used throughout this work, Bīja is said to be seated on the elephant Airāvata, which is here located. This and the other animals figured in the Chakras are intended to denote the qualities of the Tattvas there regnant. Thus, the elephant is emblematic of the strength, firmness, and solidity, of this Tattva of "Earth." They are, further, the vehicles (Vāhana) of the Devatās there. Thus in this Chakra there is the seed-mantra (Bīja) of Indra, whose vehicle is the elephant Airāvata. The Devatā of this center is, according to the Text, the creative

---

[348] This and the other lotuses hang head downwards except when Kundalī passes through them, when they turn upwards.

[349] These vrittis or qualities (see *post*) denoting four forms of bliss are not given in the text here translated, but in Tarkalangkāra's Commentary to the Mahānirvāna Tantra.

[350] In this and other cases meditation is done from the right (dakshināvartena). See v. 4, Shat-chakranirūpana cited as S.N.

[351] The Dhyānabindu Up. associates the Bījas with the five Prānas. Thus "Lang" is associated with Vyāna.

Brahmā, whose Shakti is Sāvitrī.[352] There also is the Shakti known as Dākinī,[353] who, as also the other Shaktis, Lākinī and the rest, which follow, are the Shaktis of the Dhātus or bodily substances assigned to this and the other centers. Here is the "female" triangle or Yoni known as Traipura, which is the Shaktipītha, in which is set the "male" Shivalingga known as Svayambhu, of the shape and color of a young leaf, representing, as do all Devīs and Devas, the Māyā-Shakti and Chit-Shakti, aspects of the Brahman as manifested in the particular centers (vv. 4-14). The Linggas are four—Svayambhu, Bāna, Itara, Para. According to the Yoginīhridaya[354] (Ch. I.), they are so called because they lead to Chit. They are the Pīthas, Kāmarūpa, and the rest because they reflect Chit (Chitsphurattādhāratvāt). They are Vritti of Manas, Ahangkāra, Buddhi, Chitta. To the first three are assigned certain forms and colors—namely, yellow, red, white, triangular, circular; as also certain letters—namely, the sixteen vowels, Ka to Ta (soft), Tha to Sa. Para is formless, colorless, and letterless, being the collectivity (Samashti) of all letters in the form of bliss. The Traipura is the counterpart in the Jīva of the Kāmakalā of the Sahasrāra. The Devī Kundalinī, luminous as lightning, shining in the hollow of this lotus like a chain of brilliant lights, the World-bewilderer who maintains all breathing creatures,[355] lies asleep coiled three and a half times[356] round the Linga, covering with Her head the Brahmadvāra.[357]

The Svādisthāna Chakra is the second lotus proceeding upwards, and is, according to the commentary, so called after Sva or the Parang Lingam.[358] It is a vermilion lotus of six petals placed in the spinal center of the region at the root of the genitals. On these petals are the letters like lightning: Bang (वं), Bhang (भं), Mang (मं), Yang (यं), Rang (रं), Lang (लं). "Water" (Ap) is the Tattva of this Chakra, which is known as the white region of Varuna. The Tāttvik Mandala is in the shape of a crescent moon[359] (Ardhendurūpalasitam). The Bīja of water (Varuna) is "Vang." This, the Varuna Bīja, is seated on a white Makara[360] with a noose in his hand. Hari (Vishnu) and Rākinī Shakti of

---

[352] The Creator is called Savitā because He creates.

[353] Who, according to Sammohana Tantra, Ch. II., acts as keeper of the door. See, however, *ante*, note 292.

[354] Yoginīhridaya Tantra, Ch. I.

[355] See v. 49, S.N.

[356] These correspond with the three and a half Bindus of which the Kubjikā Tantra speaks. See *ante*, p. 89.

[357] Entrance to the Sushumnā.

[358] For another definition see Dhyānabindu Up., where all the Chakras are named. Another derivation is "own abode" (of Shakti).

[359] The diagrams or mandalas symbolic of the elements are also given, as here stated, in the first chapter of the Shāradā Tilaka and in the Vishvasāra Tantra, cited at p. 25 of the Prānatoshinī, with the exception that, according to the Vishvasāra Tantra, the Mandala of water is not a crescent, but eight-cornered (Ashtāsra).

[360] An animal like an alligator. See Plate 3.

furious aspect, showing Her teeth fiercely, are here (vv. 14-18). Above it, at the center of the region of the navel, is the lotus Manipūra (Nābhipadma), so called, according to the Gautamīya Tantra, because, owing to the presence of the fiery Tejas, it is lustrous as a gem (Mani).[361] It is a lotus of ten petals on which are the letters Dang (ड), Dhang (ढ), Nang (ण), Tang (त), Thang (थ), Dang (द), Dhang (ध), Nang (न), Pang (प), Phang (फ). This is the triangular region of the Tejas Tattva. The triangle has three Svastika. The red Bīja of fire, "Rang," is seated on a ram, the carrier of Agni, the Lord of Fire. Here is the old red Rudra smeared with white ashes, and the Shakti Lākinī who as the Devatā of this digestive center is said to be "fond of animal food, and whose breasts are ruddy with the blood and fat which drop from Her mouth." Lākinī and the other special Shaktis of the centers here named are the Shaktis of the Yogī himself—that is, Shaktis of the Dhātus assigned to each of his bodily centers, and concentration on this center may involve the satisfaction of the appetites of this Devatā. The Shaktis of the higher centers are not meat-eaters. From these three centers the gross Virāt, waking body, is evolved (vv. 19-21).

Next above the navel lotus (Nābhipadma) is the Anāhata, in the region of the heart, which is red like a Bandhuka flower, and is so called because it is in this place that Munis hear that "sound (Anāhata shabda) which comes without the striking of any two things together," or the "sound" of the Shabdabrahman, which is here the Pulse of Life. For it is here that the Purusha (Jīvātmā) dwells. This lotus is to be distinguished from the Heart Lotus of eight petals, which is represented in the place below it, where in mental worship the Patron Deity (Īshtadevatā) is meditated upon. (See Plate V.) Here is the Tree which grants all desires (Kalpataru) and the jeweled altar (Manipītha) beneath it. As the Vishvasāra Tantra cited in the Prānatoshinī says: "Shabdabrahman is said to be Deva Sadāshiva. That Shabda is said to be in the Anāhatachakra. Anāhata is the great Chakra in the heart of all beings. Ongkāra is said to be there in association with the three Gunas."[362] The Mahāsvachchhanda Tantra says:[363] "The great ones declare that Thy blissful form, O Queen, manifests in Anāhata, and is

---

[361] For another derivation, derived from Samaya worship, see Commentary on the Lalitā-Sahasranāma, vv. 37, 38.

[362] P. 14.

Shabdabrahmeti tang prāha sakshād devah sadāshivah
Anāhateshu chakreshu sa shabdah parikīrttyate
Anāhatang mahāchakrang hridaye sarvvajantushu
Tatra ongkāra ityukto gunatraya-samanvitah.

[363] Cited by Bhāskararāya's Comm. on Lalitā, v. 70, on the title of the Devī as Nādarūpā; and in v. 167, where she is described as Nādarūpinī, referring also to Yoginīhridaya.

experienced by the mind inward-turned of the Blessed Ones, whose hairs stand on end and whose eyes weep with joy." This is a lotus of ten petals with the vermilion letters Kang (कं), Khang (खं), Gang (गं), Ghang (घं), Ngang (ङं), Chang (चं), Chhang (छं), Jang (जं), Jhang (झं), Nyang (ञं), Tang (टं), Thang (ठं). This is the center of the Vāyu Tattva. According to v. 22, the region of Vāyu is six-cornered (that is, formed by two triangles, of which one is inverted), and its color that of smoke by reason of its being surrounded by masses of vapor.[364] Its Bīja "Yang" is seated on a black antelope which is noted for its fleetness, and is the Vāhana of "Air" (Vāyu), with its property of motion. Here are Īsha, the Overlord of the first three Chakras; the Shakti Kākinī garlanded with human bones, whose "heart is softened by the drinking of nectar"; and the Shakti in the form of an inverted triangle (Trikona), wherein is the golden Bāna Linga, "joyous with a rush of desire" (Kāmodgamollasita), and the Hangsa as Jīvātmā, like "the steady flame of a lamp in a windless place" (vv. 22-27). The Ātmā is so described because just as the flame is undisturbed by the wind, so the Ātmā is in itself unaffected by the motions of the world.[365]

The seventeenth verse of the Ānanda-Laharī mentions that the Devatās Vashinī and others are to be worshipped in the two last-mentioned Chakras. Vashinī and others are eight in number:[366]

(1) Vashinī, (2) Kāmeshvarī, (3) Modinī, (4) Vimalā, (5) Arunā, (6) Jayinī, (7) Sarveshvarī, and (8) Kālī or Kaulinī. These are respectively the Presiding Deities of the following eight groups of letters: (1) अ to अः, 16 letters; (2) क to ङ, 5 letters; (3) च to ञ, 5 letters; (4) ट to ण, 5 letters; (5) त to न, 5 letters; (6) प to म, 5 letters; (7) य to व, 4 letters; (8) श to ष or ळ, 5 letters.

The other beings in v. 17 of Ānanda-Laharī refer to the twelve Yoginīs, who are (1) Vidyāyoginī, (2) Rechikā, (3) Mochikā, (4) Amritā, (5) Dīpikā, (6) Jnānā, (7) Āpyāyanī, (8) Vyāpinī, (9) Medhā, (10) Vyomarūpā, (11) Siddhirūpā, and (12) Lakshmīyoginī.

These twenty Deities (eight Vashinīs and twelve Yoginīs) are to be worshipped in Manipūra and Anāhata centers. In respect of this, the Commentator quotes a verse from the Taittarīyāranyaka, and gives a description of these Deities, their respective colors, place, etc.

At the spinal center of the region at the base of the throat (Kantha-

---

[364] According to the Shāradā, Ch. I. (and to the same effect Prapanchasāra Tantra), the colors of the Bhūtas are as follows: Ākāsha (ether) is transparent (svachchha); Vāyu (air) is black (Krishna); Agni (fire) is red (Rakta); Ap (water) is white (Sveta); and Prithivī (earth) is yellow (Pīta).

[365] This steady, still, state is that of the Ātmā. See Mandalabrāhmana Up., Brāhmanas II., III.

[366] Pandit Ananta Shāstri's Ānanda Laharī, pp. 47, 48, and translation of same by A. Avalon, "Wave of Bliss."

mūla) is the Vishuddha Chakra or Bhāratīsthāna,[367] with sixteen petals of a smoky purple hue, on which are the sixteen vowels with Bindu thereon—that is, Ang (अं), Āng (आं), Ing (इं), Īng (ईं), Ung (उं), Ūng (ऊं), Ring (ऋं), Rīng (ॠं), Lring (ऌं), Lrīng (ॡं). Eng (एं), Aing (ऐं), Ong (ओं), Aung (औं), and the two breathings Āng (अं), Āh (अः). According to the Devībhāgavata (VII. 35), the Chakra is so called because the Jīva is made pure (Vishuddha) by seeing the Hangsah. Here is the center of the white circular Ākāsha or Ether Tattva, the Bīja of which is "Hang." Ākāsha is dressed in white and mounted on a white elephant. Its Mandala is in the form of a circle.[368] Here is Sadāshiva in his androgyne or Arddhanārīshvara Mūrti, in which half the body is white and the other half gold. Here also is the white Shakti Shākinī, whose form is light (Jyotihsvarūpā). Here, too, is the lunar region, "the gateway of the great liberation." It is at this place that the Jnānī "sees the three forms of time" (Tri-kāladarshī). As all things are in the Ātmā, the Jnānī who has realized the Atmā has seen them (vv. 28-31). Above the Vishuddha, at the root of the palate, is a minor Chakra called Lalanā, or in some Tantras Kalāchakra, which is not mentioned in the works here translated. It is a red lotus with twelve petals bearing the following Vritti or qualities: Shraddhā (faith), Santosha (contentment), Aparādha (sense of error), Dama (self-command), Māna (anger),[369] Sneha (affection),[370] Shuddhatā (purity), Arati (detachment), Sambhrama (agitation),[371] Ūrmmi (appetite).[372] (*V. post.*)

Before summarizing the previous description, it is to be here observed that the Commentator Kālīcharana states the principle of this Yoga to be that that which is grosser is merged into that which is more subtle (Sthūlānām sukshme layah). The grosser are lower in the body than the more subtle. The gross which are in and below the Mūlādhāra or connected with it are—(1) the Prithivī Tanmātra; (2) the Prithivī Mahābhūta; (3) the nostrils with their sense of smell, which is the grossest of the senses of knowledge (Jnānendriya), and which is the quality (Guna) of the Prithivī Tanmātra; and (4) the feet, which are the grossest of the senses of action (Karmendriya), and "which have Prithivī (earth) for their support." Here the nostrils are classified as the

[367] That is, abode of the Devī of speech.

[368] This is sometimes represented as a circle with a number of dots in it, for, as the Prapanchasāra Tantra says, Ākāsha has innumerable Shushira—that is, Chhidra, or spaces between its substance. It is because of its interstitial character that things exist in space.

[369] This term is generally applied to cases arising between two persons who are attached to one another, as man and wife.

[370] Usually understood as affection towards those younger or lower than oneself.

[371] Through reverence or respect.

[372] Or it may refer to the six which are technically called ūrmmi—that is, hunger, thirst, sorrow, ignorance (moha), decay, and death.

grossest of the Jnānendriya, because therein is the sense which perceives the quality (Guna) of smell of the grossest Tanmātra (Gandha), from which is derived the Prithivī Sthūla Bhūta. Thus the Jnānendriya have a relation with the Tanmātra through their Gunas (qualities), for the perception of which these senses exist. In the case, however, of the senses of action (Karmendriya), no such relation appears to exist between them and the Tanmātras. In the order of successive merging or Laya, the feet occur in the same grade as earth, hands in the same grade as water, anus in the same grade as fire, penis in the same grade as air, and mouth in the same grade as ether; not, apparently, because there is any direct relation between earth and feet, water and hands, fire and anus, and so forth, but because these organs are in the same order of comparative subtlety as earth, water, and fire, and so forth. Hands are supposed to be subtler agents than feet; the anus[373] a subtler agent than the hands; the penis a subtler agent than the anus; and the mouth a subtler agent than the penis. This is also the order in which these agents are situated in the body, the hands coming second because they find their place between the feet and the anus when the arms are given their natural vertical position. It is to be remembered is this connection that the Tantras here follow the Sāngkhya, and state the scheme of creation as it occurs also in the Purānas, according to which the Jnānendriya and Karmendriya and the Tanmātras issue from different aspects of the threefold Ahangkāra. There is a relation between the senses and the Tanmātra in the created Jīva, according to the Vedānta, for the senses are related to the Tanmātra, but the order, in that case, in which the senses occur is different from that given in this work. For, according to the Vedāntik scheme, earth is related to the sense of smell and penis; water to the sense of taste and anus; fire to the sense of sight and feet; air to the sense of touch and hands; and ether to the sense of hearing and mouth. Another explanation seemingly artificial, however, which has been given, is as follows: The feet are associated with "earth" because the latter alone has the power of support, and the feet rest on it. "Water" is associated with the hands because in drinking water the hand is used. The word Pāni, which means hand, is derived from the root Pā, to drink (Pīyate anena iti pāni). Fire is associated with the anus because what is eaten is consumed by fire in the stomach, and the residue is passed out through the anus, whereby the body becomes pure. "Air" is associated with the penis because in procreation the Jīvātmā as Prāna Vāyu throws itself out through the penis. And so the Shruti says; "Ātmā itself is reborn in the son" (Ātmā vai jāyate putrah). "Ether" is associated with

[373] At first sight this might appear not to be so, but the importance of the anus is well known to medical experts, its sensitivity having even given rise to what has been called a "psychology of the anus."

the mouth because by the mouth sound is uttered, which is the Guna (quality) of ether (Ākāsha).

Hitherto we have dealt with the comparatively gross Tattvas. According to this work, the twenty grosser Tattvas are associated (4 × 5) as in the following table:

Centre in which dissolved.	*Grosser Tattvas.*
1. Mūlādhāra -	Gandha (smell) Tanmātra; Prithivī Tattva (earth); the Jnānendriya of smell;* the Karmendriya of feet.
2. Svādhishthāna -	Rasa (taste) Tanmātra; Ap Tattva (water); the Jnānendriya of taste; the Karmendriya of hands.
3. Manipūra -	Rūpa (sight) Tanmātra; Tejas Tattva (fire); the Jnānendriya of sight; the Karmendriya of anus.
4. Anāhata -	Sparsha (touch) Tanmātra; Vāyu Tattva (air); the Jnānendriya of touch; the Karmendriya of penis.
5. Vishuddha -	Shabda (sound) Tanmātra; Ākāsha Tattva (ether); the Jnānendriya of hearing; the Karmendriya of mouth. [374]

It will be observed that with each of the elements is associated an organ of sensation (Jnānendriya) and action (Karmendriya). In Chapter II. of the Prapanchasāra Tantra it is said: "Ether is in the ears, air in the skin, fire in the eye, water in the tongue, and earth in the nostrils." The Karmendriya are possibly so arranged because the Tattvas of the respective centers in which they are placed are, as above stated, of similar grades of subtlety and grossness. As explained below, each class of Tattvas is dissolved in the next higher class, commencing from the lowest and grossest center, the Mūlādhāra. So far the Tattvas have been those of the "matter" side of creation.

Progress is next made to the last or Ājnā Chakra, in which are the subtle Tattvas of Mind and Prakriti. The Chakra is so called because it is here that the command (Ājnā) of the Guru is received from above. It is a lotus of two white petals between the eyebrows, on which are the white letters Hang (हं), and Kshang (क्षं). This exhausts the fifty letters. It will have been observed that there are fifty petals and fifty letters in the six Chakras. In the pericarp is the great Mantra "Om." Each Lotus has either two or four more petals than the one immediately below it, and the number of the petals in the Vishuddha Chakra is the sum of the preceding differences. Here are Paramashiva in the form of Hangsa (Hangsarūpa), Siddhakālī, the white Hākinī Shakti "elated by draughts of ambrosia," the inverted triangle or Yoni (Trikona), and the Itara

[374] * The nose is a centre at which sexual excitement may be aroused or subdued. Though the reproductive organ is higher up than the Mūlādhāra, the sexual force proceeds therefrom.

Linga, shining like lightning, which is set in it. The three Lingas are thus in the Mūlādhāra, Anāhata, and Ājnā Chakras respectively; for here at these three Brahmagranthis the force of Māyā Shakti is in great strength. And this is the point at which each of the three groups of Tattva associated with fire, sun, and moon, converge.[375] The phrase "opening the doors" refers to passage through these Granthi. Here in the Ājnā is the seat of the subtle Tattvas, Mahat and Prakriti. The former is the Antahkarana with Gunas—namely, Buddhi, Chitta, Ahangkāra and its product Manas (Sangkalpavikalpaka). Commonly and shortly it is said that Manas is the Tattva of the Ājnā Chakra. As, however, it is the mental center, it includes all the aspects of mind above stated, and the Prakriti whence they derive, as also the Ātmā in the form of the Pranava (Om) its Bīja. Here the Ātmā (Antarātmā) shines lustrous like a flame. The light of this region makes visible all which is between the Mūla and the Brahmarandhra. The Yogī by contemplation of this lotus gains further powers (Siddhi), and becomes Advaitāchāravādī (monist). In connection with this Padma, the text (S.N., v. 36) explains how detachment is gained through the Yoni Mudrā. It is here that the Yogī at time of death places his Prāna, and then enters the supreme primordial Deva, the Purāna (ancient) Purusha, "who was before the three worlds, and is known by the Vedānta." The same verse describes the method (Prānāropanaprakāra). From the last center and the causal Prakriti is evolved the subtle body which individually is known as Taijasa, and collectively (that is, the Īshvara aspect) as Hiranyagarbha. The latter term is applied to the manifestation of the Paramātmā in the Antahkarana; as displayed in Prāna it is Sūtrātmā; and when manifested through these two vehicles without differentiation it is known as the Antaryāmin. The Chakras are the bodily centers of the world of differentiated manifestation, with its gross and subtle bodies arising from their causal body, and its threefold planes of consciousness in waking, sleeping, and dreamless slumber.

Above the Ājnā-chakra (vv. 32-39) there are the minor Chakras called Manas and Soma, not mentioned in the texts here translated. The Manas Chakra is a lotus of six petals, on the petals of which are (that is, which is the seat of) the sensations of hearing, touch, sight, smell, taste, and centrally initiated sensations in dream and hallucination. Above this, again, is the Soma Chakra, a lotus of sixteen petals, with certain Vritti which are detailed later.[376] In this region are "the house without support" (Nirālambapurī), "where Yogīs see the radiant Īshvara," the seven causal bodies (v. 39) which are intermediate aspects of Ādyā Shakti, the white twelve-petalled lotus by the pericarp of the Sahasrāra (vv. 32-39), in which twelve-petalled lotus is the A-ka-tha triangle,

[375] *V. post.*
[376] *V. post.*

which surrounds the jeweled altar (Manipītha) on the isle of gems (Manidvīpa), set in the Ocean of Nectar,[377] with Bindu above and Nāda below, and the Kāmakalā triangle and the Guru of all, or Paramashiva. Above this, again, in the pericarp, are the Sūryya and Chandra Mandalas, the Parabindu surrounded by the sixteenth and seventeenth digits of the moon circle. In the Chandra Mandala there is a triangle. Above the Moon is Mahāvāyu, and then the Brahmarandhra with Mahāshangkhinī.

The twelve-petalled lotus and that which is connected with it is the special subject of the short book Pādukāpanchaka Stotra here translated, which is a hymn by Shiva in praise of the "Fivefold Footstool," with a commentary by Shrī Kālīcharana. The footstools are variously classified as follows: According to the first classification they are—(1) The white twelve-petalled lotus in the pericarp of the Sahasrāra lotus. Here there is (2) the inverted Triangle, the abode of Shakti called "A-ka-tha." (3) The region of the altar (Manipītha), on each side of which are Nāda and Bindu. The eternal Guru, "white like a mountain of silver," should be meditated upon, as on the Jeweled Altar (Manipītha). (4) The fourth Pādukā is the Hangsa below the Antarātmâ; and (5) the Triangle on the Pītha. The differences between this and the second classification are explained in the notes to v. 7 of the Pādukā. According to this latter classification they are counted as follows: (1) The twelve-petalled lotus; (2) the triangle called A-ka-tha; (3) Nāda-Bindu; (4) the Manipītha-Mandala; and (5) the Hangsa, which makes the triangular Kāmakalā. This Triangle, the Supreme Tattva, is formed by the three Bindus which the text calls Chandra (Moon), Sūryya (Sun), and Vahni (Fire) Bindus, which are also known as Prakāsha, Vimarsha, and Mishra Bindu. This is the Hangsa known as the triangular Kāmakalā, the embodiment of Purusha-Prakriti. The former is the Bindu Hangkāra at the apex of the triangle, and the two other Bindus called Visargah or Sa are Prakriti. This Kāmakalā is the Mūla (root) of Mantra.

The Shabdabrahman with its threefold aspect and energies is represented in the Tantras by this Kāmakalā, which is the abode of Shakti (Abalālayam). This is the Supreme Triangle, which, like all Yonipīthas, is inverted. It may be here noted that Shakti is denoted by a triangle because of its threefold manifestation as will, action, and knowledge (Ichchhā, Kriyā, Jnāna). So, on the material plane, if there are three forces, there is no other way in which they can be brought to interact except in the form of a triangle in which, while they are each separate and distinct from one another, they are yet related to each

---

[377] In mental worship the jeweled altar is in the eight-petalled lotus below Anāhata (see Plate V.). The Isle of Gems is a supreme state of Consciousness, and the Ocean of Nectar is the infinite Consciousness Itself. As to the causal bodies, see my "Studies in the Mantra Shāstra."

other and form part of one whole. At the corners of the Triangle there are two Bindus, and at the apex a single Bindu. These are the Bindus of Fire (Vahnibindu), Moon (Chandrabindu), and Sun (Sūryyabindu).[378] Three Shaktis emanate from these Bindus, denoted by the lines joining the Bindus and thus forming a triangle. These lines are the line of the Shakti Vāmā, the line of the Shakti Jyeshthā, and the line of the Shakti Raudrī. These Shaktis are volition (Ichchhā), action (Kriyā), and cognition (Jnāna). With them are Brahmā, Vishnu, and Rudra, associated with the Gunas Rajas, Sattva, and Tamas.

The lines of the triangle emanating from the three Bindus or Hangsah are formed by forty-eight letters of the alphabet. The sixteen vowels beginning with A form one line; the sixteen consonants beginning with Ka form the second line; and the following sixteen letters beginning with Tha form the third line. Hence the triangle is known as the A-ka-tha triangle. In the inner three corners of the triangle are the remaining letters Ha, Lla, Ksha. The Yāmala thus speaks of this abode, "I now speak of Kāmakalā," and, proceeding, says: "She is the eternal One who is the three Bindus, the three Shaktis, and the three Forms (Trimūrtih)." The Brihat-Shrī-krama, in dealing with Kāmakalā, says: "From the Bindu (that is, the Parabindu) She has assumed the form of letters (Varnāvayavarūpinī)." The Kālī Ūrddhvāmnāya says: "The threefold Bindu (Tribindu) is the supreme Tattva, and embodies in itself Brahmā, Vishnu, and Shiva."[379] The triangle which is composed of the letters has emanated from the Bindu. These letters are known as the Mātrikā Varna. These form the body of Kulakundalinī[380] the Shabdabrahman, being in their Vaikharī state various manifestations of the primal unmanifested "sound" (Avyaktanāda).

They appear as manifested Shabda on the self-division of the Parabindu; for this self-division marks the appearance of the differentiated Prakriti.

The commentary on the Pādukāpanchaka (v. 3) says that the Bindu is Parashakti itself, and its variations are called Bindu, Nāda, and Bīja, or Sun, Moon, and Fire; Bindu, the sun, being red, and Nāda, the moon, being white.[381] These form the Chinmaya or Ānandamayakosha (Pādukāpanchaka, v. 3). The two Bindus making the base of the triangle are the Visargah (*ib.*, v. 4). In the Āgamakalpadruma it is said:

---

[378] The Kāmakalāvilāsa says: "Bindu-trayamayas tejas-tritaya" (three Bindus and three fires). "Tripurasundarī sits in the Chakra which is composed of Bindus (Bindumayachakre), Her abode being the lap of Kāmeshvara, whose forehead is adorned by the crescent moon. She has three eyes, which are Sun, Moon, and Fire."

[379] The Māheshvarī Sanghitā says: "Sūryya, Chandra, and Vahni, are the three Bindus; and Brahmā, Vishnu, and Shambhu, are the three lines."

[380] The Kāmakalāvilāsa says: "Ekapanchāshadaksharātmā" (she is in the form of the 51 letters).

[381] This appears to be in conflict with the previous statement of Rāghava Bhatta, that Bindu is Moon and Nāda the Sun.

"Hangkāra is Bindu or Purusha, and Visarga is Sah or Prakriti. Hangsah is the union of the male and female, and the universe is Hangsah." The triangular Kāmakalā is thus formed by Hangsah (*ib.*). The Hangsa-pītha is composed of Mantras (*ib.*, v. 6).

As this subject is of great importance, some further authorities than those referred to in the work here translated are given. In his commentary to v. 73 of the Lalitā, in which the Devī is addressed as being in the form of Kāmakalā (Kāmakalārūpā), Bhāskararāya says: "There are three Bindus and the Hārdhakalā.[382] Of these the Bindus are called Kāma, and the Hakārārdha is named Kalā."[383] He adds that the nature of Kāmakalā is set forth in the Kāmakalāvilāsa in the verses commencing "Supreme Shakti (Parā Shakti) is the manifested union of Shiva and Shakti in the form of seed and sprout," and ending with the lines "Kāma (means) desirableness, and the Kalā the same. The two Bindus are said to be the Fire and Moon."[384] Kāma, or creative will, is both Shiva and Devī, and Kalā is their manifestation. Hence it is called Kāmakalā. This is explained in the Tripurāsiddhānta: "O Pārvatī, Kalā is the manifestation of Kāmeshvara and Kāmeshvarī. Hence She is known as Kāmakalā."[385] Or She is the manifestation (Kalā) of desire (Kāma)[386]—that is, of Ichchhā. The Kālikā Purāna says: "Devī is called Kāma because She came to the secret place on the blue peak of the great mountain (Kailāsa) along with Me for the sake of desire (Kāma): thus Devī is called Kāmā. As She is also the giver or fulfiller of desire, desiring, desirable, beautiful, restoring the body of Kāma (Manmatha) and destroying the body of Kāma, hence She is called Kāma."[387] After Shiva (with whom She is one) had destroyed Kāma, when he sought by the instilment of passion to destroy His yoga; so She (with whom He is one) afterwards gave a new body to the "Bodiless One" (Ananga). They destroy the worlds and take them to themselves through the cosmic yoga path, and again by Their desire and will (Ichchhā) recreate them. These Bindus and Kalā are referred to in the celebrated Hymn

---

[382] Also called Hakārārdha—that is, half the letter Ha (ह).

[383] Bindu-trayang hārdhakalā cha ityatra prathamo binduh kāmākhyashcharamā kalā cha iti pratyāhāranyāyena kāmakaletyuchyate.

[384] Tasyāh svarūpang sphutashivashakti-samāgamabījāngkurarūpirī parāshaktirityārabhya Kāmah kamanīyatayā kalā cha dahanenduvigrahau bindū ityantena nirnītang kāmakalāvilāse tadrūpetyarthah (*ib.*).

[385] Kāmayoh kaleti vā, taduktang, Tripurāsiddhānte
Tasyakāmeshvarākhyasya kāmeshvaryāshcha Pārvvati
Kalākhyā salīlā sā cha khyātā kāmakaleti sā.

[386] Kāmashchāsau kalārūpā cheti vā.

[387] Kāmapadamātra-vāchyatāyāh Kālīpurāne pratipādanāt.
Kāmārthamāgatā yasmānmayā sārdhang mahāgirau
Kāmākhyā prochyate devī nīlakūtarahogatā
Kāmadā kāminī kāmyā kāntā kāmānggadāyinī
Kāmāngganāshinī yasmāt kāmākhyā tena kathyate
Iti shadaksharamidamnāma (*ib.*).

"Waves of Bliss" (Ānandalahari), attributed to the great Shangkarāchāryya.[388]

This Devī is the great Tripurasundarī. Bhāskararāya's Guru Nrisinghānandanātha wrote the following verse, on which the disciple commentates: "I hymn Tripurā, the treasure of Kula,[389] who is red of beauty; Her limbs like unto those of Kāmarāja, who is adored by the three Devatās[390] of the three Gunas; who is the desire (or will) of Shiva;[391] who dwells in the Bindu and who manifests the universe." She is called (says the commentator cited)[392] Tripurā, as She has three (Tri) Puras (lit., cities), but, here meaning Bindus, angles, lines, syllables, etc. The Kālikā Purāna says: "She has three angles (in the triangular Yoni) as well as three circles (the three Bindus), and her Bhūpura[393] has three lines. Her Mantra is said to be of three syllables,[394] and She has three aspects. The Kundalinī energy is also threefold, in order that She may create the three Gods (Brahmā, Vishnu, Rudra). Thus, since She the supreme energy is everywhere triple, She is called Tripurasundarī."[395] These syllables are said by the commentator last cited[396] to be the three Bījas of the three divisions (of the Panchadashī)—viz., Vāgbhava, Kāmarāja, and Shakti, which according to the Vāmakeshvara Tantra are the Jnānashakti which confers salvation, and the Kriyā and Ichchhā Shaktis.

---

[388] Mukhang bindung kritvā kuchayugamadhastasya tadadho
Hakārārdhang dhyāyet Haramahīshi te manmathakalām (v. 19).

(Let him contemplate on the first Bindu as the face of the Devī, and on the other two Bindus as Her two breasts, and below that on the half Ha.) Ha is the yoni, the womb, and origin of all. See Lalitā, v. 155.

[389] Kulanidhi. In its literal ordinary sense Kula means race or family, but has a number of other meanings: Shakti (Akula is Shiva), the spiritual hierarchy of Gurus, the Mūlādhāra, the doctrine of the Kaula Tantriks, etc.

[390] Vishnu, Brahmā, and Rudra, of the Sattva, Rajas, and Tamas qualities respectively.

[391] This is the Commentator's meaning of Ekām tām. Eka—a + i = e. According to the Vishva Dictionary, "A" has among other meanings that of Īsha or Shiva, and, according to the Anekārthadhvanimanjarī Lexicon, I = Manmatha—that is, Kāma, or desire. Ekā is therefore the spouse of Shiva, or Shivakāmā, the desire or will of Shiva.

[392] Introduction to Lalitā.

[393] The portion of the Yantra which is of common form and which encloses the particular design in its center. Reference may, however, also be here made to the three outer lines of the Shrīchakra.

[394] *V. post.* The Kāma bīja is Klīng. Klīngkāra is Shivakāma. Here Īng means the Kāmakalā in the Turīya state through which Moksha is gained, and hence the meaning of the saying (*ib.*, v. 125) that he who hears the Bīja without Ka and La does not reach the place of good actions—that is, he does not go to the region attained by good actions, but to that attainable by knowledge alone (see *ib.*, v. 138, citing Yoginīhridaya and Vāmakeshvara Tantra).

[395] Other instances may be given, such as the Tripurārnava, which says that the Devī is called Tripurā because She dwells in the three Nādīs (Sushumnā, Pinggalā, and Idā; *v. post*) and in Buddhi Manas Chitta (*v. post*).

[396] V. 126.

Three "Pāda" are also spoken of as Tripurā—white, red, and mixed.[397] Elsewhere, as in the Varāha Purāna, the Devī is said to have assumed three forms—white, red, and black: that is, the Supreme energy endowed with the Sāttvik, Rājasik, and Tāmasik qualities.[398] The one Shakti becomes three to produce effects.

In the Kāmakalā meditation (Dhyāna) the three Bindus and Hārdhakalā are thought of as being in the body of the Devī Tripurasundarī. The Commentator on the verse of the Ānanda-Laharī cited says:[399] "In the fifth sacrifice (Yajna) let the Sādhaka think of his Ātmā as in no wise different from, but as the one only Shiva; and of the subtle thread-like Kundalinī which is all Shaktis, extending from the Ādhāra lotus to Paramashiva. Let him think of the three Bindus as being in Her body (Tripurasundarī), which Bindus indicate Ichchhā, Kriyā, Jnāna—Moon, Fire, and Sun; Rajas, Tamas, Sattva; Brahmā, Rudra, Vishnu; and then let him meditate on the Chitkalā who is Shakti below it."[400]

The Bindu which is the "face" indicates Virinchi[401] (Brahmā) associated with the Rajas Guna. The two Bindus which are the "breasts," and upon which meditation should be done in the heart, indicate Hari[402] (Vishnu) and Hara[403] (Rudra) associated with the Sattva and Tamas Gunas. Below them meditate in the Yoni upon the subtle Chitkalā, which indicates all three Gunas, and which is all these three Devatās.[404] The meditation given in the Yoginī Tantra is as follows: "Think of three Bindus above Kalā, and then that from these a young girl sixteen years old springs forth, shining with the light of

---

397 According to a note of R. Anantakrishna Shāstri, editor of the Lalitā, p. 213, the three "feet" are explained in another work of Bhāskararāya as follows: White, the pure Samvit (Consciousness) untainted by any Upādhis; red, the Parāhantā (Supreme Individuality), the first Vritti (modification) from the Samvit; and the mixed—the above-mentioned as one inseparable modification (the Vritti) of "I." These are known as the "three feet" (Charana tritaya), or Indu (white), Agni (red), Ravi (mixed).

398 So also the Devī Bhāgavata Pr. says: "The Shāmbhavī is white; Shrīvidyā, red; and Shyāmā, black." The Yantra of Shrīvidyā is the Shrīchakra mentioned.

399 Shangkarāchāryyagranthāvalī (Vol. II.), ed. Shrī Prasanna Kumāra Shāstri. The editor's notes are based on the Commentary of Achyutānanda Sharmā.

400 Atha panchamayāge abhedabhudhyā ātmānang shivarūpamekātmānang vibhāvya ādhārāt paramashivāntang sūtrarūpāng sūkshmāng kundalinīng sarvashaktirūpāng vibhāvya sattvarajastamogunasūchakang brahmavishnushivashaktyātmakang sūryāgnichandrarūpang bindutrayang tasyā angge vibhāvya adhaschitkalāng dhyāyet (Comm. to v. 19).

401 That is, He who creates, from *Vi* + *rich*.

402 He who takes away (harati) or destroys all grief and sin.

403 The same.

404 Mukhang bindung kritvā rajogunasūchakang virinchyātmakang bindung kritvā, tasyādho hridayasthāne sattvatamogunasūchakang hariharātmakang bindudvayang kuchayugang kritvā, tasyādhah yonigunatrayasūchikāng hariharavirinchyātmikāng sūkshmāng chitkalāng hakārārdhang kritvā yonyantargata-trikonākriting kritvā dhyāyet (*ib.*).

millions of rising suns, illuminating every quarter of the firmament. Think of Her body from crown to throat as springing from the upper Bindu, and that her body from throat to middle, with its two breasts and three belly lines of beauty (trivali), arise from the two lower Bindus. Then imagine that the rest of Her body from genitals to feet is born from Kāma. Thus formed, She is adorned with all manner of ornaments and dress, and is adored by Brahmā, Īsha, and Vishnu. Then let the Sādhaka think of his own body as such Kāmakalā."[405] The Shrītattvārnava says: "The glorious men who worship in that body in Sāmarasya[406] are freed from the waves of poison in the untraversable sea of the world (Sangsāra).'"[405]

To the same effect are the Tantrik works the Shrīkrama[407] and Bhāvachūdāmani[408] cited in the Commentary to the Ānanda-Laharī. The first says: "Of the three Bindus, O Mistress of the Devas, let him contemplate the first as the mouth and in the heart the two Bindus as the two breasts. Then let him meditate upon the subtle Kalā Hakārārdha in the Yoni." And the second says: "The face in the form of Bindu, and below twin breasts, and below them the beauteous form of the Hakārādha." The three Devatās Brahmā, Vishnu, and Rudra, with their Shaktis, are said to take birth from the letters A, U, M, of the Ongkāra or Pranava.[409] Ma, as the Prapanchasāra Tantra[410] says, is the Sun or

[405] See p. 199, *et seq.*, Nityapūjāpaddhati, by Jaganmohana Tarkālangkāra.

[406] That is, equal feeling; or being one with; homogeneity; union of Shiva and Shakti.

[407] Tathācha Shrīkrame: Bindutrayasya deveshi prathamang devi vaktrakang Bindudvayang stanadvandvang hridi sthāne niyojayet. Hakārārdhang kalāng sūkshmāng yonimadhye vichintayet.

[408] Taduktang Bhāvachūdāmanau:

Mukhang binduvadākārang
Tadadhah kuchayugmakam
Tadadhashcha hakārārdhang
Supariskritamandalam.

The third verse is printed Tadadhah Sapārārdhangcha. But this means the same thing. Sapara is Hakāra, as Ha follows Sa. For further Dhyānas and mode of meditation, see p. 199 of the Nityapūjāpaddhati of Jaganmohana Tarkālangkāra.

[409] Phetkārinī Tantra, Ch. I.:

Tebhya eva samutpannā varnāh ye vishnu-shūlinoh
Mūrtayah shaktisangyuktā uchyante tāh kramena tu.

And so also Vishvasāra Tantra (see Prānatoshini, 14):

Shivo brahmā tathā vishnurongkāre cha pratishthitāh
Akārashcha bhaved brahmā ukārah sachchidātmakah
Makāro rudra ityukta iti tasyārthakalpanā.

[410] Ch. III.

Ātmā among the letters, for it is Bindu. From each of these ten Kalās arise.

Verse 8 of the first work translated says that in the Mūlādhāra center there is the Triangle (Trikona) known as Traipura, which is an adjective of Tripura. It is so called because of the presence of the Devī Tripurā within the Ka inside the triangle. This Ka is the chief letter of the Kāma Bīja, and Kang[411] is the Bīja of Kāminī, the aspect of Tripurasundarī in the Mūlādhāra. Here also, as the same verse says, there are the three lines Vāmā, Jyeshthā, and Raudrī, and, as the Shatchakra-vivriti adds, Ichchhā, Jnāna, and Kriyā.[412] Thus the Traipura Trikona is the gross or Sthūla aspect of that subtle (Sūkshma) Shakti which is below the Sahasrāra, and is called Kāmakalā. It is to this Kāminī that in worship the essence of Japa (Tejorūpajapa) is offered, the external Japa being offered to the Devatā worshipped in order that the Sādhaka may retain the fruits of his worship.[413] There are also two other Lingas and Trikonas at the Anāhata and Ājnā centers, which are two of the Knots or Granthis, and which are so called because Māyā is strong at these points of obstruction, at which each of the three groups converge. The Traipura Trikona is that, however, in the Mūlādhāra which is the grosser correspondence of the Kāmakalā, which is the root (Mūla) of all Mantra below the Sahasrāra, and which, again, is the correspondence in Jīva of the Tribindu of Īshvara.

Before, however, dealing in detail with the Sahasrāra, the reader will find it convenient to refer to the tables on pp. 114 and 115, which summarizes some of the details above given up to and including the Sahasrāra.

---

[411] Nityapūjāpaddhati, p. 80, by Jaganmohana Tarkālangkāra.

[412] See p. 117, Vol. II., of Tantrik Texts, where that Commentary is printed.

[413] Nityapūjāpaddhati, *loc. cit.*

Chakra.	*Situation.*	*Number of Petals.*	*Letters on Same.*	*Regnant Tattva and its Qualities.*	*Colour of Tattva.*	*Shape of Mandala.*	*Bīja and its Vāhana (Carrier).*	*Devatā and its Vāhana.*	*Shakti of the Dhātu.*	*Linga and Yoni.*	*Other Tattvas here dissolved.*
Mūlā-dhāra	Spinal centre of region below genitals	4	va, sha, *sh*a, sa	Prithivī; cohesion, stimulating sense of smell	Yellow	Square	Lang on the Airāvata elephant	Brahmā on Hangsa	Dākinī	Svayambhu and Traipura Trikona	Gandha (smell) Tattva; smell (organ of sensation); feet (organ of action)
Svādhi-shthāna	Spinal centre of region above the genitals	6	ba, bha, ma, ya, ra, la	Ap; contraction, stimulating sense of taste	White	Crescent	Vang on Makara	Vishnu on Garuda	Rākinī		Rasa (taste) Tattva; taste (organ of sensation); hand; (organ of action)
Mani-pūra	Spinal centre of region of the navel	10	*d*a, *d*ha, *n*a, ta, da, tha, na, dha, pa, pha	Tejas; expansion; producing heat and stimulating sight-sense of colour and form	Red	Triangle	Rang on a ram	Rudra on a bull	Lākinī		Rūpa (form and colour; sight) Tattva; sight (organ of sensation); anus (organ of action)

Chakra.	*Situation.*	*Number of Petals.*	*Letters on Same.*	*Regnant Tattva and its Qualities.*	*Colour of Tattva.*	*Shape of Mandala.*	*Bīja and its Vāhana (Carrier).*	*Devatā and its Vāhana.*	*Shakti of the Dhātu.*	*Linga and Yoni.*	*Other Tattvas here dissolved.*
Anā-hata	Spinal centre of region of the heart	12	ka, kha, ga, gha, nga, cha, chha, ja, jha, nya, *t*a, *t*ha	Vāyu; general movement, stimulating sense of touch	Smoky	Six-pointed hexagon	Yang on an antelope	Īsha	Kākinī	Bāna and Trikona	Sparsha (touch and feel) Tattva; touch (organ of sensation); penis (organ of action)
Vish-uddha	Spinal centre of region of the throat	16	the vowels a, ā, i, ī, u, ū, ri, rī, lri, lrī, e, ai, o, au, ang, ah	Ākāsha; space-giving, stimulating sense of hearing	White	Circle	Hang on a white elephant	Sadā-shiva	Shākinī	—	Shabda (sound) Tattva; hearing (organ of sensation); mouth (organ of action)
Ājnā	Centre of region between the eyebrows	2	ha and ksha	Manas (mental faculties)	—	—	Om	Sham-bhu	Hākinī	Itara and Trikona	Mahat, the Sūkshma Prakriti called Hiranyagarbha (v. 52)

Above the Ājnā is the causal region and the Lotus of a thousand petals, with all the letters, wherein is the abode of the Supreme Bindu Parashiva.

In the description of the Chakras given in this work, no mention is made of the moral and other qualities and things (Vritti) which are associated with the Lotuses in other books, such as the Adhyātmaviveka,[414] commencing with the root-lotus and ending with the Somachakra. Thus, the Vrittis, Prashraya, Avishvāsa, Avajnā, Mūrchhā, Sarvanāsha, Krūratā,[415] are assigned to Svādhishthāna; Lajjā, Pishunatā, Īrshā, Trishnā, Sushupti, Vishāda, Kashāya, Moha, Ghrinā, Bhaya,[416] to the Manipūra; Āshā, Chintā, Cheshtā, Mamatā, Dambha, Vikalatā, Ahangkāra, Viveka, Lolatā, Kapatatā, Vitarka, Anutāpa,[417] Kripā, Mridutā, Dhairyya, Vairāgya, Dhriti, Sampat, Hāsya, Romāncha, Vinaya, Dhyāna, Susthiratā, Gāmbhīryya, Udyama, Akshobha, Audārya, Ekāgratā,[418] to the secret Somachakra; and so forth. In the Mūlādhāra, which has been described as the "source of a massive pleasurable æsthesia," there are the four forms of bliss already mentioned; in the Vishuddha the seven subtle "tones," Nishāda, Rishabha, Gāndhāra, Shadja, Madhyama, Dhaivata, Panchama; certain Bījas, Hūng, Phat, Vaushat, Vashat, Svadhā, Svāhā, Namah; in the eighth petal "venom," and in the sixteenth "nectar";[419] and in the petals and pericarp of the Ājnā the three Gunas, and in the former the Bījas Hang and Kshang; and in the six-petalled Manaschakra above the Ājnā are Shabdajnāna, Sparshajnāna, Rūpajnāna, Āghrānopalabdhi, Rasopabhoga, and Svapna, with their opposites, denoting the sensations of the sensorium—hearing, touch, sight, smell, taste, and centrally initiated sensations in dream and hallucination. It is stated that particular Vrittis are assigned to a particular lotus, because of a connection between such Vritti and the operation of the Shaktis of the Tattva at the center to which it is assigned. That they exist at any particular Chakra is said to be shown by their disappearance when Kundalī ascends through the Chakra. Thus the bad Vritti of the lower Chakras pass away in the Yogī who raises Kundalī above them.

Moral qualities (Vritti) appear in some of the lower Chakras and in the secret twelve-petalled lotus called the Lalanā (and in some Tantras Kalāchakra), situate above the Vishuddha, at the root of the palate

---

[414] Quoted in the Dīpikā to v. 7 of the Hangsopanishad.

[415] Credulity, suspicion, disdain, delusion (or disinclination), false knowledge (lit., destruction of everything which false knowledge leads to), pitilessness.

[416] Shame, fickleness, jealousy, desire, supineness, sadness, dullness ignorance, aversion (or disgust), fear.

[417] Hope, care or anxiety, endeavor, sense of languor, mineness (resulting in attachment), arrogance or hypocrisy, egoism or self-conceit, discrimination, covetousness, duplicity, indecision, regret.

[418] Mercy, gentleness, patience or composure, dispassion, constancy, prosperity (spiritual) cheerfulness, rapture or thrill, humility or sense of propriety, meditativeness, quietude or restfulness, gravity (of demeanor), enterprise or effort, emotionlessness (being undisturbed by emotion), magnanimity, concentration.

[419] Both, were extracted at the churning of the ocean, and, as so spoken of, represent the destructive and upbuilding forces of the world.

(Tālumūla), as also in the sixteen-petalled lotus above the Manashchakra, and known as the Somachakra. It is noteworthy that the Vritti of the two lower Chakras (Svādhishthāna and Manipūra) are all bad; those of the Anāhata centers are mixed,[420] those of the Lalanā Chakra are predominantly good, and those of the Somachakra wholly so; thus indicative of an advance as we proceed from the lower to the higher centers, and this must be so as the Jīva approaches or lives in his higher principles. In the twelve-petalled white lotus in the pericarp of the Sahasrāra is the abode of Shakti, called the Kāmakalā, already described.

Between Ājnā and Sahasrāra, at the seat of the Kārana Sharīra of Jīva, are the Varnāvalirūpā Viloma Shaktis, descending from Unmanī to Bindu. Just as in the Īshvara or cosmic creation there are seven creative Shaktis from Sakala Parameshvara to Bindu; and in the microcosmic or Jīva creation seven creative Shaktis from Kundalīnī, who is in the Mūlādhāra, to Bindu, both of which belong to what is called the Anuloma order:[421] so in the region between the Ājnā Chakra and Sahasrāra, which is the seat of the causal body (Kārana Sharīra) of Jīva, there are seven Shaktis,[422] which, commencing with the lowest, are Bindu (which is in Īshvara Tattva), Bodhinī, Nāda, Mahānāda or Nādānta (in Sadākhya Tattva), Vyāpikā, Samanī (in Shakti Tattva), and Unmanī (in Shiva Tattva). Though these latter Shaktis have a cosmic creative aspect, they are not here co-extensive with and present a different aspect from the latter. They are not co-extensive, because the last-mentioned Shaktis are, as here mentioned, Shaktis of the Jīva. Hangsa Jīva or Kundalī is but an infinitesimal part of the Parabindu. The latter is in the Sahasrāra, or thousand-petalled lotus, the abode of Īshvara, who is Shiva-Shakti and is the seat of the aggregate Kundalīs or Jīva. And hence it is said that all the letters are here twentyfold (50 × 20 = 1,000). In the Sahasrāra are Parabindu, the supreme Nirvāna Shakti, Nirvāna Kalā, Amākalā,[423] and the fire of Nibodhikā. In the Parabindu is the empty void (Shūnya) which is the supreme Nirguna Shiva.

Another difference is to be found in the aspect of the Shaktis. Whilst the cosmic creative Shaktis are looking outwards and forwards (Unmukhī), the Shaktis above the Ājnā are, in Yoga, looking backwards towards dissolution. The Īshvara of the Sahasrāra is not then

---

[420] *E.g.*, with Dambha (arrogance), Lolatā (covetousness), Kapatatā (duplicity), we find Āshā (hope), Cheshtā (endeavor), Viveka (discrimination).

[421] That is, the ordinary as opposed to the reversed (viloma) order. Thus, to read the alphabet as A to Z is anuloma; to read it backwards, Z to A, is viloma. In the above matter, therefore anuloma is creation (srishti) or the forward, movement, and viloma (nivritti) the path of return.

[422] See my "Studies in Mantra Shāstra": "Causal Shaktis of the Pranava."

[423] See my "Studies in Mantra Shāstra": "Kalās of the Shaktis."

the creative aspect of Īshvara. There He is in the Nirvāna mood, and the Shaktis leading up to Nirvāna Shakti are "upward moving"—that is, liberating Shaktis of the Jīva.

These seven states or aspects of Bindumayaparashakti (S.N., v. 40) leading up to Unmanī, which are described in this and other Tantrik books, are called causal forms (Kāranarūpa). The commentary to the Lalitā[424] apparently enumerates eight, but this seems to be due to a mistake, Shakti and Vyāpikā being regarded as distinct Shaktis instead of differing names for the third of this series of Shaktis.

Below Visargah (which is the upper part of the Brahmarandhra, in the situation of the fontenelle) and the exit of Shangkinī Nādī is the Supreme White (or, as some call it, variegated) Lotus of a thousand petals (S.N., vv.40-49), known as the Sahasrāra, on which are all the letters of the Sanskrit alphabet, omitting according to some the Vaidik Lakāra, and according to others Ksha. These are repeated twenty times to make the 1,000, and are read from beginning to end (Anuloma), going round the Lotus from right to left. Here is Mahāvāyu and the Chandramandala, in which is the Supreme Bindu (O), "which is served in secret by all the Devas." Bindu as such implies Guna, but it also means the void of space, and in its application to the Supreme Light, which is formless, is symbolical of its decaylessness. This subtle Shūnya (Void), which is the Ātmā of all being (Sarvvātmā), is spoken of in S.N., vv. 42-49. Here in the region of the Supreme Lotus is the Guru, the Supreme Shiva Himself. Hence the Shaivas call it Shivasthānam, free of all illusion, and the abode of bliss where the Ātmā is realized. Here, too, is the Supreme Nirvāna Shakti, the Shakti in the Parabindu, and the Mother of all the three worlds. He who has truly and fully known the Sahasrāra is not reborn in the Sangsāra, for he has by such knowledge broken all the bonds which held him to it. His earthly stay is limited to the working out of the Karma already commenced and not exhausted. He is the possessor of all Siddhi, is liberated though living (Jīvanmukta), and attains bodiless liberation (Moksha), or Videha Kaivalya, on the dissolution of his physical body.

In the fourteenth verse and commentary thereon of the Ānandalaharī the Deity in the Sahasrāra is described.[425]

"She is above all the Tattvas. Every one of the six centers represents a Tattva. Every Tattva has a definite number of rays. The six centers, or Chakras, are divided into three groups. Each of these groups has a knot or apex where converge the Chakras that constitute that group. The names of the groups are derived from those of the Presiding Deities. The following table clearly puts the above:

---

[424] V. 70, Lalitā-Sahasaranāma.

[425] See Pandit R. Ananta Shāstri's Ānandalaharī. p. 42, *et seq.* The passage within quotation marks is taken from that work.

See "Wave of Bliss," by A. Avalon.

No.	Name of Chakra.	Name of Tattva.	No. of Rays of Tattva.	Name of Group.	Name of Converging Point.	Remarks.
1	Mūlādhāra	Bhū	56	Agni-Khanda	Rudra-granthi	In Sahasrāra the rays are numberless, eternal and unlimited by space. There is another Chandra here whose rays are countless and ever-shining.
2	Svādhishthāna	Agni	62			
3	Manipūra	Apas	52	Sūrya	Vishnu-granthi	
4	Anāhata	Vāyu	54			
5	Vishuddhi	Ākāsha	72	Chandra	Brahma-granthi	
6	Ājnā	Manas	64			
			360			

"Lakshmīdhara quotes the Taittirīyāranyaka in support of his commentary, from which we have taken the notes above given. The extracts which he makes from 'Bhairava Yāmala' are very valuable. In discoursing about Chandra, Shiva addresses (vv. 1-17, Chandrajnānavidyāprakarana) Pārvati, his consort, thus:

"'Welcome, O Beauty of the three worlds, welcome is Thy question. This knowledge (which I am about to disclose) is the secret of secrets, and I have not imparted it to anyone till now. (But I shall now tell thee the grand secret. Listen, then, with attention:)

"'Shrīchakra (in the Sahasrāra) is the form of Parāshakti. In the middle of this Chakra is a place called Baindava, where She, who is above all Tattvas, rests united with Her Lord Sadāshiva. O Supreme One, the whole Cosmos is a Shrīchakra formed of the twenty-five Tattvas—5 elements + 5 Tanmātras + 10 Indriyas + Mind + Māyā, Shuddhavidyā, Mahesha, and Sadāshiva.[426] Just as it is in Sahasrāra, so cosmically, also, Baindava is above all Tattvas. Devī, the cause of the creation, protection, and destruction, of the universe, rests there ever united with Sadāshiva, who as well is above all Tattvas and ever-shining. Uncountable are the rays that issue forth from Her body; O good one, they emanate in thousands, lacs—nay, crores. But for this light there would be no light at all in the universe . . . 360 of these rays illumine the world in the form of Fire, Sun, and Moon. These 360 rays are made up as follows: Agni (Fire) 118, Sun 106, Moon 136. O Shankari, these three luminaries enlighten the macrocosm as well as the microcosm, and give rise to the calculation of time—the Sun for the

[426] Māyā to Sadāshiva are the Shaiva Tattvas described in the Introduction.—A. A.

day, the Moon for the night, Agni (Fire) occupying a mean position between the two.'[427]

"Hence they constitute (or are called) Kāla (time), and the 360 days (rays) make a year. The Veda says: 'The year itself is a form of the Lord. The Lord of time, the Maker of the world, first created Marīchi (rays), etc., the Munis, the protectors of the world. Everything has come to exist by the command of Parameshvarī.'

"Dindima takes a quite different view of this verse. He interprets it as meaning that, having already described the Antaryāga (inner worship), the author recommends here the worship of the Āvarana Devatās—*i.e.*, Deities residing in each of the Chakras or centers—without propitiating whom it is impossible for the practitioner to lead the Kundalinī through these Chakras. He enumerates all the 360 Deities and describes the mode of worshipping each of them.

"There are other commentators who understand the 360 rays esoterically, and connect the same with the 360 days of the year, and also with the human body. Every commentator quotes the Taittarīyāranyaka, first chapter, to support his views. Thus it seems that Taittarīyāranyaka contains much esoteric matter for the mystic to digest. The first chapter of the Aranyaka referred to is chanted in worshipping the Sun. It is called Ārunam because it treats of Arunā (red-colored Devī)."[428]

An Indian physician and Sanskritist has expressed the opinion that better anatomy is given in the Tantras than in the purely medical works of the Hindus.[429] It is easier, however, to give a statement of the present and ancient physiology than to correlate them. Indeed, this is for the present a difficult matter. In the first place, the material as regards the latter is insufficiently available and known to us, and those native scholars and Sādhakas (nowadays, probably, not numerous) who are acquainted with the subject are not conversant with Western physiology, with which it is to be compared. It is, further, possible to be practically acquainted with this Yoga without knowing its physiological relations, a knowledge of which is not so important as is sometimes supposed. Working in what is an unexplored field, I can only here put forward, on the lines of the Text and such information as I have gathered, explanations and suggestions which must in some cases be of a tentative character, in the hope that they may be followed up and tested by others.

It is clear that the Merudanda is the vertebral column, which as the axis of the body is supposed to bear the same relation to it as does

---

[427] See "Wave of Bliss," ed. A. Avalon.

[428] Pp. 42-45 of Pandit Ananta Shāstri's Ānandalaharī.

[429] Dr. B. D. Basu, of the Indian Medical Service, in his Prize Essay on the Hindu System of Medicine, published in the *Guy's Hospital Gazette* (1889), cited in Vol. XVI., "Sacred Books of the Hindus," by Professor Benoy Kumar Sarkar.

Mount Meru to the earth. It extends from the Mūla (root) or Mūlādhāra to the neck. It and the connected upper tracts, spinal bulb, cerebellum, and the like, contain what has been described as the central system of spinal nerves (Nādī) and cranial nerves (Shiro-nādī). The Sushummā, which is undoubtedly a Nādī within the vertebral column, and as such is well described by the books as the principal of all the Nādīs, runs along the length of the Merudanda, as does the spinal cord of Western physiology, if we include therewith the *filum terminale.* If we include the *filum*, and take the Kanda to be between the anus and penis, it starts from practically the same (sacro-coccygeal) region, the Mūlādhāra, and is spoken of as extending to the region of the Brahmarandhra,[430] or to a point below the twelve-petalled lotus (v. 1)—that is, at a spot below but close to the Sahasrāra, or cerebellum, where the nerve Chitrinī also ends. The position of the Kanda is that stated in this work (v. 1). It is to be noted, however, that according to the Hathayogapradīpikā the Kanda is higher up, between the penis and the navel.[431] The place of the union of Sushummā and Kanda is known as the "Knot" (Granthisthānam), and the petals of the Mūla lotus are on four sides of this (v. 4). It is in this Sushummā (whatever for the moment we take it to be) that there are the centers of Prāna Shakti which are called Chakras or Lotuses. The spinal cord ends blindly in the *filum terminale*, and is apparently closed there. The Sushummā is said to be closed at its base, called the "gate of Brahman" (Brahmadvāra), until, by Yoga, Kundalī makes its way through it. The highest of the six centers called Chakra in the Sushummā is the Ājnā, a position which corresponds front ally with the space between the eyebrows (Bhrūmadhye), and at the back with the pineal gland, the pituitary body, and the top of the cerebellum. Close by it is the Chakra called Lalanā, and in some Tantras Kalāchakra, which is situate at the root of—that is, just above—the palate (Tālumūla). Its position as well as the nature of the Ājnā would indicate that it is slightly below the latter.[432] The Sushummā passes into the ventricles of the brain, as does the spinal cord, which enters the fourth ventricle.

Above the Lalanā are the Ājnā Chakra with its two lobes and the Manashchakra with its six lobes, which it has been suggested are represented in the physical body by the Cerebellum and Sensorium respectively. The Somachakra above this, with its sixteen "petals," has been said to comprise the centers in the middle of the Cerebrum above the Sensorium. Lastly, the thousand-petalled lotus Sahasrāra corresponds to the upper Cerebrum of the physical body, with its

---

[430] Sammohana Tantra, II. 7, or, according to the Tripurāsārasamuchchaya, cited in v. 1, from the head to the Ādhāra.

[431] *V. post.*

[432] And not, as I wrote in the Introduction to the Mahānirvāna Tantra, p. lxii, above it. On further consideration. I think the position as stated in the text is correct, though in any case the two are very close together.

cortical convolutions, which will be suggested to the reader on an examination of the Plate VIII., here given of that center. Just as all powers exist in the seat of voluntary action, so it is said that all the fifty "letters" which are distributed throughout the spinal centers of the Sushumnā exist here in multiplied form—that is, 50 × 20. The nectar rayed moon[433] is possibly the underpart of the brain, the convolutions or lobes of which, resembling half-moons, are called Chandrakalā, and the mystic mount Kailāsa is undoubtedly the upper brain. The ventricle connected with the spinal cord is also semi-lunar in shape.

As above stated, there is no doubt that the Sushumnā is situated in the spinal column, and it has been said that it represents the central canal. It is probable that its general position is that of the central canal. But a query may be raised if it is meant that the canal alone is the Sushumnā. For the latter Nādī, according to this work, contains within it two others—namely, Vajrinī and Chitrinī. There is thus a threefold division. It has been suggested that the Sushumnā when not considered with its inner Nādīs as a collective unit, but as distinguished from them, is the white nervous matter of the spinal cord, Vajrinī the grey matter, and Chitrinī the central canal, the inner Nādī of which is known as the Brahmanādī, and, in the Shivasanghitā, Brahmarandhra.[434] But as against such suggestion it is to be noted that v. 2 of this work describes Chitrinī as being as fine as a spider's thread (lūtā-tantūpameya), and the grey matter cannot be so described, but is a gross thing. We must therefore discard this suggestion, and hold to the opinion either that the central canal is the Sushumnā or that the latter is in the canal, and that within or part of it are two still more subtle and imperceptible channels of energy, called Vajrinī and Chitrinī. I incline to the latter view. The true nature of the Chitrinī Nādī is said in v. 3 to be pure intelligence (Shuddha-bodha-svabhāva) as a force of Consciousness. As v. 1 says, the three form one, but considered separately they are distinct. They are threefold in the sense that Sushumnā, "who is tremulous like a woman in passion," is as a whole composed of "Sun," "Moon," and "Fire," and the three Gunas. It is noteworthy in this connection that the Kshurikā Upanishad,[435] which speaks of the Sushumnā, directs the Sādhaka "to get into the white and very subtle Nāda (? Nādī), and to drive Prānavāyu through it." These three, Sushumnā. Vajrinī, and Chitrinī, and the central canal, or Brahmanādī, through which, in the Yoga here described. Kundalinī passes, are all, in any case, part of the spinal cord. And, as the Shivasanghitā and all other Yoga works say, the rest of the body is dependent on Sushumnā, as being the chief spinal

---

433 See Shiva-Sanghitā, II· 6.

434 Ch. II·, v. 18.

435 Ed. Ānandāshrama. Series XXIX., p. 145. Prāna does not here mean gross breath, but that which in the respiratory centers appears as such, and which appears in other forms in other functions and parts of the body.

representative of the central nervous system. There seems also to be some ground to hold that the Nādīs, Idā and Pinggalā, or "moon" and "sun," are the left and right Sympathetic cords respectively on each side of the "fiery" Sushumnā. It is to be noted that, according to one and a common notion reproduced in this work, these Nādīs, which are described as being pale and ruddy respectively (v. 1), do not he merely on one side of the cord, but cross it alternating from one side to the other (see v. 1), thus forming with the Sushumnā and the two petals of the Ājnā Chakra the figure of the Caduceus of Mercury, which according to some represents them. Elsewhere (v. 1), however, it is said that they are shaped like bows. That is, one is united with Sushumnā and connected with the left scrotum. It goes up to a position near the left shoulder, bending as it passes the heart, crosses over to the right shoulder, and then proceeds to the right nostril. Similarly, the other Nādī connected with the right scrotum passes to the left nostril. It has been suggested to me that Idā and Pinggalā are blood vessels representing the inferior Vena Cava and Aorta. But the works and the Yoga process itself indicate not arteries, but nerves. Idā and Pinggalā when they reach the space between the eyebrows make with the Sushumnā a plaited threefold knot called Triveni, and proceed to the nostrils. This, it has been said, is the spot in the medulla where the sympathetic cords join together or whence they take their origin.

There remains to be considered the position of the Chakras. Though this work speaks of six, there are, according to some, others. This is stated by Vishvanātha in his Shatchakra-Vivriti. Thus we have mentioned Lalanā, Manas, and Soma Chakras. The six here given are the principal ones. Indeed, a very long list exists of Chakras or Ādhāras, as some call them. In a modern Sanskrit work called "Advaitamārtanda" the author[436] gives twenty, numbering them as follows: (1) *Ādhāra*, (2) Kuladīpa, (3) Vajra or Yagna, (4) *Svādishthāna*, (5) Raudra, (6) Karāla, (7) Ghvara, (8) Vidyāprada, (9) Trimukha, (10) Tripada, (11) Kāladandaka, (12) Udāra, (13) Kaladvāra, (14) Karankaka, (15) Dīpaka, (16) Ānandalalitā, (17) *Manipūraka*, (18) Nākula, (19) Kālabhedana, (20) Mahotsāha. Then for no apparent reason, many others are given without numbers, a circumstance, as well as defective printing, which makes it difficult in some cases to say whether the Sanskrit should be read as one word or two.[437] They are

[436] Brahmānanda Svāmī, a native of Palghat, in the Madras Presidency, late Guru of H.H. the Maharāja of Kashmir. The work is printed at Jummoo.

[437] I am not sure that the author himself was aware of this in all cases. He may have been quoting himself from some lists without other knowledge on the subject. The list has, to my eyes, in some respects an uncritical aspect—*e.g.*, apart from bracketed notes in the text, Kāmarūpa and Pūrnagiri are Pīthas, the others, Jālandhara and Auddīyāna, not being mentioned. The last quotation he makes draws a distinction between the Chakras and Ādhāras.

apparently Parama, Padukam, Padam (or Pādakampadam), Kalpajāla, Paushaka, Lolama, Nādavartta, Triputa, Kangkālaka, Putabhedana, Mahāgranthivikāra, Bandhajvalana (printed as Bandhejvalana), *Ānāhata*, Yantraputa (printed Yatra), Vyomachakra, Bodhana, Dhruva, Kalākandalaka, Kraunchabherundavibhava, Dāmara, Kulapīthaka, Kulakolahala, Hālāvarta, Mahadbhaya, Ghorabhairava, *Vishuddhi*, Kantham, Uttamam (*quære* Vishuddhikantham or Kanthamuttamam), Pūrnakam, *Ājnā*, Kākaputtam, Shringātam, Kāmarūpa, Pūrnagiri, Mahāvyoma, Shaktirūpa. But, as the author says, in the Vedas (that is, Yogachudāmanī, Yogashikhā Upanishads, and others) we read of only six Chakras—namely, those underlined in the above list, and described in the works here translated—and so it is said: "How can there be any Siddhi for him who knows not the six Chakras, the sixteen Ādhāras, the five Ethers, and three Lakshas, in his own body?"

I have already pointed out that the positions of the Chakras generally correspond to spinal centers of the anatomical divisions of the vertebræ into five regions, and it has been stated that the Padmas or Chakras correspond with various plexuses which exist in the body surrounding those regions. Various suggestions have been here made. The Author of a recent work[438] identifies (commencing with the Mūlādhāra and going upwards) the Chakras with the sacral, prostatic, epigastric, cardiac, laryngeal (or pharyngeal), and cavernous plexuses, and the Sahasrāra with the Medulla. In passing it may be noted that the last suggestion cannot in any event be correct. It is apparently based on verse 120 of chapter v. of the Shiva Sanghitā.[439] But this work does not in my opinion support the suggestion. Elsewhere the Author cited rightly identifies Mount Kailāsa With the Sahasrāra, which is undoubtedly the upper cerebrum. The anatomical position of the Medulla is below that assigned to the Ājnā Chakra. Professor Sarkar's work contains some valuable appendices by Dr. Brojendranath Seal on, amongst others, Hindu ideas concerning plant and animal life, physiology, and biology, including accounts of the nervous system in Charaka and in the Tantras.[440] After pointing out that the cerebrospinal

---

[438] "The Positive Background of Hindu Sociology," by Professor Benoy Kumar Sarkar.

[439] P. 54 of the translation of Srīsha Chandra Vasu, to which I refer because the author cited does so. The rendering, however, does not do justice to the text, and liberties have been taken with it. Thus, a large portion has been omitted without word or warning, and at p. 14 it is said that Kundalinī is "of the form of electricity." There is no warrant for this in the text, and Kundalinī is not, according to the Shāstra, mere electricity.

I cannot too strongly protest against attempts to represent Indian Shāstra, not as it actually *is*, but what some who are concerned with it would *like* it to be. State accurately what is in the Shāstra, and then disapprove of it if you will.

[440] Both the work of Professor Sarkar and the Appendices of Dr. Seal are of interest and value, and gather together a considerable number of facts of importance on Indian Geography, Ethnology, Mineralogy, Zoology, Botany, and Hindu Physiology, Mechanics, and Acoustics.

axis with the connected sympathetic system contains a number of ganglionic centers and plexuses (Chakras, Padmas), from which nerves (Nādī, Shirā, and Dhamanī) radiate over the head, trunk, and limbs, the latter says, as regards the ganglionic centers and plexuses constituting the sympathetic spinal system:

"Beginning with the lower extremity, the centers and plexuses of the connected spinal and sympathetic systems may be described as follows:

"(1) The Ādhāra Chakra, the sacro-coccygeal plexus, with four branches, nine Angulis (about six inches and a half) below the solar plexus (Kanda, Brahmagranthi); the source of a massive pleasurable æsthesia; voluminous organic sensations of repose. An inch and a half above it, and the same distance below the membrum virile (Mehana), is a minor center called the Agni-sikhā. (2) The Svādhishthāna Chakra, the sacral plexus, with six branches (Dalāni—petals) concerned in the excitation of sexual feelings, with the accompaniments of lassitude, stupor, cruelty, suspicion, contempt.[441] (3) The Nābhikanda (corresponding to the solar plexus, Bhānubhavanam), which forms the great junction of the right and left sympathetic chains (Pinggalā and Idā) with the cerebrospinal axis. Connected with this is the Manipūraka, the lumbar plexus, with connected sympathetic nerves, the ten branches[442] of which are concerned in the production of sleep and thirst, and the expressions of passions like jealousy, shame, fear, stupefaction. (4) The Anāhata Chakra, possibly the cardiac plexus of the sympathetic chain, with twelve branches, connected with the heart, the seat of the egoistic sentiments, hope, anxiety, doubt, remorse, conceit, egoism, etc. (5) The Bhāratīsthāna,[443] the junction of the spinal cord with the medulla oblongata, which, by means of nerves like the pneumogastric, etc., regulate the larynx and other organs of articulation. (6) The Lalanā Chakra, opposite the uvula, which has twelve leaves (or lobes), supposed to be the tract affected in the production of ego-altruistic sentiments and affections, like self-regard, pride, affection, grief, regret, respect, reverence, contentment, etc. (7) The sensori-motor tract, comprising two Chakras: (*a*) the Ājnā Chakra—lit., the circle of command (over movements)—with its two lobes (the cerebellum); and (*b*) the Manas Chakra, the sensorium, with its six lobes (five special sensory for peripherally initiated sensations, and one common sensory for centrally initiated sensations, as in dreams and hallucinations). The Ājnā-vahā Nādīs, efferent or motor nerves, communicate motor impulses to the periphery from this Ājnā Chakra,

[441] These and other Vritti, as they are called, are enumerated in the Introduction to my edition of the Mahānirvāna Tantra.

[442] That is, petals.

[443] This is a name for the Vishuddha Chakra as abode of the Goddess of Speech (Bhāratī).

this center of command over movements; and the afferent or sensory nerves of the special senses, in pairs, the Gandhavahā Nādī (olfactory sensory), the Rūpavahā Nādī (optic), the Shabdavahā Nādī (auditory), the Rasavahā Nādī (gustatory), and the Sparshavahā Nādī (tactile), come from the periphery (the peripheral organs of the special senses) to this Manaschakra, the sensory tract at the base of the brain. The Manaschakra also receives the Manovahā Nādī, a generic name for the channels along which centrally initiated presentations (as in dreaming or hallucination) come to the sixth lobe of the Manaschakra. (8) The Somachakra, a sixteen-lobed ganglion, comprising the centers in the middle of the cerebrum, above the sensorium; the seat of the altruistic sentiments and volitional control—*e.g.*, compassion, gentleness, patience, renunciation, meditativeness, gravity, earnestness, resolution, determination, magnanimity, etc. And lastly (9) the Sahasrāra Chakra, thousand-lobed, the upper cerebrum with its lobes and convolutions, the special and highest seat of the Jīva, the soul."[444]

Then, dealing with the cerebro-spinal axis and the heart, and their respective relations to the conscious life, the Author cited says:

"Vijnānabhikshu, in the passage just quoted, identifies the Manovahā Nādī (vehicle of consciousness) with the cerebro-spinal axis and its ramifications, and compares the figure to an inverted gourd with a thousand-branched stem hanging down. The Sushumnā, the central passage of the spinal cord, is the stem of this gourd (or a single branch). The writers on the Yoga (including the authors of the various Tantrik systems) use the term somewhat differently. On this view, the Manovahā Nādī is the channel of the communication of the Jīva (soul) with the Manaschakra (sensorium) at the base of the brain. The sensory currents are brought to the sensory ganglia along afferent nerves of the special senses. But this is not sufficient for them to rise to the level of discriminative consciousness. A communication must now be established between the Jīva (in the Sahasrāra Chakra, upper cerebrum) and the sensory currents received at the sensorium, and this is done by means of the Manovahā Nādī. When sensations are centrally initiated, as in dreams and hallucinations, a special Nādī (Svapnavahā Nādī), which appears to be only a branch of the Manovahā Nādī, serves as the channel of communication from the Jīva (soul) to the sensorium. In the same way, the Ajnavahā Nādī brings down the messages of the Soul from the Sahasrāra (upper cerebrum) to the Ājnā Chakra (motor tract at the base of the brain), messages which are thence carried farther down, along efferent nerves, to various parts of the periphery. I may add that the special sensory nerves, together with the Manovahā Nādī, are sometimes generally termed Jnānavahā Nādī—lit., channel of

---

[444] The author cited refers to the Jnāna Sankalinī Tantra, Sanghitāratnākara, and for functions of Ājnā-vahā Nādī and Manovahā Nādī to Shangkara Mishra's Upaskāra.

presentative knowledge. There is no difficulty so far. The Manovahā Nādī and the Ājnāvahā Nādī connect the sensori-motor tract at the base of the brain (Manaschakra and Ājnāchakra) with the highest (and special) seat of the soul (Jīva) in the upper cerebrum (Sahasrāra), the one being the channel for carrying up the sensory, and the other for bringing down the motor messages. But efforts of the will (Ājnā, Prayatna) are conscious presentations, and the Manovahā Nādī must therefore co-operate with the Ājnāvahā in producing the consciousness of effort. Indeed, attention, the characteristic function of Manas, by which it raises sense-presentations to the level of discriminative consciousness, implies effort (Prayatna) on the part of the soul (Ātmā, Jīva), an effort of which we are conscious through the channel of the Manovahā Nādī. But how to explain the presentation of effort in the motor nerves? Shangkara Mishra the author of the Upaskāra on Kanāda's Sūtras, argues that the Nādīs (even the volitional or motor nerves) are themselves sensitive, and their affections are conveyed to the sensorium by means of the nerves of the (inner) sense of touch (which are interspersed in minute fibrillæ among them). The consciousness of effort, then, in any motor nerve, whether Ājnāvahā (volitional motor) or Prānavahā (automatic-motor), depends on the tactile nerves (or nerves, of organic sensation) mixed up with it. Thus the assimilation of food and drink by the automatic activity of the Prānas implies an (automatic) effort (Prayatna) accompanied by a vague organic consciousness, which is due to the fact that minute fibers of the inner touch-sense are interspersed with the machinery of the automatic nerves (the Prānavahā Nādīs)."

To a certain extent the localizations here made must be tentative. It must, for instance, be a matter of opinion whether the throat center corresponds with the carotid, laryngeal, or pharyngeal, or all three; whether the navel center corresponds with the epigastric, solar, or lumbar, the Ājnā with the cavernous plexus, pineal gland, pituitary body, cerebellum, and so forth. For all that is known to the contrary each center may have more than one of such correspondences. All that can be said with any degree of certainty is that the four centers, above the Mūlādhāra, which is the seat of the presiding energy, have relation to the genito-excretory, digestive, cardiac, and respiratory functions, and that the two upper centers (Ājnā and Sahasrāra) denote various forms of cerebral activity, ending in the repose of pure Consciousness. The uncertainty which prevails as regards some of those matters is indicated in the Text itself, which shows that on various of the subjects here debated differing opinions have been expressed as individual constructions of statements to be found in the Tantras and other Shāstras.

There are, however, if I read them correctly, statements in the above-cited accounts with which, though not uncommonly accepted, I disagree. It is said, for instance, that the Ādhāra Chakra *is* the sacrococcygeal plexus, and that the Svādhishthāna *is* the sacral plexus, and so forth. This work, however, not to mention others, makes it plain that the Chakras are in the Sushumnā. Verse 1 speaks of the "Lotuses inside the Meru (spinal column); and as the Sushumnā supports these (that is, the lotuses) She must needs be within the Meru." This is said in answer to those who, on the strength of a passage in the Tantrachūdāmani, erroneously suppose that Sushumnā is outside the Meru. In the same way the Commentator refutes the error of those who, relying on the Nigamatattvasāra, suppose that not only Sushumnā, but Idā and Pinggalā, are inside the Meru. Verse 2 says that inside Vajrā (which is itself within Sushumnā) is Chitrinī, on which the lotuses are strung as it were gems, and who like a spider's thread pierces all the lotuses which are within the backbone. The Author in the same place combats the view, based on the Kalpa Sūtra, that the lotuses are within Chitrinī. These lotuses are in the Sushumnā; and as Chitrinī is within the latter, she pierces but does not contain them. Some confusion is raised by the statement in v. 51, that the lotuses are in or on the Brahmanādī. But by this is meant appertaining to this Nādī, for they are in Sushumnā, of which the Brahmanādī is the central channel. The commentator Vishvanātha, quoting from the Māyā Tantra, says that all the six lotuses are attached to the Chitrinī Nādī (Chitrinī-grathitam). One conclusion emerges clearly from all this—namely, that the Lotuses are in the vertebral column in Sushumnā, and not in the nerve plexuses which surround it. There in the spinal column they exist as extremely, subtle vital centers of Prānashakti and centers of consciousness. In this connection I may cite an extract from an article on the "Physical Errors of Hinduism,"[445] for which I am indebted to Professor Sarkar's work: "It would indeed excite the surprise of our readers to hear that the Hindus, who would not even touch a dead body, much less dissect it, should possess any anatomical knowledge at all. . . . It is the Tantras that furnish us with some extraordinary pieces of information concerning the human body. . . . But of all the Hindu Shāstras extant, the Tantras lie in the greatest obscurity. . . . The Tantrik theory, on which the well-known Yoga called 'Shatchakrabheda' is founded, supposes the existence of six main internal organs, called Chakras or Padmas, all bearing a special resemblance to that famous flower, the lotus. These are placed one above the other, and connected by three imaginary chains, the emblems of the Ganges, the Yamunā, and the Saraswatī. . . . Such is the obstinacy with which the Hindus adhere to these erroneous notions, that, even when we show them by actual dissection the non-existence of the imaginary Chakras in the human body, they will rather have recourse to excuses revolting to common

[445] Published in Vol. XI., pp. 436-440, of the *Calcutta Review*.

sense than acknowledge the evidence of their own eyes. They say, with a shamelessness unparalleled, that these Padmas exist as long as a man lives, but disappear the moment he dies."[446] This, however, is nevertheless quite correct, for conscious and vital centers cannot exist in a body when the organism which they hold together dies. A contrary conclusion might indeed be described as "shameless" stupidity.[447]

The Author of the work from which this citation is made says that, though these Chakras cannot be satisfactorily identified, the Tantriks must nevertheless have obtained their knowledge of them by dissection. By this he must refer to the physical regions which correspond on the gross plane to, and are governed by, the Chakras proper, which as subtle, vital, and conscious centers in the spinal cord are invisible to any but a Yogi's vision,[448] existing when the body is alive and disappearing when vitality (Prāna) leaves the body as part of the Lingasharīra.

It is a mistake, therefore, in my opinion, to identify the Chakras with the physical plexuses mentioned. These latter are things of the gross body, whereas the Chakras are extremely subtle vital centers of various Tattvik operations. In a sense we can connect with these subtle centers the gross bodily parts visible to the eyes as plexuses and ganglia. But to connect or correlate and to identify are different things. Indian thought and the Sanskrit language, which is its expression, have a peculiarly penetrative and comprehensive quality which enables one to explain many ideas for which, except by paraphrase, there is no equivalent meaning in English. It is by the Shakti of the Ātmā that the body exists. It is the collective Prāna which holds it together as an individual human unit, just as it supports the different Principles and Elements (Tattva) of which it is composed. These Tattvas, though they pervade the body, have yet various special centers of operation. These centers, as one might otherwise suppose, lie along the axis, and are the Sūkshma Rūpa, or subtle forms of that which exists in gross form (Sthūla Rūpa) in the physical body which is gathered around it. They are manifestations of Prānashakti. In other words, from an objective standpoint the subtle centers, or Chakras, vitalize and control the gross bodily tracts which are indicated by the various regions of the vertebral column and the ganglia, plexuses, nerves, arteries, and organs, situate in these respective regions. It is only therefore (if at all) in the sense of

[446] "Physical Errors of Hinduism," *Calcutta Review*, Vol. XI., pp. 436-440.

[447] This reminds one of the story of a materialistic doctor in Calcutta who said he had done hundreds of *post-mortem* examinations, but had never yet discovered the trace of a soul.

[448] So it is said: Tāni vastūni tanmātrādīni pratyakshavishayāni (Such things as the Tanmātra and others are subject of immediate perception by Yogins only). A Yogī "sees" the Chakras with his mental eye (Ājnā). In the case of others they are the matter of inference (anumāna).

being the gross outer representatives of the spinal centers that we can connect the plexuses and so forth with the Chakras spoken of in the Yoga books. In this sense only the whole tract, which extends from the subtle center to the periphery, with its corresponding bodily elements, may be regarded as the Chakra. As the gross and subtle are thus connected, mental operation on the one will affect the other. Certain forces are concentrated in these Chakras, and therefore and by reference to their function they are regarded as separate and independent centers. There are thus six subtle centers in the cord with grosser embodiments within the cord itself, with still grosser sheaths in the region pervaded by the sympathetics Idā and Pinggalā, and other Nādīs. Out of all this and the gross compounded elements of the body are fashioned the organs of life, the vital heart of which is the subtle Chakra by which they are vivified and controlled. The spiritual aspects of the six centers according to Tantrik doctrine must not be overlooked whilst attention is paid to the gross or physiological aspect of the body. As previously and in the Commentary to the thirty-fifth verse of the Ānandalaharī explained, there are six Devas—viz., Shambhu, Sadāshiva, Īshvara, Vishnu, Rudra, Brahmā—whose abodes are the six Lokas or regions: viz., Maharloka, Tapoloka, Janaloka, Svarloka, Bhuvoloka, and Bhūrloka (the Earth). It is these Divinities who are the forms of consciousness presiding over the Shatchakra. In other words, Consciousness-feeling (Chit), as the ultimate experiencing principle, pervades and is at base all being. Every cell of the body has a consciousness of its own. The various organic parts of the body which the cells build have not only particular cell-consciousness, but the consciousness of the particular organic part which is other than the mere collectivity of the consciousness of its units. Thus there may be an abdominal consciousness. And the consciousness of such bodily region is its Devatā—that is, that aspect of Chit which is associated with and informs that region. Lastly, the organism as a whole has its consciousness, which is the individual Jīva. Then there is the subtle form or body of these Devatās, in the shape of Mind—supersensible "matter" (Tanmātra); and sensible "matter"—namely, ether, air, fire, water, earth, with their centers at the Ājnā, Vishuddha, Anāhata, Manipūra, Svādhishthāna, and Mūlādhāra. Of these six Tattvas, not only the gross human body, but the vast macrocosm, is composed. The six Chakras are therefore the divine subtle centers of the corresponding physical sheath. The seventh or supreme center is Paramashiva, whose abode is Satyaloka, the Cosmic aspect of the Sahasrāra in the human body. The Supreme, therefore, descends through its manifestations from the subtle to the gross as the six Devas and Shaktis in their six abodes in the world-axis, and as the six centers in the body-axis or spinal column. The special operation of each of the Tattvas is located at its individual center in the microcosm. But, notwithstanding all such subtle and gross transformations of and by Kula-Kundalinī, She ever remains in Her Brahman or Svarūpa aspect the One, Sat, Chit, and Ānanda, as is realized by the Yogī when drawing the Devī from Her world-abode in the earth center (Mūlādhāra) he unites Her with Paramashiva in the Sahasrāra in that blissful union which is the Supreme Love (Ānanda).

In a similar manner other statements as regards these Chakras should be dealt with, as, for instance, those connected with the existence of the "Petals," the number of which in each case has been said to be determined *by* characteristics of the gross region which the particular Chakra governs. The centers are said to be composed of petals designated by certain letters. Professor Sarkar[449] expresses the opinion that these petals point to either the nerves which go to form a ganglion or plexus, or the nerves distributed from such ganglion or plexus. I have been told that the disposition of the Nādīs at the particular Chakra in question determines the number of its petals.[450] In the five lower Chakras their characteristics are displayed in the number and position of the Nādīs or by the lobes and sensory and motor tracts of the higher portions of the cerebro-spinal system. As I have already explained, the Chakra is not to be identified with the physical ganglia and plexuses, though it is connected with, and in a gross sense represented by, them. The lotuses with these petals are within the Sushumnā, and they are there represented as blooming upon the passage through them of Kundalī. The letters are on the petals.

The letters in the six Chakras are fifty in number—namely, the letters of the Sanskrit alphabet less Ksha, according to the Kangkālamālinī Tantra cited in v. 40, or the second La (*ib.*). All these letters multiplied by 20 exist potentially in the Sahasrāra, where they therefore number 1,000, giving that Lotus its name. There are, on the other hand, 72,000 Nādīs which rise from the Kanda. Further, that these letters in the Chakras are not gross things is shown by vv. 28 and 29, which say that the vowels of the Vishuddha are visible to the enlightened mind (Dīpta-buddhi) only—that is, the Buddhi which is free of impurity resulting from worldly pursuits, as the effect of the constant practice of Yoga. Verse 19 and other verses speak of the letters there mentioned as being colored. Each object of perception, whether gross or subtle, has an aspect which corresponds to each of the senses. It is for this reason that the Tantra correlates sound, form, and color. Sound produces form, and form is associated with color. Kundalī is a form of the Supreme Shakti who maintains all breathing creatures.

---

449 *Op. cit.*, p. 292.

450 See my Mahānirvāna Tantra, p. lvii. My reference there to the lotus as a plexus of nādīs is to the gross sheath of the subtle center, which gross sheath is said to contain the determinant, though in another sense it is the effiect, of the characteristics of the subtle center.

She is the source from which all sound or energy, whether as ideas or speech, manifests. That sound Mātrikā when uttered in human speech assumes the form of letters and prose and verse, which is made of their combinations. And sound (Shabda) has its meaning—that is, the objects denoted by the ideas which are expressed by sound or words. By the impulse of Ichchhā Shakti acting through the Prānavāyu (vital force) of the Ātmā is produced in the Mūlādhāra the sound power called Parā, which in its ascending movement through other Chakras takes on other characteristics and names (Pashyantī and Madhyamā), and when uttered by the mouth appears as Vaikharī in the form of the spoken letters which are the gross aspect of the sound in the Chakras themselves (see vv. 10 and 11). Letters when spoken are, then, the manifested aspect in gross speech of the subtle energy of the Shabdabrahman as Kundalī. The same energy which produces these letters manifesting as Mantras produces the gross universe. In the Chakras is subtle Shabda in its states as Parā, Pashyantī, or Madhyamā Shakti, which when translated to the vocal organ assumes the audible sound form (Dhvani) which is any particular letter. Particular forms of energy of Kundalī are said to be resident at particular Chakras, all such energies existing in magnified form in the Sahasrāra. Each manifested letter is a Mantra, and a Mantra is the body of a Devatā. There are therefore as many Devatās in a Chakra as there are petals which are surrounding (Āvarana) Devatās or Shaktis of the Devatā of the Chakra and the subtle element of which He is the presiding Consciousness. Thus, Brahmā is the presiding Consciousness of the Mūlādhāra lotus, indicated by the Bindu of the Bīja La (Lang), which is the body of the earth Devatā; and around and associated with these are the subtle forms of the Mantras, which constitute the petals and the bodies of associated energies. The whole human body is in fact a Mantra, and is composed of Mantras.

These sound powers vitalize, regulate, and control, the corresponding gross manifestations in the regions surrounding them. Why, however, particular letters are assigned to particular Chakras is the next question. Why, for instance, should Ha be in the Ājnā and Sa in the Mūlādhāra? It is true that in some places in the Tantras certain letters are assigned to particular elements. Thus, there are certain letters which are called Vāyava Varna, or letters pertaining to the Vāyu Tattva; but an examination of the case on this basis fails to account for the position of the letters, as letters which are assigned to one element may be found in a Chakra the predominant Tattva of which is some other element. It has been said that in the utterance of particular letters the centers at which they are situated are brought into play, and that this is the solution of the question why those particular letters were at their particular center. A probable solution is that given by me in my "Shakti and Shākta." Apart from this one can only say that, it is either

Svabhāva or the nature of the thing, which in that case is as little susceptible of ultimate explanation as the disposition in the body of the gross organs themselves; or the arrangement may be an artificial one for the purpose of meditation, in which case no further explanation is necessary.

The four Bhāvas, or states of sound, in the human body are so called as being states in which sound or movement is produced or becomes, evolving from Parā Shakti in the body of Īshvara to the gross Vaikharī Shakti in the body of Jīva. As already stated, in the bodily aspect (Adhyātmā) the Kārana Bindu resides in the Mūlādhāra center, and is there known as the Shakti Pinda[451] or Kundalinī.[452] Kundalī is a name for Shabdabrahman in human bodies. The Āchāryya, speaking of Kundalinī, says: "There is a Shakti called Kundalinī who is ever engaged in the work of creating the universe. He who has known Her never again enters the mother's womb as a child or suffers old age." That is, he no longer enters the Sangsāra or world of transmigration.[453] This Kārana Bindu exists in a non-differentiated condition.[454]

The body of Kundalī is composed of the fifty letters or sound-powers. Just as there is an apparent evolution[455] in the cosmic body of Īshvara, represented in the seven states preceding from Sakala Parameshvara to Bindu, so there is a similar development in the human

---

[451] She is so called because all the Shaktis are collected or "rolled into one mass" in Her. Here is the Kendra (center) of all the Shaktis. The Svachchhanda as also the Shāradā say:

> Pindang Kundalinī-Shaktih
> Padang hangsah prakīrtitah
> Rūpang binduriti khyātang
> Rūpātītastu chinmayah.

(Kundalinī Shakti is Pinda, Hangsah is Pada; Bindu is Rūpa, but Chinmaya (Chit) is formless.) The first, as potentiality of all manifested power, is in the Mūlādhāra Chakra; the second, as Jīvātmā, is in Anāhata, where the heart beats, the life-pulse. Bindu, the causal form body, as Supreme Shakti, is in Ājnā, and the formless Consciousness passing through Bindu Tattva manifesting as Hangsa, and again resting as Kundalinī, is in the Brahmarandhra (see Tīkā of first Sangketa of Yoginīhridaya Tantra).

[452] Adhyātmantu kāranabinduh shaktipindakundalyādishabdavāchyo mūlādhārasthah (Bhāskararāya, Comm. Lalitā, v. 132).

[453] Shaktih kundalinīti, vishvajananavyāpārabaddhodyamāng jnāttvethang na punar vishanti jananīgarbhe arbhakatvang narā ityādirītyāchāryyairvyavahritah (*ib.*).

[454] Soyamavibhāgāvasthah kāranabinduh (*ib.*).

[455] Vikāra or Vikriti is something which is really changed, as curd from milk. The former is a Vikriti of the latter. Vivartta is apparent but unreal change, such as the appearance of what was and is a rope as a snake. The Vedāntasāra thus musically defines the two terms:

> Satattvato, nyathāprathā vikāra ityudīritah
> Atattvato, nyathāprathā vivarta ityudāhritah.

body in Kundalī, who is the Īshvarī therein. There are evolved by this form the following states, corresponding with the cosmic development—viz., Shakti, Dhvani, Nāda, Nirodhikā, Ardhendu, Bindu. These are all states of Kundalī Herself in the Mūlādhāra, and are known as Parā sound. Each one of the letters composing the body of Kundalī exists in four states as Parā Shakti, or in the succeeding states of sound, Pashyantī, Madhyamā, and Vaikharī, to which reference is later made. The first is a state of undifferentiated sound, which exists in the body of Īshvara; the second and third as existing in the body of Jīva are stages towards that complete manifestation of differentiated sound in human speech which is called Vaikharī Bhāva. In the cosmic aspect these four states are Avyakta, Īshvara, Hiranyagarbha, and Virāt. The Arthasrishti (object creation) of Kundalinī are the Kalās, which arise from the letters such as the Rudra and Vishnu Mūrtis and their Shaktis, the Kāmas and Ganeshas and their Shaktis, and the like. In the Sakala Parameshvara or Shabdabrahman in bodies—that is, Kundalinī Shakti—the latter is called Chit Shakti or Shakti simply, "when Sattva enters"—a state known as the Paramākāshāvastha. When She into whom Sattva has entered is next "pierced" by Rajas, She is called Dhvani, which is the Aksharāvasthā. When She is again "pierced" by Tamas, she is called Nāda. This is the Avyaktāvasthā, the Avyakta Nāda which is the Parabindu. Again, She in whom Tamas abounds is, as Rāghava Bhatta says, called Nirodhikā; She in whom Sattva abounds is called Arddhendu; and the combination of the two (Ichchhā and Jnāna) in which Rajas as Kriyā Shakti works is called Bindu. Thus it has been said: "Drawn by the force of Ichchhā Shakti (will), illumined by Jnāna Shakti (knowledge), Shakti the Lord appearing as male creates (Kriyā Shakti, or action)."

When the Kārana Bindu "sprouts" in order to create the three (Bindu, Nāda, and Bīja) there arises that unmanifested Brahman-word or Sound called the Shabdabrahman (Sound Brahman).[456] It is said: "From the differentiation of the Kārana Bindu arises the unmanifested "Sound" which is called Shabdabrahman by those learned in Shruti."[457] It is this Shabdabrahman which is the immediate cause of the universe, which is sound and movement manifesting as idea and language. This sound, which is one with the Kārana Bindu, and is therefore all-pervading, yet first appears in man's body in the Mūlādhāra. "It is said in the Mūlādhāra in the body the 'air' (Prānavāyu) first appears. That 'air' acted upon by the effort of a person desiring to speak, manifests

---

[456] Ayamevacha yadā kāryabindvāditrayajananonmukho bhidyate taddashāyāmavyaktah shabdabrahmābrndheyoravastatrotpadyate (*ib.*).

[457] Tadapyuktam bindostasmādbhidyamānādavyaktātmā ravo, bhavat, Sa ravah shrutisampannaih shabdabrahmeti gīyate (*ib.*).

the all-pervading Shabdabrahman."[458] The Shabdabrahman which' is in the form of the Kārana Bindu when it remains motionless (Nihspanda) in its own place (that is, in Kundalī, who is Herself in the Mūlādhāra) is called Parā Shakti or speech. The same Shabdabrahman manifested by the same air proceeding as far as the navel, united with the Manas, possessing the nature of the manifested Kāryya Bindu with general (Sāmānyaspanda) motion, is named Pashyantī speech.[459] Pashyantī, which is described as Jnānātmaka and Bindvātmaka (in the nature of Chit and Bindu), extends from the Mūlādhāra to the navel, or, according to some accounts, the Svādishthāna.

Next, the Shabdabrahman manifested by the same air proceeding as far as the heart, united with the Buddhi, possessing the nature of the manifested Nāda and endowed with special (Visheshaspanda) motion, is called Madhyamā speech.[460] This is Hiranyagarbha sound, extending from the region of Pashyantī to the heart. Next,[461] the same Shabdabrahman manifested by the same air proceeding as far as the mouth, developed in the throat, etc., articulated and capable of being heard by the ears of others, possessing the nature of the manifested Bīja with quite distinct articulate motion (Spashtatara), is called Vaikharī speech.[462] This is the Virāt state of sound, so called because it "comes out."

This matter is thus explained by the Āchāryya: "That sound which first arises in the Mūlādhāra is called Parā; next Pashyantī; next, when it goes as far as the heart and is joined to the Buddhi, it is called 'Madhyamā.'" This name is derived from the fact that She abides "in the midst." She is neither like Pashyantī nor does She proceed outward like Vaikharī, with articulation fully developed. But She is in the middle between these two.

---

458 Soyang ravah kāranabindutādātmyāpannatvāt sarvagatopi vyanjakayatnasangskritapavanavashāt prāninānag mūlādhāra eva abhivyajyate. Taduktang, Dehepi mūlādhāresmin samudeti samīranah, Vivakshorichchhayotthena prayatnena susangskritah. Sa vyanjayati tatraiva shabdabrahmāpi sarvagam iti (*ib.*).

459 Tadidang kāranabindvātmakamabhivyaktang shabdabrahmasvapratishthatayā nishpandam tadeva cha parā vāgityuchyate. Atha tadeva nābhiparyantamāgachchhatā tena pavanenābhivyaktam vimarsharūpena manasā yuktam sāmānyaspandaprakāsharūpakāryyabindumayang sat pashyantī vāguchyate (*ib.*).

460 Atha tadeva shabdabrahma tenaiva vāyunā hridayaparyantamabhivyajyamānang nishchayātmikayā buddhyā yuktang · visheshaspandaprakāsharūpanādamayang sat madhyamāvāgityuchyate (*ib.*).

461 Atha tadeva vadanaparyyantang tenaiva vāyunā kanthādisthāneshvabhivyajyamānamakārādivarnarūpang parashrotra-grahanayogyang spashtataraprakāsharūpabījātmakang sat vaikharī vāguchyate (*ib.*).

462 That is, Shabda in its physical form. Bhāskararāya, in his Commentary to the same verse (81) of the Lalitā, gives the following derivations: Vi = much; khara = hard. According to the Saubhagya Sudhodaya, Vai = certainly; kha = cavity (of the ear); va = to go or enter. But according to the Yoga Shāstras, the Devī who is in the form of Vaikharī (Vaikharīrūpā) is so called because she was produced by the Prāna called Vikhara.

The full manifestation is Vaikharī of the man wishing to cry out. In this way articulated sound is produced by air.[463] The Nityā Tantra also says: "The Parā form rises in the Mūlādhāra produced by 'air'; the same 'air' rising upwards, manifested in the Svādishthāna, attains the Pashyantī[464] state. The same slowly rising upwards, and manifested in the Anāhata united with the understanding (Buddhi), is Madhyamā. Again rising upwards, and appearing in the Vishuddha, it issues from the throat as Vaikharī."[465] As the Yoga Kundalī Upanishad[466] says: "That Vāk (power of speech) which sprouts in Parā gives forth leaves in Pashyantī, buds forth in Madhyamā, and blossoms in Vaikharī. By reversing the above order sound is absorbed. Whosoever realizes the great Lord of Vāk the undifferentiated illuminating Self is unaffected by any word, be it what it may."

Thus, though there are four kinds of speech, gross-minded men (Manushyāh sthūladrishah)[467] who do not understand the first three (Parā, etc.) think speech to be Vaikharī alone,[468] just as they take the gross body to be the Self, in ignorance of its subtler principles. Shruti says: "Hence men think that alone to be speech which is imperfect"—that is, imperfect in so far as it does not possess the first three forms.[469] Another Shruti also says:[470] "Four are the grades of speech—those Brāhmanas who are wise know them: three are hidden and motionless; men speak the fourth." The Sūta Sanghitā also says: "Apada (the motionless Brahman) becomes Pada (the four forms of speech), and Pada may become Apada. He who knows the distinction between Pada[471] and Apada, he really sees (*i.e.*, himself becomes Brahman)."[472]

---

[463] Taduktamāchāryyaih: Mūlādhārāt prathamamudito yashcha bhāvahparākhyah, Pashchātpashyantyathahridayago buddhiyugmadhyamākhyah, Vyakte vaikharyatha rurudishorasya jantoh sushumnā, Baddnastasmāt bhavati pavanapreritā varnasangjnā, iti (Bhāskararāya, *op. cit.*).

[464] Bhāskararāya cites Her other name, Uttīrnā (risen up), and the Saubhagya Sudhodaya, which says: "As She sees all in Herself, and as She rises (Uttīrnā) above the path of action, this Mother is called Pashyantī and Uttīrnā").

[465] Nityātantrepi: Mūlādhārāt samutpannah parākhyo nādasangbhavah. Sa evordhvatayā nītah svādhishthāne vijringbhitah, Pashyāntyākhyāmavāpnoti tathaivordhvang shanaih sbanaih, Anāhate buddhitattvasameto madhyamābhidhah, tathā tayordhvag nunnah san vishuddhau kanthadeshatah Vaikharyākhya ityādi (Bhāskararāya, *op. cit.*). See also Ch. II., Prapanchasāra Tantra, Vol. III. of Tantrik Texts, ed. A. Avalon.

[466] Ch. III.

[467] That is, men who see and accept only the gross aspect of things.

[468] Itthang chaturvidhāsu mātrikāsu parāditrayang ajānanto manushyāh sthūladrisho vaikharīm eva vāchang manvate (Bhāskararāya, *ib.*).

[469] Tathā cha shrutih: Tasmād yadvācho nāptang tanmanushyā upa jīvantiiti anāptam apūrnang tisribhirvirahitam ityartha iti vedabhāshye.

[470] Shrutyantarepi chatvāri vākparimitapadāni tāni vidurbrāhmanā ye manīshinah guhā trīni nihitā nenggayanti, turīyang vācho manushyāvadantīti (*ib.*).

[471] The Pada, or word, is that which has a termination. Pānini says (Sūtra, I., IV. 14): "That which ends in Sup (nominal endings) and in Tip (verbal terminations) is called Pada." Again, the Sup (termintion) has five divisions.

[472] Bhāskararāya, *loc. cit.*

Thus, the conclusions of Shruti and Smriti are that the "That" (Tat) in the human body has four divisions (Parā, etc.). But even in the Parā form the word Tat only denotes the Avyakta with three Gunas, the cause of Parā, and not the unconditioned Brahman who is above Avyakta. The word "Tat" which occurs in the transcendental sayings means the Shabdabrahman, or Īshvara endowed with the work of creation, maintenance, and "destruction," of the Universe. The same word also indicates indirectly (Lakshana) the unconditioned or supreme Brahman who is without attributes. The relation between the two Brahmans is that of sameness (Tadātmya). Thus, the Devī or Shakti is the one essence of consciousness (Chidekarasarūpinī)—that is, She is ever inseparate from Chit. The relation of the two Brahmans is possible, as the two are one and the same. Though they appear as different (by attributes), yet at the same time they are one.

The commentator cited then asks, How can the word Tat in the Vaikharī form indicate Brahman? and replies that it only does so indirectly. For sound in the physical form of speech (Vaikharī) only expresses or is identified with the physical form of Brahman (the Virāt), and not the pure Supreme Brahman.

The following will serve as a summary of correspondences noted in this and the previous Chapter. There is first the Nirguna Brahman, which in its creative aspect is Saguna Shabda Brahman, and assumes the form of Parabindu, and then of the threefold (Tribindu); the four who are represented in the sense above stated by the four forms of speech, sound or state (Bhāva).

The causal (Kārana) or Supreme Bindu (Parabindu) is unmanifest (Avyakta), undifferentiated Shiva-Shakti, whose powers are not yet displayed, but are about to be displayed from out the then undifferentiated state of Mūlaprakriti. This is the state of Supreme Speech (Paravāk), the Supreme Word or Logos, the seat of which in the individual body is the Mūlādhāra Chakra. So much is clear. There is, however, some difficulty in coordinating the accounts of the threefold powers manifesting upon the differentiation of the Great Bindu (Mahābindu). This is due in part to the fact that the verses in which the accounts appear are not always to be read in the order of the words (Pratishabdam), but according to the actual order in fact, whatever that may be (Yathā sambhavam).[473] Nextly, there is some apparent variance

[473] As pointed out by the author of Prānatoshinī, p. 9, when citing the verse from the Goraksha Sanghitā:

> Ichchhā kriyā tathā jnānang gaurī brāhmītu vaishnavī
> Tridhā shaktih sthitā yatra tatparang jyotirom iti.

According to this account of the Devas of different Ādhāras of Prānashakti upāsanā the order is (according to sequence of words): Ichchhā = Gaurī; Kriyā = Brahmī; Vaishnavī = Jnāna.

in the commentaries. Apart from names and technical details, the gist of the matter is simple and in accordance with other systems. There is first the unmanifested point (Bindu), as to which symbol St. Clement of Alexandria says[474] that if from a body abstraction be made of its properties, depth, breadth, and length, that which remains is a point having position, from which, if abstraction be made of position,[475] there is the state of primordial unity. There is one Spirit, which appears threefold as a Trinity of Manifested Power (Shakti). As so manifesting, the one (Shiva-shakti) becomes twofold, Shiva and Shakti, and the relation (Nāda) of these two (Tayormithasamāvaya) makes the threefold Trinity common to so many religions. The One first moves as the Great Will (Ichchhā), then as the Knowledge or Wisdom (Jnāna) according to which Will acts, and then as action (Kriyā). This is the order of Shaktis in Īshvara. So, according to the Paurānik account, at the commencement of creation Brahmā wakes. The Sangskāras then arise in His mind. There arises the desire to create (Ichchhā Shakti); then the knowledge (Jnāna Shakti) of what He is about to create; and, lastly, the action (Kriyā) of creation. In the case of Jīva the order is Jnāna, Ichchhā, Kriyā. For He first considers or knows something. Informed by such knowledge, He wills and then acts. The three powers are, though counted and spoken of as arising separately, inseparable and indivisible aspects of the One. Wherever there is one there is the other, though men think of each separately and as coming into being—that is, manifested in time—separately.

According to one nomenclature the Supreme Bindu becomes threefold as Bindu (Kāryya), Bīja, Nāda. Though Shiva is never separate from Shakti, nor Shakti from Shiva, a manifestation may predominantly signify one or another. So it is said that Bindu is in the nature of Shiva (Shivātmaka) and Bīja of Shakti (Shaktyātmaka), and Nāda is the combination of the two (Tayormithahsamavāyah). These are also called Mahābindu (Parabindu), Sitabindu (White Bindu), Shonabindu (Red Bindu), and Mishrabindu (Mixed Bindu). These are supreme (Para), subtle (Sūkshma), gross (Sthūla). There is another nomenclature—viz., Sun, Fire, and Moon. There is no question but that Bīja is Moon, that from Bīja issues the Shakti Vāmā, from whom comes Brahmā, who are in the nature of the Moon and Will-Power (Ichchhā Shakti).[476] Ichchhā Shakti in terms of the Gunas of Prakriti is

---

[474] Stromata, Book V., Ch. II., in Vol. IV., Antenicene Library. So also in "Les Mystères de la Croix," an eighteenth-century mystical work, we read: "Ante omnia punctum exstitit; non mathematicum sed diffusivum."

[475] See my "Studies in the Mantra shāstra."

[476] Raudrībindostato nādāt jyeshthā bījāda jāyata
Vāmā tābhyah samutpannāh rudrabrahmaramādhipāh
Sangjnānechchhākriyātmāno vahnīndvarka-svarūpinah.
(Shāradā Tilaka, Ch. I.)

Rajas Guna, which impels Sattva to self-display. This is Pashyantī Shabda, the seat of which is in the Svādīshthāna Chakra. From Nāda similarly issue Jyeshthā Shakti and Vishnu, and from Bindu Raudrī and Rudra, which are Madhyamā and Vaikharī Shabda, the seats of which are the Anāhata and Vishuddha Chakras respectively. According to one account[477] Bindu is "Fire" and Kriyā Shakti (action), and Nāda is "Sun" and Jnāna Shakti, which in terms of the Gunas are Tamas and Sattva respectively.[478] Rāghavabhatta, however, in his Commentary on the Shāradā, says that the Sun is Kriyā because, like that luminary, it makes all things visible, and Jnāna is Fire because knowledge burns up all creation. When Jīva through Jnāna knows itself to be Brahman it ceases to act, so as to accumulate Karma, and attains liberation (Moksha). It may be that this refers to the Jīva, as the former represents the creation of Īshvara.

In the Yoginīhridaya Tantra it is said that Vāmā and Ichchhā Shakti are in the Pashyantī body; Jnāna and Jyesthā are called Madhyamā; Kriyā Shakti is Raudrī; and Vaikharī is in the form of the universe.[479] The evolution of the Bhāvas is given in the Shāradā Tilaka[480] as follows: the all-pervading Shabdabrahman or Kundalī emanates Shakti, and then follow Dhvani, Nāda, Nirodhikā, Arddhendu, Bindu. Shakti is Chit with Sattva (Paramākāshāvasthā); Dhvani is Chit with Sattva and Rajas (Aksharāvasthā); Nāda is Chit with Sattva, Rajas, Tamas (Avyaktāvasthā); Nirodhikā is the same with abundance of Tamas (Tamah prāchuryāt); Arddhendu the same with abundance of Sattva; and Bindu the combination of the two. This Bindu is called by the different names of Parā and the rest, according as it is in the different centers, Mūlādhāra and the rest. In this way Kundalī, who is Ichchhā, Jnāna, Kriyā, who is both in the form of consciousness (Tejorūpā) and composed of the Gunas (Gunātmikā), creates the Garland of Letters (Varnamālā).

The four Bhāvas have been dealt with as coming under Nāda, itself

---

[477] Yoginīhridaya Tantra; Commentary already cited referring to Saubhāgyasudhodaya and Tattvasandoha. See also Tantrāloka, Ch. VI.

[478] The following shows the correspondences according to the texts cited:

Bīja Shonabindu	Shakti, Moon, Vāmā, Brahmā, Bhāratī, Īchchhā, Rajas, Pashyantī, Svādishthāna.
Nāda Mishrabindu	Shiva-shakti, Sun, Jyeshthā, Vishnu, Vishvambhara, Jnāna, Sattva, Madhyamā, Anāhata.
Bindu Sitabindu	Shiva, Fire, Raudrī, Rudra, Rudrānī, Kriyā, Tamas, Vaikharī, Vishuddha.

[479] Ichchhāshaktistathā Vāmā pashyantī vapushā sthitā
Jnānashaktistathā Jyeshthā madhyamā vāgudīritā
Kriyāshaktistu Raudrīyam vaikharī vishvavigrahā.
(Cited under v. 22, Comm. Kāmakalāvilāsa.)

[480] Chap. I.

one of the following nine manifestations of Devī.

Pandit Ananta Shāstrī, referring to Lakshmīdhara's commentary on v. 34 of Ānandalaharī, says:[481]

"'Bhagavatī is the word used in the text to denote Devī. One that possesses Bhaga is called a Bhagavatī (feminine). Bhaga signifies the knowledge of (1) the creation, (2) destruction of the universe, (3) the origin of beings, (4) the end of beings, (5) real knowledge or divine truth, and (6) Avidyā, or ignorance. He that knows all these six items is qualified for the title Bhagavān. Again, Bha = 9. "Bhagavatī" refers to the nine-angled Yantra (figure) which is used in the Chandrakalāvidyā.'

"According to the Āgamas, Devī has nine manifestations, which are:

"1. Kāla group—lasting from the twinkling of an eye to the Pralaya time. The sun and moon are included in this group. TIME.

"2. Kula group—consists of things which have form and color. FORM.

"3. Nāma group—consists of things which have names. NAME.

"4. Jnāna group—Intelligence. It is divided into two branches: Savikalpa (mixed and subject to change) and Nirvikalpa (pure and unchanging). CHIT.

"5. Chitta group—consists of (1) Ahangkāra (egoism), (2) Chitta, (3) Buddhi, (4) Manas, and (5) Unmanas. MIND.

"6. Nāda group—consists of (1) Rāga (desire),[482] (2) Ichchhā (desire[482] strengthened, or developed desire), (3) Kriti (action, or active form of desire), and (4) Prayatna (attempt made to achieve the object desired). These correspond, in order, to (1) Parā (the first stage of sound, emanating from Mūlādhāra), (2) Pashyantī (the second stage), (3) Madhyamā (the third stage), and (4) Vaikharī (the fourth stage of sound as coming out of the mouth). SOUND.

"7. Bindu group—consists of the six Chakras from Mūlādhāra to Ājnā. PSYCHIC ESSENCE, THE SPIRITUAL GERM.[483]

"8. Kalā group—consists of fifty letters from Mūlādhāra to Ājnā. KEYNOTES.[484]

"9. Jīva group—consists of souls in the bondage of matter.

"The Presiding Deities or Tattvas of the four constituent parts of Nāda are Māyā, Shuddhavidyā, Mahesha, and Sadāshiva. The Commentator deals with this subject fully, quoting extracts from occult works. The following is a translation of a few lines from

---

[481] Ananta Shāstri, *op. cit.*, p. 72.

[482] Rāga should be translated as "interest," as in Rāga Kanchuka. Ichchhā is the will towards action (Kriyā) in conformity therewith. Desire is a gross thing which comes in with the material world.

[483] I cite the passage as written, but these terms are not clear to me.

[484] I do not know what the Pandit means by this term.

Nāmakalāvidyā,[485] a work on phonetics, which will be of interest to the reader:

"'Parā is Ekā (without duality); its opposite is the next one (Pashyantī); Madhyamā is divided into two, gross and subtle forms: the gross form consists of the nine groups of letters; and the subtle form is the sound which differentiates the nine letters. . . . One is the cause, and the other the effect; and so there is no material difference between the sound and its gross forms.'

"Com. 'Ekā': When the three Gunas, Sattva, Rajas, and Tamas, are in a state of equilibrium (Sāmya), that state is called Parā. Pashyantī is the state when the three Gunas become unequal (and consequently produce sound). The next stage is called Madhyamā; the subtle form of this is called Sūkshmamadhyamā, and the second and gross form is called Sthūlamadhyamā, which produces nine distinct forms of sound represented by nine groups of letters: viz., अ (and all the other vowels), क (Kavarga, 5 in number), च (Chavarga, 5), ट (Tavarga, 5), त (Tavarga, 5), प (Pavarga, 5), य (Ya, Ra, La and Va), श (Sha, Sa and Ha), and क्ष (Ksha). These letters do not in reality exist, but represent only the ideas of men. Thus all the forms and letters originate from Parā, and Parā is nothing but Chaitanya (Consciousness).

"The nine groups or Vyūhas (manifestations of Devī) above enumerated are, again, classed under the following three heads: (1) Bhoktā (enjoyer)—comprises No. 9, Jīva-vyūha. (2) Bhogya (objects of enjoyment)—Comprises groups Nos. 1, 2, 3, 5, 6, 7, and 8. (3) Bhoga (enjoyment)—comprises No. 4, Jnānavyūha.

"The above is the substance of the philosophy of the Kaulas as expounded by Shrī Shankarāchārya in this shloka of Ānanda Laharī (No. 34). In commenting on this, Lakshmīdhara quotes several verses from the Kaula Āgamas, of which the following is one:

"'The blissful Lord is of nine forms. This God is called Bhairava. It is he that confers enjoyment (bliss) and liberates the souls (from bondage). His consort is Ānandabhairavī, the ever-blissful, the Chaitanya. When these two become equal (unite in harmony), the universe comes into existence.'

"The Commentator remarks here that the power of Devī predominates in creation, and that of Shiva in destruction."

---

485 "This work is not easily available to Pandits or scholars; we do not find this name in any of the catalogues prepared by European or Indian scholars. The make-secret policy has spoiled all such books. Even now, if we find any MS. dealing with occult matters in the houses of any ancient Pandits, we will not be allowed even to see the book; and actually these works have for a long time become food for worms and white ants" (Ananta Shāstrī).

VI. PRACTICE (YOGA: LAYA-KRAMA)

Yoga is sometimes understood as meaning the result and not the process which leads to it. According to this meaning of the term, and from the standpoint of natural dualism, Yoga has been described to be the union of the individual spirit with God.

But if Jīva and Paramātmā are really one, there can be no such thing as union, which term is strictly applicable to the case of the coming together of two distinct beings. Samādhi (ecstasy) consists in the realization that the Jīvātmā *is* Paramātmā; and Yoga means, not this realization, but the *means* by which it is attained. Yoga is thus a term for those physical and psychical processes which are used to discover man's inner essence, which is the Supreme.

It is thus not a result, but the *process*, method, or practice, by which this result is attained. This result is possible, according to Advaita Vedānta, because Chit, as the true being of every Jīva, is not really fettered, but only appears to be so. Were Ātmā not truly free, liberation (Moksha) would not be possible. Moksha therefore is potentially in the possession of every Jīva. His identity with Paramātmā exists now as then, but is not realized owing to the veil of Māyā, through which Jivātmā and Paramātmā appear as separate. As ignorance of the identity of the Jīvātmā and Paramātmā is due to Avidyā, the realization of such identity is attained by Vidyā or Jnāna.

The latter alone can immediately produce liberation (Sadyomukti). Jnāna is used in a twofold sense—namely, Svarūpa Jnāna and Kriyā Jnāna. The first is Pure Consciousness, which is the end and aim of Yoga; the second is those intellective processes which are the means taken to acquire the first. Jnāna considered as means or mental action (Mānasī Kriyā) is an intellective process that is the discrimination between what is and what is not Brahman; the right understanding of what is meant by Brahman, and the fixing of the mind on what is thus understood until the Brahman wholly and permanently occupies the mind to the displacement of all else. Mind is then absorbed into Brahman or Consciousness, which alone remains; this is realization or the attainment of the state of pure consciousness, which is Jnāna in its true (Svarūpa) sense. Liberating Yoga short of perfect Jnāna effects what is called Kramamukti—that is, the Yogī attains Sāyujya with Brahman in Satya-loka, which is thence perfected into complete Mukti through the Devatā with whom he is thus united. What the Siddha (complete) Jnānayogī or Jīvanmukta himself accomplishes in this life is thereafter attained as the sequel to Brahmasāyujya. But man is not only intellect. He has feeling and devotion. He is not only these, but has a body. Other processes (Yogas) are therefore associated with and in aid of it, such as those belonging to worship (Upāsanā) and the gross

(Sthūla Kriyā) and subtle processes (Sūkshma Kriyā) of Hathayoga.

Mind and body are the instruments whereby the ordinary separative worldly experience is had. As long, however, as they are so used they, are impediments in the way of attainment of the state of pure consciousness (Chit). For such attainment all screenings (Āvarana) of Chit must be cleared away. Yoga therefore is the method whereby mental intellection and feeling (Chittavritti) and Prāna are first controlled and then stayed.[486] When the Chitta, Vritti, and Prāna, are stilled, then Chit or Paramātmā stands revealed. It supervenes without further effort on the absorption of matter and mind into the primordial Power (Shakti) whence they sprang, of whom they are manifested forms, and who is Herself as Shivā one with Him who is Shiva or Consciousness. Yoga thus works towards a positive state of pure consciousness by the negation of the operation of the principle of unconsciousness which stands in the way of its uprising. This pruning action is well illustrated by the names of a Shakti which in this work is variously described as Nibodikā and Nirodhikā. The first means the Giver of Knowledge, and the second That which obstructs—that is, obstructs the affectation of the mind by the objective world through the senses. It is by the prohibition of such impressions that the state of pure consciousness arises. The arising of such state is called Samādhi—that is, the ecstatic condition in which the "equality" that is identity of Jīvātmā and Paramātmā is realized. This experience is achieved after the absorption (Laya) of Prāna and Manas and the cessation of all ideation (Sangkalpa). An unmodified state (Samarasatvam) is thus produced which is the natural state (Sahajāvasthā) of the Ātmā. Until then there is that fluctuation and modification (Vritti) which is the mark of the conditioned consciousness, with its self-diremption of "I" and "Thou." The state of Samādhi is "like that of a grain of salt, which mingled in water becomes one with it."[487] It is, in the words of the Kulārnava Tantra, "that form of contemplation (Dhyāna) in which there is neither 'here' nor 'not here,' in which there is illumination and stillness as of some great ocean, and which is the Void Itself."[488]

The all-knowing and venerable Teacher has said, "One who has attained complete knowledge of the Ātmā reposes like the still waters of the deep" (v. 31). The Māyā Tantra defines Yoga as the unity of Jīva and Paramātmā (v. 51); that by which oneness is attained with the Supreme (Paramātmā), and Samādhi, or ecstasy, is this unity of Jīva

---

[486] The Tattva (Reality) is revealed when all thought is gone (Kulār nava Tantra, IX. 10).

[487] Hathayogapradīpikā, IV. 5-7. The same simile is used in the Buddhist Demchog Tantra.

[488] IX. 9.

and Ātmā (*ib.*).[489] Others define it as the knowledge of the identity of Shiva and Ātmā. The Āgamavādīs proclaim that the knowledge of Shakti (Jnānashaktyātmaka) is Yoga. Other wise men say that the knowledge of the "Ancient of Days" (the Purāna Purusha) is Yoga, and others, again, the Prakritivādīs, declare that the knowledge of the union of Shiva and Shakti is Yoga (*ib.*). All such definitions refer to one and the same thing—the realization by the human spirit that it is the Great Spirit, the Brahman, who as the Ruler of the worlds is known as God. As the Hathayogapradīpikā says:[490] "Rājayoga, Samādhi, Unmanī,[491] Manonmanī,[491] Amaratvam (Immortality), Shūnyāshūnya (void yet non-void),[492] Paramapada[493] (the Supreme State), Amanaska (without Manas—suspended operation of mental functioning),[494] Advaita (non-dual), Nirālamba (without support—*i.e.*, detachment of the Manas from the external world),[495] Niranjana (stainless),[496] Jīvanmukti (liberation in the body), Sahajāvasthā (natural state of the Ātmā), and Turīya (Fourth State), all mean one and the same thing—that is, the cessation of both mental functioning (Chitta) and action (Karma), on which there arises freedom from joy and sorrow and a changeless (Nirvikāra) state. This on the dissolution of the body is followed by bodiless (Videhakaivalya) or supreme liberation (Paramamukti), which is the permanent existence of the real state (Svarūpāvasthānam). Whilst the aim and the end of all Yoga is the same, the methods by which it is attained vary.

There are, it is commonly said, four forms of Yoga, called Mantrayoga, Hathayoga, Layayoga, and Rājayoga.[497] In this classification Hathayoga is used as a description of the processes passing under that title other than the Laya or Kundalī Yoga. But in a more general sense Hathayoga includes the latter. The distinction, however, is not without value, because Hathayoga in its more limited sense includes some of such practices as are used as auxiliaries in other Yogas. He who is expert in Kundalī Layayoga needs no other. These are all various modes of practice (Sādhanā) whereby the feelings and intellectual activities of the mind (Chittavritti) are brought into control

---

489 As water poured into water the two are undistinguishable (Kulārnava Tantra, IX. 15).

490 Ch. IV., vv. 3, 4.

491 State of mindlessness. See Nādabindu Up.

492 See Hathayogapradīpikā, IV., v. 37. The Yogī, like the Consciousness with which he is one, is beyond both.

493 The root pad = "to go to," and Padam therefore is that to which one has access (Comm. on v. 1, Ch. IV., of Hathayogapradīpikā).

494 See Mandalabrāhmana Up., II., III.

495 This is the Nirālambapurī referred to in the Text.

496 Anjana = Māyopādhī (the Upādhi, or apparently limiting condition produced by Māyā, or appearance); therefore Niranjana = destitute of that (Tadrahitam), or Shuddham (pure)—that is, the Brahman. Comm. Hathayogapradīpikā, IV., v. 1.

497 Varāha Upanishad, Ch. V., II.; Yogatattva Up. A useful analysis of Yoga will be found in Rajendra Ghose's "Shangkara and Rāmānuja."

and the Brahman is in various ways realized (Brahmasākshātkāra). Each of these forms has the same eight subservients, which are called the "eight limbs" (Ashtāngga). Each of these has the same aim—namely, spiritual experience or realization of Brahman; they differ, however, as to the means employed and, it is said, in degree of result. The Samādhi of the first has been described as Mahābhāva, of the second as Mahabodha, of the third as Mahālaya, and by Rājayoga and Jnānayoga, it is said, the liberation called Kaivalyamukti is obtained.

It is to be noted, however, that in the estimation of the practitioners of Kundalī Yoga it is the highest Yoga in which a perfect Samādhi is gained by the union with Shiva of both mind and body, as hereafter described. In Rāja and Jnāna Yoga intellective processes are the predominant where they are not the sole means employed. In Mantra Yoga worship and devotion predominate. In Hathayoga there is more stress on physical methods, such as breathing. Each, however, of these Yogas employs some methods of the others. Thus, in Hatha Layayoga there is Kriyājnāna. But whereas the Jnāna Yogī attains Svarūpa Jnāna by his mental efforts without rousing Kundalī, the Hathayogī gets this Jnāna through Kundalinī Herself. For Her union with Shiva in the Sahasrāra brings, and in fact is, Svarūpa Jnāna.

It will be convenient, therefore, to deal with the general subservients (Ashtāngga) which are common to all forms of Yoga, and then follow with an account of Mantra and the lower Hatha Yogas as a preliminary to that form of Layayoga which is the subject of this work, and includes within itself elements to be found both in Mantra and such Hathayogas.

The prerequisites of all Yoga are the eight limbs or parts, Yama, Niyama, and others. Morality, religious disposition and practice, and discipline (Sādhanā), are essential prerequisites of all Yoga which has as its aim the attainment of the Supreme Experience.[498] Morality (Dharma) is the expression of the true nature of being. The word Dharma, which includes both ethic and religion, but has also a wider context, comes from the root *dhri*, to sustain, and is therefore both the sustainer and the act of sustaining. The Universe is sustained (Dhāryate) by Dharma, and the Lord who is its Supreme Sustainer is embodied in the eternal law and is the Bliss which its fulfillment secures. Dharma is thus the law governing the universal involution, or the path of outgoing (Pravritti), and evolution, or the path of return (Nivritti).[499] And only those can attain the liberation to which the latter

---

[498] There are forms of Yoga, such as that with the elements giving "powers" (Siddhi) over them, to which different considerations apply. This is a part of magic, and not of religion. So the uniting of Prāna with the Tejas Tattva in the navel (Āgneyīdhāranā mudrā) is said to secure immunity from fire.

[499] This grandiose concept, therefore, is a name for *all* those laws (of which religion is but one) which hold the universe together. It is the inherent law of all manifested being.

path leads who by adherence to Dharma co-operate in the carrying out of the universal scheme. For this reason it is finely said, "Doing good to others is the Supreme Duty" (Paropakāro hi paramo dharmah).

In this scheme the Jīva passes from Shabdavidyā, with its Tapas involving egoism and fruit attained through the "Path of the Gods," its Karma (rites), which are either Sakāma (with desire for fruit) or Nishkāma (disinterested), to Brahmavidyā (knowledge of the Brahman) or Theosophy as taught by the Upanishads. This transition is made through Nishkāma Karma. By Sakāma Karma is attained the "Path of the Fathers" (Pitri), Dharma, Artha (wealth), Kāma (desire and its fulfillment). But Nishkāma Karma produces that purity of mind (Chittashuddhi) which makes man competent for Brahmavidyā, or Theosophy, which leads to, and in its completest sense is, liberation (Moksha).

It is obvious that before the pure blissful state of the Ātmā can be attained the Jīva must first live that ordered life which is its proper expression on this plane.

To use theological language, only those who follow Dharma can go to its Lord. The disorder of an immoral life is not a foundation on which such a Yoga can be based. I do not use the term immorality in the absurdly limited meaning which ordinary English parlance gives it, but as the infringement of all forms of moral law. All such infringements are founded on selfishness. As the object of Yoga is the destruction of the limited self even in its more ordered manifestation, its doctrines clearly presuppose the absence of a state disordered by the selfishness which is the grossest obstacle to its attainment. The aim of Yoga is the achievement of complete detachment from the world. In a life governed by Dharma, there is that natural attachment to worldly objects and sense of separateness even in acts of merit which must exist until by the destruction of Manas the Unmanī state is attained. Where, however, there is unrighteousness (Adharma), attachment exists in its worst and most injurious form, and the sense of separateness which Yoga seeks to overcome is predominantly present in sin. The body is poisoned by the secretion of passions' poisons, and vitality or Prāna is lessened and injured. The mind under the influence of anger,[500] lust, malice, and other passions, is first distracted, and then, on the principle "what a man thinks that he becomes," is centered on, and is permanently molded into and becomes, the expression of Adharma (unrighteousness) itself. In such a case the Jīva is not merely bound to the world by the Māyā which affects both him and the virtuous Sakāma Sādhaka, but suffers Hell (Naraka), and "goes down" in the scale of

As pain follows wrong-doing, the Vaisheshika Darshana describes Dharma as "that by which happiness is attained in this and the next world, and birth and suffering are brought to an end (Mokshadharma).

[500] According to Indian notions, anger is the worst of sins.

Being.

Dharma in its devotional aspect is also necessary. Desire to achieve the highest aim of Yoga can only spring from a religious disposition, and such a disposition and practice (Sādhanā) furthers the acquisition of those qualities which Yoga requires. Indeed, by persevering devotion to the Mother, Samādhi may be achieved.

Therefore is it that the Commentator in v. 50 of the first of these works says:

"He alone whose nature has been purified by the practice of Yama and Niyama and the like (referring to the Sādhanā hereinafter described) will learn from the mouth of the Guru the means whereby the way to the great liberation is discovered."

He adds, however, that the practice of Yama and the like is only necessary for those whose minds are disturbed by anger, lust, and other evil propensities. If, however, a man through merit acquired in previous births is by good-fortune of a nature which is free of these and other vices, then he is competent for Yoga without this preliminary preparation.

All forms of Yoga, whether Mantra, Hatha, or Rāja, have the same eight limbs (Ashtāngga) or preparatory subservients: Yama, Niyama, Āsana, Prānāyāma, Pratyāhāra, Dhāranā, Dhyāna, and Samādhi.[501] Yama is of ten kinds: Avoidance of injury to all living creatures (Ahingsā); truthfulness (Satyam); restraint from taking what belongs to another, or covetousness (Asteyam); sexual continence in mind, speech, or body (Brahmacharyya);[502] forbearance, the bearing patiently of all things pleasant or unpleasant (Kshamā); fortitude in happiness or unhappiness (Dhriti); mercy, kindliness (Dayā); simplicity (Ārjavam);

---

[501] Varāha Up., Ch. V. The preliminaries are necessary only for those who have not attained. For those who have, Niyama, Āsana, and the like, are needless. Kulārnava Tantra, IX. 28, 29.

[502] As the Hathayogapradīpikā says: "He who knows Yoga should preserve his semen. For the expenditure of the latter tends to death, but there is life for him who preserves it."

> Evang sangrakshayet bindung mrityung jayati yogavit
> Maranang bindupātena jīvanang bindudhāranāt.

See also Yogatattva Up., which says that Hathayoga secures such personal beauty to the Yogī that all women will desire him, but they must be resisted. And see also v. 90, which shows the connection between semen, mind, and life. In the early stages of Hathayoga Sādhanā the heat goes upwards, the penis shrinks, and sexual powers are largely lost. Coition with emission of semen at this stage is like to prove fatal. But a Siddha regains his sexual power and can exercise it. For if fire and the other elements cannot hurt him, what can a woman do? Presumably, however, the dictum cited applies, for continence must in all cases tend to strength and longevity. It may, however, be that the physical perfection assumed negatives the ill effects observed in ordinary men.

moderation[503] in and regulation[504] of diet (Mītāhāra), suited to the development of the Sattvaguna; and purity of body and mind (Shaucham). The first form of purity is the external cleansing of the body, particularly dealt with by Hathayoga (*v. post*); and the second is gained through the science of self (Adhyātmavidyā).[505]

Niyama is also of ten kinds: Austerities, such as fasts and the like, in the nature of purificatory actions (Tapah); contentment with that which one has unasked (Santosha); belief in Veda (Āstikyam) charity (Dānam)—that is gifts to the deserving of what one has lawfully acquired; worship of the Lord or Mother (Īshvarapūjanam) according to His or Her various forms; hearing of Shāstric conclusions, as by study of the Vedānta (Siddhāntavākyashravanam); modesty and shame felt in the doing of wrong actions (Hrī); a mind rightly directed towards knowledge revealed and practice enjoined by the Shāstra (Mati); recitation of Mantra (Japa);[506] and Homa sacrifice (Hutam)[507]—that is, religious observances in general (Vrata). The Pātanjala Sūtra mentions only five Yamas—the first four and freedom from covetousness (Parigraha). Ahingsā is the root of those which follows. Shaucham, or cleanliness, is included among the Niyama. Five of the latter are stated—namely, cleanliness (Shaucham), contentment (Santosha), purificatory action (Tapah), study of the Scriptures leading to liberation (Svādhyāya), and devotion to the Lord (Īshvarapranidhāna).[508]

The statement of such obvious truths would hardly be necessary were it not that there are still some who see in Yoga mere "Shamanism," feats of breathing, "acrobatic posturing," and so forth. On the contrary, no country since the Middle Ages and until our own has laid greater stress on the necessity of the association of morality and religion with all forms of human activity, than India has done.[509]

The practice of Yama and Niyama leads to renunciation of, and detachment from, the things of this world and of the next,[510] arising

[503] Yogiyājnavalkya (Ch. I.) says: "32 mouthfuls for a householder, 16 for a forest recluse, and 8 for a Muni."

[504] For foods detrimental to Yoga, see Yogatattva Up., Yogakundalī Up.

[505] Shāndilya Up., Ch. I.; see also Mandalabrāhmana Up.

[506] Which is either spoken (which, again, is loud or soft) or mental (Shāndilya Up.).

[507] See Ch. I., vv. 16, 17 Hathayogapradīpikā, and p. 133, 2nd vol., of Tantrik Texts, ed. A. Avalon. The Shāndilya Up., Ch. I., gives Vrata as the last, which is described as the observance of actions enjoined and refraining from actions prohibited. See also Ch. V., Varāha Up.

[508] Patanjali's Yoga Sūtra, Ch. II., 30, 32.

[509] So, as was the case in our medieval guilds, religion inspires Indian Art; and Indian speculation is associated with religion as was the scholastic philosophy. In modern times in the West, the relevancy of religion in these matters has not been generally considered to be apparent, craftsmanship in the one case and intelligence in the other being usually thought to be sufficient.

[510] Such as the Sudhā (nectar) which is gained in the heavens (Hathayogapradīpikā, Comm. to v. 9, Ch. I.). Renunciation may doubtless be practiced by giving up what one

from the knowledge of the permanent and impermanent, and intense desire for and incessant striving after emancipation, which characterizes him who is Mumukshu, or longs for liberation.

Yama and Niyama are the first two of the eight accessories of Yoga (Ashtāngayoga). These accessories or limbs may be divided into five exterior methods[511] (Bahiranga), chiefly concerned with the subjugation of the body, and three inner methods[512] (Antarangga), or states affecting the development of the mind.

Attention is paid to the physical body, which is the vehicle of the Jīva's existence and activity. Purity of mind is not possible without purity of the body in which it functions and by which it is affected. Purity of mind is here used in the Hindu sense. According to English parlance, such purity merely connotes absence of irregular sexual imaginations. This, though creditable, particularly in a civilization which almost seems designed to fan every desire, is yet obviously insufficient for the purpose in hand. Proper thought and conduct in all its forms is but the alphabet of a school in which they are merely the first step to the conquest of greater difficulties to follow. What is here meant is that state of the mind or approach thereto which is the result of good functioning, clear thinking, detachment, and concentration. By these the Manas is freed of all those modifications (Vritti) which enshroud by their illusions the Ātmā from Itself. It is turned inward on the Buddhi which becomes Laya in Prakriti, and the Ātmatattva or Brahman.

Provision therefore is made in respect both of Āsana (posture) and Prānāyāma, or breath development, both of which are shortly dealt with later in connection with Hathayoga, of which they are particular processes. Pratyāhāra is the restraint of and subjection of the senses to the mind, which is thereby steadied.[513] The mind is withdrawn from the objects of the senses. The mind is by nature unsteady, for it is at every moment being affected by the sight, sounds, and so forth, of external objects which Manas through the agency of the senses (Indriyas) perceives. It must therefore be detached from the object of the senses, withdrawn from whatsoever direction it may happen to tend, freed from

wants, but renunciation or abandonment (Tyāga) here means the *want of desire* of enjoyment (Tyāgah = bhogechchhābhāvah) (*ib.*). Those who seek the joys of any heaven can never attain the end of high Yoga.

[511] Yama, Niyama, Āsana, Prānāyāma, Pratyāhāra.

[512] Dhyāna, Dhāranā, Samādhi, which is both incomplete (Savikalpa or Samprajnāta) and complete (Nirvikalpa or Asamprajnāta).

[513] See Gheranda Sanghitā, Fourth Upadesha; Shāndilya Up., Ch. I.; Amritanāda Up.; Mandalabrāhmana Up., First Brāhmana. The Shāradā Tilaka defines Pratyāhāra as "the forcible obstruction of the senses wandering over their objects" (indriyānāng vicharatāng vishayeshu balādāharanam tebhyah pratyāharah vidhīyate). The Shāndilya Up. (*loc. cit.*) speaks of five kinds of Pratyāhāra, the last of which is Dhāranā on eighteen important points of the body.

all distraction, and kept under the control of the dominant self. Steadiness (Dhairya) therefore is the aim and result of Pratyāhāra.[514] The three processes known as the "inner limbs" (Antaranga)—namely, Dhāranā, Dhyāna, and Savikalpa Samādhi—complete the psychic and mental discipline. These are concentration of the mind on an object; unity of the mind by contemplation with its object; resulting in the last or consciousness of the object only. The first is the "holding by"—that is, fixing the Chitta, or thinking principle, on—a particular object of thought or concentration (Dhāranā). The mind, having been drawn away from the objects of the senses by Pratyāhāra, is fixed on one object, such as the Devatās of the Bhūtas, alone. Uniform contemplation on the subject which the Chitta holds in Dhāranā is Dhyāna (meditation). Dhyāna has been defined to be the state of the Antahkarana (mind) of those whose Chaitanya holds to and is occupied by the thought of one object, having first cast away thought of all other objects.[515] Through Dhyāna is acquired the quality of mental realization (Pratyaksha). It is of two kinds: Saguna, or meditation of a form (Mūrti); and Nirguna, in which the self is its own object.[516]

Samādhi has been defined to be the identification of Manas and Ātmā as salt in water,[517] that state in which all is known as one (equal)[518] and the "nectar of equality" (oneness).[519] Complete Samādhi is thus the state of Parāsamvit. Of Samādhi there are two degrees, in the first of which (Savikalpa) the mind in a lesser degree, and in the second (Nirvikalpa) in a complete degree, continuously and to the exclusion of all other objects, assumes the nature and becomes one with the subject of its contemplation.

There are in Advaita Vedānta three states (Bhūmikā) of Samprajnāta (Savikalpa) Samādhi—namely, Ritambharā, Prajnālokā, Prashāntavāhitā.[520] In the first the content of the mental Vritti is Sachchidānanda. There is still a separate knower. The second is that in which every kind of Āvarana (screening) is cast away, and there is Sākshātkāra Brahmajnāna passing into the third state of Peace in which the mind is void of all Vritti and the self exists as the Brahman alone:[521] "On which being known everything is known" (Yasmin vijnāte sarvvam idam vijnātam bhavati). Entrance is here made into Nirvikalpa

[514] Shāndilya Up., Ch. I.; Amritanādā Up.; Mandalabrāhmana Up., First Brāhmana.

[515] Vijātīyapratyayatiraskārapūrvaka-sajātīyavrittikābhih nirantara (vyāpti) vishayīkritachaitanyang yasya, tat tādrishang chittam antahkaranang yeshām (Comm. on v. 28 of the Trishatī, on the title of the Devī as Ekāgrachittanirdhyātā).

[516] Shāndilya Up., Ch. I.; Mandalabrāhmana Up., First Brāhmana.

[517] Varāha Up., Ch. II.

[518] Amritanāda Up.

[519] Yogakundalī Up., Ch. III.

[520] Comm. v. 28 of Trishatī.

[521] Comm., Manaso vrittishūnyasya brahmākāratayāsthiti. The mind has always Vritti (modifications)—that is, Guna. If the Jiva's mind is freed of these, he is Brahman.

Samādhi by Rājayoga.

These three—Dhāranā, Dhyāna, Savikalpa Samādhi—called Sangyama, are merely stages in the mental effort of concentration, though, as later stated, according to the Hathayoga aspect, they are progressions in Prāṇāyāma, each stage being a longer period of retention of Prāna.[522] Thus by Yama, Niyama, Āsana, the body is controlled; by these and Prānāyāma the Prāna is controlled; by these and Pratyāhāra the senses (Indriyas) are brought under subjection. Then through the operation of Dhāranā, Dhyāna, and the lesser Samādhi (Savikalpa or Samprajnāta), the modifications (Vritti) of the Manas cease and Buddhi alone functions. By the further and long practice of dispassion or indifference to both joy and sorrow (Vairāgya) Buddhi itself becomes Laya, and the Yogī attains the true unmodified state of the Ātmā, in which the Jīva who is then pure Buddhi is merged in Prakriti, and the Brahman as salt in the waters of ocean and as camphor in the flame.

Passing then to the processes[523] peculiar to the different Yogas, Mantrayoga comprises all those forms of Sādhanā in which the mind is controlled by the means of its own object—that is, the manifold objects of the world of name and form (Nāmarūpa). The whole universe is made up of names and forms (Nāmarūpātmaka) which are the objects (Vishaya) of the mind. The mind is itself modified into the form of that which it perceives. These modifications are called its Vritti, and the mind is not for one moment devoid of ideas and feelings. It is the feeling or intention (that is, Bhāva) with which an act is done which determines its moral worth. It is on this Bhāva that both character and the whole outlook on life depend. It is sought therefore to render the Bhāva pure. As a man who falls on the ground raises himself by means of the same ground, so to break worldly bonds the first and easiest method is to use those bonds as the means of their own undoing.[524] The mind is distracted by Nāmarūpa, but this Nāmarūpa may be utilized as the first means of escape therefrom. In Mantrayoga, therefore, a particular form of Nāmarūpa, productive of pure Bhāva, is given as the object of contemplation. This is called Sthūla or Saguna Dhyāna of the five Devatās, devised to, meet the requirements of different natures. Besides the ordinary "eight limbs" (Ashtānga)[525] common to all forms of Yoga, certain modes of training and worship are prescribed. In the latter material media are utilized as the first steps whereby the formless

---

[522] See Yogatattva Upanishad.

[523] See two publications by the Shrī Bhāratadharmmamahāmandala—Mantrayoga Sanghitā and Dharma Prachāra Series. The latter in a short compass explain the main essentials of each of the four systems.

[524] This is an essentially Tantrik principle. See Kulārnava, Ch. II.

[525] *Vide ante*, p. 147.

One is by Jnānayoga attained—such as images (Mūrti),[526] emblems (Linga, Shālagrama), pictures (Chitra), mural markings (Bhittirekhā), Mandalas and Yantras (diagrams),[527] Mudrās,[528] Nyāsa.[529] With this the prescribed Mantra is said (Japa) either aloud or softly only. The source of all Bīja-Mantra (Seed-Mantra), the Pranava (Om), or Brahman, is the articulate equivalent of that primal "Sound" which issued from the first vibration of the Gunas of Mūlaprakriti, and the other Bīja-Mantras are the same equivalents of the various Saguna forms, Devas and Devīs, which thereafter appeared when Prakriti entered the Vaishamyāvasthā state. In Mantrayoga the state of Samādhi is called Mahābhāva. This is the simplest form of Yoga practice, suited for those whose powers and capacities are not such as to qualify them for either of the other methods.

Hathayoga comprises those Sādhanās, or prescribed methods of exercise and practice, which are concerned primarily with the gross or physical body (Sthūla Sharīra). As the latter is connected with the super-physical or subtle body (Sūkshma Sharīra), of which it is the outer sheath, control of the gross body affects the subtle body with its intellection, feelings, and passions. In fact, the Sthūla Sharira is expressly designed to enable the Sūkshma Sharīra to work out the Karma it has incurred. As the former is constructed according to the nature of the latter, and both are united and interdependent, it follows that operation in and upon the gross body affects the subtle body; the physical processes of this Yoga have been prescribed for particular temperaments, in order that, the physical body being first mastered, the subtle body with its mental functioning maybe brought under control.[530] These merely physical processes are auxiliary to others. As the Kulārnava Tantra says:[531] "Neither the lotus-seat nor fixing the gaze on the tip of the nose are Yoga. It is the identity of Jivātmā and Paramātmā, which is Yoga." The special features of this Yoga may be first contrasted with Mantra Yoga. In the latter there is concern with things outside the physical body, and special attention is given to outward observances of ceremonials. Due regard must be paid to the laws of the caste and stages of life (Varnāshrama Dharma), and the respective duties of men and women (Kula Dharma). So the mantra

[526] "The Deva of the unawakened (aprabuddha) is in Images; of the Vipras in Fire; of the wise in the Heart. The Deva of those who know the Ātmā is everywhere" (Kulārnava Tantra, IX. 44). "O Beautiful-Eyed! Not in Kailāsa, Meru, or Mandara, do I dwell. I am there where the knowers of Kula doctrine are" (*ib.*, v. 94).

[527] See Introduction, Mahānirvāna Tantra.

[528] *Ib.* These ritual Mudrās are not to be confused with the Yoga Mudrās later described.

[529] Sec Introduction, Mahānirvāna Tantra.

[530] See the short summary of the Hathayoga Sanghitā given in the Dharma Prachāra Series (Shrī Bhāratadharmamahāmandala, Benares).

[531] IX. 30.

which is given to the male initiate may not be given to a woman. Nor is the mantra given to a Brāhmana suitable for a Shūdra. The objects of contemplation are Devas and Devīs in their various manifestations and concrete symbols, and the Samādhi called Mahābhāva is attained by contemplation of and by means of Nāmarūpa. In Hathayoga, on the other hand, the question of the fitness or otherwise of a novice is determined from the physical point of view, and rules are prescribed to procure and increase health and to free the body of disease. In Hathayoga contemplation is on the "Light," and the Samādhi called Mahābodha is attained by the aid of control of breath and other vital Vāyus (Prānāyāma), whereby the mind is also controlled. As already observed, Āsana and Prānāyāma, which are parts of Hathayoga, are also parts of Mantrayoga. Those who practice the latter will derive benefit from taking advantage of some of the other exercises of Hathayoga, just as the followers of the latter system will be helped by the exercises of Mantrayoga.

The word Hatha is composed of the syllables Ha and Tha, which mean the "sun" and "moon"—that is, the Prāna and Apāna Vāyus. In v. 8 of the Shatchakranirūpana it is said that the Prāna (which dwells in the heart) draws Apāna (which dwells in the Mulādhāra), and Apāna draws Prāna, just as a falcon attached by a string is drawn back again when he attempts to fly away. These two by their disagreement prevent each other from leaving the body, but when they are in accord they leave it. Both their union or Yoga in the Sushumnā and the process leading thereto is called Prānāyāma. Hathayoga or Hathavidyā is therefore the science of the Life-Principle, using that word in the sense of the various forms of vital Vāyu into which Prāna is divided. Prāna in the body of the individual is a part of the Universal Breath (Prāna), or the "Great Breath." An attempt, therefore, is first made to harmonize the individual breath, known as Pinda or Vyashti Prāna, with the cosmic or collective breath, or the Brahmānda or Samashti Prāna. Strength and health are thereby attained. The regulation of the harmonized breath helps to the regulation and steadiness of mind, and therefore concentration.

In correspondence with the threefold division Adhyātma, Adhidaiva, Adhibhūta, Mind (Manas), Prāna (vitality), and Vīryya (semen), are one. Therefore the subjection of Manas causes the subjection of Prāna or Vāyu and Vīryya. Similarly, by controlling Prāna, Manas and Vīryya are automatically controlled. Again, if the Vīryya is controlled, and the force which under the influence of sexual desire develops into gross seed[532] is made to flow upwards

[532] The retention of gross seed—that is, seed already formed—effects little compared with the sexual power which has not been allowed to materialize. Semen is the projection into matter of the individual sexual will.

(Ūrddhvaretas), control is had over both Manas and Prāna. With Prānāyāma the semen (Shukra) dries up. The seminal force ascends and comes back as the nectar (Amrita) of Shiva-Shakti.

Prānāyāma is recognized as one of the "limbs" of all the (Ashtāngga) forms of Yoga. But whereas it is used in Mantra, Laya, and Rājayoga, as an auxiliary, the Hathayogī as such regards this regulation and Yoga of breath as the chief means productive of that result (Moksha), which is the common end of all schools of Yoga. This school, proceeding on the basis that the Vritti or modification of the mind always follows Prāna,[533] and of the sufficiency of that fact, held that by the aid of the union of Ha and Tha in the Sushumnā, and the leading of the combined Prānas therein to the Brahmarandhra, Samādhi was attained. Though the reciprocal action of matter and mind is common knowledge, and bodily states influence psychic or mental states as the latter the former, the Hathayoga method is preponderantly a physical one, though the gross physical acts of the preparatory stages of this Yoga are succeeded by Kriyājnāna and subtle vital processes which have Prāna as their subject.

Under the heading of gross physical training come provisions as to the place of residence, mode of life as regards eating, drinking, sexual function, exercise, and so forth.

The practice and exercises connected with Hathayoga are divided into seven parts or stages—namely, cleansing (Shodhana) by the six processes (Shatkarma); the attainment of strength or firmness (Dridhatā) by bodily postures (Āsana); of fortitude (Sthiratā) by bodily positions (Mudrā); of steadiness (Dhairya) by restraint of the senses (Pratyāhāra); of lightness (Lāghava) by Prānāyāma; of realization (Pratyaksha) by meditation (Dhyāna); and of detachment (Nirliptatva) in Samādhi.

Those who suffer from inequality of the three "humors"[534] are required to practice the "six acts" (Shatkarma) which purify the body and facilitate Prānāyāma. For others who are free from these defects they are not necessary in such case, and according to some teachers the practice of Prānāyāma alone is sufficient. These form the first steps in the Hathayoga. On this cleansing (Shodhana) of the body and Nādīs, health is gained, the internal fire is rendered more active, and restraint of breath (Kumbhaka) is facilitated. Recourse is also had, if necessary, to Oshadhiyoga, in which herbal preparations are administered to cure defective health.

Cleansing (Shodhana) is effected by the six processes known as the Shatkarmma. Of these, the first is Dhauti, or washing, which is

[533] Chitta has two causes—Vāsanā and Prāna. If one is controlled, then both are controlled (Yoga Kundalī Up., Ch. I.).

[534] Vāta, Kapha, and Pitta. These will be found described in my Introduction to the Prapanchasāra Tantra, Vol. III. of Tantrik Texts.

fourfold, or inward washing (Antardhauti), cleansing of the teeth, etc. (Dantadhauti), of the "heart" (Hriddhauti), and of the anus (Mūladhauti). Antardhauti is also fourfold—namely, Vātasāra, by which air is drawn into the belly and then expelled; Vārisāra, by which the body is filled with water, which is then evacuated by the anus; Vahnisāra, in which the Nābhigranthi is made to touch the spinal column (Meru); and Vahishkrita, in which the belly is by Kākinīmudrā[535] filled with air, which is retained half a Yāma,[536] and then sent downward. Dantadhauti is fourfold, consisting in the cleansing of the root of the teeth and tongue, the ears, and the "hollow of the skull" (Kapālarandhra). By Hriddhauti phlegm and bile are removed. This is done by a stick (Dandadhauti) or cloth (Vāsodhauti) pushed into the throat, or swallowed, or by vomiting (Vamanadhauti). Mūladhauti is done to cleanse the exit of the Apānavāyu, either with the middle finger and water or the stalk of a turmeric plant.

Vasti, the second of the Shatkarmma, is twofold, and is either of the dry (Shuska) or watery (Jala) kind. In the second form the Yogī sits in the Utkatāsana[537] posture in water up to the navel, and the anus is contracted and expanded by Ashvinī Mudrā; or the same is done in the Pashchimottānāsana,[538] and the abdomen below the navel is gently moved. In Neti the nostrils are cleansed with a piece of string. Laulikī is the whirling of the belly from side to side. In Trātaka the Yogī, without winking, gazes at some minute object until the tears start from his eyes. By this the "celestial vision" (Divya Drishti) so often referred to in the Tāntrika Upāsanā is acquired. Kapālabhāti is a process for the removal of phlegm, and is threefold: Vātakrama, by inhalation and exhalation; Vyūtkrama, by water drawn through the nostrils and ejected through the mouth; and Shītkrama, the reverse process.

These are the various processes by which the body is cleansed and made pure for the Yoga practice to follow.

Āsana, or posture, is the next, and when the Shatkarma are dispensed with, is the first stage of Hathayoga.

Dridhatā, or strength or firmness, the acquisition of which is the second of the above-mentioned processes, is attained by Āsana.

The Āsanas are postures of the body. The term is generally described as modes of seating the body. But the posture is not necessarily a sitting one; for some Āsanas are done on the belly, back,

---

[535] Gheranda Sanghitā, Third Upadesha (v. 86); see also Hathayogapradīpikā, II. 21-38.

[536] A Yāma is three hours.

[537] Gheranda Sanghitā, Second Upadesha (v. 23). That is, squatting resting on the toes, the heels off the ground, and buttocks resting on heels. A Hathayogī can give himself a natural enema by sitting in water and drawing it up through the anus. The sphincter muscles, are opened and shut, and suction established.

[538] *Ibid.*, v. 20.

hands, etc. It is said[539] that the Āsana are as numerous as living beings, and that there are 8,400,000 of these; 1,600 are declared to be excellent, and out of these thirty-two are auspicious for men, which are described in detail. Two of the commonest of these are Muktapadmāsana[540] (the loosened lotus seat), the ordinary position for worship, and Baddhapadmāsana.[541] Kundalīyoga is ordinarily done in an Āsana, in which the feet close both the genital and anal apertures, the hands closing the others—nostrils, eyes, ears, mouth (Yonimudrā). The right heel is pressed against the anus and the left against the genitals to close the aperture of the penis.

There are certain other Āsana which are peculiar to the Tantras, such as Mundāsana, Chitāsana, and Shavāsana, in which skulls, the funeral pyre, and a corpse,[542] respectively, form the seat of the Sādhaka. These, though they have other ritual and magical objects, also form part of the discipline for the conquest of fear and the attainment of indifference, which is the quality of a Yogī. And so the Tantras prescribe as the scene of such rites the solitary mountain-top, the lonely empty house and riverside, and the cremation ground. The interior cremation ground is there where the Kāmik body and its passions are consumed in the fire of knowledge.[543]

Patanjali, on the subject of Āsana, merely points out what are good conditions, leaving each one to settle the details for himself according to his own requirements.

Āsana is an aid to clear and collect the thought. The test of suitability of Āsana is that which is steady and pleasant, a matter which

---

[539] Gheranda Sanghitā, Second Upadesha. In the Shiva Sanghitā (Ch. III., vv. 84-91) eighty-four postures are mentioned, of which four are recommended—viz., Siddhāsana, Ugrāsana, Svastikāsana and Padmāsana.

[540] The right foot is placed on the left thigh, the left foot on the right thigh, and the hands are crossed and placed similarly on the thighs; the chin is placed on the breast, and the gaze fixed on the tip of the nose (see also Shiva Sanghitā, Ch. I., v. 52).

[541] The same, except that the hands are passed behind the back, and the right hand holds the right toe and the left hand the left toe. By this, increased pressure is placed on the Mūlādhāra, and the nerves are braced with the tightening of the body.

[542] In successful Shavāsana the Devī appears to the Sādhaka. In Shavasādhanā the Sādhaka sits astride on the back of a corpse (heading the north), on which he draws a Yantra and then does Japa of Mantra with Shodhānyāsa and Pujā on its head. A corpse is selected as being a pure form of organized matter, since the Devatā which is invoked into it is the Mahāvidyā whose Svarūpa is Nirgunabrahman, and by such invocation becomes Saguna. The corpse is free from sin or desire. The only Vāyu in it is the Dhananjaya, "which leaves not even a corpse." The Devatā materializes by means of the corpse. There is a possession of it (Āvesha)—that is, entry of the Devatā into the dead body. At the conclusion of a successful rite the head of the corpse turns round, and, facing the Sādhaka, speaks, bidding him name his boon, which may be spiritual or worldly advancement as he wishes. This is part of Nīla Sādhanā done by the "Hero" (Vīra), for it and Shavāsana are attended by many terrors.

[543] As the Yogakundalī Upanishad says (Ch. III.), the outer burning is no burning at all.

each will settle for himself. Posture becomes perfect when effort to that end ceases, so that there is no more movement of the body.[544] The Rajas Guna, the action of which produces fickleness of mind, is restrained. A suitable steady Āsana produces mental equilibrium. Hathayoga, however, prescribes a very large number of Āsanas, to each of which a peculiar effect is described. These are more in the nature of a gymnastic than an Āsana in its sense of a seated posture. Some forms of this gymnastic are done seated, but others are not so, but standing upright, bending, lying down, and standing on the head. This latter is Vrikshāsana. Thus, again, in Chakrāsana the Yogī stands and bends and touches his feet with his hand, a familiar exercise, as is also Vāmadakshinapadāsana, a kind of goose step, in which, however, the legs are brought up to right angles with the body. These exercises secure a fine physical condition and freedom from disease.[545] They are also said to assist in Prānāyāma, and to help to effect its object, including the rousing of Kundalinī. The author of the work last cited says[546] that as among the Niyamas the most important is Ahingsā, and among Yamas Mitāhāra, or a moderate diet (a significant choice), so is Siddhāsana (in which the Mūlādhāra is firmly pressed by the heel) among the Āsanas. Mastery of this helps to secure the Unmanī Avasthā, and the three Bandhas (*v. post*) are achieved without difficulty.

Sthiratā, Or fortitude, is acquired by the practice of the Mudrā.[547] The Mudrā dealt with in works of Hathayoga are positions of the body.[548] They are gymnastic, health-giving, and destructive of disease and of death, such as the Jālandhara[549] and other Mudrās. They also preserve from injury by fire, Water, or air. Bodily action and the health resulting therefrom react upon the mind, and by the union of a perfect mind and body Siddhi is by their means attained. The Gheranda Sanghitā describes a number of Mudrā, of which those of importance may be selected. In the celebrated Yonimudrā, the Yogī in Siddhāsana stops with his fingers the ears, eyes, nostrils, and mouth, so as to shut out all external impressions. He inhales Prānavāyu by Kākinīmudrā,[550] and unites it with Apānavāyu. Meditating in their order upon the six Chakra, he arouses the sleeping Kulakundalinī by the Mantra "Hūng

---

[544] Patanjali Yogasūtra, 46, 47 (Sthīrasukhamāsanam).

[545] See Ch. II. of Gheranda Sanghitā, and Hathayogapradīpikā, I., vv. 19-35; Shāndilya Upanishad, Ch. I.

[546] Ch. I., v. 39.

[547] According to the Commentary on the Hathayogapradīpikā (Ch. IV., v. 37), Mudrā is so called because it removes pain and sorrow (Mudrayati klesham iti mudrā). See my Introduction to Mahānirvāna Tantra, Ch. CXXVII., and Ch. III. of Gheranda Sanghitā.

[548] Gheranda Sanghitā, Third Upadesha.

[549] *Ibid.*, v. 12.

[550] The lips are formed to resemble the beak of a crow, and the air gently drawn in (Gheranda Sanghitā, III. 86, 87).

Hangsah."[551] By "Hang," or the Sun, heat is produced (for Mantra can produce fire), and this heat is made to play on Kundalī Shakti. By "Sah" the Kāma or will (Ichchhā) is made active. The vital air (Vāyu) in the Mūlādhāra is in the form of both Moon and Sun (Somasūryyarūpī). With "Hangsa" She is roused, Hang rousing Her with his heat, and Sah lifting Her upwards. He raises Her to the Sahasrāra; then deeming himself pervaded with the Shakti, and in blissful union (Sanggama) with Shiva, he meditates upon himself as, by reason of that union, Bliss itself and the Brahman.[552] Ashvinīmudrā consists of the repeated contraction and expansion of the anus for the purpose of Shodhana, or of contraction to restrain the Apāna in Shatchakrabheda. Shaktichālana employs the latter Mudrā, which is repeated until Vāyu manifests in the Sushumnā. The process is accompanied by inhalation and the union of Prāna and Apāna whilst in Siddhāsana.[553]

Yoni Mudrā is employed in the rousing of Kundalinī accompanied by Shaktichālana Mudrā,[554] which should be well practiced first before the Yoni Mudrā is done. The rectal muscle is contracted by Ashvinī Mudrā until the Vāyu enters the Sushumnā, a fact which is indicated by a peculiar sound which is heard there.[555] And with the Kumbhaka the Serpent goes upwards to the Sahasrāra roused by the Mantra "Hūng Hangsah." The Yogī should then think himself to be pervaded with Shakti and in a state of blissful union (Sanggama) with Shiva. He then contemplates: "I am the Bliss Itself," "I am the Brahman."[556] Mahāmudrā[557] and Mahāvedha are done in conjunction with Mahābandha, already described. In the first the Yogī presses the Yoni (Mūlādhāra) with the left heel, and, stretching out the right leg, takes hold of the two feet with both hands. Jālandhara Bandha is then done. When Kundalinī is awakened, the Prāna enters the Sushumnā, and Idā

---

[551] Hūng is called Kurchcha Bīja. Hūng is Kavacha Bīja = "May I be protected." Hūng stands for Kāma (desire) and Krodha (anger). Kāma here means creative will (Srīshti), and Krodha its reverse, or dissolution (Laya). So-called "angry" Devatās are not angry in the ordinary sense, but are then in that aspect in which they are Lords of dissolution, an aspect which seems angry or terrible to the worldly-minded. It is said of the Tārāmantra that the Hūng in it is the sound of the wind as it blew with force on the Chola lake to the west of Meru what time She manifested. Hangsah = Prakriti (Sa) and Purusha (Hang) or Jīvātmā. This Mantra is used in taking Kundalinī up, and So'ham (He I am) in bringing Her down. Hang also = Sun (Sūryya), and Sah = Moon (Indu), which = Kāma = Ichchhā.

[552] Gheranda Sanghitā, Third Upadesha.

[553] *Ibid.*, vv. 37, 49, 82.

[554] Gheranda Sanghitā, III., vv. 49-61.

[555] Hathayogapradīpikā, Commentary to Ch. II., v. 72.

[556] The Mantra Hangsah is the breath held in Kumbhaka.

[557] Gheranda Sanghitā, III. 37-42. The Yoni Mudrā, "which detaches the Manas from the objective world," is described in the Com. to v. 36 of the work here first translated, *post*.

and Pinggalā, now that Prāna has left them, become lifeless. Expiration should be done slowly, and the Mudrā should be practiced an equal number of times on the left and right side of the body. This Mudrā, like other Hathayoga Mudrās, is said to ward off death and disease. In Mahāvedha[558] the Yogī assumes the Mahābandha posture, and, concentrating his mind, stops by methods already described the upward and downward course of the Prāna. Then, placing the palms of his hands on the ground, he taps the ground softly with his buttocks (Sphichau), and the "Moon," "Sun," and "Fire"—that is, Idā, Pinggalā, and Sushumnā—become united upon the entry of the Prāna into the latter Nādī. Then the body assumes a death-like aspect, which disappears with the slow expiration which follows. According to another mode of rousing Kundalinī, the Yogī seated in Vajrāsana takes firm hold of his feet a little above the ankles, and slowly taps the Kanda (*v. post*) with them. Bhastra Kumbhaka is done and the abdomen is contracted.[559]

The Khecharī Mudrā,[560] which, as well as the Yoni Mudrā, is referred to in the text translated, is the cutting of the *frænum* of the tongue and the lengthening of it until it reaches the eyebrows. It is then turned back in the throat, and closes the exit of the breath previously inspired. The mind is fixed in the Ājnā[561] until with Siddhi this "path of the upward Kundalī" (Ūrddhvakundalinī) conquers the whole universe, which is realized in the Yogī's body as not different from Ātmā.[562]

The term Mudrā also includes[563] what are called Bandha (bindings), certain physical methods of controlling Prāna. Three important ones which are referred to in the texts here translated are Uddīyāna, Mūla, and Jālandhara.[563] In the first it is said the lungs are emptied by a strong expiration, and drawn against the upper part of the thorax, carrying the diaphragm along with them, and the intestines are taken up and fill the vacant space.[564] This causes the Prāna to rise and

---

[558] *Ib.*, v. 25 *et seq.*

[559] Gheranda Sanghitā, Ch. III., v. 114 *et seq.*

[560] So called, according to the Dhyānabindu Up., because Chitta moves in Kha (Ākāsha), and the tongue through this Mudrā enters Kha.

[561] Gheranda Sanghitā, Ch. III., vv. 25-27. Suspension of breath and insensibility result, so that the Yogī may be buried in the ground without air, food, or drink, as in the case of the Yogī spoken of in the accounts of Dr. McGregor and Lieut. A. H. Boileau, cited in N. C. Paul's "Treatise on the Yoga Philosophy," p. 49. In Ch. IV., v. 80, of the Hathayogapradīpikā, it is said that concentration between the eyebrows is the easiest and quickest way of attainment of Unmanī Avasthā. See Shāndilya Up., Ch. I.; Dhyānabindu Up.

[562] Yogakundalī Up., Ch. II.

[563] *Ib.*, Ch. III., vv. 55 -76. There is also the Mahābandha. Ch. II., v. 45, says that Jālandhara should be done at the end of Puraka; and Uddīyāna Bandha at the end of Kumbhaka and beginning of Rechaka. See also Yogakundalī Up., Ch. I.

[564] *Ib.*, Ch. III., v. 57; Yogatattva Up., Dhyānabindu Up. The Varāha Up., Ch. V., says that as Prāna is always flying up (Udyāna), so this Bandha, by which its flight is

enter the Sushumnā. Through Mūlabandha the Prāna and Apāna unite[565] and go into the Sushumnā. Then the inner "sounds" are heard—that is, a vibration is felt—and Prāna and Apāna, uniting with Nāda of the cardiac Anāhata Chakra, go to the heart, and are thereafter united with Bindu in the Ājnā. In Mūlabandha the perinæal region (Yoni) is pressed with the foot, the rectal muscle contracted (by Ashvinī Mudrā), and the Apāna drawn up.[566] The natural course of the Apāna is downwards, but by contraction at the Mūlādhāra it is made to go upwards through the Sushumnā when it meets Prāna. When the latter Vāyu reaches the region of fire below the navel,[567] the fire becomes bright and strong, being fanned by Apāna. The heat in the body then becomes very powerful, and Kundalinī, feeling it, awakes from Her sleep "just as a serpent struck by a stick hisses and straightens itself." Then it enters the Sushumnā. Jālandhara Bandha is done by deep inspiration and then contraction of the thoracic region (wherein is situated the Vishuddha Chakra), the chin being held firmly pressed against the breasts at the distance of four fingers (Anguli) from the heart. This is said to bind the sixteen Adhāras,[568] or vital centers, and the nectar Satravi which flows from the cavity above the palate,[569] and is also used to cause the breath to become Laya in the Sushumnā. If the thoracic and perinæal regions are simultaneously contracted, and Prāna is forced downward and Apāna upward, the Vāyu enters the Sushumnā.[570] This union of the three Nādīs, Idā, Pinggalā, and Sushumnā, may be also affected by the Mahābandha,[571] which also aids the fixation of the mind in the Ājnā. Pressure is done on the perinæal region between the anus and penis with the left ankle, the right foot being placed on the left thigh. Breath is inspired and the chin placed firmly on the breast as in Jālandhara, or alternatively the tongue is

---

arrested, is called Uddiyānabandha. Yogakundalī Up., Ch. I., says, because Prāna uddiyate (goes up) the Sushumnā in this Bandha, it is called Uddīyāna.

[565] The Shāndilya Up., Ch. I., defines Prānāyāma to be the union of Prāna and Apāna. Nāda and Bindu are thus united.

[566] See Āgamakalpadruma, cited in notes to S.N., v. 50, *post*, Comm., and Dhyānabindu Up. The Yogakundalī Up., Ch. I., says that the downward tendency of Apāna is forced up by bending down.

[567] Vahner mandalang trikonang nābheradho bhāgo (Hathayogapradīpikā, *ib.*, v. 66).

[568] See Commentary, *post*, v. 33.

[569] The "Moon" is situate in the palatal region near the Ājnā. Here is the Somachakra under the Ājnā, and from the Somachakra comes a stream of nectar which, according to some, has its origin above. It descends to the "Sun" near the navel, which swallows it. By the process of Viparītakarania these are made to change positions, and the internal fire (Jatharāgni) is increased.

[570] Hathayogapradīpikā, II., vv. 46, 47; Yogatattva Up., Dhyānabindu Up. Yogakundalī Up. (Ch. I.) says that the contraction of the upper part of the body is an impediment to the passage of the Vāyu upwards.

[571] Dhyānabindu Up., *ib.*, III., v. 19, done in conjunction with Mahāmudrā and Mahāvedha, described *post*; *ib.*, v. 25, and Yogatattva Upanishad.

pressed firmly against the base of the front teeth; and while the mind is centered on the Sushumnā the Vāyu is contracted. After the breath has been restrained as long as possible, it should be expired slowly. The breath exercise should be done first on the left and then on the right side. The effect of this Bandha is to stop the upward course of the breath through all the Nādīs except the Sushumnā.

As the Dhyānabindu Upanishad says, the Jīva oscillates up and down under the influence of Prāna and Apāna and is never at rest, just as a ball which is hit to the earth with the palm of the hand uprises again, or like a bird which, tied to its perch by a string, flies away and is drawn back again. These movements, like all other dualities, are stayed by Yoga, which unites the Prānas.

When the physical body has been purified and controlled, there follows Pratyahāra to secure steadiness (Dhairya), as already described. With this the Yogī passes from the physical plane, and seeks to acquire the equipoise of, and control over, the subtle body.

From the fifth or Prānāyāma arises lightness (Lāghava)—that is, the levitation or lightening of the body.

The air which is breathed through the mouth and nostrils is material air (Sthūla Vāyu). The breathing is a manifestation of a vitalizing force called Prāna Vāyu. By control over the Sthūla Vāyu the Prāna Vāyu (Sūkshma Vāyu or subtle air) is controlled; the process concerned with this is called Prānāyāma.

Prānāyāma is frequently translated "breath control." Having regard to the processes employed, the term is not altogether inappropriate if it is understood that "breath" means not only the Sthūla but the Sūkshma Vāyu. But the word does not come from Prāna (breath) and Yama (control), but from Prāna and Āyāma, which latter term, according to the Amarakosha, means length, rising, extensity, expansion;[572] in other words, it is the process whereby the ordinary and comparatively slight manifestation of Prāna is lengthened and strengthened and developed. This takes place firstly in the Prāna as it courses in Idā and Pinggalā, and then by its transference to the Sushumnā, when it is said to bloom (Sphurati)[573] or to display itself in its fullness. When the body has been purified by constant practice, Prāna forces its way with ease through Sushumnā in their middle.[574] From being the small path of daily experience, it becomes the "Royal Road"[575] which is the Sushumnā. Thus, Suryabheda Kumbhaka is practiced until Prāna is felt to pervade the whole of the body from head to toe; Ujjayi until the breath fills the body from throat to heart; and in Bhasra the breath is inhaled and exhaled again and again rapidly, as the blacksmith works his bellows.

---

[572] Dairghyamāyāma āroha parināho vishālatā (Amarakosha Dictionary).

[573] Comm. Hathayogapradīpikā, III., v. 27.

[574] Shāndilya Up., Ch. I.

[575] Prānasya shūnyapadavī tathā rājapathāyate (*ib.*, vv. 2, 3).

The breath is controlled only in the sense that it is made the subject of certain initial processes. These processes, however, do not control in the sense of confine, but expand. The most appropriate term, therefore, for Prānāyāma is. "breath control and development," leading to the union of Prāna and Apāna. Prānāyāma is first practiced with a view to control and develop the Prāna. The latter is then moved into Sushumnā by the stirring of Kundalinī, who blocks the entry (Brahmadvāra) thereto. With the disappearance of Prāna therefrom, Idā and Pinggalā "die,"[576] and the Prāna in Sushumnā by means of the Shakti Kundalinī pierces the six Chakras which block the passage in the Brahmanādi, and eventually becomes Laya in the Great Breath which is the final end and aim of this process.

Prānāyāma[577] should be practiced according to the instructions laid down by the Guru, the Sādhaka living on a nutritious but moderate diet, with his senses under control. As already stated, mind and breath react upon one another, and when the latter is regulated so is the mind, and therefore rhythmic breathing is sought. This. Prānāyāma is said to be successful only when the Nādis are purified, for unless this is so the Prāna does not enter the Sushumnā.[578] The Yogī, assuming the Padmāsana posture, inhales (Puraka) and exhales (Rechaka) alternately through the left (Idā) and right (Pinggalā) nostrils, retaining the breath meanwhile (Kumbhaka) for gradually increasing periods. The Devatās of these elements of Prānāyāma are Brahmā, Rudra, and Vishnu.[579] The Prāna enters Sushumnā, and if retained sufficiently long goes, after the piercing of the Chakras, to the Brahmarandhra. The Yoga manuals speak of various forms of Prānāyāma according as commencement is made with Rechaka or Pūraka, and according as the breath is suddenly stopped without Pūraka and Rechaka. There are also various forms of Kumbhaka, such as Sahita Kumbhaka, which resembles the first two above mentioned, and which should be practiced until the Prāna enters the Sushumnā; and Kevala, in which the breath is restrained without Puraka and Rechaka.[580] Then there are others which cure excess of

---

[576] That is, they are relaxed and devitalized, as every part of the body is from which the Prāna Shakti is withdrawn.

[577] The Shāndilya Up., Ch. I., says: "As lions, elephants, and tigers, are gradually tamed, so also the breath when rightly managed comes under control; else it kills the practitioner." It should not, therefore, be attempted without instruction. Many have injured themselves and some have died through mistakes made in the processes, which must be adapted to the needs of each person. Hence the necessity for an experienced Guru.

[578] Hathayogapradīpikā, Ch. II., vv. 1-6 (see p. cxxviii. of my Introduction to the Mahānirvāna Tantra).

[579] Dhyānabindu Up., and see Amritanāda Up., Varāha Up., Ch. V., Mandalabrāhmana Up.

[580] The Shāndilya Up., Ch. I., says that by Kevala the knowledge of Kundalī arises, and man becomes Ūrddhvaretas—that is, his seminal energy goes upward instead of developing into the gross seed which is thrown by Apāna downwards. Bindu (seminal

Vāta, Pitta, and Kapha,[581] and the diseases arising therefrom; and Bhasra, which is an important Kumbhaka, as it operates in the case of all three Doshas,[581] and aids the Prāna to break through the three Grant his, which are firmly placed in the Sushumnā.[582]

It will be observed that all the methods previously and subsequently described practically subserve one object, the making of the Prāna enter Sushumnā, and then become Laya in the Sahasrāra after the Prāna Devatā Kundalinī has pierced the intervening Chakras; for when Prāna flows through the Sushumnā the mind becomes steady. When Chit is absorbed in Sushumnā, Prāna is motionless.[583] This object colors also the methods Pratyāhāra, Dhāranā, Dhyāna, and Samādhi; for whereas in the Rājayoga aspect they are various mental processes and states, from the Hathayoga point of view, which is concerned with "breathing," they are progressions in Prānāyāma. Therefore it is that some works describe them differently to harmonize them with the Hatha theory and practice, and explain them as degrees of Kumbhaka varying according to the length of its duration.[584] Thus, if the Prāna is retained for a particular time it is called Pratyāhāra, if for a longer time it is called Dhāranā, and so on until Samādhi is attained, which is equivalent to its retention for the longest period.[585]

All beings say the Ajapā Gāyatrī,[586] which is the expulsion of the breath by Hangkāra, and its inspiration by Sahkāra, 21,600 times a day. Ordinarily the breath goes forth a distance of 12 fingers' breadth, but in singing, eating, walking, sleeping, coition, the distances are 16, 20, 24, 30, and 36 breadths, respectively. In violent exercise these distances are exceeded, the greatest distance being 96 breadths. Where the breathing is under the normal distance, life is prolonged. Where it is above that, it is shortened. Puraka is inspiration, and Rechaka expiration. Kumbhaka is the retention of breath between these two movements. Kumbhaka is, according to the Gheranda Sanghitā, of eight kinds: Sahita, Sūryyabheda, Ujjāyī, Shītalī, Bhastrikā, Bhrāmarī, Mūrchchhā, and Kevalī. Prānāyāma similarly varies. Prānāyāma awakens Shakti, frees from disease, produces detachment from the world, and bliss. It is of varying values, being the best (Uttama) where the measure is 20; middling (Madhyama) when at 16 it produces spinal tremor; and inferior (Adhama) when at 12 it induces perspiration. It is necessary that the Nādī should be cleansed, for air does not enter those which are

---

energy) must be conquered, or the Yoga fails. As to the Bhedas associated with Sahita, see Ch. I., Yogakundalī Upanishad.

581 See Introduction to Prapanchasāra Tantra, Tantrik Texts, Vol. III., p. 11 *et seq.*

582 Hathayogapradīpikā, II. 44-75.

583 Yogakundalī Up., Ch. I.

584 See Yoga Sūtra, ed. Manual Nabhubhai Dvivedi, Ap. VI.

585 See Comm. to Hathayogapradīpikā, Ch. II., v. 12.

586 This is the Mantra Hangsah manifested by Prāna. See Dhyānabindu Up. Hangsah is Jīvātmā, and Paramahangsa is Paramātmā. See Hangsa Upanishad.

impure. Months or years may be spent in the preliminary process of cleansing the Nādīs. The cleansing of the Nādī (Nādīshuddhi) is either Samanu or Nirmanu—that is, with or without the use of Bīja. According to the first form, the Yogī in Padmāsana does Gurunyāsa according to the directions of the Guru. Meditating on "Yang," he does Japa through Idā of the Bīja 16 times, Kumbhaka with Japa of Bīja 64 times, and then exhalation through the solar Nādī and Japa of Bīja 32 times. Fire is raised from Manipūra and united with Prithivī. Then follows inhalation by the solar Nādī with the Vahni Bīja 16 times, Kumbhaka with 64 Japa of the Bīja, followed by exhalation through the lunar Nādī and Japa of the Bīja 32 times. He then meditates on the lunar brilliance, gazing at the tip of the nose, and inhales by Idā with Japa of the Bīja "Thang" 16 times. Kumbhaka is done with the Bīja Vang 64 times. He then thinks of himself as flooded by nectar, and considers that the Nādī have been washed. He exhales by Pinggalā with 32 Japa of the Bīja Lang, and considers himself thereby as strengthened. He then takes his seat on a mat of Kusha grass, a deerskin, etc., and, facing east or north, does Prānāyāma. For its exercise there must be, in addition to Nādi Shuddhi (purification of "nerves"), consideration of proper place, time, and food. Thus, the place should not be so distant as to induce anxiety, nor in an unprotected place, such as a forest, nor in a city or crowded locality, which induces distraction. The food should be pure and of a vegetarian character. It should not be too hot or too cold, pungent, sour, salt, or bitter. Fasting, the taking of one meal a day and the like are prohibited. On the contrary, the Yogī should not remain without food for more than one Yāma (three hours). The food taken should be light and strengthening. Long walks and other violent exercise should be avoided, as also—certainly in the case of beginners—sexual intercourse. The stomach should only be half filled. Yoga should be commenced, it is said, in spring or autumn. As stated, the forms of Prānāyāma vary. Thus, Sahita, which is either with (Sagarbha) or without (Nirgarbha) Bīja, is, according to the former form, as follows: The Sādhaka meditates on Vidhi (Brahmā), who is full of Rajoguna, red in color, and the image of Akāra. He inhales by Idā, in six measures (Mātrā). Before Kumbhaka he does the Uddīyānabandha Mudrā. Meditating on Hari (Vishnu) as Sattvamaya and the black Bīja Ukāra, he does Kumbhaka with 64 Japa of the Bīja; then, meditating on Shiva as Tamomaya and his white Bīja Makāra, he exhales through Pinggalā with 32 Japa of the Bīja; then, inhaling by Pinggalā, he does Kumbhaka, and exhales by Idā with the same Bīja. The process is repeated in the normal and reversed order.

Dhyāna, or meditation, is, according to the Gheranda Sanghitā, of three kinds: (1) Sthūla, or gross; (2) Jyotih; (3) Sūkshma, or subtle.[587] In the first the form of the Devatā is brought before the mind. One form of Dhyāna for this purpose is as follows: Let the Sādhaka think of the great Ocean of Nectar in his heart. In the middle of that ocean is the island of gems, the shores of which are made of powdered gems. The island is clothed with a Kadamba forest in yellow blossom. This forest is surrounded by Mālatī, Champaka, Pārijāta, and other fragrant trees. In the midst of the Kadamba forest there rises the beautiful Kalpa tree, laden with fresh blossom and fruit. Amidst its leaves the black bees hum and the Koel birds make love. Its four branches are the four Vedas. Under the tree there is a great Mandapa of precious stones, and within it a beautiful couch, on which let him picture to himself his Ishtadevatā. The Guru will direct him as to the form, raiment, Vāhana, and the title of the Devatā.

Jyotirdhyāna is the infusion of fire and life (Tejas) into the form so imagined. In the Mūlādhāra lies the snakelike Kundalinī. There the Jīvātmā, as it were the tapering flame of a candle, dwells. The Sādhaka then meditates upon the Tejomaya (Light) Brahman, or, alternatively, between the eyebrows on the Pranavātmaka flame (the light which is Om) emitting its luster.

Sūkshmadhyāna is meditation on Kuṇḍalinī with Shāmbhavī Mudrā after She has been roused. By this Yoga (*vide post*) the Ātmā is revealed (Ātmasākshātkāra).

Lastly, through Samādhi the quality of Nirliptatva, or detachment, and thereafter Mukti (liberation) is attained.

This Samādhi Yoga is, according to the Gheranda Sanghitā, of six kinds:[588] (1) Dhyānayogasamādhi, attained by Shāmbhavī Mudrā,[589] in which, after meditation on the Bindu-Brahman and realization of the Ātmā (Ātmapratyaksha), the latter is resolved into the Mahākāsha or the Great Ether. (2) Nādayoga, attained by Khecharī Mudrā,[590] in which the *frænum* of the tongue is cut, and the latter is lengthened until it reaches the space between the eyebrows, and is then introduced in a reversed position into the mouth. (3) Rasānandayoga, attained by Kumbhaka,[591] in which the Sādhaka in a silent place closes both ears and does Pūraka and Kumbhaka until he hears Nāda in sounds varying in strength from that of the cricket's chirp to that of the large

---

[587] Gheranda Sanghitā, Sixth Upadesha. It is said by Bhāskararāya, in the Lalitā (v. 2), that there are three forms of the Devī which equally partake of both the Prakāsha and Vimarsha aspects—viz., the physical (Sthūla), the subtle (Sūkshma), and the supreme (Para). The physical form has hands, feet, etc., the subtle consists of Mantra, and the supreme is the Vāsanā, or, in the technical sense of the Mantra Shāstrā, real or own. The Kulārnava Tantra divides Dhyāna into sthūla and sūkshma (IX. 3).

[588] Seventh Upadesha.

[589] *Ibid.*, Third Upadesha, v. 65 *et seq.*

[590] *Ibid.*, v. 25 *et seq.*

[591] *Ibid.*, Fifth Upadesha, v. 77 *et seq.*

kettledrum. By daily practice the Anāhata sound is heard, and the Light (Jyotih) with the Manas therein is seen, which is ultimately dissolved in the supreme Vishnu. (4) Layasiddhiyoga accomplished by the celebrated Yonimudrā already described.[592] The Sādhaka, thinking of himself as Shakti and the Paramātmā as Purusha, feels himself in union (Sanggama) with Shiva, and enjoys with Him the bliss which is Shringārarasa,[593] and becomes Bliss itself, or the Brahman. (5) Bhakti Yoga, in which meditation is made on the Ishtadevatā with devotion (Bhakti) until, with tears flowing from the excess of bliss, the ecstatic condition is attained. (6) Rājayoga, accomplished by aid of the Manomūrchchhā Kumbhaka.[594] Here the Manas, detached from all worldly objects, is fixed between the eyebrows in the Ājnāchakra, and Kumbhaka is done. By the union of the Manas with the Ātmā, in which the Jnāni sees all things, Rājayogasamādhi is attained.

The Hathayogapradīpikā says that on perfection being attained in Hatha the body becomes lean and healthy, the eyes are bright, the semen is concentrated, the Nādīs are purified, the internal fire is increased, and the Nāda sounds above-mentioned are heard.[595] These sounds (Nāda) issue from Anāhata Chakra in the cardiac region, for it is here that the Shabdabrahman manifested by Vāyu and in association with Buddhi, and of the nature of manifested Nāda endowed with a special motion (Vishesha Spanda), exists as Madhyamā speech. Though sound (Shabda) is not distinct and heard by the gross senses until it issues in the form of Vaikharī speech, the Yogī is said to hear this subtle Nāda when, through the various Bandhas and Mudrās described, Prāna and Apāna have united in the Sushumnā. This combined Prāna and Nāda proceed upwards and unite with Bindu.

There is a particular method by which Laya (absorption) is said to be attained by hearing the various bodily sounds.[596] The Yogī in Muktāsana and with Shāmbhavīmudrā concentrates on the sounds heard in the right ear; then after closing the sense apertures by Shanmukhi Mudrā and after Prānāyāma a sound is heard in the Sushumnā. In this Yoga there are four stages. When the Brahmagranthi

---

592 In the Lalitā (v. 142) the Devī is addressed as Layakarī—the cause of Laya or absorption.

593 Shringgāra is the love sentiment or sexual passion and sexual union. Here Shringārarasa is the cosmic root of that. The first of the eight or nine rasa (sentiments)—viz., Shringgāra, Vīra (heroism), Karunā (compassion), Adbhūta (wondering), Hāsya (humor), Bhayānaka (fear), Bībhatsa (disgust), Raudra (wrath), to which Mammathabhatta, author of the Kāvyaprakāsha, adds Shānti (peace). What the Yogī enjoys is that super-sensual bliss which manifests on the earthly plane as material Shringāra.

594 *Ibid.*, Fifth Upadesha, v. 82.

595 Ch. II., v. 78.

596 As the Nādabindu Up. says, the sound controls the mind, which roves in the pleasure-garden of the senses.

has been pierced, the sweet tinkling sound of ornaments is heard in the ethereal void (Shūnya) of the heart; in the second stage the Prāna united with Nāda pierces the Vishnugranthi. In this the further void (Atishūnya) of the thoracic region, sounds are heard like those of a kettle-drum. In the third stage a drum-like sound (Mardala) is heard in the Ājnā or Mahāshūnya, the seat of all powers (Siddhis). Then the Prāna, having forced the Rudragranthi or Ājnā, goes to the abode of Īshvara. On the insetting of the fourth stage, when the Prāna goes to Brahmarandhra, the fourth or Nishpatti state occurs. During the initial stages the sounds are loud, and gradually become very subtle. The mind is kept oft all external objects, and is centered first on the loud and then on the subtle sounds. The mind thus becomes one with Nāda, on which it is fixed. Nāda is thus like a snare for catching a deer, for like a hunter it kills the mind. It first attracts it and then slays it. The mind absorbed in Nāda is freed from Vrittis.[597] The Antahkarana, like a deer, is attracted to the sound of the bells, and, remaining immovable, the Yogī like a skilful archer kills it by directing his breath to the Brahmarandhra through the Sushumnā, which becomes one with that at which it is aimed. Chit exists within these sounds, which are its Shaktis, and by union with Nāda the self-effulgent Chaitanya (Consciousness) is said to be attained. As long as sound is heard the Ātmā is with Shakti. The Laya state is soundless.[598] There are also other methods[599] by which Laya is achieved, such as Mantrayoga, or the recitation of Mantras according to a particular method.

Layayoga is the third and higher form of Hathayoga, which, in connection with other auxiliary Hatha processes, is in its Tantrik form the subject-matter of the works here translated. Both Sachchidānandā or Shiva and Sachchidānandā or Shakti are present in the body, and Layayoga consists in the control of Chittavritti by merging the Prakriti Shakti in the Purusha Shakti according to the laws which govern the Pinda (individual—Vyashti) and Brahmānda (cosmic—Samashti) bodies, and thereby gaining liberation (Moksha).

As in the case of the preceding systems, Layayoga has special features of its own.[600] Speaking in a general way, ordinary Hathayoga is specially, though not exclusively concerned, with the physical body, its power and functions; and affects the subtle body through the gross body. Mantra Yoga is specially, though not exclusively, concerned with

---

[597] As the Amritanāda Upanishad says (v. 24), the Akshara (imperishable) is that which is Aghosha (without sound), which is neither vowel nor consonant and is not uttered.

[598] Hathayogapradīpīka, Ch. IV., vv. 65-102.

[599] Amritanāda Upanishad, Ch. IV., v. 66, says that Shiva has given out a quarter of a crore (2,500,000) of ways for the attainment of Laya, though Nāda is the best of them all.

[600] See Dharma Prachāra Series, 9.

the forces and powers at work outside, though affecting the body. Layayoga deals with the supersensible Pīthas (seats or centers) and the supersensible forces and functions of the inner world of the body. These Pīthas, or seats of the Devatās, are the Chakras already described, ranging from the Sahasrāra, the abode of the unattached (Nirlipta) Sachchidānandamaya Paramātmā, to the Mūlādhāra, the seat of Prakriti-Shakti, called Kulakundalinī in the Yoga Shāstras. The object of this Yoga is therefore to take and merge this Shakti in Purusha when Samādhi is attained. In Hathayoga the contemplation of "Light" is in particular prescribed, though, as already stated, its Dhyāna is threefold. In Mantrayoga the material forms in which Spirit clothes Itself are contemplated. After Prakriti-Shakti in the form of Kulakundalinī has according to this method of Layayoga been roused by constant practice, its reflection is manifested as a Light between the eyebrows, which when it is fixed by practice and contemplation becomes the subject of Bindudhyāna. Kundalī is aroused by various Hatha and other processes hereafter described. Methods are followed which are common to all the systems, such as Yama, Niyama, Āsana, though only a limited number of these and of the Mudrā of Hathayoga are used. These belong to the physical processes (Sthūla Kriyā), and are followed by Prānāyāma,[601] Pratyāhāra, Dhāranā, Dhyāna (on Bindu), which are super-physical exercises (Sūkshmā Kriyā). In addition to these are certain features peculiar to this Yoga. There are, besides those already noted, Svarodaya, or the science relating to the Nādīs; Panchatattva Chakra, Sūkshmaprāna, and the like inner forces of nature; and the Layakriyā, leading through Nāda and Bindu to the Samādhi, which is called Mahālaya.

The hearing of the Nāda sounds is included under Pratyāhāra, and under Dhāranā the rousing of Kundalī. As Japa, or recitation of Mantra, is the chief element in Mantrayoga, and Prānāyāma in the ordinary Hathayoga, so Dhāranā is, with the last as a preliminary, the most important part of Layayoga. It is to be observed, however, that Prānāyāma is only a preliminary method to secure mastery of the breath. It is the lower door at which the already perfect in this matter need not enter. Some processes described are for practice (Sādhanā) only. An expert (Siddha) can raise and lower Kundalī Shakti within an hour.

It is said that as Ananta, the Lord of Serpents, supports the whole universe, so is Kundalinī, "by whom the body is supported,"[602] the support of all Yoga practice;[603] and that "as one forces open a door with

---

[601] Of the several forms of Prānāyāma given in Hathayoga, it is said that only two are employed in Layayoga.

[602] Varāha Upanishad, Ch. V.

[603] Hathayogapradīpikā, Ch. III., v. 1: Sarveshāng yogatantrānāng tathādharohi Kundalī.

a key," so the Yogī should force open the door of liberation (Moksha) by the aid of Kundalinī[604] (the coiled one), who is known by various names, such as the Shakti, Īshvarī (Sovereign Lady); Kutilāngī (the crooked one), Bhujanggī (serpent), Arundhatī (unstayable helper to good action.)[605] This Shakti is the Supreme Shakti (Parashakti) in the human body, embodying all powers and assuming all forms. Thus the sexual force is one of such powers and is utilized. Instead, however, of descending into gross seminal fluid, it is conserved as a form of subtle energy, and rises to Shiva along with Prāna. It is thus made a source of spiritual life instead of one of the causes of physical death. With the extinction of sexual desire, mind is released of its most powerful bond.[606]

She the "Serpent Power" sleeps coiled up in the Mūlādhāra, closing with Her mouth the entry to the Sushumnā called the "door of Brahman" (Brahmadvāra). She sleeps above what is called the Kanda or Kandayoni, which is four fingers in length and breadth, and is covered by a "soft white cloth"—that is, membrane like the egg of a bird. It is generally described as being two fingers (Anguli) above the anus (Guda) and two fingers below the penis (Medhra).[607] From this Kanda spring the 72,000 Nādīs which here both unite and separate. Kulakundalinī is the Shabdabrahman, and all Mantras are Her manifestation (Svarūpavibhūti). For this reason one of the names of this, the Mantradevatā, whose substance is "letters," is Mātrikā—that is, the Genetrix of all the universes. She is Mātrikā, for She is the Mother of all and not the child of any. She is the world-consciousness (Jagachchaitanya), the Virāta consciousness of the world as a whole.[608] Just as in space sound is produced by movements of air, so also in the ether within the Jīva's body currents flow, owing to the movements of the vital air (Prānavāyu), and its inward and outward passage as inhalation and exhalation. Verse 12 describes Kundalinī as the revered supreme Parameshvarī (Sovereign Lady), the Omnipotent Kalā in the form of Nādashakti. She, the subtlest of the subtle, holds within Herself

---

604 Hathayogapradīpikā, Ch. III., v. 105: Udghātayet kapātantu yathā kunchikayā hathāt Kundalinyā tathā yogī mokshadvārang vibhedayet. The same verse occurs in Ch. III., v. 5, of the Gheranda Sanghitā.

605 The Yogakundalī Up., Ch. I., calls Sarasvatī Arundhatī, saying that it is by arousing Her that Kundalī is aroused. When Kundalī wishes to go up nothing can stop Her. Therefore She is called Arundhatī, which is also the name of a Nādī.

606 Yogakundalī Upanishad, Ch. I.

607 As given by Yājnavalkya, cited in Commentary to v. 113, Ch. III., of Hathayogapradīpikā, which also refers to the Gorakshashataka. The verse itself appears to fix its position as between the penis and navel (Nābhi), twelve fingers (Vitasti) above the Mūlasthāna. Kanda is also applied to the seat of Prāna, the heart (see Shatchakranirūpana, v. 8).

608 See Vol. II., "Principles of Tantra," Ch. XI., XII., *et seq.* It is because She is Mantradevatā that She is roused by Mantra.

the mystery of creation,[609] and the stream of Ambrosia which flows from the attributeless Brahman. By Her radiance the universe is illumined, and by it eternal knowledge is awakened[610]—that is, She both binds as Creatrix (Avidyā Shakti) and is the means as Vidyā Shakti whereby liberation may be attained. For this reason it is said in the Hathayogapradīpikā that She gives liberation to Yogīs and bondage to the ignorant. For he who knows Her knows Yoga, and those who are ignorant of Yoga are kept in the bondage of this worldly life. As vv. 10 and 11 of the Shatchakranirūpana says, She the World-bewilderer is lustrous as lightning; "Her sweet murmur is like the indistinct hum of swarms of love-mad bees[611] and the soft cadence of sweet harmonious music. It is She who maintains all the beings of the world by means of inspiration and expiration,[612] and shines in the hollow of the Mūla lotus like a chain of brilliant lights." Mantras are in all cases manifestations (Vibhūti) of Kulakundalinī Herself, for She is all letters and Dhvani[613] and the Paramātmā Itself. Hence Mantras are used in the rousing of Kundalinī. The substance of Mantras is the Eternal Shabda or Consciousness, though their appearance and expression is in words. Words in themselves seem lifeless (Jada), but the Mantra power which they embody is Siddha—that is, the truth and capable of teaching it, because it is a manifestation of Chaitanya, which is Satya itself. So Veda, which is the formless (Amūrti) Brahman in Veda-form (Vedamūrti), is the self-illumined Principle of Experience[614] (Chit) itself, and is displayed in words (Siddhashabda) which are without human authorship (Apaurusheya),[615] incessantly revealing knowledge[616] of the nature of Brahman, or Pure Being, and of Dharmma,[617] or those principles and laws, physical and psychical and spiritual, by which the universe is sustained (Dhāryate). And so the

---

609 She is creation itself (Srishtirūpā), vv. 10, 11, *post*, in whom are creation, maintenance, and dissolution (Srishtisthitilayātmikā), *ib.*

610 For She is also beyond the universe (Vishvātītā), and is the form of knowledge itself (Jnānarūpā), *ib.* As such She is thought of as going upwards, as in descending She creates and binds.

611 Vishvanātha the Commentator says that She makes this sound when wakened. According to the Commentator Shangkara, this indicates the Vaikharī state of Kundalinī.

612 Thus, Prāna and Apāna are declared to be the maintainers of animate being (v. 8, *post*).

613 See "Principles of Tantra," Vol. II., Ch. XI. and XII.

614 Veda is one with Chaitanya. As Shangkara says (Comm. Trishatī, v. 19), dealing with the Panchadashī Mantra: Sarve vedā yatra ekam bhavanti, etc. Shrutyā vedasya ātmābhedena svaprakāshatayā.

615 And because it is without such authorship and is "heard" only it is called Shruti ("what is heard"): Shruyata eva natu kenachit kriyate (Vāchaspati Misra in Sāngkhya Tattva Kaumudī); and see the Yāmala cited in Prānatoshinī, 19: "Veda is Brahman; it came out as His breathing."

616 The term Veda is derived from the root *vid*, to know.

617 Veda, according to Vedānta, is that word without human authorship which tells of Brahman and Dharmma: Dharmmabrahmapratipādakam apaurusheya vākyam.

Divine Mother is said to be Brahman-knowledge (Brahmavidyā) in the form of that immediate experience[618] which is the fruit of the realization of the great Vedāntic sayings (Mahāvākya).[619] As, notwithstanding the existence of feeling-consciousness in all things, it does not manifest without particular processes, so, although the substance of Mantras is feeling-consciousness, that feeling-consciousness is not perceptible without the union of the Sādhaka's Shakti (derived from Sādhanā) with Mantrashakti. Hence it has been said in the Shāradā Tilaka: "Although Kulakundalinī, whose substance is Mantras, shines brilliant as lightning in the Mūlādhāra of every Jīva, yet it is only in the lotuses of the hearts of Yogīs that She reveals Herself and dances in Her own joy. (In other cases, though existing in subtle form,) She does not reveal Herself. Her substance is all Vedas, all Mantras, and all Tattvas. She is the Mother of the three forms of energy, 'Sun,' 'Moon,' and 'Fire,' and Shabdabrahman Itself." Kundalinī is therefore the mightiest manifestation of creative power in the human body. Kundalī is the Shabdabrahman—that is, Ātmā as manifested Shakti—in bodies, and in every power, person, and thing. The Six Centers and all evolved therefrom are Her manifestation. Shiva "dwells" in the Sahasrāra. The latter is the upper Shrīchakra, as the six centers are the lower. Yet Shakti and Shiva are one. Therefore the body of Kundalinī Shakti consists of eight parts (Angas)—namely, the six centers of psychic and physical force, Shakti, and Sadāshiva Her Lord.[620] In the Sahasrāra Kundalī is merged in the Supreme Ātma-Shakti. Kundalinī is the great Prānadevatā which is Nādātmā, and if Prāna is to be drawn up through the "middle path," the Sushumnā towards the Brahmarandha, it must of necessity pierce the lotuses or Chakras which bar the way therein. Kundalinī being Prānashakti, if She is moved Prāna is moved.

The Āsanas, Kumbhakas, Bandhas, and Mudrās, are used to rouse Kundalinī, so that the Prāna withdrawn from Idā and Pinggalā may by the power of its Shakti, after entry into the Sushumnā or void (Shūnya), go upwards towards the Brahmarandhra.[621] The Yogī is then said to be free of the active Karma, and attains the natural state.[622] The object, then, is to devitalize the rest of the body by getting the Prāna from Idā and Pinggalā into Sushumnā, which is for this reason regarded as the most important of all the Nādīs and "the delight of the Yogī," and then

[618] Sākshātkāra—that is, actual Spiritual Experience (Aparoksha jnāna) as opposed, to indirect (paroksha) or merely intellectual knowledge.

[619] Vedānta-mahāvākya janya-sākshātkārarūpa-brahmavidyā (Shangkara's Comm. on Trishatī, v. 8). The Vedānta here means Upanishad, and not any particular philosophy so called.

[620] See Lakshmīdhara's Comm. on v. 9, Ānandalaharī. Dindima on v. 35, *ib.*, says that the eight forms are the six (Mind to "Earth"), the Sun and Moon.

[621] Hathayogapradīpīkā, Ch. IV., v. 10.

[622] *Ib.*, v. 11; upon what follows refer also to Ch. IV., *ib.*, *passim.*

to make it ascend through the lotuses which "bloom" on its approach. The body on each side of the spinal column is devitalized, and the whole current of Prāna thrown into that column. The Manonmanī state is said to arise with the Laya of Prāna, for on this ensues Laya of Manas. By daily practicing restraint of Prāna in Sushumnā, the natural effort of the Prāna along its ordinary channels is weakened and the mind is steadied. For when there is movement (Parispanda) of Prāna there is movement of mind; that is, it feeds upon the objects (Vishaya) of the objective world.

But when Prāna is in Sushumnā "there is neither day nor night," for "Sushumnā devours time."[623] When there is movement of Prāna (Prānaspanda), there is no cessation of Vritti (mind functioning). And, as the Yogavāshishtha says, so long as Prāna does not cease to exist there is neither Tattvajnāna nor destruction of Vāsanā, the subtle cause of the will towards life which is the cause of rebirth. For Tattvajnāna, or supreme knowledge, is the destruction of both Chitta and Vāsanā.[624] Restraint of breath also renders the semen firm. For the semen fluctuates as long as Prāna does so. And when the semen is not steady the mind is not steady.[625] The mind thus trained detaches itself from the world. These various results are said to be achieved by rousing Kundalinī, and by the subsequent processes for which She is the "key." "As one forces open a door with a key, so the Yogī should force open the door of liberation by Kundalinī."[626] For it is She who sleeps in the Mūlādhāra, closing with Her mouth the channel (Sushumnā) by which ascent may be made to the Brahmarandhra. This must be opened when the Prāna naturally enters into it. "She, the young widow, is to be despoiled forcibly." It is prescribed that there shall be daily practice, with a view to acquire power to manipulate this Shakti.[627]

It generally takes years from the commencement of the practice to lead the Shakti to the Sahasrāra. At first She can only be led to a certain point, and then gradually higher. He who has led her to a particular center can reach the same center more easily at the next attempt. But to go higher requires further effort. At each center a particular kind of bliss (Ānanda) is experienced, and particular powers, such as the conquest of the elementary forms of sensible matter (Bhūta) are gained, until at the Ājnā center the whole universe is experienced. In the earlier stages, moreover, there is a natural tendency of the Shakti to return. In the continued practice facility and greater control are gained. Where the Nādīs are pure it is easy to lead Her down even from the Sahasrāra. In

[623] *Ib.*, vv. 16 and 17, Commentary thereto.

[624] *Ib.*, vv. 19-21, and Commentary (Tattvajnānang manonāsho vāsanākshaya eva cha).

[625] See *ante*, and Varāha Up., Ch. V.

[626] *Ib.*, Ch. III., v. 106. See Bhūtashuddhi Tantra cited in v. 50, *post.*

[627] *Ib.*, Ch. III., v. 112 *et seq.*

the perfection of practice the Yogī can stay as long as he will in the Sahasrāra, where the bliss is the same as that experienced in liberation (subject in this case to return), or he may transfer himself into another body, a practice known to both the Indian and Tibetan Tantras, in the latter of which it is called Phowa.

The principle of all the methods to attain Samādhi is to get the Prāna out of Idā and Pinggalā. When this is achieved these Nādīs become "dead," because vitality has gone out of them. The Prāna then enters the Sushumnā, and, after piercing by the aid of Kundalinī, the six Chakras in the Sushumnā becomes Laya or absorbed in the Sahasrāra. The means to this end, when operating from the Mūlādhāra, seem to vary in detail, but embody a common principle—namely, the forcing of Prāna downward and Apāna upwards[628] (that is, the reverse of their natural directions) by the Jālandhara and Mūlabandha, or otherwise, when by their union the internal fire is increased. The position is thus similar to a hollow tube in which a piston is working at both ends without escape of the central air, which thus becomes heated. Then the serpent force Kundalinī, aroused by the heat thus generated, is aroused from Her potential state called "sleep," in which She lies curled up; She then hisses and straightens Herself, and enters the Brahmadvāra, or entry into the Sushumnā, when by further repeated efforts the Chakras in the Sushumnā are pierced. This is a gradual process which is accompanied by special difficulties at the three knots (Granthis) where Māyāshakti is powerful, particularly the abdominal knot, the piercing of which may, it is admitted, involve considerable pain, physical disorder, and even disease. As already explained, these "knots" are the points at which converge the Chakras of each of the three groups. Some of the above-mentioned processes are described in the present work, to which we now proceed, and which on this matter may be summarized as follows:—

The preliminary verse (and in the reference to the verses I conclude the Commentary) says that only those who are acquainted with the Six Lotuses can deal with them; and the first verse says that Yoga by means of the method here described cannot be achieved without knowledge of the Chakras and Nādīs. The first verse says that the Brahman will be realized. The next question is, How is this effected? The Commentator in the preliminary verse says that the very merciful Pūrnānanda Svāmī, being wishful to rescue the world sunk in the mire of misery, has undertaken the task firstly of instructing it as regards the union of the Shakti Kundalinī with the vital centers, or Chakras, and secondly of imparting that knowledge of Brahman (Tattvajāna) which leads to liberation. The former—that is, knowledge concerning the Chakras, and so forth—is the "first shoot" of the Yoga

[628] See Varāha Upanishad, Ch. III.

plant. Brahman, as the Commentator says, is the Supreme Consciousness which arises upon the acquisition of knowledge. The first cause of such knowledge is an acquaintance with and practice of the Tantrik Yoga Sādhanā, which is concerned with the Chakras, Nādis, and Kundalinī; the next cause is the realization of that Sādhanā by the rousing of Kundalinī; and the final result is the experiential realization of the Brahman, which is the effect of the action of Kundalinī, who is the Shakti or power of will (Ichchhā), action (Kriyā), and knowledge (Jnāna), and exists in forms both subtle and gross. Mind is as much one of the forms of Kundalī as is that which is called "matter." Both are equally products of Prakritishakti, which is a grosser form of the Nādamaya Shakti. Kundalī takes the form of the eight Prakritis.[629] It is necessary to bear this well in mind, or there is likely to be uninstructed criticism of the system on the ground of its supposed "materialism," and so forth. The Power which is aroused is in itself (Svarūpa) Consciousness, and when aroused and taken to the upper cerebral center is the giver of true knowledge (Svarūpa Jnāna), which is the Supreme Consciousness.

The arousing of this force is achieved both by will and mind power (Yogabala), accompanied by suitable physical action. The Sādhaka[630] sits himself in the prescribed Āsana and steadies his mind by the Khecharī Mudrā, in which concentration is between the eyebrows. Air is inhaled (Pūraka) and then retained (Kumbhaka). The upper part of the body is then contracted by Jālandharabandha,[631] so that the upward breath (Prāna) is checked. By this contraction the air so inhaled is prevented from escape. The air so checked tends downwards. When the Yogī feels that the air within him, from the throat to the belly, is tending downwards through the channels in the Nādīs, the escape of Vāyu as Apāna is again checked by the Mūlabandha and Ashvinī Mudrā, in which the anal muscle is contracted. The air (Vāyu) thus stored becomes an instrument by which, under the direction of mind and will, the potentialities of the vital force in the Mūlādhāra may be forced to realization. The process of mental concentration on this center is described as follows: With mental Japa of the Mantra prescribed, and acquisition thereby of Mantrashakti, the Jīvātmā (individual Consciousness), which is thought of as being in the shape of the tapering flame of a lamp, is brought from the region of the heart to the Mūlādhāra. The Jīvātmā here spoken of is the Ātmā of the subtle body—that is, the Antahkarana or mind as Buddhi (including therein Ahangkāra) and Manas, the faculties of sense (Indriya) or mind operating to receive sense impression through the sense organs, and

[629] Shāndilya Upanishad, Ch. I.; Yogakundalī Up., Ch. I.

[630] The account here given follows and amplifies the text. See Commentary to v. 50, *post.*

[631] *Vide ante* and Dhyānabindu Up.

Prāna;[632] the constituents of the second, third, and fourth bodily sheaths. Following such concentration and impact of the retained Vāyu on this center, the Vāyu is again raised with the Bīja "Yang." A revolution from left to right is given to the "air of Kāma" or Kandarpa (Kāmavāyu). This is a form of Ichchhā Shakti. This, the pressure of the Prāna and Apāna held in Kumbhaka, the natural heat arising therefrom, and the Vahni Bīja (Fire Mantra) "Rang," kindle the fire of Kāma (Kāmāgni). The fire encircles and arouses the slumbering serpent Kundalinī, who is then, in the language of the Shāstra, seized with the passion of "desire" for Her Spouse, the Parahangsah or Paramashiva. Shakti thus rendered active is drawn to Shiva, as in the case of ordinary positive and negative electric charges, which are themselves but other manifestations of the universal polarity which affects the manifested world.

The Yogakundalī Upanishad[633] states the following methods and others mentioned: When Prāna is passing through Idā, assume Padmāsana and lengthen the Ākāsha of 12 points by 4—that is, as in exhalation Prāna goes out 16 measures, and in inhalation comes in 12, inhale for 16 and thus gain power. Then, holding the sides by each hand, stir up Kundalinī with all one's strength from right to left fearlessly for 48 minutes. Draw the body up a little to let Kundalī enter Sushumnā. The Yogī does a drawing-up movement in which the shoulders are raised and dropped. Prāna enters of itself with Her. Compressing above and expanding below, and *vice versa*, Prāna rises.

In the commentary[634] on verse 32 of the Ānandalaharī it is said: "The sun and the moon, as they move always in Devayāna and Pitriyāna (northern and southern orbs) in the Macrocosm, are travelling (incessantly in the Microcosm) by Idā and Pinggalā day and night. The moon, ever travelling by the left Nādī (Idā), bedews the whole system with her nectar. The sun, travelling by the right Nādī (Pinggalā), dries the system (thus moistened by nectar). When the sun and the moon meet at Mūlādhāra, that day is called Amāvasyā (new moon day). . . . The Kundalī also sleeps in Ādhārakunda. . . . When a Yogī whose mind is under control is able to confine the moon in her own place, as also the sun, then the moon and sun become confined, and consequently the moon cannot shed its nectar nor the sun dry it. Next, when the place of nectar becomes dried by the fire with the help of Vāyu, then the Kundalī wakes up for want of food and hisses like a serpent. Afterwards, breaking through the three knots, She runs to Sahasrāra and bites the Chandra (moon), which is in the middle of the same. Then

---

[632] According to the Vedāntik definition; or the five Tanmātras, according to Sāngkhya. The Chitta (mind) therefore enters Sushumnā along with Prāna (Yogatattva Upanishad and Dhyānabindu Up.).

[633] Ch. I.

[634] Ānandalaharī, ed. Pandit R. Ananta Shāstrī, pp. 69, 70.

the nectar begins to flow, and wets the (other) Chandra Mandala in Ājnāchakra. From the latter the whole body becomes bedewed with nectar. Afterwards the fifteen eternal Kalās (parts) of Chandra (moon) in Ājnā go to Vishuddhi and move thereon. The Chandra Mandala in Sahasrāra is also called Baindava. One Kalā remains there always. That Kalā is nothing but Chit Itself, which is also called Ātman. We call Her Tripurasundarī. It is understood by this that, in order to rouse the Kundalī, one should practice in the lunar fortnight alone, and not in the solar one."

Kundalinī is led upwards "as a rider guides a trained mare by the reins," through the aperture hitherto closed by Her own coils, but now open, within the entrance of the Chitrinī Nādī. She then pierces in that Nādī each of the lotuses, which turn their heads upwards as She passes through them. As Kundalinī united with the subtle Jīvātmā passes through each of these lotuses, She absorbs into Herself the regnant Tattvas of each of these centers, and all that has been above described to be in them. As the ascent is made, each of the grosser Tattvas enters into the Laya state, and is replaced by the energy of Kundalinī, which after the passage of the Vishuddha Chakra replaces them all. The senses which operate in association with these grosser Tattvas are merged in Her, who then absorbs into Herself the subtle Tattvas of the Ājnā. Kundalinī Herself takes on a different aspect as She ascends the three planes, and unites with each of the Lingas in that form of Hers which is appropriate to such union. For whereas in the Mūlādhāra She is the Shakti of all in their gross or physical manifested state (Virāt), at the stage of Ājnā She is the Shakti of the mental and psychic or subtle body (Hiranyagarbha), and in the region of the Sahasrāra She is the Shakti of the spiritual plane (Īshvara), which, though itself in its Brahman aspect undifferentiated, contains in its Power-aspect all lower planes in a concealed potential state. The Māyā Tantra (see v. 51, *post*) says that the four sound-producing Shaktis—namely, Parā, Pashyantī, Madhyamā, and Vaikharī—are Kundalī Herself (Kundalinyabhedarūpā). Hence, when Kundalī starts to go to Sahasrāra, She in Her form as Vaikharī bewitches Svayambhu Linga; She then similarly bewitches Bāna Linga in the heart as Madhyamā and Itara Linga in the eyebrows as Pashyantī. Then, when She reaches the stage of Parabindu, She attains the state of Parā (Parābhāva).

The upward movement is from the gross to the more subtle, and the order of dissolution of the Tattvas is as follows: Prithivī with the Indriyas (smell and feet), the latter of which have Prithivī (the earth as ground) as their support, is dissolved into Gandha Tattva, or Tanmātra of smell, which is in the Mūlādhāra; Gandha Tattva is then taken to the Svādishthāna, and it, Ap, and its connected Indriyas (taste and hands), are dissolved in Rasa (Taste) Tanmātra; the latter is taken to the Manipura and there Rasa Tattva, Tejas, and its connected Indriyas (sight and anus), are dissolved into Rūpa (Sight) Tanmātra; then the latter is taken into the Anāhata, and it, Vāyu, and the connected Indriyas (touch and penis), are dissolved in Sparsha (Touch) Tanmātra; the latter is taken to the Vishuddha, and there it, Ākāsha, and associated Indriyas (hearing and mouth), are dissolved in the Shabda (Sound) Tanmātra; the latter is then taken to the Ājnā, and, there and beyond, it and Manas are dissolved in Mahat, Mahat in Sūkshma Prakriti, and the latter is united with Parabindu in the Sahasrāra. In the case of the latter merger there are various stages which are mentioned in the text (v. 52), as of Nāda into Nādānta, Nādānta into Vyāpikā, Vyāpikā into Samanī, Samanī in Unmanī, and the latter into Vishnuvaktra or Pungbindu, which is also Paramashiva. When all the letters have been thus dissolved, all the six Chakras are dissolved as the petals of the lotuses bear the letters.

On this upward movement, Brahmā, Sāvitrī, Dākinī, the Devas, Mātrikās, and Vrittis, of the Mūlādhāra, are absorbed in Kundalinī, as is also the Mahimandala or Prithivī, and the Prithivī Bīja "Lang" into which it passes. For these Bījas, or sound powers, express the subtle Mantra aspect of that which is dissolved in them. Thus "earth" springs from and is dissolved in its seed (Bīja), which is that particular aspect of the creative consciousness which propelled it. The uttered Mantra (Vaikharī Shabda) or "Lang" is the expression in gross sound of that.

When the Devī leaves the Mūlādhāra, that lotus, which by reason of the awakening of Kundalinī and the vivifying intensity of the Prānik current had opened and turned its flower upwards, again closes and hangs its head downwards. As Kundalinī reaches the Svādishthāna, that lotus opens out and lifts its flower upwards. Upon Her entrance, Vishnu, Lakshmī, Sarasvatī, Rākinī, Mātrikās and Vritti, Vaikunthadhāma, Golaka, and the Deva and Devī residing therein, are dissolved in the body of Kundalinī. The Prithivī or Earth Bīja "Lang" is dissolved in the Tattva water, and water converted into its Bīja "Vang" remains in the body of Kundalinī. When the Devī reaches the Manipūra Chakra or Brahmagranthi, all that is in that Chakra merges in Her. The Varuna Bīja "Vang" is dissolved in fire, which remains in Her body as the Bīja "Rang." The Shakti next reaches the Anāhata Chakra, which is known as the Knot of Vishnu (Vishnugranthi), where also all which is therein is merged in Her. The Bīja of Fire "Rang" is sublimed in air, and air converted into its Bija "Yang" is absorbed in Kundalinī. She then ascends to the abode of Bhāratī or Sarasvatī, the Vishuddha Chakra. Upon Her entrance, Arddhanārīshvara, Shiva, Shākinī, the 16 vowels, Mantra, etc., are dissolved in Her. The Bīja of Air "Yang" is dissolved in ether, which, itself being transformed into the Bīja "Hang," is merged in the body of Kundalinī. Piercing the concealed Lalanā Chakra, the Devī reaches the Ājnā known as the "Knot of Rudra" (Rudragranthi), where Paramashiva, Siddhakālī, the Devas, and all else therein, are dissolved in Her. At length the Bīja of Vyoma (ether) or "Hang" is absorbed into the subtle Tattvas of the Ājnā, and then into the Devī. After passing through the Rudragranthi, Kundalinī unites with Paramashiva. As She proceeds upwards from the two-petalled lotus, the Nirālambapurī, Pranava, Nāda, etc., are merged in the Devī. She has thus in Her progress upwards absorbed in Herself the twenty-three Tattvas, commencing with the gross elements, and then remaining Herself Shakti, the cause of all Shaktis, unites with Paramashiva.

By this method of mental concentration, aided by the physical and other processes described, the gross is absorbed into the subtle, each dissolving into its immediate cause and all into the Chidātmā or the Ātmā which is Chit. In language borrowed from the world of human passion, which is itself but a gross reflection on our physical plane of corresponding, though more subtle, super-sensual activities and bliss, the Shakti Kundalinī who has been seized by desire for Her Lord is said to make swift way to him, and, kissing the Lotus mouth of Shiva, enjoys him (S.N., v. 51). By the term Sāmarasya is meant the sense of enjoyment arising from the union (Sāmarasya) of male and female. This the most intense form of physical delight symbolizes the Supreme Bliss arising from the union of Shiva and Shakti in the spiritual plane upon which it is enacted. So Daksha Dharmashāstrakāra says: "The Brahman is to be known by itself alone, and to know It is as the bliss of knowing a virgin."[635] Similarly, the Sādhaka in Layasiddhiyoga, thinking of himself as Shakti and the Paramātmā as Purusha, feels himself in union (Sanggama) with Shiva, and enjoys with him the bliss which is Shringārarasa, the first of the nine Rasa, or the love sentiment and bliss. This Ādirasa (Shringāra) which is aroused by Sattvaguna[636] is impartite (Akhanda), self-illuminating (Svaprakāsha) bliss (Ānanda) whose substance is Chit (Chinmaya).[637] It is so intense and all-exclusive as to render the lover unconscious of all other objects of knowledge (Vedyāntara-sparsha-shūnyah), and the own brother[638] of Brahma-bliss (Brahmasvādasahodara).[639] But as the Brahma-bliss is known only to the Yogī, so, as the Alangkāra Shastra last cited observes, even the true love-bliss of the mortal world "is known to a few knowers only" (jneyah kashchit pramātribhih), such as poets and

[635] Svasangvedyam etad brahma kumārī-strī-sukhang yathā, cited in Commentary to v. 15 of Ch. I. of the Hathayogapradīpikā.

[636] So all the eight Bhāvas commencing with Stambha, including the well-known Romāncha or thrill in which the hair stands on end (pulaka), the choking voice (svarabhanga), pallor (vaivarnya), and so forth, are all Sāttvik. The objection of an Indian friend, that these Bhāvas could not be Sāttvik inasmuch as Sattva was "spiritual," is an apt instance of the disassociation from Indian thought effected by English education.

[637] It is not a Tāmasik thing such as dream or madness, etc.

[638] Sahodara—that is, brothers born of the same mother. Sexual bliss is the reflection (faint comparatively though it be) of Brahman bliss.

[639] Sāhitya Darpana, Ch. III.

others. Sexual as well as other forms of love are reflections or fragments of the Brahman-bliss.

This union of the Shakti Kundalinī with Shiva in the body of the Sādhaka is that coition (Maithuna) of the Sāttvika Panchatattva which the Yoginī Tantra says is "the best of all unions for those who have already controlled their passions," and are thus Yati.[640] Of this the Brihat Shrīkrama (*vide* S.N., v. 51, *post*) says: "They with the eye of knowledge see the stainless Kalā, united with Chidānanda on Nāda. He is the Mahādeva, white like a pure crystal, and is the effulgent cause (Vimbarūpa-nidāna), and She is the lovely woman of beauteous limbs which are listless by reason of Her great passion." On their union nectar (Amrita) flows, which in ambrosial stream runs from the Brahmarandhra to the Mūlādhāra, flooding the Kshudrabrahmānda, or microcosm, and satisfying the Devatās of its Chakras. It is then that the Sādhaka, forgetful of all in this world, is immersed in ineffable bliss. Refreshment, increased power and enjoyment, follows upon each visit to the Well of Life.

In the Chintāmanistava, attributed to Shrī Shangkarāchāryya, it is said: "This family woman (*i.e.*, Kundalinī), entering the royal road (*i.e.*, Sushumnā), taking rest at intervals in the sacred places (*i.e.*, Chakra), embraces the Supreme Husband (Parashiva) and makes nectar to flow (*i.e.*, from the Sahasrāra)."

The Guru's instructions are to go above the Ājnā Chakra, but no special directions are given: for after this Chakra has been pierced, the Sādhaka can, and indeed must, reach the Brahmasthāna, or abode of Brahman, unaided by his own effort. Above the Ājnā the relationship of Guru and Shishya (Master and disciple) ceases. Kundalinī having pierced the fourteen "Knots" (Granthis)—viz., three Lingas, six Chakras, and the five Shivas which they contain, and then Herself drunk of the nectar which issues from Parashiva, returns along the path whence She came to Her own abode (Mūlādhāra).[641] As She returns She pours from Herself into the Chakras all that She had previously absorbed therefrom. In other words, as Her passage upwards was Layakrama, causing all things in the Chakras to pass into the Laya state (dissolution), so Her return is Srishtikrama, as She "recreates" or makes them manifest. In this manner She again reaches the Mūlādhāra, when all that has been already described to be in the Chakras appears in the positions which they occupied before Her awakening. In fact, the descending Jīvātmā makes for Himself the idea of that separated

[640] Ch. VI.:

Sahasrāropari bindau kundalyā melanam shive.
Maithunang paramang dravyang yatinām parikīrtitam.

[641] As to the Samaya practice, *v. post*, p. 182.

multiple and individualized world which passed from him as he ascended to and became one with its Cause. She as Consciousness absorbs what She as conscious Power projected. In short, the return of Kundalinī is the setting again of the Jīvātmā in the phenomenal world of the lowest plane of being after it had been raised therefrom in a state of ecstasis, or Samādhi. The Yogī thus knows (because he experiences) the nature and state of Spirit and its pathway to and from the Māyik and embodied world. In this Yoga there is a gradual process of involution of the gross world and its elements into its cause. Each gross element (Mahābhūta), together with the subtle element (Tanmātra) from which it proceeds and the connected organ of sense (Indriya), is dissolved into the next above it until the last element, ether, with the Tanmātra sound and Manas, are dissolved in egoism (Ahangkāra), of which they are Vikritis. Ahangkāra is merged in Mahat, the first manifestation of creative ideation, and the latter into Bindu, which is the Supreme Being, Consciousness, and Bliss of the Brahman. As Kundalinī ascends, the lower limbs become as inert and cold as a corpse; so also does every part of the body when She has passed through and leaves it. This is due to the fact that She as the Power which supports the body is leaving Her center. On the contrary, the upper part of the head becomes "lustrous," by which is not meant any external luster (Prabhā), but brightness, warmth, and animation. When the Yoga is complete, the Yogī sits rigid in the posture selected, and the only trace of warmth to be found in the whole body is at the crown of the head, where the Shakti is united with Shiva. Those, therefore, who are sceptical can easily verify the facts should they be fortunate enough to find a successful Yogī who will let them see him at work. They may observe his ecstasis and the coldness of the body, which is not present in the case of what is called the Dhyāna Yogī, or a Yogī operating by meditation only, and not rousing Kundalinī. This cold is an external and easily perceptible sign. Its progression may be seen, obviously denoting the passing away of something which supplied the previous heat. The body seems lifeless, indicating that its supporting power has (though not entirely) left it. The downward return of the Shakti thus moved is, on the other hand, indicated by the reappearance of warmth, vitality, and the normal consciousness. The return process is one of evolution from the highest state of attainment to the point of departure.

Though not dealt with in this work, reference may here be made to the Sādhanā accompanying the return of Kundalinī to Her resting-place in the ritual practice called Bhūtashuddhi, where the ascent and descent are imagined only.

The Sādhaka, thinking of the Vāyu Bīja "Yang" as being in the left nostril, inhales through Idā, making Japa of the Bīja sixteen times. Then, closing both nostrils, he makes Japa of the Bīja sixty-four times.

He then thinks of the "black man of sin" (Pāpapurusha[642]) in the left[643] cavity of the abdomen as being dried up (by the air), and so thinking he exhales through the right nostril Pinggalā, making Japa of the Bīja thirty-two times. The Sādhaka then, meditating upon the red-colored Bīja "Rang" in the Manipūra, inhales, making sixteen Japa of the Bīja, and then closes the nostrils, making sixteen Japa. Whilst making Japa he thinks that the body of the "man of sin" is being burnt and reduced to ashes (by the fire). He then inhales through the right nostril with thirty-two Japa, and then meditates upon the white Chandrabīja "Thang." He next inhales though Idā, making Japa of the Bīja sixteen times, closes both nostrils with Japa done sixty-four times, and exhales through Pinggalā with thirty-two Japa. During inhalation, holding of breath, and exhalation, he should consider that a new celestial body is being formed by the nectar (composed of all the Mātrikā-varna, or sound-powers, embodied in their Vaikharī form as lettered sound) dropping from the "Moon." In a similar way with the Bīja of water "Vang" the formation of the body is continued, and with the Bīja "Lang" of the cohesive Prithivī Tattva it is completed and strengthened. Lastly, with the Mantra "So'ham" ("He I am") the Sādhaka leads the Jīvātmā into its place in the heart. Some forms of meditation are given in v. 51.

Kundalī does not at first stay long in Sahasrāra. The length of stay depends on the strength of the Yogī's practice. There is then a natural tendency on the part of Kundalī to return. The Yogī will use all effort at his disposal to retain Her above, for the longer this is done the nearer approach is made to the time when She can be in a permanent manner retained there.[644] For it is to be observed that liberation is not gained by merely leading Kundalī to the Sahasrāra, and of course still less is it gained by stirring it up in the Mūlādhāra or fixing it in any of the lower centers. Liberation is gained only when Kundalī takes up Her permanent abode in the Sahasrāra, so that She only returns by the will of the Sādhaka. It is said that after staying in Sahasrāra for a time, some Yogins lead the Kundalinī back to Hridaya (heart), and worship her there. This is done by those who are unable to stay long in Sahasrāra. If they take the Kundalinī lower than Hridaya—*i.e.*, worship her in the three Chakras below Anāhata—they no longer, it is said, belong to the Samaya group.[645]

---

642 See Mahānirvāna Tantra Ullāsa, Ch. V., vv. 98, 99, where the Bhūtashuddhi process is shortly described. Also Devī Bhāgavata, cited, *post*.

643 The worse or weaker side.

644 Great power (Siddhi) is had by the man who can keep Kundalī Shakti in the Sahasrāra three days and three nights.

645 Lakshmīdhara, cited by Ananta Shāstri, *op. cit.*, p. 71. What this means is more than I can say, as I am not familiar with the views of the school which Lakshmīdhara (cited also *post*) quotes.

Thus, when by the preliminary Sādhanā purity of physical and mental function is gained, the Sādhaka learns how to open the entrance of the Sushumnā, which is ordinarily closed at the base. This is the meaning of the statement that the Serpent with its coil closes the gate of Brahmā. At the base of the Sushumnā Nādi and in the Ādhāra lotus the Shakti Kundalinī lies slumbering coiled round the Linga, the Shiva or Purusha aspect in that center of the Shabdabrahman, of which She is the Prakriti aspect. Kundalī in the form of Her creative emanations as mind and matter is the whole moving body, but She Herself exists at the Mūlādhāra or earth center as a gross aspect of Shakti in its sleeping form. This is the normal abode of the Shakti who is the Shabdabrahman Itself. For having so completely manifested Herself She rests or sleeps in what is her grossest and concluding manifestation. The residual vital force in this center there exists in a latent and potential state. If its aid towards Yoga is sought, the first process must be that by which the Serpent is aroused from its slumber. In other words, this force is raised from its latent potential state to one of activity, and there reunited with Itself in its other aspect as the Spiritual Light which shines[646] in the cerebral center.

Kundalī Shakti is Chit, or Consciousness, in its creative aspect as Power. As Shakti it is through Her activity that the world and all human beings therein exist. Prakriti Shakti is in the Mūlādhāra in a state of sleep (Prasupta)—that is, latent activity looking *outwards* (Vahirmukhī). It is because She is in this state of latent activity that through Her all the outer material world functions of life are being performed by men. And it is for this reason that man is engrossed in the world, and under the lure of Māyā takes his body and egoism to be the real self, and thus goes round the wheel of life in its unending cycle of birth and death. When the Jīva thinks the world to be different from Himself and the Brahman, it is through the influence of Kundalinī who dwells within Him. Her sleep in the Mūlādhāra is, therefore, for the bondage of the ignorant.[647] As long as She remains in the Mūlādhāra lotus—namely, in that state of Hers which is the concomitant of the cosmic appearance—so long must that appearance endure. In short, when She is asleep man is in the waking state (Jāgrat). Hence it is said[648] that the Shakti of the initiate is awake, that of the Pashu asleep. She is therefore aroused from sleep, and when awake returns to Her Lord, who is but Herself in another aspect; Her return is, in fact, the withdrawal of that activity of Hers which produces the world of appearances, and which with such withdrawal disappears. For on Her upward Path She absorbs into Herself all the Tattvas which had

[646] For this reason the Sahasrāra is also called Bhāloka (from the root *bhā*, "to shine").

[647] Shāndilya Upanishad, Ch. I.

[648] Kulārnava Tantra, Ch. V. Mandalabrāhmana Up. Tamas is destroyed there.

emanated from Her. The individual consciousness of the Yogī, the Jīvātmā, being united with the world-consciousness in Her, or Kundalī, then becomes the universal consciousness, or Paramātmā, from which it appeared to be different only by reason of the world-creating and bewildering activity of Kundalī which is thus withdrawn. The establishment through Her of the pure state of Being-Consciousness Bliss is Samādhi.

In short, Kundalī is the individual bodily representative of the great Cosmic Power (Shakti) which creates and sustains the universe. When this individual Shakti manifesting as the individual consciousness (Jīva) is merged in the consciousness of the Supreme Shiva, the world is for such Jīva destroyed, and liberation (Mukti) is obtained. Under, however, the influence of the Cosmic Shakti, the universe continues for those who are not liberated until the great dissolution (Mahāpralaya), at the close of which the universe again evolves into those Jīvas whose Karma has not been exhausted, and who have therefore not been liberated. The rousing and stirring up of Kundalī or Kundalī Yoga is thus a form of that merger of the individual into the universal consciousness which is the end of every system of Indian Yoga.

Pandit R. Ananta Shāstrī says[649] that "The Samaya method of worshipping Shakti, called the Samayāchāra,[650] is dealt with in five treatises whose reputed authors are the great sages Sanaka, Sananda, Sanatkumāra, Vashishtha, and Shuka. The following is a summary of the teachings contained in these Samaya Āgamas, each of which goes after the name of its author:

"The Shakti or energy, the development of which is the subject of these treatises, is called the Kundalinī. The place where it resides is called the Mūlādhāra (original abode). By a successful development and working of this Shakti, the liberation of the soul is attained. In the ordinary condition Kundalinī sleeps quietly at the Mūlādhāra. The first purpose of the practitioners is to awaken this sleeping snake, and this is effected in two ways:

"(1) *By* Tapas. Here Tapas refers to the process of Prānāyāma, which means the regulation of the breath and holding it for stated periods of time. This is also the course advocated by the Yoga Shāstras.

"(2) By Mantras. The pupil is initiated in the chanting of certain Mantras which he has to repeat a fixed number of times at particular hours of the day, all the while having before his mind's eye the figure of the Murti or God connoted by the Mantra he chants. The most

[649] Ānandalahari, p. 8. The passage is given by way of citation only. There are statements in it which I have not verified, and some from which I dissent, and some which I do not understand.

[650] This term is apparently of varying significance. It seems to be used here in a sense opposed to Kulāchāra, and is yet used in the Kaula Shāstrās to denote their worship with the Panchatattva.

important of these Mantras is said to be the Panchadashī.

"When it is thus roused up, the Kundalinī ascends from (i) Mūlādhāra, where it was sleeping, to the next higher center, called the (2) Svādhishthāna (own place). Thence with great effort this Shakti is carried to the following centers in regular ascending order: (3) Manipūra (full of rays); (4) Anāhata (sound, not emanating from the collision of bodies)—the Shakti here is transformed into sound; (5) Vishuddhi (place of purity)—here it becomes a pure Sattvic element; and (6) Ājnā (ā-jnā, a little knowledge). At this stage the practitioner may be said to have so far been successful in securing a command over this Shakti, which now appears to him, though only for a moment, in the form of a sharp flash of lightning.

"The passage of the Kundalinī from the Mūlādhāra through the above centers of energy up to Ājnā constitutes the first part of the ascent. The disciple who takes to this practice has to undergo a course of Upāsanā (contemplation and worship of the prescribed Deity) and Mantra Japa (chanting of incantations),[651] into which he will be initiated by his Guru (teacher and guide). The six centers of energy above enumerated from Mūlādhāra to Ājnā, joined together by imaginary straight lines, form a double-faced triangle—a hexagon, the six-pointed star—which in called the Shrīchakra in Sanskrit. The Anāhata center (the heart) is the critical point in the course of this ascent, and hence much is found written in the Āgamas about this center.

"These centers in the body of man (Pindānda) have their correspondence in the cosmic planes, and each of these has its own quality, or Guna, and a Presiding Deity. When the disciple ascends center by center, he passes through the corresponding Lokas, or cosmic planes. The following table gives the correspondences, Guna, and Presiding Deity:

---

[651] In this and other citations from the Pandit the English equivalents of Sanskrit terms are incorrect, as might be expected in one to whom English is not his own tongue. Japa is not "chanting." In fact, in Upāngsha Japa nothing is heard, and "incantations" provoke another set of ideas to the English mind.

No.	*Psychic Centre in Man's Body.*	*Loka, or Cosmic Plane.*	*Guna, or Quality.*	*Presiding Deity.*
1	Mūlādhāra at the stage when Shakti is roused up	Bhuvarloka	Tamas	Agni (Fire)
2	Svādhishthāna	Svarloka		
3	Manipūra	Maharloka	Rajas	Sun
4	Anāhata	Janaloka		
5	Vishuddhi	Tapoloka	Sattva	Moon
6	Ājnā	Satyaloka		

"If one should die after attaining any of these stages, he is born again having all the advantages of the stages gained; thus, a man dies after leading the Shakti to the Anāhata: in his next birth he begins where he has last left, and leads the Shakti onwards from the Anāhata.

"This aspiration to unify one's soul with the Eternal One has been held by some to be an attempt of a Tāmasa origin to rid itself of all Tamas and Rajas in it. Therefore the aspirant in the first and second stages is said to have more Tamas than in the succeeding stages, and to be therefore in the Tāmasic stage, which is presided over by Agni. In the next two stages he is similarly said to be in the Rājasic stage, presided over by the Sun. In the next two he is in the Sāttvic stage, presided over by the Moon, the Deity which is assigned a higher plane than the Sun and Agni. But it is to be noticed that the aspirant does not get at pure Sattva until he passes on to the Sahasrāra, and that Tamas, Rajas, and Sattva, referred to in the above table, are but relative, and bear no comparison with their common acceptation.

"Kundalinī is the grossest form of the Chit, the twenty-fourth Tattva, which lives in the Mūlādhāra; later on we shall have to speak of it in detail in our treatment of the second part of the aspirant's ascent. This Kundalinī, as soon as it is awakened, is in the Kumārī (girl) stage. On reaching the Anāhata, it attains the Yoshit stage (womanhood). Hence the indication that it is the most difficult and important step in the ascent. The next stage is in the Sahasrāra, of which we shall speak hereafter, and the Shakti in that stage is called Pativratā (devoted to husband). See Taittirīyāranyaka, 1-27-12.

"The second part of the ascent of Kundalinī consists of only one step; the Shakti should be taken into the Sahasrāra from the Ājnā, where we left her. The Sahasrāra (lit., a thousand-petalled lotus) forms in itself a Shrīchakra. The description of this place in Sanskrit is too difficult to be rendered satisfactorily into English. In the Sahasrāra there is a certain place of luster known as Chandra Loka (a world of nectar). In this place live in union the Sat (Sadāshiva) and the Chit, the twenty-fifth and the twenty-fourth Tattvas. The Chit, or Shuddhā Vidyā, is also called Sadākhyā, the 16th Kalā of the moon. These two Tattvas are always in union, and this union itself is taken to be the twenty-sixth Tattva. It is this union of Sat and Chit that is the goal of the aspirant. The Kundalinī which has been led all the way to the Sahasrāra should be merged into this union; this is the end of the aspirant's journey; he now enjoys beatitude itself (Paramānanda).

"But this Kundalinī does not stay in the Sahasrāra for a long time. It always tends to return, and does return to its original position. The process should again and again be repeated by the aspirant several times, until the Shakti makes a permanent stay with her Pati (husband)—namely, Sadāshiva—or until the union of Sadāshiva and Chit is complete, and becomes Pativratā, as already mentioned. The aspirant is then a Jīvan-mukta, or pure Sattva. He is not conscious of this material limitation of the soul. He is all joy, and is the Eternal itself. See vv. 9 and 10. So much of Samayāchāra.

"Now to the other methods of Shākta worship; the Kaulas worship the Kundalinī without rousing her from her sleep[652] in the Mūlādhāra, which is called Kula; and hence Kaulas (Sans. Ku = earth, Prithivī; so Mūlādhāra). Beyond the Mūlādhāra they do not rise; they follow the Vāmāchāra, or black magic,[653] and gain their temporal objects and enjoy; they are not liberated from birth and death; they do not go beyond this earth. Nay, more, the Kaulas are now so far degraded that they have left off altogether the worship of the Kundalinī in the Mūlādhāra, and have betaken themselves to practices most inhuman, which are far from being divine.[654] The Mishras are far above the

---

652 A statement by the same author at p. 85 is in apparent contradiction with this. He there says, citing Lakshmīdhara: "The Kaulas who worship Kundalinī in the Mūlādhāra have no other aim than *awakening* it from its sleep. When this is done, they think that they have attained their object, and there they stop. In their own words, the Kaulas have Nirvāna always near at hand." I have not come across the worship here referred to.

653 Vāmāchāra is not "black magic," the nearest Sanskrit equivalent for which is Abhichāra. There may have been, as the Mahākāla Samhitā says (Ullāsa II.), some Kaulas who, like the Vaidikas, sought enjoyment in this and the next world, and not liberation (Aihikārtham kāmayanti amrite ratim na kurvvanti). But to state baldly that Kaulas do not rouse Kundalinī and lead her to the Sahasrāra is wholly incorrect. Pūrnānanda Svāmī, the author of the Text (S.N.) here translated, was himself a Kaula, and the whole object of the work is to secure liberation (Moksha). So much ignorance of, and prejudice against, the Kaula schools prevail that statements adverse to them should always be tested.

654 The Pandit here apparently adopts the opinion of Lakshmīdhara, a follower of the so-called Samaya school, and an opponent of the Kaulas. If (as is probably the case) "inhuman" is the Pandit's phraseology it is inapt. The practices apparently referred to—namely, the worship, so little understood, with wine, meat, woman—is, in part, a continuance of the most ancient Vaidik usages in differing forms (see my "Shakti and Shākta"). It may be admitted that some forms of Sādhanā are dangerous, and that some

Kaulas. They perform all Karmas, worship the Devī or Shakti in the elements, such as the sun, air, etc., and do Upāsanā with Yantras made of gold or other metals. They worship the Kundalinī, awake her, and attempt to lead her on. Some of the Mishra worshippers rise even as far as the Anāhata.

"We learn from the Commentators that this whole subject of Shakti-worship is treated of in detail in the 'Taittarīya Āranyaka' (1st chapter). Some of them even quote from that 'Āranyaka' in support of their explanations. This subject is vast and a very difficult one. It is not possible for one to go into the intricacies of the subject unless one be a great Guru of vast learning and much personal experience;[655] great works have been written on even single points in the ascent of the aspirant up the psychic centers."[656]

"The followers of the Samaya group are prohibited from worshipping Devī in the Macrocosm. They should worship Her in any of the Chakras in the human body, choosing that center which their practice and ability permits them to reach. They should contemplate on Devī and Her Lord Shiva as (i) having the same abode (Adhishthānasāmya), (2) occupying the same position (Avasthānasāmya), (3) performing the same functions (Anushthānasāmya), (4) having the same form (Rūpa), and (5) as having the same name (Nāma). Thus, in worshipping Devī in the Ādhārachakra, Shiva and Shakti (1) have Mūlādhāra for their seat, (2) both of them occupy the position of dancers, (3) both together perform the function of creating the universe, (4) both are red in color, (5) Shiva is called Bhairava, and Shakti Bhairavī.

"Similarly for the other Chakras mentioned in the preceding Shlokas. This is the way how beginners have to practice. Advanced students worship Devī in the Sahasrāra, and not in the lower centers. How is the worship to be carried on in Sahasrāra?

"The worshipper should fix his attention on Baindava, which is the locality where the ever-existing 26th Tattva—the union of Shiva and Shakti—resides. It lies' above all the 25 Tatvas, and is situated in Chandramandala (the sphere of the moon) in Sahasrāra. He should contemplate on the said union and identify himself with it. This shows that those who carry on Bāhya Pūjā, or worship in the external world,

details of the ritual will be generally considered repellent, as will also be (I may add by way of example) the Vaidik "horse-sacrifice" (ashvamedha)—at any rate, as Mahīdhara and others interpret it. The worst charge which can be successfully maintained against some of the lower order of the class referred to is black magic proper, through improper use of the Shatkarma. As Shiva in the Kulārnava Samhitā (not the generally known Tantra) says, "In Kali all men are lustful for money, and will even destroy beings to gain it. But I will destroy all such as does fire dry grass." The abuses of some of the followers are not to be laid to the charge of the true Shāstra.

[655] Here I wholeheartedly agree with my friend the Pandit.

[656] See his edition, ed. Ānandalaharī, pp. 8-13.

do not belong to the Samaya school. As regards the identification of oneself with the union of Shiva and Shakti at Baindava just spoken of, there are two ways of realizing it; one is known as the fourfold path, and the other the six-fold path. These should be learnt from the Guru.

"A novitiate in the Samaya school has to go through the following course:

(1) He should cherish the utmost regard for and confidence in his Guru. (2) He should receive the Panchadashī Mantra from his Guru, and chant the same according to instructions, with a knowledge of its seer (Rishi), metre (Chhandas), and the Deity (Devatā).[657] (3) On the eighth day in the bright fortnight of Āshvayuja month, Mahānavamī, he should at midnight prostrate himself at his Guru's feet, when the latter will be pleased to initiate him in some Mantra and the real nature of the six Chakras and of the six-fold path of identification.

"After he is thus qualified, Lord Mahādeva[658] gives him the knowledge or capacity to see his inner soul. . . . Then the Kundalinī awakes, and, going up suddenly to Manipūra, becomes visible to the devotee-practitioner. Thence he has to take Her slowly to the higher Chakras one after another, and there performs the prescribed worship, and She will appear to him more and more clearly. When the Ājnāchakra is crossed, the Kundalinī quickly darts away like a flash of lightning to Sahasrāra, and enters the Island of Gems surrounded by the Kalpa trees in the Ocean of Nectar, unites with Sadāshiva there, and enjoys with Him.

"The practitioner should now wait outside the veil[659] until Kundalinī returns to Her own place, and on Her return continue the process until She is joined for ever with Sadāshiva in the Sahasrāra, and never returns.

"The process heretofore described and others of a similar nature are always kept secret; yet the commentator says he has out of compassion towards his disciples given here an outline of the method.

"Even in the mere expectation of the return of Kundalinī from Sahasrāra, the aspirant feels Brahmānanda (Brahma bliss). He who has once taken Kundalinī to Sahasrāra is led to desire nothing but Moksha (liberation), if he has no other expectation. Even if any of the Samaya practitioners have some worldly expectations, they must still worship in the microcosm only.

---

[657] The Rishi of the Mantra is he to whom it was first revealed; the metre is that in which it was first uttered by Shiva; and the Devatā is the Artha of the Mantra as Shabda. The Artha is fivefold as Devatā, Adhidevatā, Pratyadhidevatā, Varnādhidevatā, Mantrādhidevatā.

[658] Shiva initiates him in the knowledge of Brahman. Thus, Shiva is considered the teacher of all spiritual Gurus (Ādinātha).

[659] This, as well as some other details of this description, I do not follow. Who is waiting outside the veil? The Jīva is, on the case stated within, if there be a veil, and what is it?

"'Subhagodaya' and other famous works on Shrividyā say that the practitioner should concentrate his mind on Devī who resides in Sūryamandala (the sun's disc), and so on. This statement is not at variance with the teaching contained in this book, for the Sūryamandala referred to applies to the Pindānda (microcosm), and not to Brahmānda (macrocosm). Similarly, all the verses advocating outer worship are to be applied to the corresponding objects in the Pindānda."[660]

VII. THEORETICAL BASES OF THIS YOGA

It will now be asked what are the general principles which underlie the Yoga practice above described. How is it that the rousing of Kundalinī Shakti and Her union with Shiva effects the state of ecstatic union (Samādhi) and spiritual experience which is alleged? The reader who has understood the general principles recorded in the previous sections should, if he have not already divined it, readily appreciate the answer here given.

In the first place, the preceding section will have indicated that there are two main lines of Yoga—namely, Dhyāna or Bhāvanā Yoga, and Kundalī Yoga, the subject of this work—and that there is a marked difference between the two. The first class of Yoga is that in which ecstasy (Samādhi) is attained by intellective processes (Kriyā jnāna) of meditation and the like with the aid, it may be, of auxiliary processes of Mantra or Hathayoga[661] (other than the rousing of Kundalī Shakti) and by detachment from the world; the second stands apart as that portion of Hathayoga in which, though intellective processes are not neglected, the creative and sustaining Shakti of the whole body is actually and truly united with the Lord Consciousness. The Yogī makes Her introduce Him to Her Lord, and enjoys the bliss of union through Her. Though it is He who arouses Her, it is She who gives Jnāna, for She is Herself that. The Dhyāna Yogī gains what acquaintance with the supreme state his own meditative powers can give him, and knows not the enjoyment of union with Shiva in and through his fundamental body-power. The two forms of Yoga diner both as to method and result. The Hathayogī regards his Yoga and its fruit as the highest. Perhaps the Jnānayogī may think similarly of his own. Kundalinī is so renowned that many seek to know Her. Having studied the theory of this Yoga, I have often been asked "whether one can get on without it." The answer is: "It depends upon what you are looking for." If you want to rouse Kundalī Shakti to enjoy the bliss of union of Shiva and Shakti

---

[660] Comm. on Ānandalaharī, ed. by Pandit R. Ānanta Shāstri, p. 85 *et seq.*, who adds: "For full particulars of these principles *vide* 'Shuka Samhitā,' one of the five Samhitās of the Samaya group."

[661] Such as Prānāyāma, Āsana.

through Her, and to gain the accompanying powers (Siddhi),[662] it is obvious that this end can only be achieved by the Yoga here described. But if liberation is sought without desire for union through Kundalī, then such Yoga is not necessary, for liberation may be obtained by pure Jnānayoga through detachment, the exercise, and then the stilling, of the mind without any reference to the central bodily power at all. Instead of setting out in, and from the world, to unite with Shiva, the Jnānayogī, to attain this result, detaches himself from the world. The one is the path of enjoyment[663] and the other of asceticism. Samādhi may also be attained on the path of devotion (Bhakti), as on that of knowledge. Indeed, the highest devotion (Parabhakti) is not different from knowledge. Both are realization. But whilst liberation (Mukti) is attainable by either method, there are other marked differences between the two. A Dhyāna Yogī should not neglect his body, knowing that, as he is both mind and matter, each reacts the one upon the other. Neglect or mere mortification of the body is more apt to produce disordered imagination than a true spiritual experience. He is not concerned, however, with the body in the sense that the Hathayogī is. It is possible to be a successful Dhyānayogī and yet to be weak in body and health, sick, and short-lived. His body, and not he himself, determines when he shall die. He cannot die at will. When he is in Samādhi, Kundalī Shakti is still sleeping in the Mūlādhāra; and none of the physical symptoms, psychical bliss, or powers (Siddhi) already described as accompanying Her rousing, are observed in his case. The ecstasis, which he calls "Liberation while yet living" (Jīvanmukta), is not a state like that of real liberation. He may be still subject to a suffering body, from which he escapes only at death, when, if at all, he is liberated. His ecstasy is in the nature of a meditation which passes into the Void (Bhāvanā samādhi) effected through negation of thought (Chittavritti) and detachment from the world—a negative process in which the positive act of raising the central power of the body takes no part. By his effort the mind, which is a product of Kundalinī as Prakriti Shakti, together with its worldly desires, is stilled, so that the veil produced by mental functioning is removed from Consciousness. In Layayoga Kundalinī Herself, when roused by the Yogī (for such rousing is his act and part), achieves for him this illumination. But why, it may be asked, should one trouble over the body and its central power, the more particularly that there are unusual risks and difficulties involved? The answer has been already given—alleged completeness and certainty of realization through the agency of the power which is Knowledge itself (Jnānarūpā shakti); an intermediate acquisition of powers (Siddhi); and

---

662 Thus, by raising Kundalī Shakti to the Manipūra center, power may be acquired over fire.

663 Subject to Dharma, Yama, Niyama, etc.

intermediate and final enjoyment. This answer may, however, usefully be developed, as a fundamental principle of the Shākta Tantra is involved.

The Shākta Tantra claims to give both enjoyment[664] (Bhukti) in this and the next world, and liberation (Mukti) from all worlds. This claim is based on a profoundly true principle.[665] If the ultimate reality is the one which exists in two aspects of quiescent enjoyment of the Self in liberation from all form and of active enjoyment of objects—that is, as pure Spirit and Spirit in matter—then a complete union with Reality demands such unity in both of its aspects. It must be known both "here" (Iha) and "there" (Amutra). When rightly apprehended and practiced, there is truth in the doctrine which teaches that man should make the best of both worlds.[666] There is no real incompatibility between the two, provided action is taken in conformity with the universal law of manifestation. It is held to be false teaching that happiness hereafter can only be had by neglect to seek it now, or in deliberately sought for suffering and mortification. It is the one Shiva who is the supreme blissful experience, and who appears in the form of man with a life of mingled pleasure and pain. Both happiness here and the bliss of liberation here and hereafter may be attained if the identity of these Shivas be realized in every human act. This will be achieved by making every human function, without exception, a religious act of sacrifice and worship (Yajna). In the ancient Vaidik ritual enjoyment by way of food and drink was preceded, and accompanied by, ceremonial sacrifice and ritual. Such enjoyment was the fruit of the sacrifice and the gift of the Gods. At a higher stage in the life of a Sādhaka it is offered to the One from whom all gifts come and of whom the Devatās are inferior limited forms. But this offering also involves a dualism from which the highest Monistic (Advaita) Sādhanā of the Shākta-Tantra is free. Here the individual life and the world-life are known as one. And so the Tantrik Sādhaka, when eating or drinking,[667] or fulfilling any other of the natural functions of the body, does so, saying and believing, Shivo'ham ("I am Shiva"), Bhairavo'ham ("I am

---

[664] As there are persons who always associate with the word "enjoyment" (Bhoga) "beer and skittles, "it is necessary to say that that is not the necessary implication of the word Bhoga, nor the sense in which it is here used. Philosophically, Bhoga is the perception of objects upon which enjoyment, or it may be suffering, ensues. Here any form of sense or intellectual enjoyment is intended. All life in the world of form is enjoyment.

[665] Which it is possible to adopt without approval of any particular *application* to which it may be put. There are some dangerous practices which in the hands of inferior persons have led to results which have given the Shāstra in this respect its ill repute.

[666] "Worlds," because that is the English phrase. Here, however, the antithesis is between the world (whether as earth or heaven) and liberation from all worlds.

[667] Thus in the Shākta ritual the Sādhaka who takes the wine-cup pours the wine as a libation into the mouth of Kundalī Shakti, the Shakti appearing in the form of himself.

Bhairava"),[668] Sāham ("I am She").[669] It is not merely the separate individual who thus acts and enjoys. It is Shiva who does so *in* and *through* him. Such a one recognizes, as has been well said,[670] that his life and the play of all its activities are not a thing apart, to be held and pursued egotistically for its and his own separate sake, as though enjoyment was something to be seized from life by his own unaided strength and with a sense of separatedness; but his life and all its activities are conceived as part of the divine action in nature (Shakti) manifesting and operating in the form of man. He realizes in the pulsing beat of his heart the rhythm which throbs through, and is the sign of, the universal life. To neglect or to deny the needs of the body, to think of it as something not divine, is to neglect and deny that greater life of which it is a part, and to falsify the great doctrine of the unity of all and of the ultimate identity of Matter and Spirit. Governed by such a concept, even the lowliest physical needs take on a cosmic significance. The body is Shakti. Its needs are Shakti's needs; when man enjoys, it is Shakti who enjoys through him. In all he sees and does it is the Mother who looks and acts. His eyes and hands are Hers. The whole body and all its functions are Her manifestation. To fully realize Her as such is to perfect this particular manifestation of Hers which is himself. Man, when seeking to be the master of himself, so seeks on all the planes, physical, mental; and spiritual; nor can they be severed, for they are all related, being but differing aspects of the one all-pervading Consciousness. Who is the more divine, he who neglects and spurns the body or mind that he may attain some fancied spiritual superiority, or he who rightly cherishes both as forms of the one Spirit which they clothe? Realization is more speedily and truly attained by discerning Spirit in, and as, all being and its activities, than by fleeing from and casting these aside as being either unspiritual or illusory and impediments in the path.[671] If not rightly conceived, they *may* be impediments and the cause of fall, otherwise they become instruments of attainments; and what others are there to hand? And so the Kulārnava Tantra says: "By what men fall, by that they rise." When acts are done in the right feeling and frame of mind (Bhāva), those acts give enjoyment (Bhukti); and the repeated and prolonged Bhāva produces at length that divine experience (Tattvajnāna) which is liberation. When the Mother is seen *in* all things, She is at length realized as She is when *beyond* them all.

These general principles have their more frequent application in

[668] A name of Shiva.

[669] That is, the Mother of all appearing in the form of Her worshipper.

[670] By Sj. Arobindo Ghose in the Ārya.

[671] The first is the Tantrik method of applying Vedantic truth; the second, the ascetic or Māyāvādin method, with a greatness of its own, but less, conform, I think, to reality and to the needs of the *mass* of men.

the life of the world before entrance on the path of Yoga proper. The Yoga here described is, however, also an application of these same principles in so far as it is claimed that thereby both Bhukti and Mukti are attained. Ordinarily it is said that where there is Yoga there is no Bhoga (enjoyment), but in Kaula teaching Yoga is Bhoga and Bhoga is Yoga, and the world itself becomes the seat of liberation ("Yogo bhogāyate, mokshāyate sangsārah").[672]

By the lower processes of Hathayoga it is sought to attain a perfect physical body which will also be a wholly fit instrument by which the mind may function. A perfect mind again approaches, and in Samādhi passes into, pure Consciousness itself. The Hathayogī thus seeks a body which shall be as strong as steel, healthy, free from suffering, and therefore long-lived. Master of the body, he is master of both life and death. His lustrous form enjoys the vitality of youth. He lives as long as he has the will to live and enjoy in the world of forms. His death is the "death at will," when making the great and wonderfully expressive gesture of dissolution[673] he grandly departs. But it may be said the Hathayogīs do get sick and die. In the first place, the full discipline is one of difficulty and risk, and can only be pursued under the guidance of a skilled Guru. As the Goraksha Sanghitā says, unaided and unsuccessful practice may lead not only to disease, but death. He who seeks to conquer the Lord of Death incurs the risk on failure of a more speedy conquest by Him. All who attempt this Yoga do not, of course, succeed, or meet with the same measure of success. Those who fail not only incur the infirmities of ordinary men, but others brought on by practices which have been ill pursued, or for which they are not fit. Those, again, who do succeed, do so in varying degree. One may prolong his life to the sacred age of 84, others to 100, others yet further. In theory, at least, those who are perfected (Siddha) go from this plane when they will. All have not the same capacity or opportunity through want of will, bodily strength, or circumstance. All may not be willing or able to follow the strict rules necessary for success. Nor does modern life offer in general the opportunities for so complete a physical culture. All men may not desire such a life, or may think the attainment of it not worth the trouble involved. Some may wish to be rid of their body, and that as speedily as possible. It is therefore said that it is easier to gain liberation than deathlessness. The former may be had by unselfishness, detachment from the world, moral and mental discipline. But to conquer death is harder than this; for these qualities and acts will not

---

[672] Yogo bhogāyate sākshāt dushkritam sukritāyate
Mokshāyate hi sangsārah kauladharme kuleshvari.

(Kulārnava Tantra.)

[673] Sanghāramudrā, the gesture which signifies dissolution, "Now I am about to die."

alone avail. He who does so conquer holds life in the hollow of one hand, and if he be a successful (Siddha) Yogī, liberation in the other. He has enjoyment and liberation. He is the Emperor who is master of the world and the possessor of the bliss which is beyond all worlds. Therefore it is claimed by the Hathayogī that every Sādhanā is inferior to Hathayoga.

The Hathayogī who works for liberation does so through the Yoga Sādhanā here described, which gives both enjoyment and liberation. At every center to which he rouses Kundalinī he experiences a special form of bliss (Ānanda) and gains special powers (Siddhi). Carrying Her to the Shiva of his cerebral center, he enjoys the Supreme Bliss, which in its nature is that of liberation, and which, when established in permanence, is liberation itself on the loosening of the spirit and body. She who "shines like a chain of lights"—a lightning-flash—in the center of his body is the "Inner Woman" to whom reference was made when it was said, "What need have I of any outer woman? I have an Inner Woman within myself." The Vīra ("heroic")[674] Sādhaka, knowing himself as the embodiment of Shiva (Shivo'ham), unites with woman as the embodiment of Shakti on the physical plane.[675] The Divya ("divine") Sādhaka or Yogī unites within himself his own principles, female and male, which are the "Heart of the Lord" (Hridayamparameshituh)[676] or Shakti, and Her Lord Consciousness or Shiva. It is their union which is the mystic coition (Maithuna) of the Tantras.[677] There are two forms of union (Sāmarasya)[678]—namely, the first, which is the gross (Sthūla), or the union of the physical embodiments of the Supreme Consciousness; and the second, which is the subtle (Sūkshma), or the union of the quiescent and active principles in Consciousness itself. It is the latter which is liberation.

Lastly, what in a philosophical sense is the nature of the process here described? Shortly stated, energy (Shakti) polarises itself into two forms—namely, static or potential (Kundalinī), and dynamic (the working forces of the body as Prāna). Behind all activity there is a static background. This *static center* in the human body is the central

---

674 See my "Shakti and Shākta."

675 The statements in the Tantras that this union is liberation (Mukti) is mere Stuti—that is, praise in the Indian fashion of the subject in hand, which goes beyond the actual fact. The European reader who takes such statements *au pied de la lettre* and ridicules them makes himself (to the knowing) ridiculous. What actually happens in such case is a fugitive bliss, which, like all bliss, emanates from the Great Bliss, but is a pale reflection of it which nowise, in itself, secures immunity from future rebirth. It is the bliss of this lower Sādhanā, as the union of Kundalinī Shakti with Shiva is that of the higher.

676 As the Parāpraveshikā beautifully calls Her. Yoginīhridaya Tantra says, "She is the heart, for from Her all things issue."

677 This, as the Yoginī Tantra says, is the coition (Maithuna) of those who are Yati (who have controlled their passions).

678 This term indicates the enjoyment which arises from the union of male and female, which may be either of bodies or of their inner principles.

Serpent Power in the Mūlādhāra (root support). It is the power which is the static support (Ādhāra) of the whole body, and all its moving Pranik forces. This center (Kendra) of power is a gross form of Chit or Consciousness—that is, in itself (Svarūpa) it is Consciousness, and by appearance it is a power which, as the highest form of force, is a manifestation of it. Just as there is a distinction (though identity at base) between the supreme quiescent Consciousness and its active power (Shakti), so, when Consciousness manifests as energy (Shakti), it possesses the twin aspects of potential and kinetic energy. There can be no partition, in fact, of reality. To the perfect eye of the Siddha the process of becoming is an ascription (Adhyāsa).[679] To the imperfect eye of the Sādhaka—that is, the aspirant for Siddhi (perfected accomplishment)—to the spirit which is still toiling through the lower planes and variously identifying itself with them, becoming is tending to appear, and appearance is real. The Shākta Tantra is a rendering of Vedantic truth from this practical point of view, and represents the world-process as a polarization in Consciousness itself. This polarity as it exists in, and as, the body, is destroyed by Yoga, which disturbs the equilibrium of bodily consciousness which is the result of the maintenance of these two poles. In the human body the potential pole of energy, which is the supreme power, is stirred to action, on which the moving forces (dynamic Shakti) supported by it are drawn thereto, and the whole dynamism[680] thus engendered moves upward to unite with the quiescent Consciousness in the highest lotus.[681] This matter has been so well put by my friend Professor Pramathanātha Mukhyopādhyāya that I cannot improve on his account,[682] and therefore cite it in lieu of giving a further description of my own:

"When you say that Kundalī Shakti is the primordial Shakti *at rest*, I am led to think of an analogy (and it may be more than an analogy) in modern science. Cosmic energy in its physical aspect may be considered either as static or as dynamic, the former being a condition of equilibrium, the latter a condition of motion or change of relative position. Thus a material thing apparently at rest (there being no

---

[679] To the eye of Siddhi, to the spirit who is Udāsīna (simple witness unmindful of the external world), becoming is Adhyāsa and nothing real (in the Indian sense of that term, as used by Shangkara). Creation (Srishti) is Vivartta, or apparent and not real evolution (Parināma), Adhyāsa is attributing to something that which it does not really possess.

[680] The projecting power of consciousness withdraws its projections into the sensual world, and the power of Consciousness merges in Consciousness itself.

[681] Why here, it may be asked, seeing that Consciousness is all pervading? True; but there the tāmasik force of Māyā is at its lowest strength. Therefore Consciousness is reached there.

[682] In a letter to me, in reply to one of mine answering some inquiries made by him as regards this Yoga. He wrote that my letter had suggested certain ideas "on a subject of supreme interest philosophically and practically in the life of a Hindu," which I reproduce in the text. The bracketed translations of the Sanskrit words are mine.

absolute rest except in pure Consciousness or Chit) should be regarded as energy or Shakti equilibrated, the various elements of it holding one another in check (or, as the mathematicians will say, the algebraic sum of the forces being zero). Of course, in any given case the equilibrium is relative rather than absolute. The important thing to note is this polarization of Shakti into two forms—static and dynamic.

"In the tissues of a living body, again, the operative energy (whatever the nature of that may be, whether we believe in a special 'vital force' or not) polarizes itself into two similar forms—anabolic and katabolic—one tending to change and the other to conserve the tissues, the actual condition of the tissues being simply the resultant of these two coexistent or concurrent activities.

"In the mind or experience also this polarization or polarity is patent to reflection. In my own writings[683] I have constantly urged this polarity between pure Chit and the stress which is involved in it: there is a stress or Shakti developing the mind through an infinity of forms and changes; but all these forms and changes are known as involved in the pure and unbounded ether of awareness (Chidākāsha). This analysis therefore exhibits the primordial Shakti in the same two polar forms as before—static and dynamic—and here the polarity is most fundamental and approaches absoluteness.

"Lastly, let us consider for one moment the atom of modern science. The chemical atom has ceased to be an atom (indivisible unit of matter). We have instead the electron theory. According to this, the so-called atom is a miniature universe very much like our own solar system. At the center of this atomic system we have a charge of positive electricity round which a cloud of negative charges (called electrons) is supposed to revolve, just as myriads of planets and smaller bodies revolve round the sun. The positive and the negative charges hold each other in check, so that the atom is a condition of equilibrated energy, and does not therefore ordinarily break up, though it may possibly break up and set free its equilibrated store of energy, as probably it does in the emanations of the radium. What do we notice here? The same polarity of Shakti into a static and a dynamic partner—viz., the positive charge at rest at the center, and the negative charges in motion round about the center: a most suggestive analogy or illustration, perhaps, of the cosmic fact. The illustration may be carried into other domains of science and philosophy, but I may as well forbear going into details. For the present we may, I think, draw this important conclusion:

"Shakti, as manifesting itself in the universe, divides itself into two polar aspects—static and dynamic—which implies that you cannot

---

[683] "Approaches to Truth," "The Patent Wonder," valuable presentments in modern terms of the ancient Vedantic teaching.

have it in a dynamic form without at the same time having it in a corresponding static form, much like the poles of a magnet. In any given sphere of activity of force we must have, according to this cosmic principle, a static background—Shakti at rest or 'coiled,' as the Tantras say.

"Before I proceed, let me point out what I conceive to be the fundamental significance of our Tantric and Pauranic Kālī. This figure or Mūrti is both real and symbolic, as indeed every Mūrti in the so-called Hindu mythology is. Now, the Divine Mother Kālī is a symbol of the cosmic truth just explained. Sadāshiva, on whose breast She dances, nude and dark, is the static background of pure Chit, white and inert (Shavarūpa), because pure Chit is in itself Svaprakāsha (self-manifest) and Nishkriya (actionless). At the same time, apart from and beyond Consciousness there can be nothing—no power or Shakti—hence the Divine Mother stands on the bosom of the Divine Father. The Mother Herself is all activity and Gunamayī (in Her aspect as Prakriti composed of the Gunas). Her nakedness means that, though She encompasses all, there is nothing to encompass Herself; her darkness means that She is inscrutable, avāngmānasagocharā (beyond the reach of thought and speech). Of course, this is no partition of reality into two (there lies the imperfection of the Sāngkhya doctrine of Purusha and Prakriti, which is otherwise all right), but merely polarization in our experience of an indivisible fact which is the primordial (Ādya) Shakti itself. Thus Chit is also Shakti. Shiva is Shakti and Shakti is Shiva, as the Tantras say. It is Gunāshrayā (support of Gunas) as well as Gunamaya (whose substance is Gunas); Nirguna (attributeless) as well as Saguna (with attribute), as said in a well-known passage of the Chandī.

"Your suggestive hint[684] makes the nature of the Kundalī Shakti rather clear to me. You are quite right, perhaps, in saying that the cosmic Shakti is the Samashti (collectivity) in relation to which the Kundalī in the bodies is only the Vyashti (individual): it is an illustration, a reproduction on a miniature scale, a microcosmic plan, of the whole. The law or principle of the whole—that of macrocosmic Shakti—should therefore be found in the Kundalī. That law we have seen to be the law of polarization into static-dynamic or potential-kinetic aspects. In the living body, therefore, there must be such polarization. Now, the Kundalī coiled three times and a half at the Mūlādhāra is the indispensable and unfailing static background of the dynamic Shakti operative in the whole body, carrying on processes and working out changes. The body, therefore, may be compared to a magnet with two poles. The Mūlādhāra is the static pole in relation to the rest of the body, which is dynamic; the working, the body,

[684] That Kundalinī is the static Shakti.

necessarily presupposes and finds such a static support, hence perhaps[685] the name Mūlādhāra, the fundamental support. In one sense, the static Shakti at the Mūlādhāra is necessarily coexistent with the creating and evolving Shakti of the body, because the dynamic aspect or pole can never be without its static counterpart. In another sense, it is the Shakti *left over* (you have yourself pointed this out, and the italics are yours) after the Prithivī—the last of the Bhūtas—has been created, a magazine of power to be drawn upon and utilized for further activity, if there should arise any need for such. Taking the two senses together (yours as well as mine), Shakti at the Mūlādhāra is both coexistent with every act of creation or manifestation and is the residual effect of such act—both cause and effect, in fact—an idea which, deeply looked into, shows no real contradiction. There is, in fact, what the physicist will describe as a cycle or circuit in action. Let us take the impregnated ovum—the earliest embryological stage of the living body. In it the Kundalī Shakti is already presented in its two polar aspects: the ovum, which the mother-element represents, one pole (possibly the static), and the spermatazoon, which is the father-element, represents the other (possibly the dynamic).[686] From their fusion proceed those processes which the biologist calls differentiation and integration; but in all this process of creation the cycle can be fairly easily traced. Shakti flows out of the germinal cell (fertilized ovum), seizes upon foreign matter, and assimilates it, and thereby grows in bulk; divides and subdivides itself, and then again co-ordinates all its divided parts into one organic whole. Now in all this we have the cycle. Seizing upon foreign matter is an outwardly directed activity, assimilation is an inwardly directed activity or return current; cell division and multiplication is an outwardly directed operation, coordination is inwardly directed;[687] and so on. The force in the germ-cell is overflowing, but also continuously it is flowing back into itself, the two operations presupposing and sustaining each other, as in every circuit. The given stock of force in the germ-cell, which is static so long as the fusion of the male and female elements does not take place in the womb; is the necessary starting-point of all creative activity; it is the primordial cause, therefore, in relation to the body—primordial as well as constantly given, unceasing. On the other hand, the reaction of every creative action, the return current or flowing back of every unfolding overflow, constantly renews this starting force, changes it without changing its general condition of relative equilibrium (and this is quite possible, as in the case of any material system); the force in the germ-cell may therefore be also regarded as a perpetual effect, something left over and

---

685 Certainly.

686 The process of fertilization is dealt with in the Mātrikābheda Tantra.

687 This outflow and inflow is a common Tantrik notion.

set against the working forces of the body. Many apparently inconsistent ideas enter into this conception, and they have to be reconciled.

"1. We start with a force in the germ-cell which is statical at first (though, like a dicotyledon seed, or even a modern atom, it involves within itself both a statical and a dynamical pole; otherwise, from pure rest, involving no possibility of motion, no motion could ever arise). Let this be the Kundalī coiled.

"2. Then there is creative impulse arising out of it; this is motion out of rest. By this, the Kundalī becomes partly static and partly dynamic, or ejects, so to say, a dynamic pole out of it in order to evolve the body, but remaining a static pole or background itself all along. In no part of the process has the Kundalī really uncoiled itself altogether, or even curtailed its three coils and a half. Without this Mūlādhāra Shakti remaining intact no evolution could be possible at all. It is the hinge upon which everything else turns.

"3. Each creative act again reacts on the Mūlādhāra Shakti, so that such reaction, without disturbing the relative rest of the coiled Shakti, changes its volume or intensity, but does not curtail or add to the number of coils. For instance, every natural act of respiration reacts on the coiled Shakti at the Mūlādhāra, but it does not commonly make much difference. But Prānāyāma powerfully reacts on it, so much so that it awakes the dormant power and sends it piercing through the centers. Now, the common description that the Kundalī uncoils Herself then and goes up the Sushumnā, leaving the Mūlādhāra, should, I think, be admitted with caution That static background can never be absolutely dispensed with. As you have yourself rightly observed, 'Shakti can never be depleted, but this is how to look at it.' Precisely; the Kundalī, when powerfully worked upon by Yoga, sends forth an emanation or ejection in the likeness of Her own self (like the 'ethereal double' of the Theosophists and Spiritualists) which pierces through the various centers until it becomes blended, as you point out, with the Mahākundalī of Shiva at the highest or seventh center. Thus, while this 'ethereal double' or self-ejection of the coiled power at the Mūlādhāra ascends the Sushumnā, the coiled power itself does not and need not stir from its place. It is like a spark given from an over-saturated[688] electro-magnetic machine; or, rather, it is like the emanations of radium which do not sensibly detract from the energy contained in it. This last, perhaps, is the closest physical parallel of the case that we are trying to understand. As a well-known passage in the Upanishad has it, 'The whole (Pūrna) is subtracted from the whole, and yet the whole remains.' I think our present case comes very near to this. The Kundalī at the Mūlādhāra is the whole primordial Shakti in monad or germ or

688 Overcharged.

latency: that is why it is coiled. The Kundalī that mounts up the Nādī is also the whole Shakti in a specially dynamic form—an eject likeness of the Eternal Serpent. The result of the last fusion (there are successive fusions in the various centers also) in the Sahasrāra is also the whole, or Pūrna. This is how I look at it. In this conception the permanent static background is not really depleted, much less is it dispensed with.

"4. When again I say that the volume or intensity of the coiled power can be affected (though not its configuration and relative equilibrium), I do not mean to throw up the principle of conservation of energy in relation to the Kundalī, which is the embodiment of all energy. It is merely the conversion of static (potential) energy into dynamic (kinetic) energy in part, the sum remaining constant. As we have to deal with infinities here, an exact physical rendering of this principle is not to be expected. The Yogī therefore simply 'awakens,' and never creates Shakti. By the way, the germ-cell which evolves the body does not, according to modern biology, cease to be a germ-cell in any stage of the complicated process. The original germ-cell splits up into two: one half gradually develops itself into the body of a plant or animal—this is the somatic cell; the other half remains encased within the body practically unchanged, and is transmitted in the process of reproduction to the offspring—that is, the germ-plasm. Now, this germ-plasm is unbroken through the whole line of propagation. This is Weismann's doctrine of 'continuity of the germ-plasm,' which has been widely accepted, though it is but an hypothesis."

In a subsequent postscript the Professor wrote:

"1. Shakti being either static or dynamic, every dynamic form necessarily presupposes a static background. A purely dynamic activity (which is motion in its physical aspect) is impossible without a static support or ground (Adhāra). Hence the philosophical doctrine of absolute motion or change, as taught by old Heraclitus and the Buddhists and by modern Bergson, is wrong; it is based neither upon correct logic nor upon clear intuition. The constitution of an atom reveals the static-dynamic polarization of Shakti; other and more complex forms of existence also do the same. In the living body this necessary static background is Mūlādhāra, where Shakti is Kundalī coiled. All the functional activity of the body, starting from the development of the germ-cell, is correlated to, and sustained by the Shakti concentrated at, the Mūlādhāra. Cosmic creation, too, ending with the evolution of Prithivī Tattva (it is, however, an unending process in a different sense, and there perhaps Henri Bergson, who claims that the creative impulse is ever original and resourceful, is right), also presupposes a cosmic static background (over and above Chidākāsha—ether of Consciousness), which is the Mahākundalī Shakti in the Chinmayadeha (body of Consciousness) of Parameshvara or Parameshvarī (the Supreme Lord in male and female aspect). In the earliest stage of creation, when the world arises only as a mist in Divine Consciousness, it requires, as the principle or pole of Tat (That), the correlate principle or pole of Aham (I); in the development of the former, the latter serves as the static background. In our own experiences, too, 'apperception' or consciousness of self is the sustaining background—a string, so to say, which holds together all the loose beads of our elements of feeling. The sustaining ground or Ādhāra, as the seat of static force, therefore is found, in one form or other, in every phase and stage of creative evolution. The absolute or ultimate form is, of course, Chit-Shakti (Consciousness as power) itself, the unfailing light of awareness about which our Gāyatrī (Mantra) says: 'Which sustains and impels all the activities of Buddhi.' This fact is symbolized by the Kālī-mūrti: not a mere symbol, however.

"2. My remarks about the rising or awakening of the Serpent Power at the Mūlādhāra have been, perhaps, almost of the nature of a paradox. The coiled power, though awakened, uncoiled, and rising, never really stirs from its place; only a sort of 'ethereal double' or 'eject' is unloosed and sent up through the system of centers. Now, in plain language, this ethereal double or eject means the dynamic equivalent of the static power concentrated at the Mūla, or root. Whenever by Prāṇāyāma of Bījamantra, or any other suitable means, the Mūlādhāra becomes, like an electro-magnetic machine, over-saturated (though the Kundalī Shakti at the Mūla is infinite and exhaustless, yet the capacity of a given finite organism to contain it in a static form is limited, and therefore there may be over-saturation), a dynamic or operative equivalent of the static power is set up, possibly by a law similar to Nature's law of induction, by which the static power itself is not depleted or rendered other than static. It is not that static energy at the Mūla wholly passes over into a dynamic form—the coiled Kundalī leaving the Mūla, thus making it a void; that cannot be, and, were it so, all dynamic operation in the body would cease directly for want of a background. The coiled power remains coiled or static, and yet something apparently passes out of the Mūla—viz., the dynamic equivalent. This paradox can perhaps be explained in two ways:

"(*a*) One explanation was suggested in my main letter. The potential Kundalī Shakti becomes partly converted into kinetic Shakti, and yet, since Shakti, even as given in the Mūla-center, is an infinitude, it is not depleted: the potential store always remains unexhausted. I referred to a passage in the Upanishad about Pūrna. In this case, the dynamic equivalent is a partial conversion of one mode of energy into another. In Layayoga (here described) it is ordinarily so. When, however, the infinite potential becomes an infinite kinetic—when, that is to say, the coiled power at the Mūla becomes absolutely uncoiled—we have necessarily the dissolution of the three bodies (Sthūla, Linga, and Kārana—gross, subtle, causal), and consequently Videhamukti (bodiless liberation), because the static background in relation to a particular form of existence has now wholly given way, according to our hypothesis. But Mahākundalī remains; hence individual Mukti (liberation) need not mean dissolution of Samsāra (transmigrating worlds) itself. Commonly, however, as the Tantra says, 'Pītvā pītvā punah pītvā,' etc.[689]

"(*b*) The other explanation is suggested by the law of induction. Take an electro-magnetic machine;[690] if a suitable substance be placed near it, it will induce in it an equivalent and opposite kind of electro-magnetism[690] without losing its own stock of energy. In conduction, energy flows over into another thing, so that the source loses and the other thing gains what it has lost, and its gain is similar in kind to the loss. Not so induction. There the source does not lose, and the induced energy is equivalent and opposite in kind to the inducing energy. Thus a positive charge will induce an equivalent negative charge in a neighboring object. Now, shall we suppose that the Mūlādhāra, when it becomes over-saturated, induces in the neighboring center (say, Svādhishthāna) a dynamic (not static) equivalent?[691] Is this what the rise of the Serpent Power really means? The explanation, I am tempted to think, is not perhaps altogether fantastic."

In reply to this highly interesting and illustrative account of my friend, I wrote suggesting some difficulties in the way of the acceptance of his statement that Kundalī-Shakti did not, in fact, Herself uncoil and ascend, but projected upwards an emanation in the likeness of Her own self. The difficulty I felt was this: In the first place, the Yoga books, to which full credence must be given in this matter, unequivocally affirm that Kundalī Herself does, in fact, ascend. This is borne out by some inquiries made of a Tantrik Pandit very familiar with his Shāstra[692] after the receipt of the letter quoted. As the body of the Yogī still lives, though in an inert corpse-like condition, when consciousness of it is lost, I asked him how the body was sustained when Kundalī left Her central abode. His answer was that it was maintained by the nectar which flows from the union of Shiva and Shakti in the Sahasrāra. This nectar is an ejection of power generated by their union. If Kundalī does not ascend, but a mere emanative spark of Her, how (he further asked) is it that the body becomes cold and corpselike? Would this follow if the power still remained at its center,

[689] "Having drunk, having drunk, having again drunk," a passage in the Kulārnava Tantra signifying not actual drinking (as some suppose), but repeated raising of Kundalinī.

[690] We may say "Take a magnet" and "magnetism."

[691] Here is the seat of the first moving, or Pashyantī Shabda.

[692] Though not practicing himself, his brother, from whom he had learnt, was an adept in this Yoga. His statements I have always found of peculiar value. It must, however, be remembered that, however learned or practiced a Pandit or Yogī may be, it is possible for him to be ignorant of the scientific implications of his doctrine and practice.

and merely sent forth a dynamic equivalent of itself? There were further difficulties in the theory put forward by my friend, though it may be that there are also difficulties in the acceptance of the statement that the Mūlādhāra is entirely depleted of the great power. I suggested that Kundalī was the static center of the whole body as a complete conscious organism, and that each of the parts of the body and their constituent cells must have their own static centers, which would uphold such parts and cells; and that the life of the body, as a collection of material particles (from which the general organic consciousness as a whole was withdrawn), was sustained by the nectar which flowed from Kundalī Shakti when in union with Shiva in the Sahasrāra. In reply, Professor P. Mukhopādhyāya dealt with the matter as follows:

"According to my presentation of the case, something—viz., a dynamic equivalent or 'operative double'—is certainly sent forth from the Mūlādhāra, but this basic center or seat is not depleted or rendered void of static energy in consequence of that operation. The Mūla (root), as the seat of static or coiled power, can never be dispensed with. It is the *sine qua non* of all functions of the triple body (gross, subtle, causal). It is, so to say, the buffer or base against which any activity of the Jīva (embodied consciousness) must react or recoil, like a naval or any other kind of heavy gun against its base or emplacement. Thus, while the dynamic or uncoiled Shakti ascends the axis, the static or coiled Shakti retains its place at the Mūla, and remains as the very possibility of the dynamic upheaval. The ascending power is simply the dynamic counterpart of the static ground. To say that Kundalī leaves its place and ascends is only to say that it ceases to be Kundalī and becomes dynamic. The ascending power is therefore uncoiled or non-Kundalī power; it is the dynamic expression of the Kundalī power. So far all can agree. But the question is: Is the Mūla depleted or deprived of all power (especially coiled power) when that dynamical expression leaves it and ascends the axis? Is the dynamic expression wholly at the expense of the static ground? Should the latter cease in order that the former may commence?

"Here, I think, I must answer in the negative. It is a case of power leaving as well as remaining—leaving as dynamic and remaining as static; it is the case of the Kundalī being uncoiled in one aspect or pole and remaining still coiled in another aspect or pole. A paradox, perhaps, but, like most paradoxes, it is likely to be true.

"Is scriptural authority, which, by-the-by, I hold in utmost reverence, really challenged by this interpretation? The nature of the dynamic equivalent and its relation to the static background have been indicated in the previous two communications, and I need not dilate on them. I have claimed throughout that the Mūlādhāra, as the seat of static (*i.e.*, coiled) power, can never be rendered a vacuum in relation to such power except in the circumstances of Videhamukti (bodiless liberation), when the triple body (gross, subtle, causal) must dissolve. I think, also, that the point of view which you have taken can be reconciled with this interpretation of the matter. The Kundalī Shakti is the static aspect of the life of the whole organized body, as you say rightly. The relation between the lives of the individual cells and that of the whole organism is not clearly understood in science. Is the common life a merely mechanical resultant of the lives of the individual cells, or are the lives of the individual cells only detailed manifestations of the common life? In other words, is the common life-cause and the cell-lives effects or *vice versa*? Science is not yet settled on this point. As a subscriber to the Shaktivāda (doctrine of Shakti) I am inclined, however, to give primacy to the common life; in the germ-cell itself the common life is given in substance, and the whole development of the Jīvadeha (Jīva body) is only the detailed carrying out in particulars of what has been already given in substance, according to the principle of Adrishta (Karma). Nevertheless, I am quite willing to concede to the individual cells lives of semi-independence. 'Semi,' because they require to be sustained to a considerable degree by the life of the whole. Benefit or injury to the life of the whole reacts on the condition of the cells; the death of the whole life is followed by the death of the cells, and so on.

"Now, in every cell there is, of course, static-dynamic polarity; in the whole organism, also, there is such polarity or correlation. In the whole organism the static pole or correlate is the coiled power at the Mūlādhāra, and the dynamic correlate is the operative power (the five Prānas—viz., Prāna, Apāna, Samāna, Udāna, and Vyāna), which actually carries on the various functions of the body. Ordinarily, therefore, this dynamic power is distributed over the whole body, vitalizing not merely the larger tissues, but the microscopic cells. Now, the devitalization (as you say) of the body in Kundalīyoga or Shatchakrabheda is due, I venture to think, not to the depletion or privation of the static power at the Mūlādhāra, but to the concentration or convergence of the dynamic power ordinarily diffused over the whole body, so that the dynamic equivalent which is set up against the static background or Kundalī Shakti is only the diffused fivefold Prāna gathered home—withdrawn from the other tissues of the body—and concentrated in a line along the axis. Thus ordinarily the dynamic equivalent is the Prāna diffused over all the tissues; in Yoga it is converged along the axis, the static equivalent or Kundalī Shakti enduring in both cases. Thus also the polarity or correlation is maintained: in the former case between Shakti at Mūlādhāra and the diffused Prāna; in the latter case between Shakti at Mūla and the converged Prāna along the axis. This will perhaps adequately explain coldness, increased inertia, insensibility, etc., of the rest of the body in Kundalī Yoga of which you write. Commonly in Yoga this withdrawal and convergence of Prāna is incomplete; the residual Prāna, together with the lives of the cells, keeps the body alive, though inert or corpselike. In the case of complete withdrawal and focusing, the cells will die and the body disintegrate.

"On the other hand, if the coiled power were simply and wholly uncoiled (*i.e.*, dynamized) in Kundalī Yoga, then there should be an excess rather than a defect of vitality all over the body; nothing would be subtracted from the already available dynamic energy of the body, but something would be added to it on account of the static power at the Mūla being rendered kinetic, and going up the axis and influencing neighboring tissues.

"Hence I should venture to conclude that the static power at the base of the axis, without itself being depleted or rendered other than static, induces or produces a dynamic equivalent which is the diffused Prāna of the body gathered and converged along the axis. The states in the process may thus be summarily indicated:

"1. To begin with, there is coiled power at the base of the axis and its necessary correlate, the dynamic Prāna, diffused all over the body in the five forms.

"2. In Kundalī Yoga some part of the already available dynamic Prāna is made to act at the base of the axis in a suitable manner, by which means the base—or particularly the four-petalled Padma (lotus) which represents this center—becomes over-saturated, and reacts on the whole diffused dynamic power (or Prāna) of the body by withdrawing it from the tissues and converging it along the line of the axis. In this way the diffused dynamic equivalent becomes the converged dynamic equivalent along the axis. This is what the rising of the serpent perhaps means.

"(*a*) In thus reacting, the coiled power has not lost its general equilibrium or static condition.

(*b*) The *modus operandi* of this reaction is difficult to indicate, but it is probably (as suggested in my previous communications) either (i.) a partial conversion of the infinite coiled power into the sort of influence that can thus gather the diffused Prāna, and converge it in its own resultant line along the axis, or (ii.) an inductive action, analogous to electro-magnetic action, by which the Prānas are collected and converged. In this latter case there is no need for conversion of the static energy. We shall have perhaps to choose between, or rather coordinate, these two explanations in understanding the *modus operandi*. In mathematical language, the diffused Prāna is a scalar quantity (having magnitude, but no direction), while the converged Prāna is a vector quantity (having both magnitude and definite direction).

"Suppose, lastly, we are witnessing with a Divyachakshu (inner eye) the progress of Kundalī Yoga. There something like condensed lightning (Tadit) is rising from the Mūlādhāra, and gathering momentum in going up from Chakra to Chakra, till the consummation is reached at the Paramshivasthāna (abode of the Supreme Shiva). But look back, and behold the Kulakundalinī is also there at the Mūla coiled three times and a half round the Svayambhu Linga. She has left and yet remained or stayed, and is again coming back to Herself. Is not this vision supported by scriptural authority and the experience of the Yogī?"

Putting aside detail, the main principle appears to be that, when "wakened," Kundalī Shakti either Herself (or as my friend suggests in Her eject) ceases to be a static power which sustains the world-consciousness, the content of which is held only so long as She "sleeps," and, when once set in movement, is drawn to that other static center in the thousand-petalled lotus (Sahasrāra), which is Herself in union with the Shiva-consciousness, or the consciousness of ecstasy beyond the world of forms. When Kundalī "sleeps" man is awake to this world. When She "awakes" he sleeps—that is, loses all consciousness of the world and enters his causal body. In Yoga he passes beyond to formless Consciousness.

I have only to add, without further discussion of the point, that practitioners of this Yoga claim that it is higher than any other,[693] and that the Samādhi (ecstasy) attained thereby is more perfect. The reason which they allege is this: In Dhyānayoga ecstasy takes place through detachment from the world and mental concentration, leading to vacuity of mental operation (Vritti), or the uprising of pure Consciousness unhindered by the limitations of the mind.[694] The degree to which this unveiling of consciousness is effected depends upon the meditative powers (Jnānashakti) of the Sādhaka and the extent of his detachment from the world. On the other hand Kundalī, who is all Shaktis, and who is therefore Jnānashakti itself, produces, when awakened by the Yogī, full Jnāna for him. Secondly, in the Samādhi of Dhyānayoga there is no rousing and union of Kundalī Shakti, with the accompanying bliss and acquisition of special powers (Siddhi). Further, in Kundalī Yoga there is not merely a Samādhi through meditation, but through the central power of the Jīva, a power which carries with it the forces of both body and mind. The union in that sense is claimed to be more complete than that enacted through mental methods only. Though in both cases bodily consciousness is lost, in Kundalī Yoga not only the

---

[693] I do not say either that this is admitted or that it is a fact. Only he who has had both true spiritual experience and has been through this Yoga can say. I merely here state the facts. See the criticism *ante* at p. 19. Another is perhaps suggested by the distinction made in the Buddhist Tantras between natural and artificial Samādhi.

[694] What, I believe, the Christian Scientist calls the "mortal mind." In Indian doctrine mind is a temporal and limited manifestation of the unlimited eternal Consciousness. As the states are different, two terms are better than one.

mind, but the body in so far as it is represented by its central power (or, may be, its eject), is actually united with Shiva. This union produces an enjoyment (Bhukti) which the Dhyānayogī does not possess. Whilst both the Divya Yogī and the Vīra Sādhaka have enjoyment (Bhukti), that of the former is infinitely more intense, being an experience of Bliss itself. The enjoyment of the Vīra Sādhaka is but a reflection of it on the physical plane, a welling up of the true bliss through the deadening coverings and trammels of matter. Again, whilst it is said that both have liberation (Mukti), this word is used in Vīra Sādhanā in a figurative sense only, indicating a bliss which is the nearest approach on the physical plane to that of Mukti, and a Bhāva or feeling of momentary union of Shiva and Shakti which ripens in the higher Yoga Sādhanā into the literal liberation of the Yogī. He, in its fullest and literal sense, has both enjoyment (Bhukti) and liberation (Mukti). Hence its claim to be the Emperor of all Yogas.

However this may be, I leave at this point the subject, with the hope that others will continue the inquiry I have here initiated. It, and other matters in the Tantra Shāstra, seem to me (whatever be their inherent value) worthy of an investigation which they have not yet received.

Description of the Six Centers

(*SHAT*CHAKRA NIRŪPA*N*A.)

PRELIMINARY VERSE.

Now I speak of the first sprouting shoot (of the Yoga plant) of complete realization of the Brahman, which is to be achieved, according to the Tantras, by means of the six Chakras and so forth in their proper order.

COMMENTARY.

He alone who has become acquainted with the wealth[695] of the six Lotuses[696] by Mahā-yoga is able to explain the inner principles[697] thereof. Not even the most excellent among the wise, nor the oldest (in experience), is able, without the mercy of the Guru,[698] to explain the inner principles[697] relating to the six Lotuses, replete as they are with

[695] Parichita-s*had*ambhoja-vibhava.

[696] That is, the *Shat*-chakra; six centers, which are: mūlādhāra svādhis*hth*āna, ma*n*ipūra, anāhata, vishuddha, and ājnā.

[697] Antas-tattva—*i.e.*, relating to the s*hat*-chakra.

[698] K*r*ipā-nātha, Lord of Mercy—*i.e.*, the Guru.

the greatness of *Sha*, Sa, and Ha.[699] Now, the very merciful Pūr*n*ānanda Svāmī, wishful to rescue the world sunk in the mire of misery, takes that task upon himself. He does so to guide Sādhakas[700]; to impart Tattva-jnāna,[701] which leads to liberation; and also with the desire of speaking of the union of Ku*nd*alinī[702] with the six Chakras.[703]

"*Now*" (Atha).—The force of this particle is to show the connection of this book with the Author's work entitled Shrī-tattva-chintāma*n*i, the first five chapters of which deal with the rites and practices preliminary to *Shat*-chakra-nirūpa*n*a.[704] In this book he speaks of the first shoot of the realization of the Brahman.

Paramānanda (Supreme Bliss) means Brahman, who, says the Shruti, is Eternal (Nityam), and is knowledge (Vijnānam and Bliss (Ānandam).

"*Following the Tantras*" (Tantrānusārena)—*i.e.*, following the authority of the Tantras.[705]

"*First sprouting shoot*" (Prathamāngkura)—*i.e.*, the first steps which lead to realization of the Brahman. The first cause of such realization is achieved by knowledge of the six Chakras, the Nā*d*īs,[706] and so forth, which is the Tāntrika Yoga Sādhanā.

"*Complete realization*" (Nirvāha).—The Sanskrit word means "accomplishment" here; it is "the accomplishment of the immediate experiential realization of the Brahman."[707]

"*Achieved by means of the six Chakras and other things*" (*Shat*-chakrādi-kramodgata)—*i.e.*, attained by[708] meditating on the six Chakras, viz.: Mūlādhāra, Svādhis*hth*āna, Ma*n*ipūra, Anāhata, Vishuddha, and Ājnā and other things,[709] viz.: on the Nā*d*īs,[710] the

---

[699] *Sha*., Sa, Ha. *Sha* = Final Liberation. Sa = Knowledge. Ha = Supreme Spirit; also Brahmā, Vi*sh*nu, and Shiva, respectively.

[700] Those who practice Sādhanā, or spiritual discipline; here aspirants for Yoga:

[701] Tattva-jnāna = Brahma-jnāna, or Brahman knowledge.

[702] The Devī as Shabda Brahman (Shabda-brahma-rūpā Ku*nd*alinī, v. 2, *post*) in the world of the body (Pi*nd*ā*nd*ā), or K*sh*udra-brahmā*nd*a (microcosm). Verse 10 describes Her as She who maintains all beings in the world by inhalation and exhalation. Unmanifested "sound" assumed the form of Ku*nd*alī in the animal body (vv. 10, 11).

[703] Mūlādhāra, etc.

[704] *Shat*-chakra-nirūpa*n*a. Nirūpa*n*a = investigation, ascertainment into, and of, the six Chakras. This forms the sixth chapter of Pūr*n*ānanda's Svami-Shri-tattva-chintāma*n*i.

[705] In which is to be found a detailed description of the process here described, known as *Shat*-Chakra-bheda, or piercing of the six Chakras.

[706] The "nerves," or channels of energy (see v. 2). Nā*d*ī is derived from the root *nad*, "motion," and means a channel (Vivara).

[707] Brahma-sāk*sh*ātkāra-rūpa-ni*sh*patti*h*.

[708] "Attained by." This is Udgata, which literally means "sprung out of" or "sprouted out of."

[709] According to Shangkara, by "other things" are meant the Sahasrāra, etc. This Shangkara here and hereafter referred to is a commentator on this work, and not the philosopher Shangkarāchāryya.

[710] See note 725.

Linggas,[711] the five Elements,[712] Shiva, Shakti, etc., connected with the six Chakras, in their order.

The *order* (Krama) is, first, meditation on them, next awakening of Ku*nd*alinī, and Her passage to the Brahmalotus and then Her return therefrom; the union of Shiva and Shakti, etc., and so forth.

"*Order*" (Krama) by which it is attained, and this is the same as Yoga practice.

The Author in substance says: "I speak of the first step (Angkura) of the practice which is the First Cause of the immediate or experiential realization[713] of the Brahman, brought about by a knowledge of the six Chakras, as is laid down in the Tantras."

VERSE 1.

In the space outside the Meru,[714] placed on the left and the right, are the two Shirās,[715] Shashī[716] and Mihira.[717] The Nā*d*ī Su*sh*umnā, whose substance is the threefold Gu*n*as,[718] is in the middle. She is the form of Moon, Sun, and Fire;[719] Her body, a string of blooming Dhūstūra[720] flowers, extends from the middle of the Kanda[721] to the Head, and the Vajrā inside Her extends, shining, from the Me*dh*ra[722] to the Head.

COMMENTARY.

Now, Yoga like that which is about to be spoken of cannot be achieved without a knowledge of the six Chakras and the Nā*d*īs; the Author therefore describes the relative Nā*d*īs in this and the following two verses.

"*In the space outside*" (Vāhya-pradesha) the two Nā*d*īs. Shashī and Mihira (Shashi-mihira-shire = the two Nā*d*īs or Shirās, Shashī and Mihira). Shashī = Chandra (Moon); Mihira = Sūryya (Sun). These two Nā*d*īs, which are in the nature of the Moon and Sun,[723] are the Nā*d*īs, Ī*d*ā and Pinggalā.

---

711 In three of the Chakras—viz., Svayambhū, Vā*n*a, and Itara.

712 Vyoma-panchaka.

713 Brahma-sāk*sh*āt-kāra.

714 The spinal column.

715 *I.e.*, Nā*d*īs.

716 Moon—that is, the feminine, or Shakti-rūpā Nā*d*ī Ī*d*ā, on the left.

717 Sun, or the masculine, Nā*d*ī Pinggalā, on the right.

718 Meaning either (*v. post*) the Gu*n*as, Sattva, Rajas, and Tamas; or, as "strings," the Nā*d*ī Su*sh*umnā with the Nā*d*ī Vajrā inside it, and the Nā*d*ī Chitri*n*ī within the latter.

719 That is, as Chitri*n*ī, Vajri*n*ī and Su*sh*umnā.

720 *Dhatura fastuosa*, a white flower.

721 The root of all the nā*d*īs (*v. post*).

722 Penis.

723 Chandrasvarūpi*n*ī and Sūryyarūpā.

"*Meru.*"—This is the Meru-da*n*da, the backbone or spinal column, extending from the Mūla (root) or Mūlādhāra to the neck. This will be explained later.

"*Placed on the left and the right*" (Savya-dak*sh*e-nis*h*anne).

"*These two Nādīs.*—"The Īdā is placed on the left, and the Pinggalā on the right" of the Meru (Bhūta-shuddhi Tantra). The Sammohana Tantra[724] speaks of their likeness to the Sun and Moon as follows:

"The Ī*d*ā Nā*d*ī on the left is pale, and is in the nature of the Moon[725] (Chandrasvarūpi*n*ī). She is the Shakti-rupā Devī,[726] and the very embodiment of nectar (Am*r*ita-vigrahā). On the right is the masculine Pinggalā, in the nature of the Sun. She, the great Devī, is Rudrātmikā,[727] and is lustrous red like the filaments of the pomegranate flower."[728]

These two Nā*d*īs go upward singly from the Mūla (*i.e.*, Mūlādhāra), and, having reached the Ājnā Chakra, proceed to the nostrils.

The Yāmala says: "On its (*i.e.*, the Meru's) left and right are Ī*d*ā and Pinggalā. These two go straight up, alternating from left to right and right to left, and, having thus gone round all the Lotuses, these auspicious ones proceed to the nostrils."

The above passage shows the twofold and differing positions of the two Nā*d*īs. They go upward alternating from left to right and right to left, and going round the Lotuses Padma) they form a plait and go to the nostrils.

Elsewhere they are described as being placed like bows: "Know that the two Nā*d*īs Ī*d*ā and Pinggalā are shaped like bows."

Also: "She who is connected with the left scrotum is united with the Su*sh*umnā, and, passing near by the right shoulder-joint, remains bent like a bow by the heart, and having reached the left shoulder-joint passes on to the nose. Similarly, She that comes from the right scrotum passes on to the left nostril."

These two Nā*d*īs which come from the left and right scrotum, when they reach the space between the eyebrows, make with the Su*sh*umnā a plaited knot of three (Trive*n*ī) and proceed to the nostrils.

They are also thus described: "In the Ī*d*ā is the Devī Yamunā, and

[724] The seventh verse, which is not quoted by the Commentator, runs: "Inside the Meru, she who extends from the Mūla to the place of Brahman is the fiery Su*sh*umnā, the very self of all knowledge."

[725] *Cf.* Rudrayāmala, Ch. XXVII., v. 51.

[726] Shakti-rūpā—the Devī as Shakti or "female."

[727] Rudrātmikā—that is, of the nature of Rudra or "male."

[728] Ch. II., 5 and 6.

in Pinggalā is Sarasvatī, and in Su*sh*umnā dwells Gangā.[729] They form a threefold plait[730] united at the root of the Dhvaja,[731] they separate at the eyebrows, and hence it is called Trive*n*ī-yoga, and bathing there[732] yields abundant fruit."

"*Whose substance is the threefold Gunas*" (Tritaya-gu*n*a-mayī).—The compound word here used is capable of different interpretations. Reading Gu*n*a to mean "a string," it would mean "made up of three strings"—viz., Su*sh*umnā, Vajrā, and Chitri*n*ī.[733] These three form one, but considered separately they are distinct. If Gu*n*a be read to mean "quality," then it would mean "possessed of the qualities Sattva, Rajas, and Tamas." Now, the substance of Chitri*n*ī is Sattva (Sattvagu*n*amayi), of Vajrā Rajas, and of Su*sh*umnā Tamas.

"*Is in the middle*" (Madhye)—*i.e.*, in the middle or inside the Meru.

"She who is inside the Meru from the Mūla to the region of the Brahma-randhra,"[734] etc.

Tripurā-sāra-sāmuchchaya says: "She who is within the hollow of the Da*n*da., extending from the head to the Ādhāra," etc. (*i.e.*, Mūlādhāra).

Some persons rely on the following passage of the Tantrachū*d*āma*n*i, and urge that it shows that the Su*sh*umnā is outside the Meru: "O Shivā, on the left of Meru is placed the Nā*d*ī Ī*d*ā, the Moon-nectar, and on its right the Sun-like Pinggalā. Outside it (tad-vāhye)[735] and between these two is the fiery Su*sh*umnā."

But this is merely the opinion of these persons. Our Author speaks (in the following verse) of the Lotuses inside the Meru; and as the Su*sh*umnā supports these she must needs be within the Meru.

"*Form of Moon, Sun, and Fire*" (Chandra-sūryyāgni-rūpā).—Chitri*n*ī is pale, and is the form of the Moon, Vajri*n*ī,[736] is Sun-like, and hence has the luster of the filaments of the pomegranate flower; Su*sh*umnā is fiery, and hence red. The Bhūtashuddhi Tantra, in

[729] Sammohana Tantra, Ch. II., 13, thus: "In the Ī*d*ā is the Devī Jāhnavī, and Yamunā is in Pinggala, and Sarasvatī is in Su*sh*umnā"—all names of Indian sacred rivers.

[730] This is also interpreted to mean that the three Nā*d*īs conjoin at the three Granthis—Brahma-granthi, Vis*h*uu-granthi, and Rudragranthi.

[731] The penis.

[732] By "bathing there," etc., in the "rivers"—*i.e.*, when the mind is suffused with a full knowledge of this Chakra—great benefit is thereby attained.

[733] Sus*h*umnā is the outermost sheath, and Chitrinī the innermost, and within Chitrinī is Brahmanā*d*i, the channel along which Ku*nd*alī goes.

[734] Sammohana Tantra, II. 7; also occurs in Ch. XXVII., v. 52, of Rudrayāmala.

[735] If Tad-vāhye be interpreted to mean outside these two, then this apparent contradiction is removed. Tadvāhye is formed either by Tasya vāhye or Tayor vāhye; if the latter, then the meaning would be outside the two. Those who rely upon this passage read Tad-vāhye as equa to Tasya vāhye.

[736] Vajri*n*i = vajrā.

describing the Sushumnā, supports these three descriptions. Sushumnā is the outermost and Chitrinī the innermost.

"Inside it, at a height of two fingers' breadth, is Vajrā, and so is Chitrinī; hence it is that Sushumnā is Trigunā; she is tremulous like a passionate woman; she is the receptacle of the three Gunas, Sattva, etc., and the very form of Moon, Sun, and Fire."

"*From the middle of the Kanda to the Head*" (Kanda-madhyāchchhirahsthā).—Kanda is the root of all the Nādīs. It is spoken of as follows: "Two fingers above the anus and two fingers below the medhra[737] is the Kanda-mūla, in shape like a bird's egg, and four fingers' breadth in extent. The Nādīs, 72,000 in number, emanate from it." The Nādīs come out of this Kanda.

Shirahsthā (placed in the head): By this is to be understood that she ends in the middle of the Lotus of twelve petals which is near the pericarp of the Sahasrāra, hanging downwards in the head. See the opening verse of Pādukā-panchaka: "I adore the twelve-petalled Lotus that is at the top of the Nādī, along the channel (Randhra)[738] within which the Kundalī passes."

As the Chitrinī ends here, her Container, Sushumnā, also ends here. If it be taken to mean that she exists above the Sahasrāra, then there will be a contradiction to the description in the fortieth verse, where the Sahasrāra is spoken of as "showing in vacant space" (Shūnyadeshe prakāsham). If Sushumnā passes over it, there can be no vacant space.

There are some who contend that all the three Nādīs—Īdā, Pinggalā, and Sushumnā—are inside the Meru, and quote the following as their authority from the Nigama-tattva-sāra: "The three Nādīs are said to be inside the Meru, in the middle of the back." But this cannot be; all the Tantras say that the Īdā and Pinggalā are outside the Meru, and on the authority of these our Author speaks of their being outside the Meru. Further, if they were inside the Meru they could not be bow-shaped and touch the hip and shoulder joints. The Nigama-tattva-sāra by the "three Nādīs" apparently means Sushumnā, Vajrā, and Chitrinī, and not Idā, Pinggalā, and Sushumnā.

The position of the Sushumnā from the Mūlādhāra to the head is thus described: "Sushumnā goes forward, clinging like a Chavya-creeper[739] to the Meru, and reaching the end of the neck, O Beauteous One, she emerges and deflects, and, supporting herself on the stalk of the Shangkhinī,[740] goes towards the region of Brahman (Brahma-sadana)."

Also *cf.*: "The other two are placed like bows. Sushumnā is the

[737] Medhra = penis.
[738] This channel or passage within Chitrini is Brahmanādī.
[739] *Tetranthera Apetala* (Colebrooke's Amarakosha).
[740] Nādī of that name; *v. post.*

embodiment of Pra*n*ava;[741] emerging from the backbone, she goes to the forehead. Passing between the eyebrows and united with Ku*nd*alī,[742] she with her mouth[743] approaches the Brahma-randhra."

By this it becomes apparent that the backbone extends to the end of the back of the neck.

Supporting herself on Shangkhinī (Shangkhinī-nālamā-lambya). Shangkhinī is thus described:

Ishvara said: "Sarasvatī and Kuhu are on either side of Su*sh*umnā; Gāndhārī and Hastijihvā again are on the right and left of I*d*ā."

And again: "Between Gāndhārī and Sarasvatī is Shangkhinī. The Nā*d*ī named Shangkhinī goes to the left ear."

And also again: "Shangkhinī, emerging from the hollow of the throat, goes obliquely to the forehead, and then, O Ambikā,[744] united with and twisted round Chitri*n*ī, she thereafter passes to the head."

Hence she (Shangkhinī) starts from Kanda-mūla, proceeds between Sarasvatī and Gāndhārī and reaches the throat, and then one of her branches proceeds obliquely to the left ear and the other goes to the top of the head.

"*Vajra inside Her*" (Madhyame)—*i.e.*, inside Su*sh*umnā.

There are some who contend that the Meru-da*nd*a extends from the feet to the Brahma-randhra, and quote in support the following passage from Nigama-tattva-sāra: "The bony staff which goes from the feet[745] to the Brahma-randhra is called the Meru-da*nd*a of the fourteen Lokas."

But the backbone is the spinal bone (Meru-da*nd*a). It extends from the Mūla-kanda to the end of the back of the neck. This is self-evident, and no authority can alter things which are patent. Moreover, it is impossible for one piece of bone to go to the end of the feet, for then the legs could not be bent or stretched. The Meru therefore does not go below the Mūla (Mūlādhāra). The meaning of the passage from the Nigama-tattva-sāra becomes clear if we read Pāda to mean "leg," and not "foot." "Beginning of the pāda" (Pādādi) would then mean "where the legs begin." The sense would then be that the bone which controls the whole body from the feet right up to the head is the Meru-da*nd*a, which is like a stick, and begins from the penis two fingers breadth above the Mūla-kanda. The Bhūtashuddhi Tantra says: "Within it and two fingers' breadth above it are Vajrā and Chitrinī."

[741] Pra*n*avākr*i*ti—the mantra Ong. This means that Pra*n*ava manifests as the Su*sh*umnā.

[742] Devī Ku*nd*alinī; *v. ante.*

[743] Her mouth has neared the Brahmarandhra. The locative here is Sāmīpye saptamī—that is, locative in sense of proximity. Su*sh*umnā does not actually reach Brahmarandhra, but goes near it, ending near the twelve-petalled lotus. *Cf.* v. 1, Pādukāpanchaka.

[744] "Mother," a title of the Devī.

[745] Lit., beginning of the pāda; *v. post.*

VERSE 2.

Inside her[746] is Chitri*n*ī, who is lustrous with the luster of the Pra*n*ava[747] and attainable in Yoga by Yogīs. She (Chitri*n*ī) is subtle as a spider's thread, and pierces all the Lotuses which are placed within the backbone, and is pure intelligence.[748] She (Chitri*n*ī) is beautiful by reason of these (Lotuses) which are strung on her. Inside her (Chitri*n*ī) is the Brahma-nā*d*ī,[749] which extends from the orifice of the mouth of Hara[750] to the place beyond where Ādideva[751] is.

COMMENTARY.

"*Inside Her*" (Tanmadhye)—*i.e.*, inside Vajrā.

"*Lustrous with the luster of the Pranava*" (Pranava-vilasitā).—She absorbs the luminous character of the Pra*n*ava in Ājnā-chakra when she passes through it. *Cf.* v. 37, *post.*

"*Like a spider's thread*" (Lūtā-tantūpameyā).—She is fine like the spider's thread.

"*She pierces all the Lotuses,*" *etc.* (Sakala-sarasijān meru-madhyāntara-sthān bhittvā dedīpyate).—She pierces the pericarp of the six Lotuses, and shines like a thread strung with gems.

There is a passage quoted as from the fourth Kā*nd*a, of the Kalpa-Sūtra, and explained to mean: "In the hollow channel within Chitri*n*ī are six Lotuses, and on the petals of these the Mahādevī Bhujangī move about (viharanti)."

But this text, as it has given a plural verb to Bhujang-gī[752] in the singular, seems to be incorrect. But if it be said that it is the word of Shiva, and that the plural is used as singular, it would then have to be understood that the locative in the phrase "in the channel within Chitri*n*ī" is used as an instrumental, and the correct meaning of the passage would in that case be "that Bhujang-gī goes along the channel within Chitri*n*ī. And as She passes in her upward movement She pierces the Chakras, and moves about on the petals of the Chakras." Or it may also mean "that Bhujang-gī goes along the hollow of the Chitri*n*ī, and moves about on the petals of the six Lotuses within Su*sh*umnā, and at length goes to Sahasrāra."

---

[746] That is, inside Vajrā, which is, again, within Su*sh*umnā.

[747] The mantra "Om."

[748] Shuddhabodhā svarūpā.

[749] The Brahmanā*d*ī is not a Nā*d*ī separate from Chitri*n*ī, but the channel in the latter.

[750] Shiva; the Svayambhu-lingga.

[751] The Parama Bindu; *v. ib.* The Brahmanā*d*ī reaches the proximity of, but not the Ādi-deva Himself.

[752] Lit., "serpent," a name of Ku*nd*alinī.

From the above authority it is not to be concluded that the six Lotuses are in the hollow of Chitri*n*ī.[753]

"*Inside her*" (Tan-madhye).—Within Chitri*n*ī is Brahmanā*d*ī. The word Nā*d*ī here means a channel (vivara). It is derived from the root Na*d*, motion. The word Brahmanā*d*ī expresses the channel by which Ku*nd*alinī goes from the Mūlādhāra to the place of Parama-shiva. Ku*nd*alinī is a form of the Shabda-Brahman.[754] From this it is certain that the inside of Chitri*n*ī is hollow, and there is no other Nā*d*ī inside her.

"*The orifice of the mouth of Hara*" (Hara-mukha-kuhara).—The orifice at the top of the Svayambhu-lingga in the Mūlādhāra. Ādideva is the supreme Bindu in the pericarp of the thousand-petalled Lotus.

The rest of the verse requires no explanation.[755]

VERSE 3.

She[756] is beautiful like a chain of lightning and fine like a (lotus) fiber, and shines in the minds of the sages. She is extremely subtle; the awakener of pure knowledge; the embodiment of all bliss, whose true nature is pure consciousness.[757] The Brahma-dvāra[758] shines in her mouth. This place is the entrance to the region sprinkled by ambrosia, and is called the Knot, as also the mouth of Su*sh*umnā.

COMMENTARY.

By this Shloka she is further described:

"*Fine like a (lotus) fiber and shines*" (Lasat-tantu-rūpā)—*i.e.*, She is luminous, albeit fine like the fiber in the lotus-stalk; she shines because of the presence of Ku*nd*alinī.

"*Embodiment of all bliss*" (Sakala-sukha-mayī).—Sukha is here used as the equivalent of Ānanda, which means Spiritual Bliss. She is the source of all bliss.[759]

"*Whose true nature is pure consciousness*" (Shuddha-bodha-

---

753 Vishvanātha, quoting from Māyā Tantra, says that all the six lotuses are attached to the Chitri*n*ī (Chitri*n*ī-grathitang).

754 Shabda-Brahma-rūpā Ku*nd*alinī. The Shabdabrahman (see Introduction) is the Chaitanya in all beings.

755 Shangkara reads this verse in a slightly modified form, but the meaning is practically the same, the modifications being of a verbal character only.

756 That is, Chitri*n*ī, the interior of which is called the Brahma-nā*d*ī.

757 Shuddha-bodha-svabhāvā.

758 See Commentary.

759 Because, according to Vishvanātha, She drops nectar, and therefore contains all kinds of bliss. Shangkara says it is also capable of the interpretation, "It is blissful to all."

svabhāvā).—Shuddha-bodha is Tattva-jnāna, She whose Nature[760] is pure consciousness.

"*Brahma-dvāra*"[761] is the entrance and exit of Ku*nd*ali*n*ī in her passage to and from Shiva.

"*Her mouth*" (Tadāsye)—the mouth of Brahmanā*d*ī, the orifice in the mouth of Hara.

"*This place*" (Tadetat)—*i.e.*, the place near the entrance.

"*The entrance to the region sprinkled by ambrosia*" (Sudhā-dhāra-gamya-pradesha).—The region which is sprinkled by the ambrosia (sudhā) which flows from the union[762] of Parama Shiva and Shakti, and which is attained by the help of Shiva and Shakti dwelling in the Mūlādhāra.

"*Knot*" (Granthi-sthānam).—The place of the union[763] of Su*sh*umnā and Kanda.[764]

"*Is called*"—that is, by those versed in the Āgamas.

VERSE 4.

Now we come to the Ādhāra Lotus.[765] It is attached to the mouth of the Su*sh*umnā, and is placed below the genitals and above the anus. It has four petals of crimson hue. Its head (mouth) hangs downwards. On its petals are the four letters from Va to Sa, of the shining color of gold.

COMMENTARY.

After having described the Nā*d*īs, the Author describes the Mūlādhāra Chakra in detail in nine verses beginning with the present.

"*It is attached to the mouth of Sushumnā*" (Su*sh*umnāsya-lagnam).—The petals[766] are on four sides of the place where the Kanda[767] and Su*sh*umnā meet.

"*Below the genitals and above the anus*" (Dhvajādho gudorddhvam).—From below the root of the genitals to Su*sh*umnā.

"*Four petals of crimson hue*" (Chatu*h* sho*n*apatram).—The four petals are red in color. Sho*n*a is the crimson color of the red lotus.

---

[760] Sva-bhāva is interpreted by Kālīchara*n*a to mean one's nature. Shangkāra interprets the word to mean the Jnāna which is the Paramātmā, or, in other words, divine or spiritual Jnāna. According to Shangkara, the reading is Shuddha-bhāva-svabhāvā.

[761] Door of Brahman.

[762] Sāmarasya, a term which is ordinarily applied to sexual union (Strīpungyogāt yat saukhyang tat sāmarasyam)—here and elsewhere, of course, used symbolically.

[763] *Vide ante*, note 735.

[764] The root of all the Nā*d*īs; see v. 1, *ante*.

[765] That is, mūlādhāra chakra, so called from its being at the root of the six Chakras; see hence to v. 12, *post*.

[766] See Introduction.

[767] *V.* p. 212, *ante*.

"*On its petals are the four letters from Va to Sa*" (Vakārādisāntai*h* veda[768]-var*n*ai*h*).—The four letters are Va, Sha (palatal), *Sh*a. (cerebral), and Sa.[769] On each of the petals of the six Lotuses the letters of the alphabet are to be meditated upon, going round in a circle from the right (dak*sh*inā-vartena). *Cf.* Vishva-sāra Tantra: "The petals of the Lotuses are known to contain the letters of the alphabet, and should be meditated upon as written in a circle from the right to the left."

VERSE 5.

In this (Lotus) is the square region (Chakra) of P*r*ithivī,[770] surrounded by eight shining spears.[771] It is of a shining yellow color[772] and beautiful like lightning, as is also the Bīja of Dharā[773] which is within.

COMMENTARY.

In the pericarp of this Lotus is the square region of P*r*ithivī, which is described in detail. On the eight sides of the square are eight shining spears. The region is of yellow color.

Cf. "O Thou of dulcet speech, in the Mūlādhāra is the four-cornered region of Dharā, yellow in color and surrounded by eight spears (shūla) like Kulāchalas."

Kulāchala is by some interpreted to mean the breast of a woman. According to this view, the tips of these spears are shaped like a woman's breasts. Others understand by the expression the seven Kula Mountains.[774]

Cf. Nirvā*n*a Tantra: "O Devī, the seven Kula Mountains—viz., Nīlāchala, Mandara, Chandra-shekhara, Himālaya, Suvela, Malaya, and Suparvata—dwell in the four corners." According to this notion, the eight spears are likened to the seven Kula Mountains on Earth.

---

768 Veda-var*n*a: Veda stands for "four." There are four Vedas, and the learned sometimes use the word Veda to mean four—*i.e.*, the number of the Vedas.

769 See Introduction.

770 Earth element, which is that of this Chakra. The form of this tattva is a square.

771 The as*ht*a vajra are shown thus: 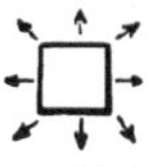

772 The color of the earth element which presides in this Chakra. Each Tattva manifests the form, color, and action, of its particular vibration.

773 That is, the Bīja of P*r*ithivī, the earth Tattva or "Lang." See Introduction.

774 Mahendro Malaya*h* Sahya*h* Shuktimān *Rik*sh*a*parvata*h*
Vindhyashcha Pāripātrashcha Saptaite Kulaparvatā*h*

(quoted in Shabdastomamahānidhi). Some read Pāriputrashcha in place of Paripātra*h*. Shangkara says that the spears are here because the Chakra is inhabited by Dākinī, who is one of the great Bhairavīs.

"*Within it*" (Tad-angke).—Inside the region of P*ri*thivī (Dharā-ma*nd*ala) is the Bīja of Earth—viz., "Lang." This Bīja is also of a yellow color. The phrase "shining yellow color" (Lasat-pīta-var*n*a) is descriptive of the Bīja also.

"Inside it is the Aindra Vīja (Bīja of Indra),[775] of a yellow color, possessed of four arms, holding the thunder in one hand, mighty[776] and seated on the elephant Airāvata."[777]

Verse 6.

Ornamented with four arms[778] and mounted on the King of Elephants,[779] He carries on his lap[780] the child Creator, resplendent like the young Sun, who has four lustrous arms, and the wealth of whose lotus-face is fourfold.[781]

Commentary.

This is the Dhyāna of the Dharā Bīja. The Bīja of Dharā or P*ri*thivī is identical with that of Indra.

"*On his lap*" (Tad-angke)—*i.e.*, in the lap of Dharā Bīja. The sense of this verse is that the Creator Brahmā dwells in the lap of Dharā Bīja. By "angka" (lap) is to be understood the space within the Bindu of Dharā Bīja. *Cf.* "In the Mūlādhāra is the Dharā Bīja, and in its Bindu dwells Brahmā, the image of a Child, and the King of the Immortals[782] is mounted on an Elephant."

Some read the above passage to mean "the King of the Immortals is in the lap of Dharā Bīja." But according to our view the description of the Dharā Bīja and Indra Bīja is the same, as the two are identical; and it is also said "the letters of the Mantra are the Devatā; the Devatā is in the form of the Mantra (Mantra-rūpi*n*ī)." Hence both are there.

Also *cf.* Nirvā*n*a Tantra: "O beautiful one, the Indra Bīja is near by the genitals. The very perfect and beautiful dwelling of Brahmā is above Nāda, and there dwells Brahmā the Creator,[783] the Lord Protector of Being."[784]

---

775 The Bīja of Indra and the Bīja of Earth are the same.

776 Mahā-bāhu, "possessed of great long arms"—sign of prowess. *Cf.* Ājānu-lambita-bāhu (arms reaching the knees).

777 The elephant of Indra. This and other animals figured in the Chakras denote both qualities of the Tattva and the Vehicles (Vāhana) of the Devatā therein. See Introduction.

778 These two adjectival phrases qualify Dharā Bīja.

779 Airāvata.

780 That is, the Bindu of the Bīja (Dharā) or "Lang." This is explained *post*.

781 Brahmā is represented with four heads.

782 *I.e.*, Indra Deva.

783 S*rishti*kartā.

784 Prajā-pati.

By "above Nāda" in this passage, we must understand that the abode of Brahmā is within the Bindu which is above Nāda. Some read "below the genitals," and thus there is a difference of opinion. The Shāradā says that the Ādhāras are various according to different views.

"*Four lustrous arms*" (Lasad-veda[785]-bāhu).—Some interpret the Sanskrit compound word to mean "in whose arms shine the four Vedas Sāma and others," thus thinking of Brahmā as being possessed of two arms only. But Brahmā is nowhere described as holding the Vedas in his hands, and that he should be meditated upon as having four arms is clear from the following passage in Bhūta-shuddhi Tantra:

"Know, O Shivā, that in its lap is the four-armed, red-colored child[786] Brahmā, who has four faces and is seated on the back of a swan."[787]

"*The wealth of whose lotus-face is fourfold*" (Mukhāmbhoja-laks*h*mī*h* chatur-bhāga-bheda).—By this is to be understood that Brahmā has four faces.

Some read the passage as "chatur-bhāgaveda"; thus read the meaning practically is the same. If the Sanskrit text is read "mukhāmbhoja-laks*h*mī-chatur-bhāgaveda," the meaning would be, "the four different Vedas enhance the beauty of his lotus-faces."[788]

As opposed to the opinion that Brahmā holds the four Vedas in his arms, the Vishva-sāra Tantra in the Brāhmī-dhyāna says: "Meditate on Brāhmī (Shakti) as red in color and garbed in the skin of the black antelope, and as holding the staff,[789] gourd,[790] rosary of Rudrāks*h*a beads,[791] and making the gesture dispelling fear."[792] And in the Sapta-shatī Stotra[793] it has been said that Shiva and Shakti are to be meditated upon as having the same weapons.

Also *cf.* Yāmala: "The Ādi-Mūrti[794] should be meditated upon as making the gestures of dispelling fear and granting boons,[795] as also holding the Ku*nd*ikā[796] and rosary of Rudrāks*h*a beads, and adorned

---

785 Veda is used to mean four, there being four Vedas.

786 *I.e.*, Hira*n*ya-garbha.

787 Hangsa, or, as some say, goose or flamingo.

788 The allusion is to the belief that the four Vedas came out of the four mouths of Brahmā.

789 Da*n*da.

790 Kama*nd*alu.

791 Aks*h*a-sūtra.

792 That is, the Abhaya-mudrā. The hand is uplifted, the palm being shown to the spectator. The four fingers are close together, and the thumb crosses the palm to the fourth finger.

793 Mārka*nd*eya Cha*nd*ī.

794 Brāhmī Shakti.

795 That is, the Varadamudrā, the hand being held in the same position as in note 792, but with the palm held horizontally instead of vertically.

796 Kama*nd*alu: a peculiar vessel with a gourd-shaped body, and handle at the top, used for carrying water, generally by ascetics.

with fine ornament."

This is how She should be meditated upon. The rest requires no explanation.

VERSE 7.

Here dwells the Devī *D*ākinī[797] by name; her four arms shine with beauty, and her eyes are brilliant red. She is resplendent like the luster of many Suns rising at one and the same time.[798] She is the Carrier of the revelation of the Ever-pure Intelligence.[799]

COMMENTARY.

In this Shloka the Author speaks of the presence of *D*ākinī Shakti in the Ādhāra-padma. The sense of this verse is that in this Lotus the Devī *D*ākinī dwells.

"*She is the Carrier of the revelation of the ever-pure-Intelligence*"[800] (Prakāsham vahantī sadā-shuddha-buddhe*h*)—that is, She, *D*ākinī Shakti, enables the Yogī to acquire knowledge of the Tattva (tattva-jnāna). By meditating on her, which is part of Yoga-practice, one acquires Tattva-jnāna. This Devī is the presiding Divinity of this region.

Cf. "The mouth (the lotus) has the letters Va, Sha (palatal), *Sh*a (lingual), and Sa, and is presided over by *D*ākinī."

"*D*ākinī, Rāki*n*ī, Lākinī, Kākinī, as also Shākinī and Hākinī, are the queens of the six respective Lotuses."[801] Elsewhere is given the Dhyāna of *D*ākinī: "Meditate on her, the red, the red-eyed *D*ākinī, in the Mūlādhāra, who strikes terror into the hearts of Pashus,[802] who holds in her two right hands the Spear[803] and the Kha*t*vānga,[804] and in her two left hands the Sword[805] and a drinking-cup filled with wine. She is fierce of temper and shows her fierce teeth. She crushes the whole host of enemies. She is plump of body, and is fond of Pāyasānna.[806] It is thus that she should be meditated upon by those who

---

797 *D*ākini and the other Shaktis of this class are in some Tantras called the Queens of the Chakras, and in others the door-keepers thereof.

798 That is, according to Vishvanātha She is very red.

799 Shuddha-buddhi—*i.e.*, tattva-jnāna.

800 If the word "sadā" is read separately from "shuddha-buddhi," it becomes an adverb qualifying "vahantī," and the passage would then mean that "she ever carries revelation of Divine Knowledge."

801 The Shāktānanda-taranggi*n*ī places them in a different order. See P. K. Shāstrī's edition, p. 75.

802 The unillumed. See Introduction to Author's Mahānirvā*n*a.

803 Shūla.

804 A staff surmounted by a human skull.

805 Kha*d*ga, a kind of sword used in the sacrifice of animals.

806 A kind of milk pudding made of rice boiled in milk with ghee and sugar.

desire immortality." Elsewhere she is described as "bright with a Tilaka[807] of vermilion, her eyes ornamented with collyrium, clad in black (antelope's skin) and decked with varied jewels," etc.

On the authority of the above passage, which occurs in a Dhyāna of *D*ākinī, she should be meditated upon as clad in black (antelope skin).

The Devas Brahmā and others are to be meditated upon as having their faces down or up according to the frame of mind (bhāva) of the Sādhaka.

The Shāktānanda-taranggi*n*ī[808] quotes the following from the Māyā Tantra:

"Pārvatī asked: How can they be in the Lotuses which have their heads downward bent?

"Mahādeva said: The Lotuses, O Devī, have their heads in different directions. In the life of action[809] they should be thought of as having their heads downward, but in the path of renunciation[810] they are always meditated upon as having their heads upward turned."

The rest is clear.

VERSE 8.

Near the mouth of the Nā*d*ī called Vajrā, and in the pericarp (of the Ādhāra Lotus), there constantly shines the beautifully luminous and soft, lightning-like Kāmarūpa,[811] which is the triangle known as Tripura.[812] There is always and everywhere the Vāyu called Kandarpa,[813] who is of a deeper red than the Bandhujīva flower,[814] and is the Lord of Beings and resplendent like ten million suns.

COMMENTARY.

In this Shloka is described the triangle in the pericarp of the Mūla-Chakra.

"*Near the mouth of the Nādi called Vajrā*" (Vajrākhyāvaktradeshe).—The mouth of the Vajrā is two fingers above

[807] Here the mark borne by woman between the eyebrows showing that her husband is living—an auspicious mark.

[808] Fourth chapter; Prasanna Kumāra Shāstrī's edition, pp. 78, 79.

[809] Pravr*i*tti-mārga: the outgoing path as distinguished from the Nivr*i*tti-mārga, or path of return to the Parabrahman.

[810] Nivr*i*tti-mārga.

[811] See Commentary, *post.*

[812] This triangle, says Vishvanātha, citing Gautamīya Tantra, is Ichchhājnānakriyātmaka—that is, the powers of will, knowledge, and action. See Introduction.

[813] A form of the Apāna vāyu.

[814] *Pentapœtes Phœnicea.*

that of the Sushumnā and below the base of the genitals.

"*The triangle known as Traipura*" (Trikonam traipurākhyam).—The triangle is so called because of the presence of the Devī Tripurā within the Ka inside the triangle, and the letter Ka is the chief letter of the Kāmavīja.[815]

Cf. Shāktānanda-taranggin̄ī[816]: "Inside dwells the Devī Sundarī,[817] the Paradevatā."

"*Soft*" (Komala)—*i.e.*, oily and smooth.

"*Kāma-rūpa*"[818]: that by which Kāma is caused to be felt—*i.e.*, it is Madanāgārātmaka.[819]

Cf. "Therefore the triangle should be known as the charming Shaktipītha."

This triangle is above the Dharā-vīja. *Cf.* Sammohana Tantra, speaking of Dharā-vīja: "Above it (Dharā-vīja) are three lines—Vāmā, Jyeshthā, and Raudrī."

"*Kandarpa.*"—Next the presence of the Kandarpa Vāyu is spoken of. It is everywhere (samantāt) extended through the triangle.

"*Lord of Beings*" (Jīvesha).—He is so called because the continuance of life depends on him.

It is said that "In the Kanda (heart) region dwells Prāna; and Apāna dwells in the region of the anus. The air in the region of the anus is therefore Apāna, and Kandarpa Vāyu accordingly is a part of Apāna Vāyu."[820] It is also said that[821] "Apāna draws Prāna, and Prāna draws Apāna—just as a falcon attached by a string is drawn back again when he flies away; these two by their disagreement prevent each other from leaving the body, but when in accord they leave it."

The two Vāyus Prāna and Apāna go different ways, pulling at one another; and neither of them, therefore, can leave the body, but when the two are in accord—that is, go in the same direction—they leave the body. Kandarpa Vāyu, being a part of Apāna, also pulls at Prāna Vāyu, and prevents the latter from escaping from the body; hence Kandarpa Vāyu is the Lord of Life.

In v. 10 the Author describes Kundalinī as "She who maintains all the beings of the world by Inhalation and Exhalation." He himself has thus said that Prāna and Apāna are the maintainers of animate being.

---

815 That is, the Mantra "Klīng"; Tantrarāja says, "letter Ka is in my form." The Nityapūjāpaddhati, p. 80, mentions in this connection "Kang," the Vīja of Kāminī. See Introduction.

816 When dealing with the Kakāra-tattva, p. 165, Prasanna Kumāra Shāstrī's edition.

817 Sundarī—*i.e.*, Tripura-Sundarī, a name of the Devī.

818 Shangkara defines this as "the embodiment of the devotee's desire" (Bhaktābhilāsha-svarūpam).

819 Chamber of Madana (Deva of Love)—the yoni.

820 Vāyu here is a name for a manifestation of prāna, the five most important of such manifestations being Prāna, Apāna, Samāna, Vyāna, Udāna. See Introduction.

821 This is an oft-repeated passage (Shāktānanda, p. 5).

VERSE 9.

Inside it (the triangle) is the Svayambhu[822] in his Linggaform,[823] beautiful like molten gold, with his head downwards. He is revealed by Knowledge[824] and Meditation,[825] and is of the shape and color of a new leaf. As the lightning-like cool rays of the moon charm, so does His beauty. The Deva who resides happily here as in Kāshī is in form like a whirlpool.[826]

COMMENTARY.

In this verse he speaks of the presence of the svayambhulinga in the triangle.

"*Svayambhu in his Lingga-form*" (Lingga-rūpī svayambhu)—*i.e.*, here dwells the Shivalingga whose name is Svayambhu.

"*Beautiful like molten gold*" (Druta-kanaka-kalā-komala).—His body has the soft luster of molten gold.

"*His head downwards*" (Pashchimāsya).—*Cf.* Kālī-kulā-m*ri*ta: "There is placed the great Lingga Svayambhu, who is ever blissful, his head downward, active when moved by Kāma-Bīja."

"*Revealed by Knowledge and Meditation.*" (Jnāna-dhyāna-prakāsha).—Whose existence is apprehended by us by Knowledge (Jnāna) and Meditation (Dhyāna). By Jnāna we realize the attributelessness, and by Dhyāna the attributefullness (of the Brahman). Such is Svayambhu.

"*The shape and color of new leaves*" (Prathama-kisha layākārarūpa).—By this is conveyed the idea that the shape of the Svayambhu Lingga is tapering like a new unopened leaf-bud. Like the pistil inside the Champaka flower, it is broad at the bottom and tapers to a point at the end; this also shows that the Svayambhu-lingga is of a blue-green color (shyāma).

Cf. Shāktānanda-tarangi*n*ī: "O Maheshāni, meditate inside it (the triangle) upon the Svayambhu-lingga, who holds his head with an aperture therein downward—the beautiful and blue-green Shiva (Shivang shyāmala-sundaram)."

In the Yāmala occurs the following passage: "Meditate upon the very beautiful celestial triangle (triko*n*a) in the Mūlādhāra; within its three lines is Ku*nd*alī, charming like ten million lightning flashes in the

---

[822] "Self-originated," "self-existent," the Shiva Linga of that name.

[823] As the human phallus.

[824] Jnā*n*a.

[825] Dhyāna.

[826] This refers to a depression on the top of the linga.

dark blue[827] clouds."

This passage, which describes Ku*nd*alī as lightning in the dark blue clouds, goes to show that the Svayambhu-Lingga is also blue; but nīla (blue) and shyāma (dark green) belong to the same category, and hence there is no contradiction.

"*As do the lightning-like cool rays of the moon, his beauty charms*" (Vidyut-pūr*n*ēndu-bimba-prakarakara-[828]chaya-snigdha-santāna-hāsī).—As the light of the moon even when bright as lightning emits no heat, so is the light which emanates from the Svayambhu linga cool and pleasing, bringing gladness into the hearts of men.

"*The Deva who resides happily here as in Kāshī*"[829] (Kāshīvāsī vilāsī).—Kāshī is the place sacred to Shiva, his favorite abode. By these two adjectives it is implied that the Svayambhu in the Ādhāra Lotus is happy as he is in his image of Vishveshvara in Kāshī, and he is as pleased to live here as at Kāshī. "Vilāsī" may also mean amorous because it has been said above, "moved by Kāma Vāyu."

"*Like a whirlpool*" (Sarid-āvarta-rūpa-prakāra).—The water on its outer edge creates a depression in the middle like the shape of a conch.[830]

This Svayambhu is placed on the Kāma-bīja. *Cf.* Kālī-Kulām*ri*ta: "There with a cavity in his head, surrounded by the filaments of the lotus, exists the beautiful Mahā-lingga Svayambhu, ever happy, holding his head downwards, and active when moved by the Kāma-bīja."

Elsewhere the following occurs: "There in the pericarp is the above-mentioned *D*ākinī, and the triangle (triko*n*a) within which is the subtle space and the red Kāma-bīja. There is also the Svayambhu Lingga, his head downward and of a ruddy hue." This is, however, a different conception.

VERSES 10 AND 11.[831]

Over it[832] shines the sleeping Ku*nd*alinī, fine as the fiber of the lotus-stalk. She is the world-bewilderer,[833] gently covering the mouth of Brahma-dvāra[834] by Her own. Like the spiral of the conch-shell, Her

---

[827] Nīla.

[828] Vishvanātha for Kara (ray) reads Rasa—that is, the nectar flowing from the Moon.

[829] Benares.

[830] Shangkara says that he is so described because of his restless motion.

[831] Shangkara, unlike Kālīchara*n*a, has annotated the two verses separately.

[832] Svayambhu Lingga—that is, round It with Her body and over It with Her head.

[833] Ku*nd*alinī is the Shakti whereby the Māyik world exists, at rest. In the Kūrma Purā*n*a Shiva says: "This Supreme Shakti is in me, and is Brahman Itself. This Māyā is dear to me, by which this world is bewildered." Hence the Devī in the Lalitā is called "Sarvamohinī" (all-bewildering).

[834] See Commentary.

shining snake-like form goes three and a half times round Shiva,[835] and her luster is as that of a strong flash of young strong lightning. Her sweet murmur is like the indistinct hum of swarms of love-mad bees[836] and the soft cadence of sweet harmonious music. It is She who maintains all the beings of the world by means of inspiration and expiration,[837] and shines in the cavity of the root (Mūla) Lotus like a chain of brilliant lights.

COMMENTARY.

In these two verses the author speaks of the presence of Ku*nd*alinī Shakti in the Svayambhu Lingga. It is the Devī Ku*nd*alinī who maintains the existence of individual beings (Jīva Jīvātmā) by the functions of inspiration and expiration. She places them in individual bodies; She produces the humming sound resembling that of a swarm of bees, and She, as described below, dwells in the triangular hollow in the pericarp of the Mūlādhāra Lotus resting upon the Svayambhu Lingga.

"*Shines fine as the fibers of the Lotus-stalk*" (Bisa-tantu-sodara-lasat-sūks*h*mā)—*i.e.*, She is fine like the fiber of the Lotus-stalk.

"*World-bewilderer*" (Jagan-mohinī)—*i.e.*, who is Māyā in this world.

"*Gently.*"[838]—Madhuram.

"*The mouth of Brahma-dvāra*" (Brahma-dvāra-mukha)—the hollow on the head of Svayambhu Linga.

"*A strong flash of young lightning*" (Navīna-chapalā-mālāvilāsāspadā).—Lit., "possessed of the wealth of a strong flash of young lightning." In youth every thing and person shows the characteristic qualities in a state of vigorous perfection. Hence a "young flash of lightning" means a strong flash.

"*The soft cadence of sweet harmonious music*" (Komalakāvya-bandha-rachanā-bhedātibheda-krama).—This shows the mode in which words are produced. The soft music produced by a combination of soft and melodious words descriptive of beauty, virtue, etc., in all its modulations, resulting from perfection of composition and regularity in the disposition of words. By *Bandha* is here meant descriptive poetical composition in prose or verse; and by *Atibheda* the author alludes to all

---

835 Shivōpari.

836 Vishvanātha says She makes this sound when awakened. According to Shangkara, this indicates the Vaikharī state of Ku*nd*alinī.

837 Vishvanātha quotes Daks*hin*āmūrti as stating that during day and night man breathes in and out 21,600 times, taking both expiration and inspiration as the unit. See Introduction.

838 Madhuram: this is used as an adjective, according to Shangkara, and means sweet. He says She is drinking nectar by the Brahmadvāra; as the nectar is coming through it, the Brahmadvāra is sweet.

the words in Sangskrita and Prākrita. By using the word "order, sequence," the author emphasizes the fact that these compositions and words come out in the order laid down in the Shāstras. Kundalinī produces, not at random, but in set forms. Kundalinī produces words, Sangskrita and Prākrita, distinct and indistinct. She is the source from which all sound emanates.

Cf. Shāradā[839]: "Upon the bursting (unfolding) of the supreme Bindu arose unmanifested Sound[840] (Avyakta-rava). It assumed the form of Kundalī in the animal body, and manifested itself in prose and verse by the aid of the letters of the Alphabet (lit., the essence of the letters)."

It has distinctly been said in Kādimata[841]: "By the motion of the Ichchhā-Shakti acting through Prāna-vāyu of the Ātmā is produced in the Mūlādhāra the excellent Nāda Sound called Parā.[842] In its ascending movement it is thrown up from the Svadhishthāna,[843] receiving the name of Pashyantī; and again gently led up as before-mentioned, it becomes united in the Anāhata with Buddhi-tattva, and is named Madhyamā. Going upward again, it reaches the Vishuddha in the throat, where it is called Vaikharī; and from there it goes on towards the head, (upper part) of the throat, the palate, the lips, the teeth. It also spreads over the tongue from root to tip, and the tip of the nose; and remaining in the throat, the palate, and the lips, produces by the throat and the lips the letters of the Alphabet from A to Ksha."

It is needless to quote more.

Elsewhere has Kundalinī been thus described: "Meditate upon Devī Kundalinī, who surrounds the Svayambhu-Lingga, who is *Shyāma*[844] and subtle, who is Creation itself,[845] in whom are creation, existence, and destruction,[846] who is beyond the universe[847] and is consciousness[848] itself. Think of Her as the One who goes upwards."[849]

---

[839] Ch. I., second line of v. 11 and v. 14, the intermediate verses are omitted. These run as follows: "That sound is called, by those versed in the Āgamas, Shabdabrahman. Some teachers define Shabdabrahman to mean Shabdārtha, others (grammarians) define it to mean Shabda; but neither of them is correct, because both Shabda and Shabdārtha are Jada (unconscious things). In my opinion, Shabdabrahman is the Chaitanya of all beings." The Āgama in the text is Shruti; Rāghava quotes Shangkarāchāryya in Prapanchasāra, which speaks of men versed in Shruti. Chaitanya is the Brahman considered as the essence of all beings—that is, Chit and Shakti, or Chit in manifestation.

[840] That is, the Principle or Cause of Sound. See Introduction.

[841] The mata in which the Devatā is Kālī; also a name for Tantrarāja in that part dealing with this mata.

[842] At pp. 120-122, Vol. II., Tantrik Texts, Vishvanātha speaks of Parā Pashyantī, and the others Shaktis.

[843] Pashyantī is sometimes associated with Manipūra. See Introduction.

[844] *Vide post.*

[845] Srishtirūpā.

[846] Srishti-sthiti-layātmikā.

[847] Vishvātītā. She is not only immanent, but transcends the universe.

[848] Jnāna-rūpā.

Also: "Meditate upon the Devī Ku*nd*alinī as your Is*ht*a-devatā,[850] as being ever in the form of a damsel of sixteen in the full bloom of her first youth, with large and beautifully formed breasts, decked with all the varied kinds of jewels, lustrous as the full moon, rosy in color, with ever restless eyes."[851]

"*Rosy*" (Raktā), says the Author of the Shāktā-nandatarangini, is an attribute applicable to all beautiful women. Ku*nd*alinī as a matter of fact should always be meditated upon as rosy (Raktā) in color.[852]

Shyāmā (which ordinarily denotes "color") is here meant to signify something different. In all Tantras and all Tāntrika collections Ku*nd*alinī is described to be like lightning. "Shyāmā is the name given to a woman who is warm in winter and cool in summer, and has the luster of molten gold."[853] Thus the apparent discrepancy is removed.

The Kangkāla-mālinī Tantra describes Ku*nd*alinī in the Brahma-dvāra, and before the piercing of the Chakras, thus: "She, the Brahman Itself, resplendent like millions of moons rising at the same time, has four arms and three eyes. Her hands make the gestures[854] of granting boons and dispelling fear, and hold a book and a Vī*n*ā.[855] She is seated on a lion, and as She passes to her own abode[856] the Awe-inspiring One (Bhīmā) assumes different forms."

VERSE 12.

Within it[857] reigns dominant Parā,[858] the Shrī Parameshvarī, the Awakener of eternal knowledge. She is the Omnipotent, Kalā[859] who is wonderfully skilful to create, and is subtler than the subtlest. She is the receptacle of that continuous stream of ambrosia which flows from the Eternal Bliss. By Her radiance it is that the whole of this Universe and this Cauldron[860] is illumined.

---

849 Ūrddhvavāhinī, for Ku*nd*alinī ascends to the Sahasrāra.

850 Is*ht*a-deva-svarūpi*n*ī. The Is*ht*adevatā is the particular Devatā of the Sādhaka's worship.

851 These in women indicate a passionate nature.

852 The Shāktānandatarangi*n*ī says She is only to be meditated upon as red when the object of worship is a Devī. The text may also be read as meaning that "rosy" is an attribute applicable to Shrī Sundarī—that is, the Devī.

853 This is a quotation from the Alangkāra (rhetorical) Shāstra.

854 That is, the Mudrās Abhaya and Vara; *v. ante*, p. 219.

855 The musical instrument of that name.

856 The Mūlādhāra.

857 Svayambhu lingga, round which Ku*nd*alī is coiled.

858 According to Shangkara, Parā is in Ku*nd*alinī. She is called Brahmā*n*ī by Vishvanātha, who quotes the Svachchhandasanggraha. In Ku*nd*alī is the Parā state of Shabda.

859 *Vide post.*

860 Ka*t*āha—that is, the lower half of the Brahmā*nd*a, and as such cauldron-shaped.

COMMENTARY.

He is now speaking of the Staff-like Parā Shakti, who is like a straight thread above Ku*nd*alinī, who is coiled round Svayambhu-Lingga. The Shrī Parameshvarī, whose radiance illumines this Universe[861] and its cauldron, dwells in the Svayambhu Lingga above where Ku*nd*alinī is coiled and holds supreme sway.

"*Omnipotent*" (Paramā).—She is the Māyā who is able to do that which is impossible.[862]

"*Kalā*" is in the form of Nāda Shakti (Kalā is Nāda-shaktirūpā); by this Her identity with Ku*nd*alinī is implied.[863]

The Shāktānanda-taranggi*n*ī says: "Kalā is Ku*nd*alinī, and She, Shiva has said, is Nāda-shakti."[864]

And it has also been elsewhere said: "Above it, meditate in your mind on Chitkalā united with Lak*sh*mī, who is tapering of shape like the flame of a lamp, and who is one with Ku*nd*alī." This is what has been said by author of this Lalitārahasya.

Cf. Kālikā-Shruti: "Man becomes freed of all sins by meditating upon Ku*nd*alinī as within, above, and below the flame, as Brahmā, as Shiva, as Shūra,[865] and as Parameshvara Himself; as Vi*sh*nu, as Prā*n*a, as Kālāgni,[866] and as Chandra."[867]

By "within the flame" is meant the excellent Kalā (= Nādarūpā) above Ku*nd*alinī's coil.

"*She (parā) is wonderfully skilful to create*" (Ati-kushalā)—*i.e.*, She it is who possesses the wonderful skill and power of creation.

"*She is the receptacle of that continuous stream of ambrosia flowing from Eternal Bliss* (*Brahman*)" (Nityānanda-paramparāti-vigalat-pīyū*sha*-dhārā-dharā).—By Eternal Bliss (Nityānanda) is meant the Nirgu*n*a or Attributeless Brahman. *Paramparā* means "connected step by step." From Nityānanda, which is Nirgu*n*a Brahman, there arises (in Its aspect as) Sagu*n*a Brahman; Shakti; from Shakti, Nāda;

861 Brahmā*nd*a—egg of Brahmā.

862 So the Devī Purā*n*a (Ch. XLV.), speaking of this power of the Supreme, says:

> Vichitra-kāryyakāra*n*ā chintitaphalapradā
> Svapnendrajālavalloke māyā tena prakīrtitā.

Paramā may also mean Parang mīyate anayā iti Paramā—*i.e.*, She by whom the Supreme "measured," in the sense (for the Supreme is immeasurable) that She who is one with the Supreme, is formative activity. See Introduction. Vishvanātha, quoting an unnamed Tantra, says that this Māyā is within Ku*nd*alinī, and this Paramā is Paramātmasvarūpā.

863 Ku*nd*alinyabheda-sharīri*n*ī.

864 Nāda-shakti = Shakti as Nāda. See Introduction.

865 Shūra = Sūryya, or Sun.

866 The fire which destroys all things at the time of dissolution (Pralaya).

867 Moon.

from Nāda, Bindu; and from Bindu, Ku*nd*alinī.[868] Chit-kalā is another form of Ku*nd*alinī. It is thus that the ambrosia comes step by step to Parameshvarī, the Chit-kalā. She is Nityānandaparamparā—that is, She belongs to the chain of emanation from Nityānanda downwards; and She is Ativigalat-pīyū*sh*a-dhārādharā —that is, She is the receptacle of the stream of ambrosia which flows copiously from Nityānanda.[869]

This compound word may be interpreted to mean that She holds the copious flow of ambrosia caused by her union with the Brahman. From Nityānanda this nectar comes to Para-Bindu, and passes through the Ājnā Chakra, Vishuddha Chakra, etc., till it reaches the Mūlādhāra, and this is what She is the receptacle of. To interpret it to mean this, the entire word is read as one.

VERSE 13.

By meditating thus on Her who shines within the Mūla Chakra, with the luster of ten million Suns, a man becomes Lord of speech and King among men, and an Adept in all kinds of learning. He becomes ever free from all diseases, and his inmost Spirit becomes full of great gladness. Pure of disposition by his deep and musical words, he serves the foremost of the Devas.[870]

COMMENTARY.

In this verse the Author speaks of the benefit to be derived from meditating on Ku*nd*alinī. By *Mūla Chakra* is meant the Mūlādhāra. "It is the root of the six Chakras—hence its name."

"*Within*" (Mūla-chakrāntara-vivara-lasat-ko*t*i-sūryya-prakāsham). —She shines in the Mūlādhāra Chakra like ten million suns shining at one and the same time.

"*His deep and musical words*" (Vākyai*h* kāvya-prabandhai*h*).— His speech is musical and full of meanings, as in a poetical composition.

"*He serves*" (Sevate).—He uses his words in hymns of praise and for purposes of a like nature. He pleases them by words of adoration.

"*All the foremost of the Devas*" (Sakala-sura-gurūn).—The word Guru here means excellent, and the Author means Brahmā, *Vishnu*, and Shiva, the principal Devas. Amara says that "adding the words Singha (lion), Shārdūla (tiger), Nāga (serpent), etc., to a male name implies excellence."

---

[868] See Introduction.

[869] That is, if the compound be read in two sections—viz., Nityānanda-paramparā, and then separately, Ativigalatpīyūs*h*adhārādharā. The translation adopted in the text is that which is referred to in the paragraph which follows.

[870] That is, Brahmā, Vi*shn*u, Shiva, etc.

SUMMARY.

The Mūlādhāra is a Lotus of four petals. The petals are red, and have the letters Va, Sha (palatal), *Sha*. (cerebral), Sa, in colors of gold. In the pericarp is the square Dharā-ma*nd*ala surrounded by eight spears, and within it and in the lower part is the Dharā-bīja,[871] who has four arms and is seated on the elephant Airāvata. He is yellow of color, and holds the thunderbolt[872] in his hands. Inside the Bindu of the Dharā-bīja is the Child Brahmā, who is red in color, and has four hands with which he holds the staff,[873] the gourd,[874] the Rudrāk*sh*a rosary, and makes the gesture which dispels fear.[875] He has four faces. In the pericarp there is a red lotus on which is the presiding Divinity of the Chakra (Chakrādhis*hth*ātrī), the Shakti *D*ākinī. She is red and has four arms, and in her hands are Shūla,[876] Kha*t*vāngga,[877] Kha*d*ga,[878] and Cha*sh*aka.[879] In the pericarp there is also the lightning-like triangle, inside which are Kāma-vāyu and Kāma-bīja,[880] both of which are red. Above this is the Svayambhu Lingga which is Shyāma-var*n*a,[881] and above and round this Lingga is Ku*nd*alinī coiled three and a half times, and above this last upstands, on the top of the Lingga, Chit-kalā.[882]

(This is the end of the first section.)[883]

VERSE 14.

There is another Lotus[884] placed inside the Su*sh*umnā at the root of the genitals, of a beautiful vermilion color. On its six petals are the letters from Ba to Purandara,[885] with the Bindu[886] superposed, of the shining color of lightning.

---

871 "Lang."
872 Vajra.
873 Da*n*da.
874 Kama*nd*alu.
875 Abhayamudrā; *v. ante*, n. 792.
876 Spear.
877 Skull-mounted staff.
878 Sword. Kha*d*ga is a heavy sacrificial sword.
879 Drinking-cup.
880 "Klīng."
881 Its color.
882 Described in v. 12 as another form of Ku*nd*alinī.
883 Prakarana. The commentator divides his commentary into eight sections.
884 That is, the Svādhi*sh*t*h*āna Chakra. See Introduction.
885 The letter La; *v. post*.
886 The anusvāra.

COMMENTARY.

Having described the Mūlādhāra, he describes the Svādhi*shth*āna, Chakra in five verses beginning with the present one. This verse says that at the root of the genitals there is, distinct from the Mūlādhāra, another Lotus, of a beautiful vermilion color.

"*Placed inside the Sushumnā*" (Sau*sh*umna[887]-madhyagha*t*itam).—The place of this Chakra or Padma is within Su*sh*umnā.

"*At the root of the genitals*" (Dhvaja-mūladeshe).

"*Of a beautiful vermilion color*" (Sindūra-pūra-ruchirāru*n*a).—This Lotus is of the charming red color of vermilion.

"*On its six petals*" (Angga-chhadai*h*).—It is surrounded by its six petals.[888]

"*The letters*" (Bādyai*h* savindu-lasitai*h* Purandarāntai*h*).—By Purandara is meant the letter Lă, it being the Bīja of Purandara or Indra. Each of these letters from Ba to La is on each petal of the lotus. They have the Bindu over them, and are of the shining color of lightning. The above may also mean that the luster of the letter is caused by their union with the Bindus placed over them.

VERSE 15.

Within it[889] is the white, shining, watery region of Varu*n*a, of the shape of a half-moon,[890] and therein, seated on a Makara,[891] is the Bīja Văng, stainless and white as the autumnal moon.

COMMENTARY.

Here the Author speaks of the presence of the watery region of Varu*n*a in the pericarp of the Svādhi*shth*āna. This watery region (Ambhoja-ma*n*dalam) is in shape like the half-moon (Ardhendurūpalasitam), and is luminously white (Vishadaprakāsham).

The Shāradā says: "The Lotus of the region of water is four-cornered,[892] and has the thunderbolt (Vajra) and so forth." Rāghava-bha*tt*a,[893] in describing it, says: "Draw a half-moon, and draw two

---

[887] Sau*sh*umna: Shangkara reads this word to mean the Brahmanā*d*ī and which is within Su*sh*umnā, and says that the suffix "in" by which the change is affected is used in the sense of "relating to," and not "placing within."

[888] *V. ante*, Introduction.

[889] Svādhi*shth*āna.

[890] Water is the element of this Chakra, which is represented by the crescent.

[891] An animal of a legendary form, somewhat like an alligator. See Plate.

[892] Ch. I., v. 24, Chaturasram; *sed qu.*, for ordinarily the Ma*n*dala is semicircular.

[893] The famous Commentator on the Shāradā-tilaka.

Lotuses on its two sides." The Great Teacher[894] speaks of it as "the ray of the Lotus-united Half-Moon."

Then he speaks of the Varu*n*a-bīja. This Bīja is also white, and is seated on a Makara, which is the Carrier[895] of Varu*n*a. He has also the noose in his hand.

Cf. "(Meditate) upon the white Bīja of Varu*n*a (within the Lotus). Varu*n*a is seated on a Makara, and carries the noose (Pāsha). And above him[896] (that is, in the Bindu) meditate on Hari,[897] who is blue of color (Shyāma) and four-armed."

The Va in Varu*n*a Bīja belongs to the Ya class—*i.e.*, to Ya, Ra, La, Va. This becomes clear from the arrangement of the letters in Kulākula Chakra and in Bhūtalipi Mantra.

The rest is clear.

VERSE 16.

May Hari, who is within it,[898] who is in the pride of early youth, whose body is of a luminous blue beautiful to behold, who is dressed in yellow raiment, is four-armed, and wears the Shrī-vatsa[899] and the Kaustubha,[900] protect us!

COMMENTARY.

The Author here speaks of the presence of Vi*sh*nu in the Varu*n*a Bīja.

"*Within it*" (Angke)—*i.e.*, in the Bindu above Varu*n*a Bīja, in the same way as Brahmā is in the lap of Dharā Bīja. The same explanation applies by analogy to the description of the other Lotuses.

"*Whose body*" (Nīla-prakāsha-ruchira-shriyam).—Lit., He possesses the enchanting beauty of blue effulgence; *i.e.*, his body is of a luminous blue beautiful to behold.

"*Wears Shrīvatsa and Kaustubha.*"—The following is his Dhyāna in the Gautamīya Tantra: "On his heart is the gem Kaustubha, lustrous as ten thousand Suns shining at the same time, and below it is the

894 Apparently Shangkarāchāryya, vol. iii. 3, 3. Prapanchasāra, i. 24.

895 Vāhana.

896 Tadūrddhvam. See Comm. to next verse.

897 Vi*sh*nu.

898 *I.e.*, Vi*sh*nu, is within "the lap" of the Bindu of Vang.

899 Lit., Favorite of Shrī or Lak*sh*mī—an auspicious curl on the breast of Vi*sh*nu and his Avatāra *Krishn*a. It is said to symbolically represent Prakriti. See Ahirbudhnya Samhitā 52, 92, citing also the Astrabhūshana Adhyāya of Vi*sh*nu Purā*n*a I., 22.

900 A great gem worn by Vi*sh*nu, which is said to symbolically signify the souls (see authorities in last note). These are said to be united with the Kaustabha of the Lord (Vi*sh*nutilaka II., 100).

garland[901] with the luster of ten thousand moons. Above Kaustubha is Shrī-vatsa, which also is luminous like ten thousand moons."

The Tantrāntara speaks of the weapons in the hands of Hari: "(Meditate on) Him who has the noose in his hand, and Hari who is in his lap, and has four arms, and holds the Conch,[902] Discus,[903] Mace,[904] and Lotus,[905] is dark blue (Shyāma) and dressed in yellow raiment."

By "who has the noose in his hand" is meant Varu*n*a as he has been described in the preceding verses.

Elsewhere he (Hari) is spoken of as "clad in yellow raiment, benign of aspect, and decked with a garland."[906]

We have seen that, in the Mūlādhāra, Brahmā is seated on the Hangsa, and we should therefore think of Vi*sh*n*u as seated on Garu*d*a.[907]

VERSE 17.

It is here that Rāki*n*ī always dwells.[908] She is of the color of a blue lotus.[909] The beauty of Her body is enhanced by Her uplifted arms holding various weapons. She is dressed in celestial raiments and ornaments, and Her mind is exalted[910] with the drinking of ambrosia.

---

[901] Vanamālā: the name for a large garland descending to the knee. It is defined as follows:

> Ājānulambinī mālā sarvartu-kusumojjvaiā
> Madhye sthūlakadambādyā vanamāleti kīrtitā.

(That is said to be Vanamālā which extends down to the knee, beauteous with flowers of all seasons, with big Kadamba flowers and the like in the middle.) This garland is celestial because in it the flowers of all the seasons are contained.

[902] Shangkha.

[903] Chakra.

[904] Gadā.

[905] Padma.

[906] The garland symbolizes the elements; as the club, Mahat; the couch, Sāttvika Ahangkāra; the bow, Tāmasika Ahangkāra; the sword, knowledge; its sheath, ignorance; discus the mind and the arrows the senses. See authorities cited at p. 233, *ante*.

[907] The Bird King, Vāhana of Vi*sh*nu.

[908] Dwells (Bhāti): the Sanskrit word literally means "shines"—that is, in the Svādhi*shth*āna.

[909] Of the color of a blue lotus (Nīlāmbujodara-sahodarakāntishobhā); lit., Her radiant beauty equals the interior of the blue lotus.

[910] Matta-chittā; for she drinks the nectar which drops from Sahasrāra. She is exalted with the divine energy which infuses Her.

COMMENTARY.

In this Shloka the Author speaks of the presence of Rākin*ī* in the Svādhi*shthā*na.

Cf. Rāki*n*ī-dhyāna elsewhere: "Meditate on Rāki*n*ī, who is blue of color (Shyāmā). In Her hands are a spear,[911] a lotus, a drum[912] and a sharp battle-axe.[913] She is of furious aspect. Her three eyes are red, and her teeth[914] show fiercely. She, the Shining Devī of Devas, is seated on a double lotus, and from one of her nostrils there flows a streak of blood. She is fond of white rice,[915] and grants the wished-for boon."

As Rāki*n*ī is within another lotus[916] in this Lotus, therefore should the six Shaktis everywhere be understood to be in a red lotus as in the Mūlādhāra.

VERSE 18.

He who meditates upon this stainless Lotus, which is named Svādhi*shth*āna, is freed immediately from all his enemies,[917] such as the fault of Ahangkāra[918] and so forth. He becomes a Lord among Yogīs, and is like the Sun illumining the dense darkness of ignorance.[919] The wealth of his nectar-like words flow in prose and verse in well-reasoned discourse.

COMMENTARY.

In this verse is described the benefit derived from the contemplation of the Svādhi*shth*āna Lotus.

"*Svādhishthāna.*"—"By *Sva* is meant the Para-Linga (Supreme Linga), and hence the Lotus is called Svādhi*shth*āna."[920]

"*Fault of Ahangkāra and so forth*" (Ahang-kāra-dos*h*ādi).—By this is implied the six evil inclinations: Kāma (lust), Krodha (anger), etc. These six,[921] which are the six enemies of Man, are destroyed by

---

911 Shūla.

912 *Damaru.*

913 Tangka.

914 Dang*shtra*—*i.e.*, She has long projecting teeth.

915 Shuklānna.

916 There is another smaller Lotus in each of the main lotuses on which the Shakti sits.

917 That is, his enemies the six passions.

918 Egoism. See Introduction.

919 Moha.

920 This is from v. 58 of Ch. XXVII. of the Rudra-yāmala.

921 Viz., Kāma (lust), Krodha (anger), Lobha (greed), Moha (delusion) Mada (pride), Mātsaryya (envy).

contemplation on the Svādhi*shth*āna Lotus. By contemplation upon it are also destroyed the darkness of Māyā, and Moha,[922] and the Sun of knowledge (Jnāna) is acquired. The rest is clear.

SUMMARY OF VERSES 14 TO 18.

The Svādhi*shth*āna Chakra is of the color of vermilion, and has six petals. On its six petals are the six letters Ba, Bha, Ma, Ya, Ra, and La, with the Bindu placed thereon. They are of the color of lightning. In the pericarp of this Lotus is the region of water in the form of an eight-petalled Lotus, with a half-moon in its center. This region is white. Inside this latter is the Varu*n*a Bīja "Vang," seated on a Makara, with a noose in his hand. In the lap of the latter (*i.e.*, in the hollow of the Bindu) is Vi*shn*u seated on Garu*d*a. He has four hands, and is carrying the Shangkha (conch shell), Chakra (discus), Gadā (mace), and Padma (lotus). He is dressed in yellow raiment, wears a long garland (Vanamālā) round his neck, the mark Shrīvatsa and the gem Kaustubha on his breast, and is youthful in appearance. On a red lotus in the pericarp is the Shakti Rāki*n*ī. She is Shyāma-var*n*ā,[923] and in her four hands she holds the Shūla (spear or trident), Abja (lotus), *D*amaru (drum), and Tangka (battle-axe). She is three-eyed and has fierce projecting fangs,[924] and is terrible to behold. She is fond of white rice,[925] and a stream of blood runs from Her nostril.

(*Here ends the second section.*)

VERSE 19.

Above it,[926] and at the root of the navel, is the shining Lotus of ten petals,[927] of the color of heavy-laden rain-clouds. Within it are the letters *D*a to Pha, of the color of the blue lotus with the Bindu above them. Meditate there on the region of Fire, triangular in form and shining like the rising sun. Outside it are three Svastika marks,[928] and within, the Bīja of Vahni himself.[929]

---

[922] Ignorance, illusion, infatuation.

[923] See note to v. 11.

[924] Ku*t*ila-dan*gsht*ra.

[925] Shuklānna.

[926] Svādhi*shth*āna.

[927] The Ma*n*ipūra Chakra, the seat of the Element of Fire the sign of which is a triangle. See Introduction.

[928] An auspicious mark; *v. post.*

[929] That is, "Rang," the Seed-mantra of Fire.

COMMENTARY.

The Ma*n*ipūra Chakra is described in this and the two following verses.

"*Shining lotus of ten petals*" (Dashadala-lashite)[930]—*i.e.*, the Lotus which shines by reason of its ten petals.

"*Of the color of heavy rain-clouds*" (Pūr*n*amegha-prakāshe)—*i.e.*, of a dark hue.

"*Within it are the letters*," *etc.* (Nīlāmbhoja-prakāshai*h* upahitaja*th*are *d*ādi-phāntai*h* sachandrai*h*).

The ten letters from *D*a (cerebral) to Pha, with the Bindu placed above them, are of the color of the blue lotus, and are each of them on the ten several petals. The letters are *D*a, *Dh*a, *N*a, Ta, Tha, Da, Dha, Na, Pa, Pha.

"*Like the rising Sun*" (Aru*n*a-mihira-samam)—*i.e.*, like the young sun.

"*Svastika Marks.*[931]—These three marks or signs are on three sides of the triangle.

Rāghava-bha*tt*a says[932]: "A Svastika sign is one made by two straight lines going in four different directions."[931]

VERSE 20.

Meditate upon Him (Fire) seated on a ram, four-armed, radiant like the rising Sun. In His lap ever dwells Rudra, who is of the hue of vermilion. He (Rudra) is white with the ashes with which He is smeared; of an ancient aspect and three-eyed, His hands are placed in the attitude of granting boons and of dispelling fear.[933] He is the destroyer of creation.

COMMENTARY.

Cf. the Dhyāna of Vahni elsewhere: "Seated on a ram, a Rudrāk*sh*a rosary in one hand, and the Shakti[934] in the other."

From this it is to be inferred that the other two hands are in the attitude of granting boons and of dispelling fear; that is how He is described to be in other Dhyānas of Him.

Rudra should here be meditated upon as seated on a bull.

---

[930] Shangkara reads it as dasha-dala-lalite—*i.e.*, the charming lotus of ten petals.

[931] *I.e.*, like a cross 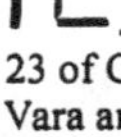.

[932] In the note to v. 23 of Ch. I. of the Shāradā Tilaka.

[933] That is, making Vara and Abhaya Mudrās; *v. ante*, p. 219.

[934] Vahni's or Fire's weapon.

"*He is white . . . smeared*" (Bhasmāliptāngga-bhūs*h*ā-bhara*n*a-sita-vap*u*).—The ashes with which his body is smeared and the ornaments he is wearing make him look white (though his hue is red).

VERSE 21.

Here abides Lākinī, the benefactress of all. She is four-armed, of radiant body, is dark[935] (of complexion), clothed in yellow raiment and decked with various ornaments, and exalted with the drinking of ambrosia.[936] By meditating on this[937] Navel lotus[938] the power to destroy and create (the world) is acquired. Vā*n*ī[939] with all the wealth of knowledge ever abides in the lotus of his face.

COMMENTARY.

"*Decked with various ornaments*" (Vividha-virachan-ālang*kri*tā).—She who is decorated with gems and pearls arranged in varied and beautiful designs.

Cf. Lākinī-dhyāna elsewhere: "Let the excellent worshipper meditate upon the Devī Lakinī, who is blue and has three faces, and three eyes (to each face), fierce of aspect, and with Her teeth protruding.[940] In Her right hand She holds the thunderbolt and the Shakti,[941] and in the left She makes the gestures[942] of dispelling fear and of granting boons. She is in the pericarp of the navel lotus, which has ten petals. She is fond of meat (Māngsāshī), and her breast is ruddy with the blood and fat which drop from Her mouth."

The navel lotus is called Ma*n*i-pūra. The Gautamīya Tantra says: "This Lotus is called Ma*n*ipūra because it is lustrous like a gem."[943]

SUMMARY OF VERSES 19 TO 21.

The Nābhi-padma (Navel Lotus) is of the color of the rain-cloud, and has ten petals; on each of its petals are each of the ten letters *D*a, *Dh*a, *N*a., Ta, Tha, Da, Dha, Na, Pa, and Pha, of a lustrous blue color, with the Bindu above each of them. In the pericarp of this Lotus is the

---

935 Shyāmā; see *ante*, note to v. 11.

936 Matta-chittā; *vide ante*, n. 910.

937 Etat: a variant reading is evam, "in this manner."

938 Nābhi-Padma.

939 That is, the Devī of Speech, Sarasvatī.

940 Vishvanātha quotes a dhyāna in which She is described as humpbacked (kubjinī) and as carrying a staff.

941 The weapon of Vahni (Fire).

942 Mudrā.

943 Ma*n*i-vad-bhinnang. Bhinna here means "distinguished," for in the Ma*n*ipūra is the Region of Fire. See also Rudrayāmala, Ch. XXVII., v. 60.

red Region of Fire, which is triangular in shape, and outside it, on its three sides, are three Svastika signs. Within the triangle is the Bīja of Fire—"Rǎng." He is red in color and is seated on a ram, is four-armed, and holds in his hands the Vajra (thunderbolt) and the Shakti weapon, and makes the signs of Vara and of Abhaya.[944] In the lap of Vahni Bīja is Rudra, red of color, seated on the bull, who, however, appears to be white on account of the ashes which He smears on his body. He is old in appearance. On a red lotus in the pericarp of this Lotus is the Shakti Lākinī. She is blue, has three faces with three eyes in each, is four-armed, and with Her hands holds the Vajra and the Shakti weapon, and makes the signs of dispelling fear and granting boons. She has fierce projecting teeth, and is fond of eating rice and dhal, cooked and mixed with meat and blood.[945]

(*Here ends the third section.*)

VERSE 22.

Above that, in the heart, is the charming Lotus,[946] of the shining color of the Bandhūka flower,[947] with the twelve letters beginning with Ka, of the color of vermilion, placed therein. It is known by its name of Anāhata, and is like the celestial wishing-tree,[948] bestowing even more than (the supplicant's) desire. The Region of Vāyu, beautiful and with six corners,[949] which is like unto the smoke in color, is here.

COMMENTARY.

The Anāhata Lotus is described in the six verses beginning with this one.

This Lotus should be meditated upon in the heart; the verb *dhyāyet* is in the next verse. The twelve letters beginning with Ka and the letters Ka to *Tha* are on the petals.

"*It is known by its name Anāhata*" (Nāmnānāhata-sangjnakam).—It is so called by the Munis because it is here that the sound of Shabdabrahman is heard, that Shabda or sound which issues without

---

944 Vara and Abhaya—*i.e.*, the Mudrās dispelling fear and granting boons.

945 Khecharānna—that is, meat mixed with rice and dhal, such as Khecharānna (Khichri), Pilau, etc.

946 The Anāhata, or heart Lotus, seat of the air element, the sign of which is described as hexagonal, is here. See Introduction.

947 *Pentapœtes Phœnicea.*

948 Kalpa-taru. Shangkara says the Kalpa-taru, one of the celestial trees in Indra's heaven, grants what is asked; but this gives more, since it leads him to Mok*sha*.

949 *Shatkona*—that is, interlacing triangles. See Plate V. See Introduction and Rudrayāmala, Ch. XXVII., v. 64.

the striking of any two things together.[950]

"*Wishing-tree*"[951] is the tree in Heaven which grants all one asks; as it is like the Kalpataru, so it bestows more than is desired.

"*Region of Vāyu*" (Vāyor Ma*n*dala*m*).—In the pericarp of this Lotus is the Vāyu Ma*n*dala.

VERSE 23.

Meditate within it on the sweet and excellent Pavana Bīja,[952] grey as a mass of smoke,[953] with four arms, and seated on a black antelope. And within it also (meditate) upon the Abode of Mercy,[954] the Stainless Lord who is lustrous like the Sun,[955] and whose two hands[956] make the gestures which grant boons and dispel the fears of the three worlds.

COMMENTARY.

In this verse the Author speaks of the presence of the Vāyu Bīja in the Anāhata Chakra.

"*Pavana Bīja*" (Pavanāk*sh*ara)—*i.e.*, the Bīja Yang.

"*Grey as a mass of smoke*" (Dhūmāvalī-dhūsara).—It has the greyish color of smoke by reason of its being surrounded by masses of vapor.

"*A black antelope*," which is noted for its fleetness, is the Vāhana (carrier) of Vāyu. Vāyu carries his weapon, "Angkusha,"[957] in the same way that Varu*n*a carries his weapon, "Pāsha."[958]

He next speaks of the presence of Īsha in the Vāyu Bīja. Everywhere Shiva is spoken of as having three eyes,[959] hence Īsha also has three eyes.

Elsewhere it is said: "Meditate upon him as wearing a jeweled

---

950 Vishvanātha quotes (p. 121, Vol. II., Tantrik Texts) the following: "Within it is Vā*n*a Lingga, lustrous like ten thousand suns, also Sound which is Shabdabrahmamaya (whose substance is Brahman), and is produced by no cause (Ahetuka). Such is the lotus Anāhata wherein Puru*sh*a (that is, the Jivātmā) dwells."

951 Surataru = Ka'pa-taru.

952 *I.e.*, Vāyu, whose Vīja is "Yang."

953 This smoke, Shangkara says, emanates from the Jīvātmā which is in the form of a flame.

954 Shangkara reads ocean of mercy.

955 Hangsa, the Sun—a name also of the Supreme. *Cf.* "Hrīng the Supreme Hangsa dwells in the brilliant heaven." See the Hangsavatī Rik of Rigveda in Mahānirvā*n*a Tantra, vv. 196, 197, Ch. V. Hangsa is from Han = Gati, or motion. It is called Āditya because it is in perpetual motion (Sāyana). Hangsa is also the form of the Antarātmā; see v. 31, *post.*

956 This shows that the Bīja has hands and feet (Shangkara).

957 Goad.

958 Noose.

959 The third eye, situate in the forehead in the region of the pineal gland, is the Eye of Wisdom (Jnānachak*sh*u).

necklet and chain of gems round his neck, and bells on his toes, and also clad in silken raiment." "The beautiful One possessed of the soft radiance of ten million moons, and shining with the radiance of his matted hair."

Īsha should therefore be thought of as clad in silken raiment, etc.

VERSE 24.

Here dwells Kākinī, who in color is yellow like unto new lightning,[960] exhilarated and auspicious; three-eyed and the benefactress of all. She wears all kinds of ornaments, and in Her four hands She carries the noose and the skull, and makes the sign of blessing and that which dispels fear. Her heart is softened with the drinking of nectar.

COMMENTARY.

In this verse the Author speaks of the presence of the Shakti Kākinī.

"*Exhilarated*"[961] (Mattā)—that is, She is not in an ordinary, but in a happy, excited mood.

"*With the drinking of nectar,*" *etc.* (Purā*n*a-sudhā-rasārdrah*ri*dayā).—Her heart is softened to benevolence by the drinking of nectar; or it may be interpreted to mean that Her heart is softened by the supreme bliss caused by drinking the excellent nectar which drops from the Sahasrāra. Her heart expands with the supreme bliss. Kākinī should be thought of as wearing the skin of a black antelope.

Compare the following Dhyāna of Kākinī where She is so described: "If thou desirest that the practice of thy Mantra be crowned with success, meditate on the moon-faced, ever-existent[962] Shakti Kakinī, wearing the skin of a black antelope, adorned with all ornaments."[963]

VERSE 25.

In the pericarp of this Lotus is the Shakti in the form of a triangle (Triko*n*a), whose tender body is like ten million flashes of lightning. Inside the triangle is the Shiva-lingga known by the name of Vā*n*a. This

---

960 Nava-ta*d*it-pītā—*i.e.*, where there is more thunder than rain, when the lightning shows itself very vividly. Pīta is yellow; Kākinī is of a shining yellow color.

961 Shangkara gives *unmattā* (maddened or exalted) as equivalent of Mattā.

962 Nityām. If this is not stutī, possibly the word is nityam, "always."

963 Vishvanātha, in his commentary on the S*hat*chakra, gives the following Dhyāna of Kākinī: "Meditate on Kākinī as seated on a cloud holding in Her hands Pāsha (noose), Shūla (trident), Kapāla (skull), *D*amaru (drum). She is yellow in color, fond of eating curd and rice (Dadhyanna). Her beautiful body is in a slightly bending pose (Svavayavanamitā). Her heart is made joyous by the draught of rice wine (Vāru*n*ī)."

Lingga is like shining gold, and on his head is an orifice minute as that in a gem. He is the resplendent abode of Lak*sh*mī.

COMMENTARY.

In this Shloka is described the triangle Triko*n*a which is in the pericarp of this Lotus.

"*Shakti in the form of a triangle*" (Triko*n*ābhidhā Shakti*h*).—By this we are to understand that the mouth or head of the Triko*n*a is downward.[964]

This Triko*n*a is below the Vāyu Bīja, as has been said elsewhere. "In its lap is Īsha. Below it, within the Triko*n*a is Vā*n*a-Lingga."

"*On his head*," *etc.* (Maulau Sūk*sh*ma-vibheda-yuk ma*nih*).—This is a description of Vā*n*a-Lingga. The orifice is the little space within the Bindu which is within the half-moon which is on the head of the Lingga.

Cf. the following description: "The Vā*n*a-Lingga within the triangle, decked in jewels made of gold—the Deva with the half-moon on his head; in the middle is an excellent red lotus."

The red lotus in this quotation is one below the pericarp of the heart lotus; it has its head turned upwards, and has eight petals. It is in this that mental worship (Mānasapūjā) should be made.[965] Compare the following: "Inside is the red eight-petalled lotus, there is the Kalpa-tree and the seat of the Ī*sht*a-deva under an awning (Chandrātapa), surrounded by trees laden with flowers and fruits and sweet-voiced birds. There meditate on the Ī*sht*a-deva according to the ritual[966] of the worshipper."

"*Orifice minute as.*"—He here speaks of the Bindu which manifests on the head of the Vā*n*a Lingga. As a gem has a minute orifice in it (when pierced to be threaded), so has this Lingga.[967] By this is meant that the Bindu is on the head of the Shiva Lingga.

"*The resplendent abode of Lak*shm*ī.*"[968]—By this one must know the great beauty of the Lingga, due to a rush of desire.[969]

---

964 As it is a Triko*n*a Shakti, it must have its apex downwards as in the case of the Yoni.

965 This is not one of the six Chakras, but a lotus known as Ānandakanda, where the I*sht*adevatā is meditated upon. See Ch. V., v. 132, Mahānirvā*n*a Tantra.

966 Kalpa.

967 The Lingga itself is not pierced, but it carries the Bindu, which has an empty space (Shūnya) within its circle.

968 That is, here, beauty.

969 Kāmodgama.

VERSE 26.

He who meditates on this Heart Lotus becomes (like) the Lord of Speech, and (like) Īshvara he is able to protect and destroy the worlds. This Lotus is like the celestial wishing-tree,[970] the abode and seat of Sharva.[971] It is beautified by the Hangsa,[972] which is like unto the steady flame of a lamp in a windless place.[973] The filaments which surround its pericarp, illumined by the solar region, charm.

COMMENTARY.

In this and the following verse he speaks of the good to be gained by meditating on the Heart Lotus.

"*He who meditates on this Lotus in the Heart becomes like the Lord of Speech*"—*i.e.*, Bri̍haspati, the Guru of the Devas—and able like Īshvara the Creator to protect and destroy the worlds. Briefly, he becomes the Creator, Protector, and Destroyer, of the Worlds.

He speaks of the presence of the Jivātmā in the pericarp of this Lotus by speaking of the Hangsa,[974] which is like the steady flame of a lamp in a windless place, and enhances the beauty of this Lotus (Anila-hīna-dīpa-kahkā-hangsena sangshobhitam). *Hangsa* is the Jīvātmā. He also speaks of the presence of the Sūryya-ma*nd*ala in the pericarp of this Lotus.

"*The filaments which surround its pericarp, illumined by the solar region, charm*" (Bhānorma*nd*ala-ma*nd*itāntara-lasatkinjalka-shobhādharam).—It is beautified by reason of the filaments which surround the pericarp being tinged by the rays of the Sun. The rays of the Sun should be read to qualify the filaments, and not the space within the pericarp. The filaments of the other Lotuses are not so tinged, and it is the distinctive feature of this Lotus. By the expression "the Mandala of Sūrya (Bhānu)" the reader is to understand that all the filaments in the pericarp are beauteous with the rays of the Sun, and not a portion of them.

All over the pericarp is spread the region of Vāyu. Round it is the Region of Sūryya; and above these the Vāyu Bīja and Triko*n*a. etc., should be meditated upon. This is quite consistent. In mental worship the *mantra* is "Mang[975]—salutation to the Region of Fire with his ten

[970] Sura-taru = kalpa-taru.
[971] Mahā-deva, Shiva.
[972] Here the Jīvātmā.
[973] See Introduction.
[974] Vishvanāthā quotes a verse in which this Hangsa is spoken of as Puru*sh*a.
[975] *Sic* in the text, which is possibly a mistake for "Rang."

Kalās,"[976] etc. And we therefore see from this[977] that the regions of Vahni (Fire), Arka (Sun), and Chandra (Moon), are placed one above the other.

"*Īshvara*"—*i.e.*, Creator.

"*Able to protect, and destroy the world*" (Rak*sh*ā-vināshe k*sh*amah)—*i.e.*, it is he who protects and destroys. The idea meant to be conveyed by these three attributes is that he becomes possessed of the power of creating, maintaining, and destroying, the Universe.[978]

VERSE 27.

Foremost among Yogīs, he becomes dearer than the dearest to women.[979] He is pre-eminently wise and full of noble deeds. His senses are completely under control. His mind in its intense concentration is engrossed in thoughts of the Brahman. His inspired speech flows like a stream of (clear) water. He is like Vi*shn*u Himself,[980] and he is able at will to enter another's body.[981]

COMMENTARY.

"*Dearer than the dearest to women*" (Priyāt priyatama*h* kāntākulasya)—*i.e.*, because he is skilful to please them.[982]

"*His senses are completely under control*" (Jitendriyaga*nah*)—*i.e.*, he is one who should be counted among those that have completely subjugated their senses.

"*His mind . . . Brahman*" (Dhyānāvadhāna-k*sh*ama*h*).—Dhyāna is Brahma-chintana, and Avadhāna means steady and intense concentration of the mind. The Yogī is capable of both.

"*His inspired speech flows like a stream of (clear) water*" (Kāvyāmbu-dhārā-vaha).—The flow of his speech is compared to an uninterrupted flow of water, and it is he from whom it flows.

"*He is like Vi*shnu" (Lak*sh*mī-ranggana-daivata*h*).—He becomes like the Deva who is the beloved of Laks*h*mī. Lak*sh*mī, the Devi of Prosperity, is the spouse of Vi*shn*u. This compound word is capable of another meaning. It may mean: One who has enjoyed all prosperity (Lak*sh*mī) and bliss (Rangga*na*) in this world goes along the path of liberation. It has therefore been said: "Having enjoyed in this world the

---

[976] Kalā = digits or portions of Shakti.

[977] Literally "following the maxim (Nyāya) which draws inferences from previous experience" (dri*sh*taparikalpanā-nyāya).

[978] By reason of his unification with the Brahma-substance.

[979] Priyāt priyatama*h*—more beloved than those that are dear to them.

[980] According to Shangkara's reading, Lak*sh*mī becomes his family Devatā—that is, his family is always prosperous.

[981] Parapure; *v. post.*

[982] Karmmakushala*h*. "Dearer than their husbands" (Shangkara).

best of pleasures, he in the end goes to the abode of Liberation."[983]

"*Another's body*" (Para-pura).—He is able at will to enter the enemy's fort or citadel (Durga), even though guarded and rendered difficult of access. And he gains power by which he may render himself invisible, fly across the sky, and other similar powers. It may also mean "another man's body."[984]

SUMMARY OF VERSES 22 TO 27.

The Heart Lotus is of the color of the Bandhūka[985] flower, and on its twelve petals are the letters Ka to *Tha*., with the Bindu above them, of the color of vermilion. In its pericarp is the hexagonal[986] Vāyu-Ma*nd*ala, of a smoky color, and above it Sūryya-Ma*nd*ala, with the Triko*n*a lustrous as ten million flashes of lightning within it. Above it the Vāyu Bīja, of a smoky hue, is seated on a black antelope, four-armed and carrying the goad (angkusha). In his (Vāyu-bīja's) lap is three-eyed Īsha. Like Hangsa (Hangsābha), His two arms extended in the gestures of granting boons and dispelling fear. In the pericarp of this Lotus, seated on a red lotus, is the Shaktī Kākinī. She is four-armed, and carries the noose (Pāsha), the skull (Kapāla), and makes the boon (Vara) and fear-dispelling (Abhaya) signs. She is of a golden hue, is dressed in yellow raiment, and wears every variety of jewel and a garland of bones. Her heart is softened by nectar. In the middle of the Triko*n*a is Shiva in the form of a Vā*n*a-Lingga, with the crescent moon and Bindu on his head. He is of a golden color. He looks joyous with a rush of desire.[987] Below him is the Jīvātmā like Hangsa. It is like the steady flame of a lamp.[988] Below the pericarp of this Lotus is the red lotus of eight petals, with its head upturned. It is in this (red) lotus that there are the Kalpa Tree, the jeweled altar surmounted by an awning and decorated by flags, which is the place of mental worship.[989]

(*Here ends the fourth section.*)

[983] Iha bhuktvā varan bhogān ante mukti-padam brajet.

[984] The Siddh by which Yōgīs transfer themselves into another's body, as Shangkarāchāryya is said to have done. The latter interpretation is preferable, for such an one will not have enemies, or if he have will not seek to overcome them.

[985] *Pentapœtes Phœnicea.*

[986] See Introduction.

[987] Kāmodgamollasita.

[988] See Introduction.

[989] See Mahānirvā*n*a Tantra, Ch. V., vv. 129, 130, p. 85, where the Mantra is given.

VERSES 28 AND 29.

In the throat is the Lotus called Vishuddha, which is pure and of a smoky purple hue. All the (sixteen) shining vowels on the sixteen petals, of a crimson hue, are distinctly visible to him whose mind (Buddhi) is illumined. In its pericarp there is the Ethereal Region, circular in shape, and resembling the full Moon.[990] On an elephant white as snow is seated the Bīja[991] of Ambara,[992] who is white of color.

Of His four arms, two hold the noose[993] and goad,[994] and the other two make the gestures[995] of granting boons and dispelling fear. These add to His beauty. In His lap[996] there ever dwells the snow-white Deva, three-eyed and five-faced, with ten beautiful arms, and clothed in a tiger's skin. His body is united with that of Girijā,[997] and he is known by what his name, Sadā-shiva,[998] signifies.

COMMENTARY.

The Vishuddha Chakra is described in four verses beginning with these.

"Because by the sight of the Hangsa the Jīva attains purity, this Padma (Lotus) is therefore called Vishuddha (pure)—Ethereal, Great, and Excellent."[999]

"*In the region of the throat is the Lotus called Vishuddha.*"—Pure (amala, without impurity) by reason of its being *tejo-maya*[1000] (its substance is *tejas*), and hence free from impurity.

"*All the vowels*" (Svarai*h* sarvai*h*)—*i.e.*, all the vowels beginning with *ă-kāra* and ending with visarga—altogether sixteen in number.

"*Shining on the petals*" (Dala-parilasitai*h*).—The vowels being sixteen in number, the number of petals which this lotus possesses is

---

990 Ether is the element of this Chakra, the sign (Ma*nd*ala) of this Tattva being a circle (V*ri*tta-rūpa). See Introduction.

991 "Hang."

992 Ambara = the Ethereal Region; the word also means "apparel"—"Vyomni, vāsasi" (Amara-ko*sh*a). On an elephant of the color of snow is seated Ambara, white in color in his Bīja form. The Sansk*ri*t is capable of another meaning: "On an elephant is seated the Bija whose raiment is white."

993 Pāsha.

994 Angkusha.

995 Mudrā; *v.* p. 219, *ante*.

996 Of the Nabhovīja or "Hang."

997 "Mountain-born," a title of the Devī as the daughter of the Mountain King (Himavat—Himālaya). The reference is here to the Androgyne Shiva-Shakti form. See Commentary.

998 Sadā = ever. Shiva = the Beneficent One.

999 See Rudrayāmala, Ch. XXVII., v. 67.

1000 Fire purifies.

shown by implication to be sixteen also.

Elsewhere this has been clearly stated: "Above it is the Lotus of sixteen petals, of a smoky purple color; its petals bear the sixteen vowels, red in color, with the Bindu above them. Its filaments are ruddy, and it is surrounded by Vyoma-ma*nd*ala."[1001]

"*Distinctly visible*" (Dīpitam).—These letters are lighted up, as it were, for the enlightened mind (Dīpta-bud*dh*i).

"*Whose mind (buddhi) is illumined*". refers to the person whose *buddhi*, or intellect, has become free from the impurity of worldly pursuits as the result of the constant practice of Yoga.

"*The Ethereal Region circular in shape, and resembling the full Moon*" (Pūr*n*endu-prathita-tama-nabhoma*nd*alam v*r*itta-rūpam).—The Ethereal Region is circular in shape (V*r*itta-rūpa), and its roundness resembles that of the full Moon, and like the Moon it is also white. The Shāradā says: "The wise know that the Ma*nd*alas participate in the luster of their peculiar elements."[1002] The Ma*nd*alas are of the color of their respective Devatās and elements: Ether is white, hence its Ma*nd*ala is also white.

"*In this pericarp is the circular Ethereal Region*" (Nabhōma*nd*alam v*r*ita-rūpam).—In the lap of this white Ambara (or Ethereal Region) ever dwells Sadā-shiva, who is spoken of in the second of these two verses.

"*On an elephant white as snow is seated*" (Hima-chchhāyā nāgopari lasit-tanu).—This qualifies Ambara.

Nāga here means an Elephant, and not a serpent. The Bhūta-shuddhi clearly says: "Inside it is the white Bīja of Vyoma on a snow-white elephant." Literally, "His body shows resplendent on an elephant," because He is seated thereon.

"*The Bīja of Ambara*" (Tasya mano*h*).—Tasya mano*h* means literally "His mantra," which is the Bīja of Ether or Hang.[1003]

"*His four arms, (two of) which hold the pāsha (noose), angkusha (goad), and (the other two) are in the gesture granting boons and dispelling fear, add to his beauty*" (Bhujai*h* pāshā bhayang-kusha-vara-lasitai*h* shobhitānggasya).—The meaning, in short, is that in His hands He is carrying the *pāsha* and *angkusha*, and making the gestures of dispelling fear and granting boons.

"*In the lap of his Bīja*" (Tasya manorangke).—He is here in His Bīja form—in the form of Hang which is Ākāsha-Bīja. This shows the presence of the Bīja of Ether in the pericarp of this Lotus, and we are to meditate upon it as such.

"*The snow-white Deva whose body is united with (or inseparable*

[1001] The Ethereal Circle.

[1002] That is, each Ma*nd*ala (*i.e.*, square, circle, triangle, etc.) takes after the characteristics of its elements.

[1003] The Bīja of a thing is that thing in essence.

from) that of Giri-jā" (Girijābhinna-deha).—By this is meant the Arddha-nārīshvara.[1004] The Deva Arddha-nārīshvara is of a golden color on the left, and snow white on the right. He dwells in the lap of Nabho-bīja. He is described as "the Deva Sadā-shiva garbed in white raiment. His half-body inseparate from that of Giri-jā is both silvern and golden." He is also spoken of as "possessed of the down-turned digit (Kalā) of the Moon which constantly drops nectar."[1005]

The Nirvā*n*a Tantra,[1006] in dealing with the Vishuddha Chakra, says: "Within the Yantra is the Bull, and on his back the great lion-seat (Singhāsana). On this is the eternal Gaurī, and on Her right is Sadā-Shiva. He has five faces, and three eyes to each face; His body is smeared with ashes, and He is like a mountain of silver. The Deva is wearing the skin of a tiger, and garlands of snakes are His ornaments."

The Eternal Gaurī (Sadā Gaurī) is there as half of Shiva's body. She is in the same place spoken of as "the Gaurī, the Mother of the Universe, who is half the body of Shiva."

"*With ten beautiful arms*" (Lalita-dasha-bhuja).—The Author here has said nothing of what the Deva has in His hands. In a Dhyāna elsewhere He is spoken of as carrying in His hands the Shūla (trident), the Tangka (battle-axe), the *Kr*ipā*n*a (sword), the Vajra (thunderbolt), Dahana, the Nāgendra (snake-king), the Gha*n*t*ā (bell), the Angkusha (goad), Pāsha (noose), and making the gesture dispelling fear (Bhītihara). In meditating on Him, therefore, He should be thought of as carrying these implements and substances and making these gestures in and by His ten arms. The rest can be easily understood.

VERSE 30.

Purer than the Ocean of Nectar is the Shakti Shākinī who dwells in this Lotus. Her raiment is yellow, and in Her four lotus-hands She carries the bow, the arrow, the noose, and the goad. The whole region of the Moon without the mark of the hare[1007] is in the pericarp of this Lotus. This (region) is the gateway of great Liberation for him who desires the wealth of Yoga and whose senses are pure and controlled.

[1004] Hara-Gaurī-mūrti (Shangkara).

[1005] This is, the Amākalā.

[1006] Patala VIII. In Rasikamohana Cha*tt*opādhyāya's Edition there is some difference in the wording: "Within the Yantra is the bull, half whose body is that of a lion." This is consistent with the Arddha-nārīshvara, as the bull is the Vāhana (carrier) of Shiva, and the lion of the Devī.

[1007] The "Man in the Moon."

COMMENTARY.

Here the Author speaks of the presence of Shākinī in the pericarp of the Vishuddha Lotus.

"*Purer than the Ocean of Nectar*" (Sudhāsindhoh[1008] Shuddhā).—The Ocean of Nectar is white and cool. Shākinī, who is the form of light itself (Jyoti*h*-svarūpā), is white and heatless.

In the following Dhyāna of Shākinī She is described in detail: "Let the excellent Sādhaka meditate in the throat lotus on the Devī Shākinī. She is light itself (Jyoti*h*-svarūpā); each of Her five beautiful faces is shining with three eyes. In Her lotus hands She carries the noose, the elephant hook, the book, and makes the Jnāna-mudrā.[1009] She maddens (or distracts) all the mass of Pashus,[1010] and She is seated on bones.[1011] She is fond of milk food, and elated with the nectar which She has drunk."

By the expression "She is light itself" in the above Dhyāna, it is meant that She is white, whiteness being characteristic of light. The two Dhyānas differ as regards the weapons the Devī has in her hands. This is due to differences in the nature of the Sādhaka's aim.[1012]

The Devī is in the lunar region (Chandrama*nd*ala) within the pericarp. The Prema-yoga Taranggi*n*ī says: "Here dwells the Shakti Shākinī in the auspicious region of the Moon."

"*In this Lotus*" (Kamale)—*i.e.*, in the pericarp of the Vishuddha Chakra.

"*In this pericarp is the spotless region of the Moon, without the mark of a hare*" (Shasha-parirahita), conveys the same meaning. The spots on the moon are called "the sign of the hare," "the stain on the moon." She is likened to the Stainless Moon.

"*The gateway of great liberation*" (Mahā-moks*h*a-dvāra).—This is attributive of Ma*nd*ala, the lunar region, and is used in praise of the Ma*nd*ala. It is the gateway of Liberation, of Nirvā*n*a-mukti, for those who have purified and conquered their senses, among other practices; by meditating on this in the path of Yoga they attain liberation (Mukti).

[1008] Sudhāsindhu, says Shangkara, is Chandra (Moon). She is purer and whiter than the nectar in the moon. The translation here given is according to the construction of Shangkara and Vishvanātha, who read Sudhāsindhoh in the ablative. Kālīchara*n*a, however, reading it in the possessive case, gives the meaning "pure like the ocean of Nectar," which is the innermost ocean of the seven oceans, which surrounds the jeweled island (Ma*n*idvīpa).

[1009] Made by touching the thumb with the first finger.

[1010] See Introduction to A. Avalon's Mahānirvā*n*a Tantra. Apparently the sense is that She makes it very difficult for the Sādhaka to pierce this Lotus.

[1011] *I.e.*, She is the Devatā of the Asthi Dhātū.

[1012] The nature of the Dhyāna (meditation) varies with the aim which a Sādhaka vises by his worship.

"*Who desires the wealth of Yoga*" (Shriyam-abhimata-shīlasya).—By Shrī is meant "the wealth of Yoga." For him who by his very nature desires the wealth of Yoga, that is the gateway of Liberation. This clearly explains the meaning of Shuddhendriya, whose senses are pure and controlled.

In the pericarp of this Lotus is the Nabho-ma*nd*ala (ethereal region): inside the latter is the triangle (triko*n*a); inside the triangle is the Chandra-ma*nd*ala; and inside it is the Nabhovīja[1013]; and so forth. *Cf.* "Think of the full moon in the triangle within the pericarp; there think of the snowy Ākāsha seated on an elephant, and whose raiment is white. There is the Deva Sadā-Shiva." "Whose raiment is white" qualifies Ākāsha.

VERSE 31.

The Sādhaka who has attained complete knowledge of the Ātmā (Brahman) becomes by constantly concentrating his mind (Chitta) on this Lotus a great Sage,[1014] eloquent and wise, and enjoys uninterrupted peace of mind.[1015] He sees the three periods,[1016] and becomes the benefactor of all, free from disease and sorrow and long-lived, and, like Hangsa, the destroyer of endless dangers.

COMMENTARY.

In this verse he speaks of the good gained by meditating on the Vishuddha Chakra.

"*Who has attained,*" *etc.* (Ātmā-sampūr*n*a-yoga).[1017]—He whose knowledge of the Ātman is complete by realization of the fact that it is all-pervading.

According to another reading (Ātta-sampūr*n*a-yoga), the meaning would be "one who has obtained perfection in Yoga." Hence the all-knowing and venerable Teacher has said: "One who has attained complete knowledge of the Ātmā reposes like the still waters of the deep." The Sādhaka who fixes his *Chitta* on this Lotus, and thereby acquires a full knowledge of the Brahman, becomes a knower (Jnānī)—*i.e.*, becomes possessed of the knowledge of all the Shāstras without instruction therein. His *Chitta* becomes peaceful; "he becomes merciful towards all, not looking for any return therefore. He is constant, gentle, steady, modest, courageous, forgiving, self-controlled, pure, and free

---

[1013] The Bīja of Ether—Hăng.

[1014] Kavi.

[1015] Shānta-chetā*h*. Shama, says Shangkarāchāryya, in his Ātmānātmaviveka, is Antarindriya-nigraha—*i.e.*, subjection of the inner sense.

[1016] Past, present, and future.

[1017] The word Yoga is here used as equivalent of Jnāna.

from malice and pride."[1018]

"*He sees the three periods*" (Tri-kāla-darshī)—*i.e.*, by the knowledge acquired by Yoga he sees everything in the past, present, and future. Some say that the meaning of this is that the Yogī has seen the Self (Ātmā), and, as all things are therein, they become visible to him.

"*Free from disease and sorrow*"—*i.e.*, by having attained Siddhi in his *mantra* he becomes free from diseases and long-lived, and by reason of his having freed himself from the bonds of Māyā he feels no sorrow.

"*Like Hangsa, the destroyer of endless dangers*" (Niravadhivipadāng dhvangsa-hangsa-prakāsha*h*).—From acts good and evil various dangers (Vipat) arise. The Sādhaka becomes like the Hangsa which is the Antarātmā that dwelleth by the pericarp of the Sahasrāra,[1019] for he can destroy all such dangers and open the gate of liberation" (Mok*sh*a). Hangsa is the form of the Antarātmā. The rest is clear.

SUMMARY OF THE VISHUDDHA CHAKRA.

At the base of the throat[1020] is the Vishuddha Chakra, with sixteen petals of smoky purple hue. Its filaments are ruddy, and the sixteen vowels, which are red and have the Bindu above them, are on the petals. In its pericarp is the ethereal region (Nabho-ma*nd*ala), circular and white. Inside it is the Chandra-ma*nd*ala, and above it is the Bīja Hang. This Bīja is white and garmented in white, seated on an elephant, and is four-armed. In his four hands he holds the Pāsha (noose) and the Angkusha (goad), and makes the Vara-mudrā and the Abhaya-mudrā. In his lap is Sadā-shiva, seated on a great lion-seat which is placed on the back of a bull. He is in his form of Ardhanārīshvara, and as such half his body is the color of snow, and the other half the color of gold. He has five faces and ten arms, and in his hands he holds the Shūla (trident), the Tangka (battle-axe), the Kha*d*ga (sacrificial sword), the Vajra (thunderbolt), Dahana,[1021] the Nāgendra (great snake), the Gha*n*tā (bell), the Angkusha (goad), the Pāsha (noose), and makes the Abhaya-mudrā. He wears a tiger's skin, his whole body is smeared with ashes, and he has a garland of snakes round his neck. The nectar dropping from the down-turned digit of the Moon is on his forehead. Within the pericarp, and in the Lunar Region and seated on bones, is the Shakti Shākinī, white in color, four-armed, five-faced and three-eyed, clothed in yellow, and carrying in Her hand a bow, an arrow, a noose, and a

---

[1018] The portion within inverted commas is from the Bhagavadgītā, XVI.—2, 3.
[1019] That is, the Hangsa is in the twelve-petalled Lotus below the Sahasrāra.
[1020] Ka*nth*a-mūle.
[1021] Āgneya astra.

goad.

VERSE 31A.[1022]

The Yogī, his mind constantly fixed on this Lotus, his breath controlled by Kumbhaka,[1023] is in his wrath[1024] able to move all the three worlds. Neither Brahmā nor Vi*sh*nu, neither Hari-Hara[1025] nor Sūryya[1026] nor Ga*n*apa,[1027] is able to control his power (resist him).

COMMENTARY.

"*His breath controlled by Kumbhaka*" (Ātta-pavana).—Literally it means, who has taken the air in, which is done by Kumbhaka.

"*Hari-Hara.*"—The Yugala (coupled) form, consisting of Vi*sh*nu and Shiva combined.

"*Sūryya*" (Kha-ma*n*i).—This word means the jewel of the sky, or Sūryya.

(*Here ends the fifth section.*)

VERSE 32.

The Lotus named Ājnā[1028] is like the Moon, beautifully white. On its two petals are the letters Ha and *Ksha*, which are also white and enhance its beauty. It shines with the glory of Dhyāna.[1029] Inside it is the Shakti Hākinī, whose six faces are like so many moons. She has six arms, in one of which She holds a book; two others are lifted up in the gestures of dispelling fear and granting boons, and with the rest She holds a skull, a small drum,[1030] and a rosary.[1031] Her mind is pure (Shuddha-chittā).

[1022] This verse has not been taken into account either by Kālīchara*n*a or Shangkara. It is given by Bala-deva in his text, and his Commentary is also here given.

[1023] Retention of breath in Prā*n*āyāma is Kumbhaka.

[1024] This is praise (Stutivāda) of his great powers—that is, were he to get angry he could move the three worlds.

[1025] See Commentary.

[1026] Sun. See Commentary.

[1027] Ga*n*esha.

[1028] Ājnā—command. See Commentary. The Tantrāntara Tantra calls this Chakra the house of Shiva (Shivageha).

[1029] The state of mind which is acquired by meditation (Dhyāna).

[1030] *D*amaru.

[1031] Rosary with which "recitation" (japa) of mantra is done.

COMMENTARY.

The Author now describes the Ājnā Chakra between the eyebrows in the seven verses beginning with this present one.

"*Lotus named Ājnā*" (Ājnā-nāma).—"Ājnā is communicated there between the eyebrows, hence it is called Ājnā." Here between the eyebrows is the Ājnā (Command), which is communicated from above, hence it is called Ājnā. This Lotus which is well known is here.[1032]

This Lotus is between the eyebrows, as the following shows: "Going upwards after entering the throat and palate, the white and auspicious Lotus between the eyebrows is reached by Kundali. It has two petals on which are the letters Ha and K*sha.*, and it is the place of mind (Manas)."

The following are descriptions of the Lotus:

"*Like the Moon, beautifully white*" (Hima-kara-sad*r*ishang).—This comparison with Chandra (Himakara) may also mean that this Lotus is cool like the moonbeams (the moon being the receptacle of Am*r*ita, or Nectar, whose characteristic is coolness), and that it is also beautifully white.

It has been said in "Īshvara-kārtikeya-sangvāda"[1033]: "Ājnā Chakra is above it; it is white and has two petals; the letters Ha and K*sha.*, variegated in color, also enhance its beauty. It is the seat of mind (Manas)."

"*Two petals*" (Netra-patra).—The petals of the lotus.

"*The letters Ha and K*sha*, which are also white*" (Ha-k*sh*ā-bhyāng kalābhyām parilasatavapu*h* su-shubhram).—These two letters are by their very nature white, and by their being on the white petals the whiteness thereof is made more charming by this very excess of whiteness. The letters are called Kalās because they are Bījas of Kalās.[1034]

"*It shines with the glory of Dhyāna*" (Dhyāna-dhāma-pramāsham)—that is, its body shines like the glory of Dhyāna Shakti.

"*Hākinī.*"—He next speaks of the presence of the Shakti Hākinī here. The force of the pronoun Sā (she) in addition to Her name is that She is the well-known Hākinī.

"*The gestures of dispelling fear and granting boons*" (Mudrā).—This word stands for both. There should be six weapons in Her hands, as She has six hands. There are some who read Vidyā and Mudrā as one word, Vidyā-mudrā, and interpret it to mean "the gesture of

---

[1032] It is here that the Ājnā of the Guru is communicated (Gautamīya Tantra, cited by Vishvanātha). See Rudrayāmala, Ch. XXVII., v. 68, which says that the Guru's Ājnā is communicated (gurorajneti). The text has Bhruvorājneti.

[1033] *I.e.*, the Sammohana Tantra.

[1034] See Introduction, Prapanchasāra Tantra, Vol. III., Tantrik Texts, ed. A. Avalon.

explanation"—the gesture that conveys learning or knowledge—and speak of Her as possessed of four arms. Different manuscripts give different readings. Various manuscripts read these as two words. The wise reader should judge for himself.

In a Dhyāna in another place She is thus described: "Meditate upon Her, the divine Hākinī. She is placed within the Chakra and is white. In Her hands are the *D*amaru, the Rudrāk*sh*a rosary, the skull, the Vidyā (book), the Mudrā (gesture of granting boons and dispelling fear). She is placed in the yellow filaments round the pericarp, and is elated by drinking ambrosia. She is well seated on a white Lotus, and Her mind is exalted by the drink of the King of the Devas gathered from the Ocean."

The rest is clear.

VERSE 33.

Within this Lotus dwells the subtle mind (Manas). It is well known. Inside the Yoni in the pericarp is the Shiva called Itara,[1035] in His phallic form. He there shines like a chain of lightning flashes. The first Bīja of the Vedas,[1036] which is the abode of the most excellent Shakti, and which by its luster makes visible the Brahma-sūtra,[1037] is also there. The Sādhaka with steady mind should meditate upon these according to the order (prescribed).

COMMENTARY.

He speaks of the presence of Manas in this Lotus.

"*Subtle*" (Sūk*sh*ma-rūpa).—The Manas is beyond the scope of the senses; that being so, it may be asked, What is the proof of its existence? The answer is, It is well known or universally accepted (Prasiddha) from eternity by generation after generation as a thing realized, and is hence well known. The evidence of the Shāstras, also, is that this Manas selects and rejects.[1038] Here is the place of the Manas. The presence of Manas is above the first Bīja of the Vedas as will appear from what is about to be spoken of.

"*Phallic form.*"—He next speaks of the presence of the Shiva-lingga[1039] in the Yoni which is within the pericarp. The Itara-Shiva who is there is in His phallic form, and within the Yoni. Within the triangle

---

[1035] Ing—*i.e.*, Kālang tarati iti Itara (Vishvanātha). "Itara" is that which enables one to cross Kāla. Ing—that is, here, the world.

[1036] Om.

[1037] The Nā*d*ī Chitri*n*ī.

[1038] Sangkalpavikalpātmaka. This is the lower Manas, and not that referred to in the Commentary to v. 40, *post.* As to the metal faculties, see Introduction.

[1039] Phallic emblem of Shiva.

in the pericarp dwells Itara-shiva-pada[1040]—*i.e.*, the corpse-like form known by the name of Itara. This Lingga is in the phallic form and white. As has been said in the Bhūta-shuddhi Tantra: "Inside it is the Lingga Itara, crystalline and with three eyes." This Lingga resembles continuous streaks of lightning flashes (Vidyun-mālāvilā-sam).

"*First Bīja of the Vedas*" (Vedānām ādivījam).—He then speaks of the presence of the Pra*n*ava[1041] in the pericarp of this Lotus. In the pericarp there is also the first Bīja—*i.e.*, Pra*n*ava.[1041]

"*Which is the abode of the most excellent Shakti*" (Parama kula-pada).—Kula = shakti. Parama means most excellent, by reason of its resembling lightning; and *Pada* means place—*i.e.*, the triangular space. Hence this Bīja—namely, the Pra*n*ava—we perceive is within the triangle. This is clearly stated in the following text:

"Within the pericarp, and placed in the triangle, is Ātmā in the form of the Pra*n*ava, and above it, like the flame of a lamp, is the charming Nāda, and Bindu which is Makāra,[1042] and above it is the abode of Manas."

Now, if the Paramakulapada[1043] be the container (Ādhāra) of the Pra*n*ava, how is it that it is not mentioned as one of the sixteen Ādhāras spoken of in the following passage? For it has been said that "the sixteen Ādhāras hard of attainment by the Yogī are Mūladhāra, Svādhi*shth*āna, Ma*n*i-pura, Anāhata, Vishuddha, Ājnā-chakra, Bindu, Kalāpada, Nibodhikā, Addhendu, Nāda, Nādānta, Unmanī, Vi*shn*u-vaktra Dhruvama*nd*ala,[1044] and Shiva."

The answer is that the second Kalāpada is not the one in the Ājnā Chakra, but is placed in the vacant space above Mahānāda which is spoken of later. This will become clear when dealing with the subject of Mahānāda.

"*Which makes manifest the Brahma-sūtra*" (Brahma-sūtra-prabodha).—Brahma-sūtra = Chitri*n*ī-nā*d*ī. This Nā*d*ī is made visible by the luster of the Pra*n*ava. In v. 3 this Nā*d*ī has been described as "lustrous with the luster of the Pra*n*ava."

The Sādhaka should with a steady mind meditate upon all these—viz., Hākinī, Manas, Itara Lingga, and Pra*n*ava—in the order prescribed. This is different to the order in which they are placed in the text by the Author. But the arrangement of words according to their import is to be preferred to their positions in the text. The order as

---

[1040] According to Vishvanātha, this is an Angsha (part) of the Nirgu*n*a Para Shiva in the Sahasrāra.

[1041] Om.

[1042] The letter Ma; that is, it is Makārarūpa or Ma before manifestation.

[1043] Shangkara says that Paramakula = Mūlādhāra Padma, and Paramakulapada = He who has his abode in the Mūlādhāra.

[1044] See Shāradā Tilaka, Ch. V., 135, Ch. XII., v. 117 *et seq.*; Kular nava Tautra, Ch. IV., and Introduction.

shown here should prevail. Thus, first Hākinī in the pericarp, in the triangle; above her Itara Lingga; in the triangle above him another; and above the last the Pra*n*ava; and last of all, above the Pra*n*ava itself, Manas, should be meditated upon.

VERSE 34.

The excellent Sādhaka, whose Ātmā is nothing but a meditation on this Lotus, is able quickly to enter another's body[1045] at will, and becomes the most excellent among saints and sages, and all-knowing and all-seeing. He becomes the benefactor of all, and is versed in all the Shāstras. He realizes his unity with the Brahman and acquires excellent and unknown powers.[1046] Full of fame and long-lived, he ever becomes the Creator, Destroyer, and Preserver, of the three worlds.

COMMENTARY.

In this verse he speaks of the good to be gained by the Dhyāna of this Lotus.

"*Most excellent among saints and sages*" (Munīndra).—A Muni is one who is possessed of the wealth of Dhyāna and Yoga and other excellent acquirements. The suffix Indra means King or Chieftain, and is added to names to signify excellence.

"*Versed in all the Shāstras*" (Sarva-shāstrārthavettā).—Such an one becomes proficient in the Shāstras and in Divine knowledge, and thus he becomes all-seeing (Sarva-darshī)—*i.e.*, able to look at things from all points by reason of his being possessed of wisdom and knowledge which harmonizes with Shāstras, manners, and customs.

"*He realizes,*" *etc.* (Advaitāchāra-vādi).—He knows that this Universe and all material existence is the Brahman, from such sayings of Shruti as, "The worlds are Its feet: all that exists is the Brahman"[1047]; and, "I am the Deva, and no one else; I am the very Brahman, and sorrow is not my share."[1048] He knows that the Brahman alone is the Real (Sat), and everything else is unreal (Asat), and that they all shine by the light of the Brahman.[1049] The man who by such knowledge is able to realize the identity of the Individual with the Supreme Spirit[1050] (Jīvātmā and Paramātmā), and preaches it, is an Advaitavādī.

"*Excellent and unknown powers*" (Paramāpūrva-siddhi)—that is,

[1045] Para-pura—another's body or house. See p. 244, *ante*.

[1046] Siddhi.

[1047] Pādo 'sya vishvā bhūtānīti tadidang sarvvang Brahma.

[1048] Ahang devo na chānyo'smi Brahmaivāsmi na shokabhāk.

[1049] Brahmaivaikang sad-vastu tadanyadasat prapancha samudāyastu Brahma-bhāsatayā bhāsate.

[1050] Jīvātma-paramātmanoraikyachintana.

most exalted and excellent powers.

"*Full of fame*" (Prasiddha)—*i.e.*, famous by reason of his excellence.

"*He ever becomes*," *etc.* (So 'pi kartā tri-bhuvana-bhavane sanghr*i*tau pālane cha).—This is the highest Prashangsāvāda[1051]; or it may mean that such Sādhaka becomes absorbed in the Supreme on the dissolution of the body, and thus becomes the source of Creation, Preservation, and Destruction.

VERSE 35.

Within the triangle in this Chakra ever dwells the combination of letters[1052] which form the Pra*n*ava. It is the inner Ātmā as pure mind (Buddhi), and resembles a flame in its radiance. Above it is the half (crescent) moon, and above this, again, is Ma-kāra,[1053] shining in its form of Bindu. Above this is Nāda, whose whiteness equals that of Bala-rāma[1054] and diffuses the rays of the Moon.[1054]

COMMENTARY.

The author desires to speak of the presence of the Pranava in the Ājnā Chakra and says that in this Chakra, and within the triangle which has already been spoken of, ever dwells the combination of letters which by the rules of Sandhi makes the thirteenth vowel O. This combination of letters is Shuddha-buddhyantarātmā—*i.e.*, the innermost Spirit manifesting as pure intelligence (Buddhi).

He next gives its attributes:

"*Resembles the flame in its radiance*" (Pradīpābhajyoti*h*).—But how can this thirteenth vowel by itself be Shuddha-buddhyantarātmā? He therefore says:

"*Above it is the crescent moon*" (Tadūrdhve chandrārdha).

"*And above this, again, is Ma-kāra, shining in its bindu form*" (Tad-upari vilasad Bindu-rūpī *Ma*-kāra*h*).—It is thus shown that by the placing of the crescent moon and the Bindu[1055] over the thirteenth vowel the Prar*n*ava is completely formed.

"*Above this is Nāda*" (Tadūrdhve nādo'sau)—*i.e.*, above the Pra*n*ava is the Avāntara (secondary) *N*āda, which challenges as it were

---

[1051] *I.e.*, Stuti-vāda, or praise; or, as we should say, compliment, which, while real in the sense of the presence of a desire to praise that which is in fact praiseworthy, is unreal so far as regards the actual words in which that desire is voiced.

[1052] That is, *a* and *u*, which by Sandhi becomes *O*, and with anusvāra (*m*) thus form the Pra*n*ava, or mantra Om.

[1053] The letter M in its bindu form in Chandra-vindu.

[1054] Shangkara reads it as "Jaladhavala, etc.," and explains it by "white like water." The last portion may also mean "smiling whiteness equals that of the Moon."

[1055] That is, Anusvāra.

the whiteness of Baladeva and the Moon (Baladhavala-sudhādhāra-santāna-hāsī). By this he means to say that it is extremely white, excelling in whiteness both Baladeva and the Moon.

Some read Tadādye nādo'sau (in the place of Tadūrdhve nādo'sau), and interpret it as, "Below Bindu-rūpī Ma-kāra is Nāda." But that is incorrect. The text says, "Above this, again, is Ma-kāra, shining in its form of Bindu," and there is Nāda below it; that being so, it is useless to repeat that Nāda is below.

Besides, this Nāda is beyond the Nāda which forms part of the Prar*n*ava, and is part of the differentiating Bhidyamāna Parabindu placed above the Pra*n*ava. If, however, it be urged that it is necessary to state the details in describing the special Pra*n*ava (Vishi*sht*a-Pra*n*ava), and it is asked, "Why do you say a second *N*āda is inappropriate?" then the reading Tadādye nādo'sau may be accepted.

But read thus it should be interpreted in the manner following: "This Nāda shown below the Bindu-rūpī Ma-kāra is Bala-dhavala-sudhādhāra-santāna-hāsī (*v. ante*), and the Nāda first spoken of is also so described. Such repetition is free from blame on the authority of the maxim that "the great are subject to no limitations."

VERSE 36.

When the Yogī closes the house which hangs without support,[1056] the knowledge whereof he has gained by the service of Parama-guru, and when the Chetas[1057] by repeated practice becomes dissolved in this place which is the abode of uninterrupted bliss, he then sees within the middle of and in the space above (the triangle) sparks of fire distinctly shining.

COMMENTARY.

Having described the Pranava, he now speaks of its union (with chetas).

The Yogī should close the house (Pur)—*i.e.*, he should, with his mind set on the act, close the inner house; or, in other words, he should make Yoni-mudrā[1058] in the manner prescribed, and thus effectually close the inner house. The word *Pur* here used shows that the Yoni-mudrā is meant. Then, when his Chetas by repeated practice (Abhyāsa) or meditation on the Pra*n*ava becomes dissolved (Līna) in this place (the Ājnā-chakra), he sees within and in the space above the triangle

---

[1056] Nirālamba-purī. Nirālamba (*v. post*) means that which has no support—viz., that from which the mind's connection with the world has been removed. Ākāshamāngsī = whose flesh or substance is Ākāsha (Rājanirgha*n*ta Dict.).

[1057] See next page and Introduction.

[1058] *I.e.*, closes the avenues of the mind and concentrates it within itself.

sparks of Fire[1059] (Pavana-suh*ri*dāng ka*n*ān), or, to put it plainly, sparks of light resembling sparks of fire appear before his mental vision above the triangle on which the Pra*n*ava rests. It is by Yoni-mudrā that the inner self (Anta*h*-pur) is restrained and detached from the outside world, the region of material sense. The Manas cannot be purified and steadied unless it is completely detached from the material sphere. It is therefore that the mind (Manas) should be completely detached by Yoni-mudrā.

Yoni-mudrā, which detaches the Manas from the outside world, is thus defined: "Place the left heel against the anus, and the right heel on the left foot, and sit erect with your body and neck and head in a straight line. Then, with your lips formed to resemble a crow's beak,[1060] draw in air and fill therewith your belly. Next[1061] close tightly your ear-holes with the thumbs, with your index-fingers the eyes, the nostrils by your middle fingers, and your mouth by the remaining fingers. Restrain the air[1062] within you, and with the senses controlled meditate on the Mantra whereby you realize the unity (Ekatvam) of Prā*n*a and Manas.[1063] This is Yoga, the favorite of Yogi*s*."

"That steadiness of mind is produced by restraint of breath through the help of Mudrā," has been said by Shruti. The mind under the influence of Hangsa[1064] moves to and fro, over different subjects; by restraining Hangsa the mind is restrained.

"*Closes the house*" (Purang baddhvā).—This may also mean Khecharī Mudrā.[1065] This latter also produces steadiness of mind.

As has been said, "As by this the Chitta roams in the Brahman (Kha),[1066] and as the sound of uttered word[1067] also roams the Ether (Kha), therefore is Khecharī Mudrā honored by all the Siddhis."

The Chitta is Khe-chara[1068] when, disunited from Manas and

1059 Pavana-suh*ri*d—"He whose friend is air" = Fire. When the wind blows fire spreads.

1060 That is, by Kākī-mudrā. Shruti says that when Vāyu is stopped by this Mudrā steadiness of mind is produced.

1061 These and following verses occur in Shāradā Tilaka, Ch. XXV., vv. 45, 46. The first portion of this passage describes Siddhāsana.

1062 That is, by Kumbhaka.

1063 That is, recite the Hangsa or Ajapāmantra, or breathing in Kumbhaka.

1064 The Jīvātmā manifesting as Prāna.

1065 One of the Mudrās of Ha*th*a-yoga. See Introduction.

1066 Kha has three meanings—viz., Ether, Brahman, and space between eyebrows (Ājnā). Brahmānanda, the Commentator of the Ha*th*ayogapradīpikā, adopts the last meaning in interpreting this verse, and in commenting on v. 55 of the Ha*th*ayogapradīpikā gives it the meaning of Brahman.

1067 Lit., tongue.

1068 What moves about in the sky or ether. It is Manas which deprives the Chitta of freedom by causing attachment to the world. On being disunited from Manas it moves freely in the ether, going its own way.

devoid of all attachment to all worldly things, it becomes Unmanī.[1069]

As has been said,[1070] "the Yogī is united with Unmanī; without Unmanī there is no Yogī." Nirālambā means that which has no support—namely, that from which the mind's connection with the world has been removed.

"*The knowledge whereof he has gained by the service of his Parama-guru*" (Parama-guru-sevā-suviditām).—Parama is excellent in the sense that he has attained excellence in Yoga practice (by instructions) handed down along a series of spiritual preceptors (Gurus), and not the result of book learning.[1071]

"*Serving the Guru.*"—Such knowledge is obtained from the Guru by pleasing him by personal services (Sevā). *Cf.* "It can be attained by the instructions of the Guru, and not by ten million of Shāstras."

"*The abode of uninterrupted bliss*" (Su-sukha-sadana)—*i.e.*, this is the place where one enjoys happiness that nothing can interrupt. This word qualifies *place* (Iha-sthāne—*i.e.*, Ājnā-chakre).

"*Sparks of fire distinctly shining*" (Pavana-suh*ri*dām pravilasita-rūpān ka*n*ān).—These sparks of Fire shine quite distinctly.

Elsewhere it is clearly stated that the Pra*n*ava is surrounded by sparks of light: "Above it is the flame-like Ātmā, auspicious and in shape like the Pra*n*ava, on all sides surrounded by sparks of light."

VERSE 37.

He then also sees the Light[1072] which is in the form of a flaming lamp. It is lustrous like the clearly shining morning sun, and glows between the Sky and the Earth.[1073] It is here that the Bhagavān manifests Himself in the fullness of His might.[1074] He knows no decay, and witnesseth all, and is here as He is in the region of Fire, Moon, and Sun.[1075]

[1069] Unmanī is there where, to coin a word, the "Manasness" of manas ceases. See note to v. 40. Ut = without, and manī is from Manas.

[1070] This is from Jnānār*n*ava Tantra, Ch. XXIV., v. 37.

[1071] Which is well recognized to be insufficient in these matters.

[1072] Jyoti*h*.

[1073] See Commentary, *post*.

[1074] Pūr*n*a-vibhava, which, however, as Kālīchara*n*a points out *post*, may be interpreted in various ways. According to Vishvanātha, the second chapter of the Kaivalya Kalikā Tantra contained a verse which says that the presence of the all-pervading Brahman is realized by His action as we realize the presence of Rāhu by his action on the sun and moon.

[1075] That is, the A-ka-tha triangle. See v. 4 of the Pādukāpanchaka.

COMMENTARY.

Yogīs such as these see other visions beside the sparks of light. After seeing the fiery sparks they see the light.

"*Then*" (Tadanu)—*i.e.*, after seeing the sparks spoken of in the preceding Shloka.

He then describes this Light (Jyoti*h*).

"*Glows between the Sky and the Earth*" (Gagana-dhara*n*ī-madhyamilita).—This compound adjective qualifies *Jyoti*h or Light.

Gagana (sky) is the sky or empty space above Shangkhinī Nā*d*ī (see Shloka 40, *post*), and Dhara*n*ī is the Dharā-ma*nd*ala in the Mūlādhāra. This light extends from the Mūlādhāra to the Sahasrāra.[1076]

He next speaks of the presence of Parama-Shiva in the Ājnā-Chakra.

"*It is here*" (Iha sthāne)—*i.e.*, in the Ājnā Chakra; Parama-Shiva is here, as in the Sahasrāra. Bhagavān is Parama-Shiva.

"*Manifests Himself*" (Sāk*s*hād bhavati)—*i.e.*, He is here.[1077]

"*In the fullness of His might*" (Pūr*n*a-vibhava).—This compound word which qualifies *Bhagavān* is capable of various interpretations.

Pūrna-vibhava may also be interpreted in the following different ways:

(*a*) *Pūrna* may mean complete in Himself, and *vibhava* infinite powers, such as the power of creation, etc. In that case the word would mean: "One who has in Him such powers, who is the absolute Creator, Destroyer, and Supporter, of the Universe."

(*b*) *Vibhava*, again, may mean "the diversified and limitless creation," and *pūrna* "all-spreading." In this sense *Pūrna-vibhava* means "He from whom this all-spreading and endless (vast) creation has emanated." *Cf.* "From whom all these originated, and in whom having originated they live, to whom they go and into whom they enter" (Shruti).

(*c*) *Vibhava*, again, may mean "omnipresence," and *Pūrna*[1078] "all-spreading." It would then mean: "He who in His omnipresence pervades all things."

(*d*) *Pūrna* may also mean the quality of one whose wish is not moved by the result and is not attached to any object. *Pūrna-vibhava* would then mean one who is possessed of that quality.

All things except Ātmā pass away. The ethereal region, etc., though omnipresent, are not ever-existent. The Nirvā*n*a Tantra (Ch.

[1076] The particle *vā* in the text is used in a collective sense.

[1077] He is seen here.

[1078] Phalānupahita-vi*sh*ayitā-nāspadechchhākatvang: He whose wish is not moved by the result, and is not attached to any object; or, in other words, He whose ways are inscrutable to us, subject as we are to limitations (Māyā).

IX.) speaks of the presence of Parama-Shiva in the Ājnā Chakra in detail.

"Above this (*i.e.*, Vishuddha) Lotus is Jnāna Lotus, which is very difficult to achieve; it is the region[1079] of the full Moon, and has two petals." Again: "Inside it, in the form of *Hangsah*, is the Bīja of Shambhu"; and again: "Thus is *Hangsah* in *Mani-dvīpa*,[1080] and in its lap is Parama-Shiva, with Siddha-kālī[1081] on his left. She is the very self of eternal bliss." By *lap* is meant the *space* within the *Bindus* which form the Visarga*h* at the end of Hangsa*h*.[1082]

Cf. what has been said in describing the Sahasrāra: "There are the two Bindus which make the imperishable Visarga.[1083] In the space within is Parama-shiva." As It is in the Sahasrāra so It is represented here.[1084]

We are to understand that these two, Shiva and Shakti, are here united (Bandhana) in the form of Parabindu, as the letter Ma (Makārātmā), and that they are surrounded (Āchchhādana) by Māyā.[1085] *Cf.* "She the Eternal One stays here (Ājnā-chakra) in the form of a grain of gram,[1086] and creates beings (Bhūtas)." Here the Paramashiva in the form of gram dwells, and according to the Utkalādimata[1087] also creates.

"*The region of Fire, Moon, and Sun.*"—As the presence of Bhagavān in these regions is well known, so is He here. Or it may be that the Author means that as He in the shape of a grain of gram dwells in the regions of Fire, Moon, and Sun, in the Sahasrāra, so does He dwell here also. We shall describe the Arka, Indu, and Agni Ma*nd*ala in the Sahasrāra later. Pī*th*a-pūjā and Pūjā of Paramātmā and Jnānātmā should be performed on the Ma*nd*alas of Sun (Arka), Moon (Indu), and Fire (Agni). By Paramātmā Paramashiva is meant, and by Jnānātmā Jnāna-Shakti. The Bindu should be meditated upon as like the grain of gram, consisting of the inseparable couple[1088]—namely, Shiva and Shakti.

[1079] Pūr*n*a-chandrasya ma*nd*alam.

[1080] The isle of gems in the Ocean of Ambrosia. The Rudrayāmala says that it is in the center of the Ocean of nectar outside and beyond the countless myriads of world systems, and that there is the Supreme abode of Shrīvidyā.

[1081] A form of Shakti.

[1082] *I.e.*, the two dots which form the aspirate breathing at the end of *Hangsah*.

[1083] Imperishable visarga—Visargarūpam avyayam.

[1084] That is, the Parabindu is represented in the Ājnā by the Bindu of the Ongkāra, which is its Pratīka.

[1085] Bindu is the nasal sound of Ma, which is a male letter. Bindu is here the unmanifest Ma.

[1086] Cha*n*akākāra-rūpinī. See Introduction.

[1087] Apparently a school of that name.

[1088] The grain referred to is divided in two under its encircling sheath.

VERSE 38.

This is the incomparable and delightful abode of Vi*sh*nu. The excellent Yogī at the time of death joyfully places his vital breath (Prā*n*a)[1089] here, and enters (after death) that Supreme, Eternal, Birthless, Primeval Deva, the Puru*sh*a, who was before the three worlds, and who is known by the Vedānta.

COMMENTARY.

He now speaks of the good to be gained by giving up the Prā*n*a by Yoga in the Ājnā Chakra.

This verse means: The excellent Yogī (Yogīndra) at the time of death (Prā*n*a-nidhane) joyfully (Pramuditamanā*h*) places his Prā*n*a (Prā*n*ang samāropya) in the abode of Vi*sh*nu in the Ājnā Chakra (Iha sthāne Vi*sh*no*h*—*i.e.*, in the abode of Bhagavān in the Bindu already described), and passes away, and then enters the Supreme Puru*sh*a.

"*At the time of death*" (Prā*n*a-nidhane)—*i.e.*, feeling the approach of death.

"*Joyfully*" (Pramudita-manā*h*).—Glad in the enjoyment of the blissful frame of his own mind.

"*Vishnu*" = Bhagavān = Paramashiva (see previous Shloka).

"*Here*" (Iha sthāne)—*i.e.*, Bindu spoken of above.

"*Places the prāna here*" (Iha sthāne prā*n*ang samāropya)—*i.e.*, he places it on the Bindu already spoken of. He describes Puru*sh*a as Eternal, etc.

"*Eternal*" (Nitya).—Indestructible.

"*Birthless*" (Aja).

"*Primeval*" (Purā*n*a).—He is the one known as the Purā*n*a Puru*sh*a.[1090]

"*Deva*" means he whose play is creation, existence, and destruction.

"*Who was before the three worlds*" (Tri-jagatām ādyam).[1091]—By this the implication is that He is the Cause of all.

"*Known by the Vedānta*" (Vedānta-vidita).[1092]—Vedānta are sacred texts dealing with the inquiry concerning the Brahman.

The way the Prā*n*a is placed (Prā*n*āropa*n*a-prakāra) in the place of

---

[1089] Compare Bhagavadgītā, Ch. VIII., vv. 9 and 10, and the commentary of Shangkarāchāryya and Madhusūdana Sarasvatī on those verses.

[1090] According to Shangkara, it is an adjective, and means "He who is the cause of Creation," and the like.

[1091] That is, the three spheres Bhū*h*, Bhuva*h*, Sva*h* the Vyāh*r*iti of the Gāyatrī.

[1092] Shangkara reads Vedānta-vihita, and explains the expression to mean "this is the teaching of the Vedānta."

Vi*sh*nu is described below: Knowing that the time for the Prā*n*a to depart is approaching, and glad that he is about to be absorbed into the Brahman, the Yogī sits in Yogā-sana and restrains his breath by Kumbhaka. He then leads the Jīvātmā in the heart to the Mūlādhāra, and by contracting the anus[1093] and following other prescribed processes rouses the Ku*nd*alinī. He next meditates upon the lightning-like, blissful Nāda, which is thread-like and whose substance is Ku*nd*alī (Ku*nd*alinī-maya). He then merges the Hangsa which is the Paramātmā in the form of Prā*n*a[1094] in the Nāda, and leads it along with the Jīva through the different Chakras according to the rules of Chakra-bheda to Ājnā-Chakra. He there dissolves all the diverse elements from the gross to the subtle, beginning with Prithivi, in Ku*nd*alinī. Last of all he unifies Her and the Jīvātmā with the Bindu whose substance is Shiva and Shakti (Shiva-shakti-maya); which having done, he pierces the Brahma-randhra and leaves the body, and becomes merged in the Brahman.

SUMMARY OF THE ĀJNĀ CHAKRA, VERSES 32 TO 38.

The Ājnā Chakra has two petals and is white. The letters Ha and K*sh*a, which are white,[1095] are on the two petals. The presiding Shakti of the Chakra, Hākinī, is in the pericarp. She is white, has six faces each with three eyes, and six arms, and is seated on a white lotus. With Her hands She displays Vara-mudrā and Abhaya-mudrā,[1096] and holds a Rudrak*sh*a rosary, a human skull, a small drum, and a book. Above Her, within a Triko*n*a, is Itara-Lingga, which is lightning-like, and above this, again, within another Triko*n*a, is the inner Ātmā (Antarātmā), lustrous like a flame. On its four sides, floating in air, are sparks surrounding a light which by its own luster makes visible all between Mūla and the Brahma-randhra. Above this, again, is Manas, and above Manas, in the region of the Moon, is Hangsa*h*, within whom is Paramashiva with His Shakti.

(*Here ends the sixth section.*)

[Vishvanātha,[1097] in the Commentary to the *Shat*chakra, gives under this verse a description, taken from the Svachchhandasanggraha, of the region beyond the Ājnā—that is, beyond the Sama*sht*i or collective Ājnā: "Within the Bindu is a space a hundred million

---

[1093] Gudamākunchya—that is, by Ashvinī Mudrā.

[1094] Prā*n*arūpashvāsaparamātmakam. See Jnanār*n*ava Tantra, Ch. XXI. vv. 13-18.

[1095] Karbura = white, and also means *variegated.*

[1096] *V.* p. 219, *ante.*

[1097] The portion in brackets is my note.—A. A.

Yojanas[1098] in expanse, and bright with the brightness of ten million suns. Here is the Lord of the State beyond Shānti (Shāntyatīteshvara), with five heads and ten arms and lustrous as a mass of lightning flashes. On His left is Shāntyatītā Manonmanī. Surrounding them are Nivr*i*tti, Prati*shth*ā, Vidyā, and Shāntī.[1099] Each of these is adorned with a moon and has five heads and ten arms. This is Bindu Tattva. Above Bindu is Arddhachandra, with the Kalās of the latter—namely, Jyotsnā, Jyotsnāvatī, Kāntī, Suprabhā, Vimalā. Above Arddhachandra is Nibhodikā, with the Kalās of the latter—Bandhatī, Bodhinī, Bodhā, Jnānabodhā, Tamopahā. Above Nibhodikā is Nāda and its five Kalās—Indhikā, Rechikā, Ūrddhvagā, Trāsā, and Paramā. On the lotus above this last is Īshvara, in extent a hundred million Yojanas, and lustrous as ten thousand moons. He is five-headed, and each head has three eyes. His hair is matted, and he holds the trident (Shūla). He is the one who goeth upwards (Ūrddhvagāmī), and in His embrace (Utsangga) is the Kalā Ūrddhvagāminī."]

VERSE 39.

When the actions of the Yogī are through the service of the Lotus feet of his Guru in all respects good, then he will see above it (*i.e.*, Ājnā-chakra) the form of the Mahānāda, and will even hold in the Lotus of his hand the Siddhi of Speech.[1100] The Mahānāda which is the place of dissolution of Vāyu[1101] is the half of Shiva, and like the plough in shape,[1102] is tranquil and grants boons and dispels fear, and makes manifest pure intelligence (Buddhi).[1103]

[1098] A Yojana is about eight miles.

[1099] See, as to the Kalās, Introduction to Vol. III., Tantrik Texts, ed. by A. Avalon. See also Introduction to this volume; and "Studies in the Mantrāshāstrā," by A. Avalon.

[1100] That is, all powers of speech.

[1101] Vāyo*h* layasthānam. Shangkara defines it by saying: Etat sthānam vāyoh virāma-bhūtam—this is the place where vāyu ceases to be.

[1102] That is, Shiva is Hakāra; and if the upper part of Ha is removed, the remaining portion of the letter has the form of an Indian plough.

[1103] Shuddha-buddhi-prakāsha.

COMMENTARY.

He now wishes to describe the intermediate causal body (Kāra*n*āvāntara-sharīra)[1104] situate above Ājnā Chakra and below Sahasrāra, and says: When the actions of the Yogī are, through the service of the Lotus feet of his Guru, in all respects good—that is, when he excels by intense concentration of the mind in Yoga practice—he then sees the image of Mahānāda above it (above Ājnā-chakra), and he becomes accomplished in speech (Vāksiddha).

"*Actions in all respects good*" (Sushīla).—The good inclination for Yoga practice rendered admirable by strong and undivided application thereto. This result is obtained by serving the Guru.

The Author then qualifies Nāda, and says it is the place of dissolution of Vāyu (Vāyor laya-sthānam). The Rule is "things dissolve into what they originate from." Hence, although in Bhūta-shuddhi and other practices it has been seen that Vāyu dissolves into Sparsha-tattva,[1105] and the latter in Vyoma,[1106] Vāyu dissolves in Nāda also. We have the authority of revelation (Shruti) for this:

"P*ri*thivī the possessor of Rasa (Rasa-vatī) originated from Ī-kāra.[1107] From Ka-kāra,[1107] who is Rasa, the waters and Tīrthas[1108] issued; from Repha (Ra-kāra)[1107] originated Vahnitattva[1109]; from Nāda[1107] came Vāyu,[1110] which pervades all life (Sarva-prā*n*amaya). From Bindu[1107] originated the Void[1111] (that which is empty of all things), and is the Sound-container. And from all these[1112] issued the twenty-five *Tattvas* which are Gu*n*a-maya. All this Universe (Vishva), which is the mundane egg of Brahmā, is pervaded by Kālikā."

We should therefore realize in our mind that at the time the letters

---

1104 Kāra*n*āvāntarasharīra. Kāra*n*a = cause; Avā*n*tara = secondary or intermediate or inclusive; Sharīra = body. Body is so called because it wastes and fades. It is derived from the root Shri, to wane. Kāra*n*āvāntara-Sharīra would thus mean "the intermediate Sharīra of the cause." The primary cause is the Great Cause. Its effects are also intermediate causes of that which they themselves produce; they are thus secondary or intermediate causal bodies. Taking the Sakala Parameshvara to be the first cause, Mahānāda is one of its effects and a Kāra*n*āvāntarasharīra as regards that which it produces and which follows it.

1105 The "touch principle," also called Tvak-tattva. As to Bhūtashuddhi, see the same described in Author's Introduction to the Mahānirvā*n*a Tantra.

1106 Ether.

1107 The Bīja Krīng is here being formed. Kakāra = Kālī; Ra-kāra = Brahma as fire; Īkāra = Mahāmāyā. Anusvāra or Chandrabindu (Ng) is divided into two—viz., Nāda, which is Vishvamātā, or Mother of the Universe; and Bindu, which is Du*h*khaharā, or remover of pain (Bījako*sh*a).

1108 Places of pilgrimage where the devotees bathe. It also means sacred waters.

1109 Fire.

1110 Air.

1111 Gagana, or Ether.

1112 That is, from Krīng as composed of Ka + Ra + Ī + Ng.

of the Kālī-mantra[1113] are merged into that which is subtle, Vāyu is absorbed in Nāda.

"*Half of Shiva*" (Shivārddha).—By this is meant that here Shiva is in the form of Addha-nārīshvara. Half is Shakti which is Nāda.

"*Like a plough*" (Sirākāra).—The word Sirā is spelt here with a short *i*, and in Amara-Ko*sh*a it is spelt with a long *i*; but it is clearly the same word, as it begins with a dental *s*.

Cf. "Above it is Mahānāda, in form like a plough, and lustrous" (Īshvara-kārttikeya-Sangvāda).[1114]

If the text is read as "Shivākāra instead of Sirākāra," then the meaning would be that the Nāda is Shiva-Shaktimaya.[1115]

Cf. Prapancha-sāra: "That Shakti which tends towards the seat of Lliberation[1116] is called male (Pungrūpā—that is, Bindu) when, quickened by Nāda, She turns towards Shiva[1117] (Shivonmukhī). It is therefore that Rāghava-Bha*tt*a has said that the Nāda and Bindu are the two conditions under which She creates."[1118]

It has elsewhere been said: "She is eternal[1119] existing as Chit (Chinmātrā)[1120]: when being near the light She is desirous of change She becomes massive (Ghanī-bhūya) and Bindu."

So in the word of the great (Shrīmat) Āchāryya: "Nāda becomes massive and the Bindu." Now, taking all these into consideration, the conclusion is that Shakti manifests herself as Nāda-bindu, like gold in ear-rings made of gold.[1121]

Nāda and Bindu again are one—that is the deduction.

[1113] Krīng.

[1114] *I.e.*, Sammohana Tantra.

[1115] That is, its substance is Shiva and Shakti.

[1116] Nirāmaya-padōnmukhī = she who is turned to the place of Liberation: that is Shakti in the supreme state.

[1117] Tending towards, intent on, or with face uplifted to, Shiva, that is here tending to creation. That is, the first state is Chit. Nāda is the Mitha*h* samavāya of Shakti and Bindu. The establishment of this relation quickens Her to turn to Shiva for the purpose of creation when She appears as male, or Bindu.

[1118] Reading the text as Tasyā eva shakternādabindū *srisht*yupayogyarūpau (Upayoga is capacity or fitness for creation). If, however, it be read as *Prish*atyupayogyarūpau, then the translation would be: "That the Nāda and Bindu aspects of Shakti are both feminine (p*rish*atī) and masculine (upayogya)—fit companion of that or male."

[1119] According to another reading this part would mean "She who is the Tattva." The passage is from Prapanchasāra Tantra.

[1120] She is there, existing as Chit, with whom she is completely unified. She "measures Chit"—that is, coexists with and as Chit, and is also formative activity. The above translation is that of the text, but the verse has been quoted elsewhere as if it were Chinmātra jyoti*shah*, and not Chinmātrā jyotisha*h*, in which case the translation would be: "She who when near Jyoti*h*, which is mere consciousness, becomes desirous of change, becomes massive and assumes the form of Bindu."

[1121] That is, they are both gold in the form of an ear-ring.

VERSE 40.

Above all these, in the vacant space[1122] wherein is Shangkhinī Nā*d*ī, and below Visarga is the Lotus of a thousand petals.[1123] This Lotus, lustrous and whiter than the full Moon, has its head turned downward. It charms. Its clustered filaments are tinged with the color of the young Sun. Its body is luminous with the letters beginning with A, and it is the absolute bliss.[1124]

COMMENTARY.

The Āchāryya enjoins that Sādhakas who wish to practice Samādhi Yoga should before such time with every effort dissolve all things in their order from the gross to the subtle in Chidātmā.[1125] All things, both gross and subtle, which make up creation should first be meditated upon. As the knowledge thereof is necessary, they are here described in detail.

The five gross elements—P*ri*thivī[1126] and so forth—have been spoken of in the five Chakras from Mūlādhāra to Vishuddha. In the Bhūma*nd*ala[1127] in the Mūlādhāra there are the following—viz., feet, sense of smell, and Gandha-tattva,[1128] for this is their place. In the Jala-ma*nd*ala,[1129] similarly, are the hands, sense of taste, and Rasa-tattva.[1130] In the Vahni-ma*nd*ala[1131] are the anus, the sense of sight, and Rūpa-tattva.[1132] In the Vāyuma*nd*ala,[1133] the penis, sense of touch, and Sparsha-tattva.[1134] In the Nabho-ma*nd*ala[1135] are speech, the sense of hearing, and Shabda-tattva.[1136] These make fifteen tattvas. Adding these fifteen to P*ri*thivī and so forth, we get twenty gross tattvas.

We next proceed to the subtle forms. In the Ājnā Chakra the subtle

1122 This place is called the Supreme Ether (Parang-vyoma) in the Svachchhandasanggraha, cited by Vishvanātha. Parama-vyoma is the name given in the Pancharātra to the Highest Heaven or Vaikuntha. See Ahirbudhnya, 49.

1123 The Sahasrāra is called Akula, according to the Svachchhanda sanggraha, cited by Vishvanātha.

1124 Kevalānanda-rūpam.

1125 The Ātmā considered as Chit.

1126 Earth, water, fire, air, ether.

1127 Region of the Earth Element, or Mūlādhāra Chakra.

1128 Smell principle or Tanmātra.

1129 Svādhi*shth*āna, which is the region of water (Jala).

1130 Principle of taste.

1131 Ma*n*i-pūra, which is the region of fire (Vahni).

1132 Principle of sight.

1133 Anāhata, which is the region of air (Vāyu).

1134 Principle of touch.

1135 Vishuddha, which is the region of ether (Nabhas).

1136 Principle of sound.

Manas has been spoken of. Others have been spoken of in the Kangkāla-mālinī Tantra when dealing with the Ājnā Chakra: "Here constantly shines the excellent Manas, made beautiful by the presence of the Shakti Hākinī. It is lustrous, and has Buddhi[1137], Prak*r*iti,[1138] and Ahang-kāra,[1139] for its adornment."

From the above the presence of the three subtle forms—viz., Buddhi, Prak*r*iti, and Ahang-kāra—in this place becomes clear. We must, however, know that Ahang-kāra is not placed in the order shown in the above quotation. We have seen that from the Mūlādhāra upwards the generated is below the generator; that which is dissolved is below what it is dissolved into, and we also know that the Shābdakrama is stronger than Pā*th*akrama.[1140] We must remember that Vyoma is dissolved in Ahang-kāra, and hence the latter is next above Vyoma. *Cf.* "In Ahang-kāra, Vyoma with sound should be dissolved, and Ahangkāra again in Mahat." Ahangkāra, being the place of dissolution, comes first above Vyoma, and above it are Buddhi and Prak*r*iti.

The Shāradātilaka speaks of their connection as Janya (effect, generated) and Janaka (cause, generator).

"From the unmanifested (Avyakta) Root-Being (Mūlabhūta), when Vik*r*ita, of the Supreme (Paravastu)[1141] originated Mahat-tattva,[1141] which consists of the Gu*n*as and Anta*h*kara*n*a. From this (Mahat-tattva) originated Ahangkāra, which is of three kinds according to its source of generation"[1142]—Variation (Vik*r*ita). By this is meant reflection or image (Prativimba)[1143] of the Paravastu, and as such reflection it is Vik*r*iti; but as it (Vik*r*iti) is the Prak*r*iti of Mahat-tattva, etc., it is also called Prak*r*iti.[1144] *Cf.* "Prak*r*iti is the Paramā (Supreme) Shakti, and Vik*r*iti is the product thereof."[1145] It has also been shown before that "the Prak*r*iti of the Para Brahman is but another aspect of Him" (Prativimbasvarūpi*n*ī).

According to Shāradātilaka, Mahat-tattva is the same as Buddhi.[1146] Īshāna Shiva says: "The objective Prak*r*iti,[1147] which is

---

1137 See next note.

1138 See Introduction, and *post*, Commentary.

1139 Egoism—self-consciousness.

1140 That is, the actual arrangement of things as compared with the order in which they are stated.

1141 Mahat-tattva is a Vik*r*iti of Prak*r*iti. The Mūlabhūta avyakta (unmanifested root-being) corresponds with the Sāngkhyan Mūlaprak*r*iti. Here, as Rāghava Bha*tt*a says, Tattva*srishti* is indicated (Comm. to Ch. I., vv. 17, 18 of Shāradā).

1142 *Srishti*bheda—that is, one Āhangkāra is the result of the predominance of Sattva, another of Rajas, and a third of Tamas.

1143 That is in the sense of product. In Shaivashāktadarshana Mula prakriti is itself a product of the Shivashāktitattva for the Self becomes abject to itself.

1144 That is, as regarded from the point of view of the Paravastu it is an effect, but regarded in relation to that which it produces it is a cause.

1145 Vik*r*iti*h* prativimbatā—in a mirror one is seen, but the image is not oneself.

1146 Rāghavabha*tt*a says that this is so according to Shaiva doctrine.

evolved by Shakti and which is associated with the Sattva-gu*n*a, is the manifested Buddhi-tattva. It is this Buddhi that is spoken of as Mahat in Sānkhya Philosophy."

Mahat-tattva consists of the Gu*n*as and the Anta*h*-kara*n*a. The Gu*n*as are Sattva, Rajas, and Tamas. The Shāradātilaka says: "Anta*h*-kara*n*a is the Manas, Buddhi, Ahangkāra, and Chitta, of the Ātmā.[1148] All these are comprised in the term Mahat-tattva.

Now, a question may be raised—namely, If Manas be within Mahat-tattva, what of that which has been said in v. 33, where Manas has been spoken of as having an independent existence? But the answer to that is, that that Manas is the product of Ahangkāra, and Rāghava-Bha*tt*a says: "In so much as the other Manas is the one which selects and rejects (Sa-sangkalpavikalpaka),[1149] it is known to be the product of Tejas."[1150] Thus it is that, as Manas and other Tattvas in the Ājnā Chakra are placed in their order, Ahang-kāra and others should be known as being placed above them. In the Ājnā Chakra are Hākinī, Itara-lingga, Prar*n*ava, Manas, Ahang-kāra, Buddhi, and Prak*riti*, placed consecutively one above the other, no place being assigned to Chandra-ma*nd*ala, which has been spoken of before. It should be taken to be placed above all these. If it be asked, Why is it not below all these? then the reply is that it has been said in the Sammohana Tantra: "Moon (Indu) is in the forehead, and above it is Bodhinī Herself." From this it would appear that Indu and Bodhinī are above Ājnā Chakra, placed one above the other without anything intervening between them. Bodhinī is above all the rest.

The Sammohana Tantra speaks of the Cause (Kāra*n*arūpa) as above Ājnā Chakra: "Indu (the Moon, here—Bindu) is in the region of the forehead, and above it is Bodhinī Herself. Above Bodhinī shines the excellent Nāda, in form like the half (crescent) moon; above this is the lustrous Mahānāda, in shape like a plough; above this is the Kalā called Ānjī, the beloved of Yogīs. Above this last is Unmanī,[1151] which having reached one does not return."

In the above passage, in the words "above it is Bodhinī," the word "it" stands for the forehead or Ājnā-chakra.

The Bhūta-shuddhi Tantra speaks of the existence of the Bindu below Bodhinī: "Devi, above Vindu and Mātrārdhā is Nāda, and above this, again, is Mahānāda, which is the place of the dissolution of Vāyu."

1147 Boddhavya-lak*shan*ā—that is, that which can be known; the objective or manifested Prak*ri*ti.

1148 See Introduction.

1149 As to Sa-sangkalpa-vikalpa, see Introduction.

1150 That is, Taijasa ahangkāra, which is the source of the Indriyas.

1151 *Sic.* In this passage Samanī is omitted.

Mātrārddhā is Mātrārddhā Shakti.[1152]

The following passage from B*r*ihat-tri-vikrama-sanghitā proves that the Ardha-mātrā means Shakti: "Lustrous like the young Sun is Aks*h*ara, which is Bindumat (Bindu itself); above it is Ardhamātrā, associated with the Gāndhārarāga."[1153]

As both the above passages point to the same thing, we must take it that Arddha-mātrā and Bodhinī are identical. Bindu, Bodhinī, and Nāda, are but different aspects of the Bindu-maya-para-shakti.

The Shāradā-tilaka says: "From the Sakala Paramēshvara,[1154] who is Sat, Chit, and Ānanda, Shakti emanated; from Shakti, again, emanated Nāda; and Bindu has its origin from Nāda. He who is Para-shakti-maya manifests Himself in three different ways. Bindu and Nāda and Bīja are but His different aspects. Bindu is Nādātmaka,[1155] Bīja is Shakti, and Nāda, again, is the union or relation of the one to the other.[1156] This is spoken of by all who are versed in the Āgamas."[1157]

"Para-shakti-maya": Para = Shiva; hence Shiva-shaktimaya = Bindu. The Bindu who is above the forehead is Nādātmaka—that is, Shivātmaka.[1158] Bīja is Shakti as Bodhinī (Bodhinī-rupam). Nāda is the connection between the two whereby the one acts upon the other; hence it is Kriyāshakti. Above these three is Mahānāda. This has already been shown.

"Above it is Kalā," etc.: Kalā = a line. Ānjī = crooked, awry, bent.

[1152] Mātrārddhā. In the Devī Bhāgavata there occurs the expression Arddha-mātrā (which is a name for Nāda) in I, 1, v. 55, and III. 5, v. 29, and Nīlaka*nth*a defines it to mean Parampadam = the supreme state, or the Brahman. The expression Arddha-mātrā also occurs in Cha*nd*ī I. 55, in practically the same sense. Gopāla Chakravartī quotes a passage which says "Arddhamātrā is attributeless (Nirgu*n*a), and realizable by the Yogī." He quotes another passage which says: "Om—this is the three Vedas, three Lokas, and after the three Lokas Mātrārddha is the fourth—the Supreme Tattva." See Cha*nd*ī "Tvamudgīthe arddhamātrāsi," and Devībhāgavata, I. 5, v. 55. Shruti says: "Thou art the Arddhamātrā of Pra*n*ava, Gāyatrī, and Vyāh*r*iti." Here the unity of Devī and Brahman is shown. She is Brahman united with Māyā (Māyāvishi*sht*abrahmarūpi*n*ī). The Nādabindu Upanishad (v. 1) says: "A-kāra is the right wing (of Om figured as a bird), U-kāra is the other (left) wing, Ma-kāra the tail, and Arddhamātrā the head. Sattva is its body, and Rajas and Tamas are its two feet. Dharma is its right eye, and Adharma is its left eye. The Bhūr-loka is on its feet, the Bhuvarloka on its knees; the Svarloka is in its middle, the Maharloka in its navel; Janaloka is in the heart, Tapoloka in its throat, and Satyaloka between the eyebrows." See also Brahmavidyā Up., v. 10.

[1153] The third of the seven primary subtle tones.

[1154] Shāradā, Ch. I., vv. 7-9. Sakala, as opposed to Ni*sh*kala or Nirgu*n*a, means united with Kalā, which according to Sāngkhya is Sāmyāvasthā of the Gu*n*as which is Prak*r*iti. According to the Vedantists (of the Māyā Vāda), Kalā is Avidyā. In the Shaiva Tantra Kalā is Shakti (Rāghava Bha*tt*a).

[1155] Another text has Shivātmaka—that is, Vindu is the Shiva aspect.

[1156] Samavāya = ks*h*obhya-ks*h*obhaka-sambandha— lit., connection which is the connection of reciprocity.

[1157] See Introduction.

[1158] In Rasika Mohana Chattopādhyāya's edition of the Shāradātilaka the text reads Shivātmaka, as if qualifying Vīja, which seems erroneous.

This is in shape like a bent or crooked line. This Shakti appeared in the beginning of creation. *Cf.* Pancha-rātra: "Having thus seen, the Supreme Male in the beginning of creation makes manifest the eternal Prak*ri*ti who is the embodiment of Sat, Chit, and Ānanda, in whom are the Tattvas, and who is the presiding (Adhi*shth*ātrī) Devī of creation."

Also elsewhere: "From the unmanifested (Avyakta) Parameshvara, the united Shiva and Shakti, emanated the Ādyā (first) Devī Bhagavatī, who is Tripura-sundarī, the Shakti from whom came Nāda, and thence came Bindu."

"Above it is Unmanī," etc.: *Cf.* "By going where 'Manas-ness' (Manastva) of Manas ceases to be, is called Unmanī, the attainment of which is the secret teaching of the Tantras."[1159]

It is the Tattva which means the dispelling of that attachment prompted by Manas towards worldly objects.

Unmanī, again, is of two kinds: (1) Nirvā*n*a-kalā-rūpā, which also has its place in the Sahasrāra[1160]; (2) Var*n*āvalī-rūpā, which also has its place in the region (here dealt with). *Cf.* Kangkāla-mālinī: "In the pericarp of the Sahasrāra, placed within the circle of the moon, is the seventeenth Kalā, devoid of attachment.[1161] The name of this is Unmanī, which cuts the bond of attachment to the world."

Cf. also: "By mental recitation of the Mālā-var*n*a (rosary of letters) is Unmanī the granter of liberation (attained)." Mālā-var*n*a =Var*n*āvalī-rūpa.

The Bhūta-shuddhi speaks of the Samanī below Unmanī. "Next is the Vyāpikā Shakti (Diffusive Energy) which people know as Ānjī. Samanī[1162] is over this, and Unmanī is above all." This (Samanī) also is an intermediate aspect (Avāntararūpa) of Parashakti.

We now get the following:

Above Ājnā Chakra is the second Bindu—which is Shiva (Shiva-svarūpa). Above Bindu is Bodhinī in shape like an Arddha-mātrā; next is Nāda which is the union of Shiva and Shakti, in shape like a half (crescent) moon; next (above this) is Mahānāda, shaped like a plough; above Mahānāda is the Vyāpikā Shakti, crooked (Ānjī) in shape; above this last is Samanī and highest of these all is Unmanī. This is the order in which the seven causal forms (Kāra*n*a-rūpa) are placed.

There is no need to go into further detail. Let us then follow the text.

[1159] Vishvanātha, quoting Svachchhandasangraha, which speaks of Unmanī as above Samanā, says that in the Unmanī stage no distinction is made between Kāla and Kalā; there is no body, and no Devatās, and no cessation of continuity. It is the pure and sweet mouth of Rudra. *Cf.* V*ri*ttihinam mana*h* in the Shiva Sanghitā, V., 219.

[1160] Sahasrārādhārā. See Introduction.

[1161] Sarva-sangkalpa-rahitā—*i.e.*, who is free from all attachment, not prompted by anything in any action.

[1162] Vishvanātha speaks of it as Samanā, and says that She is Chidānandasvarūpā (that is, Chit and Ānanda), and the cause of all causes (Sa rvakāra*n*akāra*n*am.)

Wishing to describe the Sahasrāra he speaks of it in ten more verses.

"*Above all these*" (Tadūrddhve).—Above every other that has been described or spoken before.

"*Over the head of the Shangkhinī Nādī*"—a sight of which has been given to the disciple.

"*Vacant space*" (Shūnya-desha)—that is, the place where there are no Nādīs; the implication is that it is above where Sus*h*umnā ends.

"*Below visarga is the lotus of a thousand petals.*"—This is the purport of the Shloka. Visarga is in the upper part of the Brahma-randhra. *Cf.* "Meditate in that aperture on Visarag*h* the ever blissful and stainless." There are other similar passages.

"*Its body is luminous with,*" *etc.* (Lalā*t*ādyai*h* var*n*ai*h* pravilasitavap*u*).—The word Lalā*t*a stands for the first vowel, A. By this we are to understand that the second *L*akāra (L) is to be left out in counting the letters of the Alphabet. In counting the fifty letters, the second *L*akāra[1163] is always left out.

If the text is read as "*L*akārādyai*h* var*n*ai*h*," as is done by some, we must leave K*sh*a-kāra out in counting the letters. The fifty-one letters cannot be taken to be in the petals of the Sahasrāra.[1164] With fifty-one letters repeated twenty times, the number is 1,020, and repeated nineteen times is 969. By leaving out K*sh*a-kāra we are freed of this difficulty. By "*L*akārādyai*h*" it is not meant that the letters are to be read Viloma.[1165] The Kangkāla-mālinī in the following passage distinctly says that it is to be read Anuloma[1166]: "The Great Lotus Sahasrāra is white, and has its head downward, and the lustrous letters from Akāra (A), ending with the last letter before K*sh*akāra (K*sh*a), decorate it." Here it is distinctly stated that the letter Ks*ha* is left out.

Akārādi-k*sh*a-kārāntai*h*: This compound, K*sh*a-kārānta, if formed by Bahu-vrīhi samāsa,[1167] would mean that K*sh*akāra is left out of calculation.

There is nothing said of the color of the letters, and, as the Māt*r*ikā (letters) are white, they are to be taken as being white on the Sahasrāra petals. These letters go round the Sahasrāra from right to left.[1168]

Some read Pravilasita-tanu*h* in place of pravilasita-vapu*h*, and say that, as the word *padma* alternatively becomes masculine in gender (vā pungsi padmam), therefore the word Tanu, which qualifies a word in the masculine gender, is itself masculine. That cannot be. The verb Nivasati (= is, dwells) has for its nominative Padmam, and, as it ends

---

[1163] Vaidika *L*akāra (*L*a).

[1164] *I.e.*, fifty-one letters cannot be arranged in the Sāhasrāra.

[1165] *I.e.*, from end to beginning.

[1166] From beginning to end.

[1167] A form of Sanskrit verbal compound.

[1168] Dak*shin*āvarta—the opposite way to that in which the hands of a clock work.

with the *Bindu* (*m*), it is in the neuter gender and not masculine. For in that case it would have ended with *visarga* (*i.e.*, *h*), and its adjective, *tanu*, would also end with a *visarga*. The word *tanu* (if their reading is accepted) would be in the neuter; therefore it cannot end with a *Bindu*. And if there is no Bindu the metre becomes defective. Therefore the correct reading is vapu*h*.

The rest is clear.

VERSE 41.

Within it (Sahasrāra) is the full Moon, without the mark of the hare,[1169] resplendent as in a clear sky. It sheds its rays in profusion, and is moist and cool like nectar. Inside it (Chandra-ma*nd*ala), constantly shining like lightning, is the Triangle,[1170] and inside this, again, shines the Great Void[1171] which is served in secret by all the Suras.[1172]

COMMENTARY.

He here speaks of the existence of the Chandra-ma*nd*ala in the pericarp of the Sahasrāra.

"*Resplendent as in a clear sky*" (Shuddha)—seen in a cloudless sky.

"*Is moist and cool,*" *etc.* (Parama-rasa-chaya-snigdha-santānahāsī).—Snigdha implies the moisture of the nectar. Parama-rasa (Am*ri*ta) is free from heat. Hence the meaning of this compound word: Its rays are cool and moist, and produce a feeling of smiling gladness.

The Kangkāla-mālinī speaks of the presence of Antarātmā, etc., in the upper portion of the space below Chandra-ma*nd*ala. In dealing with the Sahasrāra, it says: "In its pericarp, O Deveshī, is the Antarātmā. Above it is the Guru. The Ma*nd*alas of Sūryya and Chandra are also there. Above this is Mahāvāyu, and then the Brahma-randhra. In this aperture (Randhra) is Visarga, the ever blissful and stainless. Above this (Tadūrddhve) last is the Devī Shangkhinī, who creates, maintains, and destroys."

"*Within Chandra-mandala constantly shines, like lightning, the triangle*" (Triko*n*a).

"*Great Void*" (Tadanta*h* shūnyam).—That is, the body of the

---

[1169] The man in the moon.

[1170] The akathādi triangle according to Vishvanāthā.

[1171] Shūnya = Bindu—that is, the Parabindu, or Īshvara, having as its center the abode of Brahman (Brahmapada). In the northern Shaiva and Shākta schools Sadāshiva and Īshvara are the nimes*h*a and unmes*h*a aspects of the experience intermediate between Shiva Tattva and Shuddhavidyā, the former being called Shūnyātishūnya. The positions of the Sun and Moon circles in the Sahasrāra and of the twelve-petalled lotus with the Kāmakalā are given in the Text.

[1172] = Devas.

Parabindu (Paravindusharīram). Within the triangle the excellent Bindu (Shūnya) shines, or within the triangle the Shūnya which is the excellent Bindu shines.

Cf. To*d*ala Tantra, 6th Ullāsa: "The Supreme Light is formless (Nirākāra), and Bindu is imperishable." Bindu means the void (Shūnya), and implies Gu*n*a also.[1173]

"*Served in secret*" (Sevitang chātiguptam).—The rule is, "Eating (Āhāra), evacuation (Nirhāra), sexual intercourse (Vihāra), and Yoga, should be done in secret by him who knows the Dharma." Hence Suras (Devas) serve or worship It in secret.

VERSE 42.

Well concealed, and attainable only by great effort, is that subtle Bindu (Shūnya) which is the chief root of Liberation, and which manifests the pure Nirvā*n*a Kalā with Amā Kalā.[1174] Here is the Deva who is known to all as Paramashiva. He is the Brahman and the Ātmā of all beings. In Him are united both Rasa and Virasa,[1175] and He is the Sun which destroys the darkness of nescience[1176] and delusion.[1177]

COMMENTARY.

The sense is that the void (Shūuya) is very secret and subtle, being, as described later, like the ten millionth part of the end of a hair. It is attainable only by great effort consisting of long and incessant performance of Dhyāna and like practices. It makes manifest the purity of the sixteenth Kalā of the moon along with Nirvā*n*a Kalā—*i.e.*, the void (Antā*h* shūnya) along with the Amā Kalā and Nirvā*n*a Kala within the triangle is realized (prakāsham bhavati) by meditation (Dhyāna). It is the source of all the mass of great Bliss, which is Liberation. If Sugopya be read in place of Suguptām, then the word yatnāt would qualify it. Some, however, read Sakala-shashi-kala-shuddha-rupā-prakāsham as qualifying the great Void within the triangle, and read sakala to mean with all the sixteen kalās and say that the Para Bindu manifests the moon with such kalās. This requires consideration. When it was said that the Trikona (triangle) is within the full moon, the repetition of it is useless. Furthermore, in the previous verse we have

---

[1173] When it assumes the form of Bindu, It is with the operating Gu*n*as, for then It is Sakala.

[1174] There are seventeen Kalās (digits) of the Moon, but the nectar-dropping Amā and the Nirvā*n*akalā are only at this stage revealed. The other Kalās are mentioned in Skanda Purā*n*a Prabhāsa Kha*nd*a.

[1175] The Bliss of liberation and that arising from the union of Shiva and Shakti; *vide post.*

[1176] Ajnāna.

[1177] Moha.

got "served by the Suras." The term "service" as applied to a void is inappropriate. The object of service is the Bindu within the triangle. If it be said that the Void should be worshipped by reason of the presence of the Para Bindu, then the Para Bindu being there present there is no void.

"*Well concealed*" (Sugupta).—By reason of its being like the ten millionth part of a hair.

"*By great effort*" (Yatnāt)—*i.e.*, by long-continued practice of meditation (Dhyāna) and so forth.

"*Chief root*" (Parang kandam.[1178])—Para usually means supreme, excellent; here chief, principal. Kanda = mūla.

"*Liberation,*" *etc.* (Atishaya-paramāmodasantāna-rāshi).—The compound word means literally combination of all the mass of great and supreme bliss, and this is Liberation (Mok*sh*a).

"*Manifests*" (Sakala-shashi-kalā-shuddha-rūpa-prakāsha).—This compound word is to be broken up as follows:

Sakala = with the Kalā, Kalā here meaning Nirvā*n*a Kalā. In the word Shashi-kalā the Kalā means Amākalā, the sixteenth Kalā, or digit, of the moon. *Shuddha* = pure; the luster is not obscured by anything.

The sense is that the Parabindu, though subtle and otherwise imperceptible, is seen by meditation (Dhyāna) with the Amākalā and Nirvā*n*a Kalā in the Triko*n*a. If Sugopyam be read in place of Suguptam, then it would be qualified by Yatnāt.

Some read Sakala-shashi-kalā-shuddha-rūpa-prakāsha to qualify Shūnya in the previous verse, and say Shūnya means "vacant space," but that is absurd.[1179]

Next he speaks of the presence of Paramashiva in the pericarp of the Sahasrāra.

"*Paramashiva*"[1180] (Paramashiva-samākhyāna-siddha). He who is known by the name Paramashiva.

"*The Brahman*" (Svarūpī).—Sva = Atmā, the spirit.

"*The Ātmā of all beings*" (Sarvātmā).—Sarva = all (beings). He is the Jīvātmā, but in fact there is no distinction between Jīvātmā and Paramātmā. The Ātmā is the Jīva. The Adhyātma-Rāmāya*n*a says: "The Jīvātmā is merely another name for (Paryyāya) the Paramātmā. When by the instructions of the Āchāryya and the Shāstras their oneness is known, then the disciple possesses Mūlavidyā (essential knowledge) concerning Jīvātmā and Paramātmā."

The Shruti also, when it says Tat tvam asi,[1181] identifies the Tvam

---

[1178] Kanda means bulb or root. The Yoginīh*r*idaya says that this Kanda is the subtle Parānanda kandabindurūpa, or the root of supreme bliss in Bindu form (Vishvanātha).

[1179] According to the Commentator, it qualifies Kanda. Bindu is the circle O; the void is the Brahmapada or space within.

[1180] Vishvanātha says that this Shiva is the Sagu*n*a Shiva.

[1181] "That Thou art." See Introduction.

with the Tat.

"*Rasa and Virasa*" (Rasa-virasamita).—Rasa is Paramānanda-rasa—*i.e.*, the essence of supreme bliss.[1182] Virasa is the bliss which is the product of the union of Shiva and Shakti. He has both these in Him. Or Rasa may mean the attachment to worldly enjoyment, and Virasa detachment from it. The meaning would then be: in Him is detachment from worldly enjoyment.[1183]

"*The Sun*" = Hangsa. As the sun dispels darkness, so does he dispel nescience (Ajnāna) and delusion (Moha).

VERSE 43.

By shedding a constant and profuse stream of nectar-like essence,[1184] the Bhagavān[1185] instructs the Yati[1186] of pure mind in the knowledge by which he realizes the oneness of the Jīvātmā and the Paramātmā. He pervades all things as their Lord, who is the ever-flowing and spreading current of all manner of bliss known by the name of Hangsa*h* Parama (Parama-hangsa*h*).

COMMENTARY.

"*Constant and profuse*" (Niravadhi atitarām).

"*Stream of nectar*" (Sudhā-dhārāsāram).—The compound word can be made up and interpreted in four different ways:

1. Shedding a constant and profuse stream of nectar-like essence.

2. The Ādhāra (receptacle) of Sudhā (nectar) is Sudhādhāra, by which is meant the Moon; Āsāra is what flows therefrom a stream. Now, what flows from the Moon is Nectar, which is silvery; hence the whole word means "the silvery beams of the moon." This adjective proves that the qualified noun is white or transparent like the moon. Shedding = Vimunchan.

3. Asāra may, again, mean "what is uttered," "word." Sudhādhāra = receptacle of sweetness, which is a quality of nectar; hence Sudhādhārāsāram = nectar-like or ambrosial word. The meaning of Niravadhi would then be "at all times," and Atitarā would mean "powerful in destroying the darkness of ignorance or delusion." Vimunchan should then mean "uttering."

[1182] *I.e.*, Moksha.

[1183] That is, the Rasa in Him has become Virasa.

[1184] As appears from the Commentary *post*, this may be variously translated as follows: "By shedding a constant and profuse stream of nectar resembling the silvery beams of the Moon," *or* "By unremitting and nectar-like words strong for the destruction of the darkness of delusion," *or* "By constant repetition of the word which is nectar-like in its mercy and contains the essence of the Brahma-mantra."

[1185] That is, the Lord as the possessor of the six forms of Aishvaryya.

[1186] Self-controlled, whose mind is unified with the object of worship.

4. Sudhā, again, may mean "nectar of mercy," and Sara is "essence"—*i.e.*, the essence of Brahma-mantra; and Dhārā is a stream (continuous repetition) of the merciful word containing the essence of the Brahma-mantra.

"Instructs the Yati," *etc.* (Bhagavān nirmala-materyate*h* svātma-jnānam dishati).

"Yati."—He whose mind intently rests upon the Devatā of his worship.

Svātma-jnāna: Svam = Jīvātmā and Ātmā = Paramātmā; and Jnāna[1187] that by which one knows—namely, the Tāraka-brahma-mantra, which leads to a knowledge of the Paramātmā, and thereby helps the worshipper to realize the oneness of the Jīvātmā and Paramātmā. Dishati = upadishati (instructs). The above qualifying expressions imply that the qualified noun is the Guru, as instructions regarding Tāraka-brahma Mantra proceed from Him. So it qualifies "Parama-shiva" in the preceding verse, as He is the Guru. *Cf.* Guru-tattvanirūpa*n*a in Lalitā-rahasya.

After describing Guru as "the well-known and excellent Puru*sh*a who is ever fond[1188] of enjoyment with the Self (Ātmarati-priya)," it goes on to say: "His beloved is the lustrous One who may be gained with difficulty by the Brahma-vartma (Brahma road). The Parama Brahma is but the effulgence of Her lotus feet."[1189]

By the above passage is meant that the great beauty of Her lotus feet overspreads the heart-lotus of the Guru. The fit place for the feet of the lustrous (Tejo-rūpā) Beloved (Shakti) of the Guru is on the breast of the Guru,[1190] and not on that of any other Puru*sh*a. Hence Parama-shiva and the Guru are one and the same.

The Nirvā*n*a Tantra also says[1191]: "In the Lotus in the head is Mahādeva—the Parama Guru: there is in the three worlds no one, O

[1187] Jnānā is spiritual knowledge or wisdom, and Vijnānā is the knowledge of the material world (science).

[1188] *I.e.*, who is engrossed in.

[1189] The second part of the passage from Lalitā-Rahasya should be translated as follows: "It is hard to reach his lustrous Beloved even following the Brahman-road; the Parama Brahma is but the effulgence of Her lotus feet." The translation in the Text is according to the reading given in the Sanskrit Edition of the *Shat*chakra Nirūpa*n*a here translated, which seems to be inaccurate. Brahma-vartma-sudurlabhā should be read as one word. The Edition cited in Text reads it as two words. The meaning is that as the Guru in the twelve-petalled lotus bears the imprint of His Shakti's feet upon his breast, so, in so far as the Guru is the Paramabrahman, the latter may be said to do so.

[1190] This is in praise of Shakti, who is made to appear superior.

[1191] This passage occurs in the 3rd Pa*t*ala of the Nirvā*n*a Tantra (Rasika Mohana Cha*tt*opādhyāya's Edition, p. 3), and is in answer to the following question of the Devī: "The Deva who is in the Turīyadhāma (the fourth state) is unquestionably the Paramātmā: if he be placed in the Lotus in the head, how can obeisance be made to him outwardly?" That is, How can the Sādhaka bow to him who is in the head which is itself bowed?

Deveshi, who is so deserving of worship as He. O Devi, meditate on His form,[1192] which includes all the four Gurus."[1193]

This Parama-shiva is outside and below the triangle in the pericarp, and above the Hangsa*h* of which we are speaking.

The Kangkāla-mālinī Tantra[1194] says: "In the pericarp of this Lotus, O Deveshī, is the Antarātmā, and above it the Guru. The Ma*nd*alas of Sun and Moon are also there." And after having spoken of the presence of different things in their order up to Mahā-shangkhinī, it then proceeds: "Below it, O Deveshi, is the Triko*n*a (triangle), placed in the Ma*nd*ala of Moon; and having meditated there on the undecaying Kalā, (one should meditate) within it upon the seventeenth Kalā, by name Nirvā*n*a, which is like a crescent" (Ku*t*ita).[1195]

The above passage speaks of the presence of Amā-kalā, and so forth, within the triangle in the Chandra-Ma*nd*ala. The Guru therefore is below them and above Antarātmā. Now, if it be asked how it is that, the Kangkāla-malinī having placed the Guru over the Antarātmā, the Guru is spoken of as placed above Hangsa*h*? the answer is that the Antarātmā and the Hangsa*h* are one and the same.

Cf. Guru-dhyāna in Kangkāla-malinī[1196]: "Meditate on your Guru seated on a shining throne (Singhāsana) placed on the excellent Antarātmā between Nāda and Bindu," etc. Also elsewhere: "Meditate on your Guru, who is the image of Shiva Himself, as seated on the Hangsa-pī*th*a which is Mantramaya." Also *cf.* the Annadā-kalpa Tantra[1197]: "Meditate on your Guru in the white Lotus of a thousand petals in the head; He is Parama Shiva seated on the Hangsa among the filaments."

On a careful consideration of the above authorities, the identity of

[1192] The passage as quoted by the Commentator reads "Tadangsham" (his part); in R. M. Cha*tt*opādhyāy's Edition it reads "Tadrūpam" (his form), which reading is here adopted.

[1193] *I.e.*, Guru, Paramaguru, Parāparaguru, and Parame*shth*iguru.

[1194] This passage occurs in Pa*t*ala II. (p. 3 of R. M. Cha*tt*opādhyāya's Edition), which in its entirety runs thus: "In it (Sahasrāra), O Deveshī, is the Antarātmā, and above it Vāyu, and above Mahānāda is Brahmarandhra. In the Brahmarandhra is Visarga, which is Eternal Peace and Bliss. (Peace—niranjana, which also means stainless, free from delusion.) Above it is the Devī Shangkhinī, the Creator, Maintainer, and Destructress. Having meditated on the Triangle placed below, He thinks that Kailāsa (the paradise of Shiva) is there. O Mahādevī, by placing the undisturbed Chetas (heart or mind) here one lives to the full term of one's life (Jīva-jīvī), free from all ills, and for such a one there is no rebirth. Here constantly shines Amākalā, which knows neither increase nor decay, and within it, again, is the seventeenth digit, known as Nirvā*n*a Kalā. Within Nirvā*n*a Kalā is the fiery Nibodhikā. Above it is unmanifested Nāda, effulgent as ten million suns. It is the excellent Nirvā*n*a Shakti, the cause of all. In this Shakti should be known that Shiva who is changeless and free from illusion."

[1195] See Jnānārnava Tantra XXIV. 36.

[1196] Pa*t*ala III.

[1197] This quotation is not traceable in Prasannakumāra Shāstri's Edition of this Tantra.

Hangsa*h* with Antarātmā becomes clear. By the expression "one's own Guru, who is Parama Shiva," it is to be understood that Parama Shiva Himself is the Guru.

The following passage, which relates to the Sahasrāra, shows that Parama Shiva is in the triangle: "Within (or near) it (Sahasrāra) is the lightning-like Triangle, and within the triangle are the two Bindus which make the imperishable Visarga. There in the empty void is Parama Shiva."

These conflicting views lead to the conclusion that the Guru is within the triangle in the pericarp of the upturned Lotus of twelve petals, below the pericarp of the Sahasrāra and inseparable from it. This has been made clear in the Pādukā-panchaka Stotra.[1198] From these passages it is not to be inferred that the Guru is within the triangle in the pericarp of the Sahasrāra. The triangular Hangsa is below the middle triangle; otherwise it would conflict with the authority of the Kangkāla-mālinī Tantra.

"*He pervades all things as their Lord*" (Samāste sarvesha*h*)—*i.e.*, in this pericarp dwells He who is the Lord of All. Now, by saying that Parama Shiva is there it has been said that Īshvara (Lord) is there; then why this repetition? But there is an object in so doing, as the following qualifying expressions will show. The Sarvesha (Lord of All) is the Hangsa*h*—*i.e.*, He is the Mantra "Hang-sa*h*."

Cf. Prapancha-sāra: "She whose name is Tattva is Chinmātrā[1199]: when by proximity to the Light she wishes to create,[1200] She becomes massive (Ghanībhūya) and assumes the form of Bindu. Then in time She divides Herself in two: the one on the right is Bindu, and that on the left side is Visarga. The right and left are respectively distinguished as *male* and *female*. Hang is the Bindu, and Sa*h* is the Visarga; Bindu is Puru*sh*a, and Visarga is Prak*ri*ti; Hangsa*h* is the union of Prak*ri*ti and Puru*sh*a, who pervades the Universe."

The Mahākālī Tantra speaks clearly on the subject (Pa*t*ala I.): "In the empty space[1201] in the Chandra-Ma*nd*ala[1202] which is within the Sahasrāra, adorned with a celestial gateway, are the letters Hang and Sah, over which meditate on Him who is pure like rock crystal and dressed in silken raiment, and so forth." Here the letters Hang and Sa*h* are explicitly spoken of.

Or if Hangsa and Parama be read separately as Hangsa and Parama, it would mean "He who is known as Hangsa and Parama." The

[1198] See notes to v. 7 of the Pādukā Panchaka.

[1199] *Vide ante*, v. 39.

[1200] Vichikīr*sh*u—"wishes to distort herself." Here "distortion," or stress, is creation. See Introduction. For a different reading *vide ante*, p. 266.

[1201] Shūnya. The Shūnya is the empty space within the Bindu.

[1202] The locative is to be read Sāmīpye saptamī—that is, the space is not in, but near, the Chandrama*nd*ala; otherwise there appears to be a contradiction.

Author himself speaks of Him as Hangsa*h* in the forty-ninth verse. Or if the two words be read together, then the meaning would be "He who is known by the name of Parama-hangsa*h*, or by one of the exceptional rules of Karmadhāraya Samāsa this word has been formed, the word anta*h* being omitted. *Cf.* Āgama-kalpa-druma: "He is called Parama-hangsa*h*, pervading all that is moving and motionless."

"*Who is the ever flowing,*" *etc.* (Sakala-sukha-santānalaharī-parīvaha)—*i.e.*, in Him becomes manifest in every possible way all kinds of imperishable and increasing happiness; that is, He is, as it were, an interminable chain of happiness.

VERSE 44.

The Shaivas call it the abode of Shiva[1203]; the Vai*shn*avas call it Parama Puru*sha*[1204]; others, again, call it the place of Hari-Hara.[1205] Those who are filled with a passion for the Lotus feet of the Devī[1206] call it the excellent abode of the Devī; and other great sages (Munis) call it the pure place of Prak*ri*ti-Puru*sha*.[1207]

COMMENTARY.

As Hangsa*h*, who has in Him all the Devatās (Sarvadevatāmaya), and others, are in this pericarp, it is the place of the Devatās of worship of all classes of worshippers, such as Shaivas, Shāktas, etc.

"*The Shaivas*"—*i.e.*, the worshippers of Shiva—call it the place of Shiva.

"*The Vaishnavas*[1208] *call it Parama Purusha*"—*i.e.*, the place of the Parama Puru*sha*, or Vi*shn*u.

"*Others, again*" (Kechidapare)—*i.e.*, others who are worshippers of Hari-Hara, or, in other words, United Vi*shn*u and Shiva in coupled (Yugala) form, call it the place of Hari-Hara. They do not call it either the place of Hari (Vi*shn*u) or of Shiva (Hara), but the place of their united selves.

"*Other great sages*" (Munīndrā apyanye).—By "the Munis" the author here means the worshippers of "the Hangsa*h*" Mantra, who call it the pure place of Prak*ri*ti-Puru*sha*. Hangsa*h* is the union of Prak*ri*ti and Puru*sha*,[1209] hence it is the place of Prak*ri*ti and Puru*sha*.

1203 Shiva-sthānam.

1204 *I.e.*, the place of Parama Puru*sha*—Vi*shn*u.

1205 Vi*shn*u and Shiva.

1206 Shakti, or the Goddess.

1207 Shakti-shiva.

1208 Worshippers of Vi*shn*u.

1209 Hangsasya prak*ri*ti-puru*sh*obhaya-rūpa-tvāt. Hang is the Puru*sha*, and Sa*h* is Prak*ri*ti.

The above shows that, as this Lotus is the dwelling-place of the Para Bindu, in which are all the Devatās, each worshipper calls it the place of the Devatā of his own separate worship.

VERSE 45.

That most excellent of men who has controlled his mind[1210] and known this place is never again born in the Wandering,[1211] as there is nothing in the three worlds which binds him. His mind being controlled and his aim achieved, he possesses complete power to do all which he wishes, and to prevent that which is contrary to his will. He ever moves towards the Brahman.[1212] His speech, whether in prose or verse, is ever pure and sweet.

COMMENTARY.

In this verse he speaks of the fruit of a complete knowledge of the Sahasrāra. The idea sought to be conveyed is that a knowledge of this place should be gained as a whole and in detail.

"*Who has controlled his mind*" (Niyata-nija-chitta)—*i.e.*, he who has controlled and concentrated the inner faculties on this place. Such an one becomes free from Sangsāra, or, in other words, he is released from bondage, as there is nothing to bind or attract him in these worlds. By bondage is meant the Māyik bonds of virtue (Pu*n*ya) and sin (Pāpa).

The Bhāgavata says: "If the action which is the product of the operation of the Gu*n*as is attributed to the self, then such (false) attribution is bondage and Sangsāra and servitude." Also *cf.* Bhagavad Gītā: "O Son of Kuntī, Man is bound by action which is the product of his own nature (Sva-bhāva)."[1213]

To inhabit this body for the purpose of undergoing Pāpa (sin) and Pu*n*ya (virtue) is bondage. In heaven one enjoys (the fruit of) Pu*n*ya, and in the nether world (Pātāla) one suffers sorrow, and on earth man is subject to both Pāpa and Pu*n*ya. For the Tattva-jnānī (him who knows the truth) there is neither Pu*n*ya nor Pāpa, which are the causes of bondage; his accumulated (Sanchita) Karma of merit (Pu*n*ya) and demerit (Pāpa) is also destroyed. He is in consequence under no bondage whether in heaven (Svarga), earth (Martya), or nether world

---

[1210] Chitta.

[1211] Sangsāra, the world of birth and rebirth to which men are impelled by their Karma.

[1212] The interpretation of Vishvanātha is here adopted, according to which Kha = Brahman. As the term also means the "air" or "ether," the text is capable of translation as "He is able to roam the sky."

[1213] Ch. XVIII. v. 60.

(Pātāla), and he is not truly embodied.[1214] Such a one stays on earth so long only as he has not worked out what he has begun. He is liberated though living (Jīvanmukta), and attains complete liberation on the dissolution of the body.

The Kulār*n*ava Tantra says: "Those who have the Brahman in the heart can acquire neither merit by performing a hundred horse sacrifices, nor demerit by killing a hundred Brāhma*n*as." The Gītā also says: "In this world there is nothing that should or should not be done. For such a one there is no dependence on any being" (III. 18).[1215]

The Subodhinī[1216] interprets this verse to mean that the "knower" (Tattvajnānī) acquires no merit by the performances of actions nor demerit by the omission thereof.

Shruti speaks of the destruction of accumulated (sanchita) Pu*n*ya and Pāpa: "When Manas, which is now selecting and now rejecting, is dissolved in That; when Pāpa and Pu*n*ya are destroyed (lit., burnt), Sadāshiva, who is Shakti and Ātmā (*cf.* Hangsa*h*, *ante*), is Shānta."[1217] *Cf.* Bhagavadgītā: "And so the fire of knowledge destroys all actions."[1218]

"*Complete power*" (Samagrā shakti)—*i.e.*, power which enables him to do everything. By power, or Shakti, is meant ability to do all he desires to do[1219] and counteract all harm, to fly across the air,[1220] and to become possessed of great powers of speech.

VERSE 46.

Here is the excellent (supreme) sixteenth Kalā of the Moon. She is pure, and resembles (in color) the young Sun. She is as thin as the hundredth part of a fiber in the stalk of a lotus. She is lustrous[1221] and soft like ten million lightning flashes, and is down-turned. From Her, whose source is the Brahman, flows copiously the stream of nectar[1222]

[1214] Na sharīrī bhavati—though he has a body, he is not of it.

[1215] Telang's Translation: "He has no interest at all in what is done, and none whatever in what is not done, in this world; nor is any interest of his dependent on any being" (p. 54, Sacred Books of the East, Vol. VIII.).

[1216] That is, Shrīdhara-svāmī's Commentary on the Gītā.

[1217] That is, peace and quietude like the still surface of an ocean, characteristic of the supreme state.

[1218] IV., 37.

[1219] Such an one may have such a power but will not wrongly exercise it.

[1220] Khagati; this is Kālīchara*n*a's interpretation as to Vishvanāthā, see n. 1212, *ante*.

[1221] Kālīchara*n*a reads "Vidyotitā," but Shangkara reads "Nityoditā," constantly shining.

[1222] Alternative reading of Commentator: Pūr*n*ānanda-paramparātivigalat-pīyū*sh*a-dhārā-dharā. Paramparā may mean "in a continuous course," or Param may mean Shiva and Parā, Shakti. This difference in meaning is due to the different ways in which these words may be read.

(or, She is the receptacle of the stream of excellent nectar which comes from the blissful union of Para and Parā).[1223]

COMMENTARY.

Shlokas 41 and 42 speak of the presence of Amākalā, Nirvā*n*a-kalā, and Para Bindu, within the triangle in the pericarp of the Sahasrāra. He now desires to describe them by their distinctive attributes, and speaks in this verse of the distinctive features of Amākalā.

"*Excellent or supreme*" (Parā)—*i.e.*, She is Chit Shakti. In the Prabhāsa-kha*nd*a occurs the following passage: "The excellent Māyā who maintains the body of all that have bodies." This is attributive of Amā.

"*The sixteenth Kalā of the Moon*" (Chandrasya *sh*o*d*ashī).—By this we are to understand that he is speaking of Amākalā.[1224]

"*Pure*" (Shuddhā)—*i.e.*, stainless.

"*She resembles*," *etc.* (Shishu-sūryya-sodara-kalā).—By this the redness of this Kalā is indicated.

"*Thin as the hundredth part of a fiber in the stalk of the lotus*" (Nīraja-sūks*h*ma-tantu-shatadhā-bhāgaika-rūpā).—Thin like a hundredth part of the fiber in the lotus-stalk split lengthwise.

"*Whose source is the Brahman*" (Pūr*n*ānanda-paramparā).—Pūr*n*ānanda = Brahman.

"*Flows*," *etc.* (Ativigalat-pīyū*sh*a-dhārā-dharā).—If the last two compound words be read as one long compound word, as follows, Pūr*n*ānanda-param-parā-ativigalat-pīyū*sh*a-dhārā-dharā, the meaning of it will be as given within brackets at the end of the verse. Ānanda will then mean the joys of union, and Param-parā will then mean Shiva and Shakti.

Para = Bindurūpa, Shiva. Parā = Prak*r*iti, Shakti. Ānanda is the joy which arises from the union of the two, and from such union flows the nectar of which Amākalā is the receptacle.

VERSE 47.

Inside it (Amākalā) is Nirvā*n*a-kalā, more excellent than the excellent. She is as subtle as the thousandth part of the end of a hair, and of the shape of the crescent moon. She is the ever-existent Bhagavatī, who is the Devatā who pervades all beings. She grants divine knowledge, and is as lustrous as the light of all the suns shining

---

[1223] Parā, according to Shangkara, may mean Parā, Pashyantī, Madhyamā, and Vaikharī collectively. Para and Parā are the Bindurūpa Shiva and Shakti.

[1224] Vishvanātha says that this Amākalā is Ūrddhvashaktirūpā, or the upward (towards the Brahman) moving Shakti.

at one and the same time.

COMMENTARY.

In this verse the Nirvā*n*a Kalā is described.

"*Inside it*" (Tadantargatā)—*i.e.*, placed in the lap[1225] of Amākalā. This Kalā has already been described[1226] as the "crescent seventeenth Kalā placed within Amā, and known by the name of Nirvā*n*a-kalā."

"*More excellent than the excellent*" (Parā paratarā).—The Amākalā is excellent; this is more excellent than Amā. If Parātparatarā be accepted for Parā paratarā, then the meaning will be that She is the most excellent.

"*She is as subtle . . . hair*" (Keshāgrasya sahasradhā vibhajitasyaikāngsha-rūpā).—She is equal in dimension to the thousandth part of the end of a hair, so very subtle is She.

"*That Devatā who pervades all beings*" (Bhūtānām adhidaivatam).—Adhi-daivatam = Hārddha-chaitanyam,[1227] and this Kalā is Hārdda-chaitanya-svarūpā of all beings.

"*She grants divine knowledge*" (Nitya-prabodhodayā)—*i.e.*, She who grants Tattva-jnāna, or knowledge of the Brahman.

"*And is lustrous*" (Sarvārka-tulya-prabhā).—There are twelve suns (Dvādashāditya). "When all the twelve suns are shining"—such is Her luster. This adjective also implies that She is red.

VERSE 48.

Within its middle space (*i.e.*, middle of the Nirvā*n*a-kalā) shines the Supreme and Primordial Nirvā*n*a Shakti[1228]; She is lustrous like ten million suns, and is the Mother of the three worlds. She is extremely subtle, and like unto the ten-millionth part of the end of a hair. She contains within Her the constantly flowing stream of gladness,[1229] and is the life of all beings. She graciously carries the knowledge of the Truth (Tattva)[1230] to the mind of the sages.

[1225] That is, within the curve of Amākalā. Vishvanātha says, not within Amākalā, but within the Chandrama*nd*ala, of which the Amākalā is one of the digits. Nirvā*n*akalā is, he says, Vyāpinītattva.

[1226] See p. 274, *ante*.

[1227] Hārdda-chaitanyam. Amara defines Hārdda to mean prema, sneha—*i.e.*, affection, love. That is the I*sh*tadevata worshipped in the heart; the Shakti who is Herself the heart of the Lord. The word is derived from h*ri*d = heart. The Devatā also exists as what is called the Hārddhakalā. See Introduction.

[1228] This is, according to Vishvanātha, the Samanāpada or Samanī Shakti. This state is not altogether free from the multitude of bonds (Pāshajāla).

[1229] Prema. See notes, *post*.

[1230] This word "Tattva" has by Vishvanāthā been said to be Shivā-bhedajnānam—*i.e.*, the non-distinction between Shiva and Shivā.

COMMENTARY.

He now speaks of the Para Bindu.

"*Its*"—*i.e.*, the Nirvā*n*a Kalā.

"*Middle*" (Madhya-deshe).—Within the lap.[1231]

"*The Supreme and Primordial Nirvāna Shaktī*" (Paramā-pūrva-nirvā*n*a-shakti = paramā apūrva-nirvā*n*a-shakti).—Paramā[1232]—*i.e.*, the Supreme Brahman as Shakti. Apūrvā—*i.e.*, She before whom there was nothing, She having come into being at the beginning of creation.

"*Shines*" (Vilasati)—*i.e.*, dwells resplendent.

"*Mother of the three worlds*" (Tri-bhuvana-jananī)—*i.e.*, She is the origin of the Universe which comprises Svarga, Martya, and Pātāla.[1233]

"*She is extremely subtle, like unto the ten-millionth part of the end of a hair*" (Keshāgrasya ko*t*i-bhāgaikarūpā 'tisūksh*m*ā).—As She is like the ten-millionth part of the end of a hair, She is extremely subtle.

"*She contains within Her the constantly flowing stream of gladness*" (Niravadhi-vigalat-prema-dhārā-dharā).—Prema is the tenderness of mind produced by the feeling of gladness; that is, She holds within Her the stream of excellent nectar which has its origin in the blissful union of Shiva and Shakti, and which flows incessantly.

"*Is the life*" (Sarvesh*ā*ng jīva-bhūtā)—*i.e.*, animated being is but a part of Her.

Cf. "O Devī, as sparks fly forth from a flame, so does the Parabindu (as Jīva) issue from Her (Nirvā*n*a Shakti), and becomes knowing[1234] when it touches the Earth."[1235]

By "Her" is meant the Shakti who is in the Parabindu, who is both Shiva and Shakti; and from Her emanates the Jīva (embodied being).

Nirvā*n*ā-Shakti is situated below Nirvā*n*a-kalā, and over Nibodhikā,[1236] which is Nāda-rūpā.[1237] *Cf.* "Placed within Nirvā*n*a (Kalā) is the fiery (Vahnirūpā) Nibodhikā, who is the unmanifested Nāda[1238]; above it is the supreme Nirvā*n*a-Shakti, who is the cause of all and is possessed of the luster of ten million suns. It is in Her that

[1231] That is, within the crescent. According to Vishvanātha the locative indicates proximity and means near the middle but slightly above it.

[1232] This word has been defined by Shangkara to mean "She who is as great as the Para, or Supreme." Vishvanātha says it means "She who measures futurity" (uttarakāla)—that is, all future time is in Her control.

[1233] Heaven, Earth, and Netherworld.

[1234] *I.e.*, Jīva-consciousness.

[1235] Yadā bhūmau patati tadā sangjnāyukto bhavati. The creation of Jīva is here spoken of.

[1236] See Introduction, and note to v. 40, particularly the portion dealing with Nāda, Bodhinī, and Bindu.

[1237] That is, Shakti as Nāda.

[1238] Avyakta-nāda—unmanifested sound.

there is Shiva who is stainless[1239] and without change[1240]; it is here that Ku*nd*alī Shakti enjoys with Paramātmā."

Nibodhikā is a phase of Avyakta-nāda (Avyakta-nādātmikā), and is fire-like. Rāghava-bha*tt*a says: "Nāda exists in three states. When Tamo-gu*n*a is dominant, it is merely sound unmanifest (Avyakta-nāda)[1241] in the nature of Dhvani; when Rajo-gu*n*a is more dominant, there is sound in which there is somewhat of a placing of the letters[1242]; when the Sattvaguna preponderates, Nāda assumes the form of Bindu."[1243] Hence Nāda, Bindu, and Nibodhikā, are respectively the Sun, the Moon, and Fire,[1244] and their activities are Jnāna, Ichchhā, and Kriyā. Jnāna, again, is like Fire, Ichchhā like the Moon, and Kriyā like the Sun. This has been said in the Shāradā. Therefore, insomuch as it has been said that Nirvā*n*a Shakti is above the fiery (Vahnirūpā) Nibodhikā, the wise should conclude that Nirvā*n*a-Shakti is placed above the Ma*nd*alas of the Sun, the Moon, and Fire.

This has been clearly stated in the Kulār*n*ava Tantra, in the Para-Brahma-dhyāna, which begins, "The Bindurūpa Para Brahma in the Sahasrāra," and ends, "Beautified by the three Ma*nd*alas within the triangle in the pericarp." By three Ma*nd*alas are meant the Ma*nd*alas of Sun, Moon, and Fire. We shall show that the Nirvā*n*a-Shakti is in the form of Para-bindu (Parabindurūpā).

[1239] Niranjana. This word may either be equal to Ni*h* + anjana (*i.e.*, stainless) or Ni*h* + ranjana (unaffected by pleasure or pain, unmoved).

[1240] Nirvikāra. Some read nirvikalpa, or of unconditioned consciousness. Nirvikalpa is also the last stage of Samādhi, in which there are no (Nir) specific distinctions (Vikalpa): and no this and that.

[1241] Tamo-gu*n*ādhikyena kevaladhvanyātmako' vyaktanāda*h*.

[1242] Raja ādhikyena kinchit var*n*a-baddha-nyāsātmaka*h*. The sense appears to be that the letters exist anyhow together in massive undifferentiated form.

[1243] Sattvādhikyena vindu-rūpa*h*.

[1244] Tatashcha nāda-vindu-nibodhikā arkendu-vahni-rupā*h*. Jnāna is Fire, because it burns up all action. When the result of action is realized, action ceases (see note to v. 45). Ichchhā is the Moon, because Ichchhā is the precursor of creation and is eternal. The Moon contains the Amā-kalā, which knows neither increase nor decay. Kriyā is the Sun, because like the Sun it makes everything visible. Unless there is striving there cannot be realization and manifestation. *Cf.* "As one Sun makes manifest all the Lokas" (Gītā).

The Text will be made clearer if an arrangement be made in the following groups: (1) Nāda, Sun, Kriyā; (2) Bindu, Moon, Ichchhā; (3) Nibodhikā, Fire, Jnāna. But see Introduction.

VERSE 49.

Within Her is the everlasting place called the abode of Shiva,[1245] which is free from Māyā, attainable only by Yogīs, and known by the name of Nityānanda. It is replete with every form of bliss,[1246] and is Pure Knowledge itself.[1247] Some call it the place of Brahman; others call it the Hangsa. Wise men describe it as the abode of Vi*shn*u, and righteous men[1248] speak of it as the ineffable place of knowledge of the Ātmā, or the place of liberation.

COMMENTARY.

He speaks of the Para-Brahma-sthāna (place of Para Brahma) in the Void within Nirvā*n*a Shakti.

"*Within Her*" (Tasyā*h* madhyāntarāle)—*i.e.*, within Nirvā*n*a[1249] Shakti, or the empty space (within the Bindu).

"*Abode of Shiva*" (Shivapadam).—This is the place of the Brahman.

"*Free from Māyā*" (Amala)—*i.e.*, free from the impurity of Māyā.

"*Called*"—*i.e.*, called by those who know the Tattva.

"*Attainable only by Yogīs*" (Yogi-gamyam).—On account of its extreme subtlety, it is beyond the scope of word and mind, is attainable by Yogīs by pure Jnāna[1250] only.

"*Some call it*"—*i.e.*, the Vedāntists (Vaidāntikas) call it.

"*Ineffable*" (Kimapi)—*i.e.*, wonder-inspiring.

"*Place of the knowledge of the Ātmā*" (Ātma-prabodham).—The place where the Ātmā is seen or realized.

"*Liberation*" (Mok*sh*a)—*i.e.*, where one is liberated from Māyā by which one is surrounded. Now be good enough to mark the following: the Parabindu which is Prak*ri*ti and Puru*sh*a is surrounded[1251] by Māyā, and is within the triangle in the pericarp of the Lotus of a thousand petals.

[1245] Shiva-padam or state of Shiva. This, Vishvanātha says, is the Unmanī state of Shakti where there is neither Kāla nor Kalā, time nor space. It is the body of Shiva (Shivatanu). It is then said Unmanyante Parashiva*h*.

[1246] Sakalasukhamayam. Vishvanātha reads here Paramakulapadam, which he interprets as param-akula-padam, or the abode of the Supreme Shiva, who is known as Akula, as Kula is Shakti. It is so called because it is here that the universe finds its rest.

[1247] Shuddha-bodha-svarūpam.

[1248] Suk*ri*tī. Such qualifications are without importance. Apparently this and some other adjectives are put in for the sake of the metre.

[1249] Vishvanāthā says Samanā.

[1250] Spiritual knowledge, as it is said: Mok*sh*e dhirjnānam anyatra vijnānang shilpashāstrayo*h*. The knowledge which gains Mok*sh*a (liberation) is called Jnāna, other forms of knowledge, such as fine arts, etc., being Vijnāna.

[1251] Māyābandhanāchchhādita-prak*ri*ti-purus*h*ātmaka-para-vindu*h*.

Also *cf.* "In the Satya-loka is the formless and lustrous One; She has surrounded Herself by Māyā, and is like a grain of gram; devoid of hands, feet, and the like. She is Moon, Sun, and Fire. When casting off (Uts*ri*jya) the covering (Bandhana) of Māyā, She becomes of two-fold aspect (Dvidhā bhitvā) and Unmukhī[1252]; then on the division or separation of Shiva and Shakti[1253] arises creative ideation."[1254] The word "Satya-loka" in the above passage means Sahasrāra.

Also *cf.* "The attributeless Bindu is without doubt the Cause (of the attainment) of Siddhis. Some say that the Devatā who is in the form of a grain of gram[1255] is Brahmā, and by some, again, He is called Vi*sh*nu; by others, again, He is called the One Mahāpūr*n*a,[1256] Niranjana[1257] Deva Rudra. Others call Him the Primordial Shakti."

The luminous empty space within the Nirvā*n*a Shakti (*i.e.*, the outer circle of the Parabindu), which is more minute than the ten-millionth part of the end of a hair, is, according to the author, the abode of Brahman (Brahmapada). *Cf.* "Within it[1258] is Parabindu, whose nature it is to create, maintain, and destroy. The space within is Shiva Himself and Bindu[1259] is Parama-ku*nd*alī."

Also: "The circumference (V*ri*tta) is the Ku*nd*alinī-Shakti, and She possesses the three Gu*n*as. The space within, O Beloved Maheshāni, is both Shiva and Shakti."[1260] This Bindu is, according to some, Īshvara, the Cause of All. Some Paurā*n*ikas call Him Mahā-Vi*sh*nu; others call Him Brahma-Puru*sh*a.

Cf. "There was neither day nor night, neither the firmament nor the earth, neither darkness nor light; there was *That* the Brahma-Male,[1261] imperceptible to hearing, and the other sources of knowledge united with Pradhāna."[1262]

The Shāradā[1263] says: "The eternal Shiva should be known both as Nirgu*n*a (attributeless) and Sagu*n*a (possessed of attributes). He is Nirgu*n*a when (considered as) disassociated from the workings of Prak*ri*ti, but when Sakala (*i.e.*, so associated with Prak*ri*ti) He is

[1252] By Unmukhī is meant that She becomes intent on creation.

[1253] Shiva-shaktivibhāgena. By division or separation is not meant that Shiva is really divided or separated from Shakti—for the two are ever one and the same—but that Shakti, which exist latently as one within the Brahman in dissolution, appears to issue from It on creation as the manifested universe.

[1254] S*rishti*-kalpanā. That is, the subject knows itself as object.

[1255] Cha*n*aka, which under its outward sheath contains two undivided halves.

[1256] All-embracing.

[1257] Stainless—that is, free from Māyā.

[1258] Apparently Nirvā*n*a-Kalā.

[1259] That is, the circumference as opposed to the inner space.

[1260] Jnānārnava Tantra, XXIV., 21.

[1261] Prādhānikang Brahma-pumān.

[1262] Kālikā Purāna, XXIV., v. 125.

[1263] Ch. I.

Saguna."[1264] This shows that the Bindu is Saguna Brahman. We should know that Saguna Brahma is in reality but one, though He is called by different names according to the inclinations of men. There is no need to go into further details.

SUMMARY OF VERSES 41 TO 49.

Above (the end) of the Sushumnā Nādī is the Lotus of a thousand petals; it is white and has its head downward turned; its filaments are red. The fifty letters of the Alphabet from A to La, which are also white, go round and round its thousand petals twenty times. On its pericarp is Hangsah, and above it is the Guru who is Parama-Shiva Himself. Above the Guru are the Sūryya and Chandra Mandalas, and above them Mahāvāyu. Over the latter is placed Brahmarandhra, and above it Mahāshangkhinī. In the Mandala of the Moon is the lightning-like triangle within which is the sixteenth Kalā[1265] of the Moon, which is as fine as the hundredth part of the lotus-fiber, and of a red color, with its mouth downward turned. In the lap of this Kalā is the Nirvāna-Kalā, subtle like the thousandth part of the end of a hair, also red and with the mouth downward turned. Below Nirvāna-Kalā is the Fire called Nibodhikā, which is a form of Avyaktanāda.[1266] Above it (Nibodhikā), and within Nirvānakalā, is Para-Bindu, which is both Shiva and Shakti. The Shakti of this Parabindu is the Nirvāna Shakti, who is Light (Tejas) and exists in the form of Hangsa (Hangsarūpā), and is subtle like the ten-millionth part of the end of a hair. That Hangsah is Jīva. Within the Bindu is the void (Shūnya) which is the Brahmapada (place of the Brahman).

According to the view expressed in the fifth chapter of the Āgama-kalpa-druma and other works, the triangle A-ka-tha[1267] is in the pericarp of the Sahasrāra. At its three corners are three Bindus: the lower Bindu at the apex of the triangle is Ha-kāra,[1268] and is male (Purusha); and the two Bindus at the corners constitute the Visarga in the form Sa[1269] and represent Prakriti. Hangsah which is Purusha and Prakriti thus shows itself in the form of three Bindus. In its middle is Amākalā, and in Her lap is Nirvāna-Shakti, and the vacant space within Nirvāna-Shakti is Parabrahman. And the authority in support of the

[1264] And so, also, the Shāktānandataranggini (Ch. I.) says of the Devī that Mahāmāyā without Māyā is Nirgunā, and with Māyā Sagunā.

[1265] That is, Amākalā.

[1266] Avyakta-nādātmaka-nibodhikākhya-vahni.

[1267] That is, the letters arranged in the form of the triangle referred to in v. 4 of Pādukā-panchaka. The Devi is Mātrikā-mayī.

[1268] Viz., Hang representing the "male" Bindu.

[1269] That is, literally "standing Sa," or Visargah in the form Sa. The letter Sa, or more strictly Sa without the vowel, changes into Visargah; thus, Tejas become Tejah, Rajas Rajah.

above is: "Within the White Lotus of a thousand petals shines like lightning the triangle A-ka-tha united with Ha-la-k*sh*a.[1270] Within it is the excellent (Para) Bindu (Shūnya), placed below Visarga. In this region is the downward-turned sixteenth Kalā, of the color of the rising Sun, in shape like the crescent moon who discharges a stream of nectar, and within Her is Parā-shakti, possessing the effulgence of ten million suns. She is as subtle as the thousandth part of the Lotus fiber, and is Chidātmikā.[1271] Within Her is Bindu who is the Niranjana Puru*sh*a, who is beyond mind and speech and is Sachchidānanda, and Visarga (who is also there) is Prak*ri*ti. Hangsa who is both Pung[1272] and Prak*ri*ti shines by His own effulgence."

Those who follow this view, place Sa-kāra over the Bindu, and place the Guru above Visarga[1273] and Bindu which together make Hangsa*h*. But this cannot be right. The Nirvā*n*a Tantra speaks of the Guru as worshipping the Para Bindurūpa-Shakti, and as being close to Her and in the act of worshipping Her. The worshipper should always sit at a level lower than, and facing, the object of worship, and never at a higher level than, and with his back towards, the object of worship. *Cf.* Nirvā*n*a: "Meditate upon the Niranjanā Devī within the Satya-loka in the Chintāma*n*ig*ri*ha[1274] as placed on the jeweled lion-throne (Singhāsana), and on your Guru as being near Her and worshipping Her."

The Mahākālī Tantra, moreover, speaks explicitly of the presence of the Guru over the two letters Hang and Sa*h*.[1275] It is to be understood that if there be any texts which differ from, or add to those here adopted, then they must be taken to refer to different methods and opinions.

This is the end of seventh section.

[1270] These Var*n*as are inside the triangle A-ka-tha.

[1271] Of the nature of Chit. *Cf.* definition of Māyā-Shakti in Tattva Sandoha 14.

[1272] The male, Puru*sh*a.

[1273] Lit., Generator of Visarga*h* (see note 1269, *ante*), for from Sa Visarga comes.

[1274] The room made of Chintāma*n*i stone which grants all desires, described in the Rudrayāmala and Brahmā*n*da Purā*n*a. The Lalitā refers to it as being the place of origin of all those Mantras which bestow all desired objects (Chintita).

[1275] In the Jnānār*n*ava Tantra (I., v. 13) it is said: "O Pārvatī, in Ha-kāra with Bindu (Hang) is Brahmā, and, O Maheshvarī, the two Bindus of Visarga (Sa*h*) are Hari and Myself. By reason of this inseparable connection men in this world speak of Hari-Hara."

VERSE 50.

He whose nature is purified by the practice of Yama, Niyama, and the like,[1276] learns from the mouth of his Guru the process which opens the way to the discovery of the liberation. He whose whole being is immersed in the Brahman then (rouses) the Devī by Hūng-kāra, pierces the center of the Lingga, the mouth of which is closed, and is therefore invisible, and by means of the Air and Fire (within him) places Her within the Brahmadvāra.[1277]

COMMENTARY.

Having described the Chakras ending with the Sahasrāra, he now wishes to speak of the union of Ku*nd*alinī, and preliminary to that he refers to the mode of rousing Ku*nd*alinī.[1278]

The sense conveyed by this verse is that the man who has attained success in Yoga learns from his Guru the process, which consists of contracting the heart, rousing Ku*nd*alinī by the power of the air and fire, and so forth[1279]; and having learned it from the mouth of his Guru, he rouses Ku*nd*alinī, attacking Her with air and fire, and by uttering the Kūrchcha "Hūng" and piercing the mouth of the Svayambhu Linga places Ku*nd*alinī within Brahmadvāra, or, in other words, within the mouth of the Nā*d*ī-Chitri*n*ī.

"*He whose nature is purified*" (Sushīla)—*i.e.*, the man who regularly practices Yama and so forth, and has trained himself.

"*By practicing Yama, Niyama,*" *etc.* (Yama-niyama-sama-bhyāsa-shīla).—It must be observed that it is not merely by the practice of Yama and Niyama that perfection in the preliminary Yoga practices[1280] is attained. But the Sādhaka has by practice to destroy such inclinations as lust, anger, and the like, which interfere with Yoga, and cultivate others, such as controlling the inner air, steadiness of mind, and so forth, which are helpful in Yoga practice. It is because of this that in v. 54 the Author has used the word "Yamādyai*h*" in the plural. Practicing Yama and the like is necessary, however, for those whose minds are disturbed by lust and other propensities. If, however, a man by reason of merit and good fortune acquired in a previous birth, or by his nature,

[1276] See Introduction.

[1277] That is, within Chitri*n*ī Nā*d*ī.

[1278] In the Yoga-process known as S*hat*chakrabheda, generally described in the Introduction, but which practically must be learned of the Guru.

[1279] The Commentator Shangkara, citing Goraks*h*a Sanghitā, says that air makes the fire go upwards, and the fire awakens Ku*nd*alinī and She also goes upwards.

[1280] Angga-yoga. See Introduction, and Vishvanātha citing Gautamīya Tantra (Tāntrik Texts, Vol. III., p. 133, ed. A. Avalon).

is free from anger, lust, and other passions, then he is capable of real Yoga without the preliminary practices. This must be well understood.

"*From the mouth of his Guru*" (Shrī-nātha-vaktrāt).—The process cannot be learnt without the instructions of the Guru. Hence it has been said: "It can be learnt from the Guru alone, and not from ten million Shāstras."

"*Process*" (Krama).—Steps, order.

"*Which opens the way to the discovery of the great liberation*" (Mahā-mok*sh*a-vartma-prakāsha).—By this is meant the process by which the entrance into the channel of the Nā*d*ī Chitri*n*ī is opened out.

"*He*" (Sa*h*)—*i.e.*, the man who has distinguished himself by his success in Yoga practices.

"*Whose whole being is immersed in the Brahman*" (Shuddha-buddhi-svabhāva).[1281]—Shuddha-buddhi means the Brahman, and he whose Svabhāva (own being) is in Him. This compound word may also mean "He whose being (Bhāva) by reason of the purity of his mind (Shuddha-buddhi) is immersed in the Spirit (sva-ātmā)."

"*Rouses the Devī by Hūng-kāra*" (Hung-kāre*n*aiva Devīm).—The Āgama-kalpa-druma says: "Then having mentally recited Hangsa, gently contract the secret part."[1282] It therefore follows that in moving Ku*nd*alinī the Hangsa Mantra should be uttered. The Author of the Lalitārahasya, following this, says that in moving Ku*nd*alinī the mantra "Hung Hangsa*h*" should be employed. But, from the fact that the part is to be contracted after the Hangsa Mantra is recited, the intention appears to be that the Jīvātmā, which is of the shape of the flame of a lamp, should by the recitation of the Hangsa Mantra be brought from the heart to the Mūlādhāra, and then moved along with Ku*nd*alinī.

The Āgama-kalpa-druma in a subsequent passage says: "Raising and again raising the Shakti with the Ātmā from the abode of Brahmā,[1283] the excellent Sādhaka should (and so forth)." This shows that She should be led away along with Ātmā or Jīvātmā. The Kālī-Kulām*ri*ta has: "Having led Jīva from the heart by the Hangsa Mantra to the Mūla Lotus,[1284] and having roused the Paradevatā Ku*nd*alinī by Hūng-kāra." The Kangkāla-mālinī says: "O daughter of the King of Mountains, having drawn the Jīvatmā by the Pra*n*ava, let the Sādhaka move Prā*n*a and Gandha[1285] with Ku*nd*alinī by the aid of the 'So 'ham' Mantra, and make the Devī enter the Svādhi*shth*āna."

The wise should, from the above texts, understand that the Jīvātmā should be brought from the heart by the aid of either the Prar*n*ava or

---

[1281] Shangkara reads prabhāva, and renders the passage as "He whose power is due to the purity of the Buddhi."

[1282] Shanai*h* sangkochayedgudam—that is, by Ashvinī-mudrā.

[1283] Brahmā is in Mūlādhāra.

[1284] Mukhāmbhuja.

[1285] *I.e.*, P*ri*thivī.

Hangsa Mantra, and then Ku*nd*alinī should be roused by the Kūrchcha-bīja alone.

"*The mouth of which is closed*," *etc.* (Guptam).—This word may be read either as an adjective qualifying Lingga, and mean unmanifested by reason of its mouth being closed,[1286] or may be read as an adverb qualifying "places," and then the word would mean "imperceptibly."

In the Āgama-kalpa-druma, Panchamashākhā, the mode of rousing the Ku*nd*alinī, is described in detail thus: "Having seated oneself in the Padmāsana posture, the two hands should be placed in the lap. Thereafter, having mentally recited the Hangsa Mantra, the anus should be gently contracted. One should then repeatedly raise the air by the same way,[1287] and having raised it let him pierce the Chakra. I now speak of its process. In the Mūlādhāra Lotus is a very beautiful triangle. Inside it is Kāma,[1288] (lustrous) like ten million young suns; above Him (Kāma), and surrounding Svayambhu-Lingga, is Ku*nd*alī Shakti." Also *cf.* "As the result of excitation by the Kāmāgni and the action of the Kūrchcha-mantra on Her, She is seized with desire for Para-Hangsa."[1289]

The Bhūta-shuddhi[1290] also says: "O Shivā, the Sādhaka should contract the chest (lit., heart), letting his breath remain there,[1291] and he should control the base of the throat and other parts of the body,[1292] and then suddenly opening the door by means of a key-like motion (Kunchikā)[1293] the fire should be kindled, O Parameshvari, by means of the air (Pavana)." "Then the Serpent,[1294] who is sleeping on the Lingga in the Mūladhara and who is stung by the heat of the fire, should be awakened in the Lingga at the mouth of the Yoni and be led forcibly upwards.[1295] Move the air into the Nā*d*ī according to the rules of Kumbhaka (retention of breath) and the method shown by the Guru. Let the Jīva thus controlled be led by the concealed passage, and by the upward breath make all the Lotuses turn their heads upwards. Having

1286 On the top of the Lingga is Nādabindu—*i.e.*, Chandra Bindu. The mouth is the Bindu which Ku*nd*alinī pierces.

1287 Tena vartmanā—that by which Ku*nd*alinī is to go.

1288 The Kāmāgni, or fire of Kāma.

1289 Parang Hangsābhilā*s*hinī—*i.e.*, passion is excited in Her, and She is impelled by the fire of Kāma towards the Parang Hangsa in the Sahasrāra.

1290 This passage is obscure, and cannot be traced in the only published edition of the Tantra, but is similar to certain passages in the Ha*th*ayo-gapradīpikā. It seems to contain passages from various texts to illustrate the process of Bhūtashuddhi. The Commentator has, however, more clearly described the process in his own words.

1291 He thus closes the passage of the upward breath.

1292 That is, the chest and the anus, thus closing the passage of the upward and downward airs.

1293 That is, the motion of the Kāma vāyu spoken of *post.*

1294 Nāginī, one of the names of Ku*nd*alī.

1295 That is, the Triko*n*a in the Mūlādhāra which surrounds the Svayambhū Linga.

fully awakened Her, let the wise one lead Her to Bhānu (the Sun) at the summit of the Meru (the Spine)."

Now pay attention to the procedure established by a careful consideration of the above texts[1296]: The Yogī should sit in the proper posture and place his two hands with palms upwards in his lap, and steady his mind (Chitta) by the Khecharī Mudrā. He should next fill the interior of his body with air and hold it in by Kumbhaka,[1297] and contract the heart.[1298] By so doing the escape of the upward breath is stopped. Then, when he feels that the air within him from the belly to the throat is tending downward through the channels in the Nā*d*īs, he should contract the anus and stop the downward air (Apāna); then, again having raised the air, let him give the Kāma[1299] within the triangle in the pericarp of the Mūlādhāra Lotus a turn from the left to the right (Vāmāvartena); by so doing the fire of Kāma there is kindled, and Ku*nd*alinī gets heated (excited) thereby. He should then pierce the mouth of the Svayambhu Lingga, and through its aperture lead Her with the aid of the "Hūng" Bīja, who desires union[1300] with Parama-Shiva, within the mouth of the Chitri*n*ī-Nā*d*ī. This is the clear sense of the text.

VERSE 51.

The Devī who is Shuddha-sattva[1301] pierces the three Linggas, and, having reached all the lotuses which are known as the Brahma-nā*d*ī lotuses, shines therein in the fullness of Her luster. Thereafter in Her subtle state, lustrous like lightning and fine like the lotus fiber, She goes to the gleaming flame-like Shiva, the supreme bliss, and of a sudden produces the bliss of Liberation.

COMMENTARY.

Now he speaks of the mode of the Union of Ku*nd*alinī (with Shiva). The meaning of this verse, in brief, is that the Devī Ku*nd*alinī pierces the three Linggas—viz., Svayambhū, Bā*n*a, and Itara[1302]—and by so doing makes a passage for herself; and when she reaches the lotuses in (or appertaining to) the Nā*d*ī called Brahma-nā*d*ī she shines in the fullness of her luster in these lotuses. Then, when in Her subtle

---

1296 The passages in quotation marks are here cited from different books on Ha*th*ayoga.

1297 Retention of breath in Prā*n*āyāma.

1298 H*r*idayamākunchayet—that is, by Jālandhara Bandha, etc. See Introduction.

1299 Kāma-vāyu.

1300 Sāma-rasya, a term used on the material plane to denote sexual union.

1301 A form of embodied Chaitanya. See Commentary, *post.*

1302 In the Mūlādhāra, Anāhata and Ājnā Chakras respectively.

form, fine like the lotus fiber, She approaches Shiva, who is Supreme Bliss itself, and who is in His Bindu form in the pericarp of the Sahasrāra, She brings to the Sādhaka the Bliss of eternal Liberation when that is least expected.

"*Pierces*" (Bheda) means making a passage through that which is obstructed.

"*Shuddha-sattvā.*"—Sattva, Ati-sattva, Parama-sattva, Shuddha-sattva, and Vishuddha-sattva, are the five different degrees of Chaitanya pervading the body.[1303] Shuddha-sattvā is therefore the fourth (Turīyā) stage. By Brahmanā*dī* is meant Chitri*nī*. The Lotuses are the six Lotuses which are strung upon Chitri*nī*.

"*The three Linggas*" (Lingga-trayam).—By this we are to understand that the six Chakras and five Shivas are included. She pierces all these, which altogether make fourteen knots (Granthi).

The Shāktānanda-tarangi*nī* speaks of "Her who goes along the Channel of Brahman[1304] having pierced the fourteen knots."[1305]

The Svatantra Tantra speaks of the distinctive features of Lingga and Shiva.

"The Devī goes to Brahman (Ni*sh*kala)[1306] after having pierced the Shivas placed in the six Chakras. As She reaches each of the different Chakras, She acquires the beauty and characteristic of each and bewitches Maheshāna[1307]; and having there repeatedly enjoyed Him who is filled with joy, She reaches the Eternal One (Shāshvata). He is called Bhinna, or the Transpierced, as He is bewitched by Parā."

The Māyā Tantra says: "The Devī goes along the Shakti-mārga, piercing the three Linggas in the Chakras in each of Her different forms[1308] (Tattadrūpe*na*), and having attained union (in the Sahasrāra) with Nis*h*kala (Brahman) She is satisfied." Tat-tadrūpe*na*—*i.e.*, in the forms Vaikharī, Madhyamā, and Pashyantī.

It has been said that[1309] "The first state (Bhāva) is Vaikharī, and Madhyamā is placed in the heart; between the eyebrows is the Pashyantī state, and the Parā state is in the Bindu."[1310] The meaning of the above quotation is that the four sound-producing (Shabdotpādikā)

[1303] Sharīrāvachchhinna-chaitanya.

[1304] Brahma-randhra, the channel within Chitri*nī*, is called Brahma-nādī and Brahma-randhra.

[1305] That is 3 Linggas, 6 Chakras, and the 5 Shivas—viz., Brahmā and the rest—in the 5 Chakras.

[1306] The Supreme or Nirgu*na* Brahman.

[1307] That is, the Shiva in the particular Chakra.

[1308] That is, She unites, in Her passage along the Nādi, with each of the Linggas in that form of Hers which is appropriate to such union.

[1309] See Commentary on v. 11, *ante.*

[1310] According to v. 11, Parā is in Mūlādhāra, Pashyantī in Svādhi*shth*āna, Madhyamā in Anāhata, and Vaikharī in the mouth. What is, however, here described is Layakrama.

Shaktis—viz., Parā, Pashyantī, Madhyamā, and Vaikharī—are identical with Ku*nd*alinī (Ku*nd*alinyabheda-rūpā). Hence at the time when Ku*nd*alinī starts to go to Sahasrāra She in Her form of Vaikharī bewitches Svayambhū Lingga; She then similarly bewitches Vā*n*a-Lingga in the heart as Madhyamā, and Itara Lingga between the eyebrows as Pashyantī, and then when she reaches Para Bindu She attains the stage of Parā (Parā-bhāva).

The Method of Chakra-bheda is thus described: "O Parameshvarī, let the Sādhaka carry along with Her the Lotuses which are on the Chitri*n*ī, and which have their origin in the mud of blood and fat.[1311] Let him[1312] enter the channel (Nāla)[1313] on the left, from below, and in this way Chakra-bheda (piercing the Chakra) is affected. After having thus pierced the six Chakras, She along with Jīva should be led as the rider guides a trained mare by the reins."

Also *cf.* "The Devī should be led by the Hangsa Mantra to the Sahasrāra through the points of union of the six Chakras (with the Nā*d*ī) along the road of Su*sh*umnā."

"*Gleaming flame-like*" (Sūk*sh*ma-dhāmni pradīpe).—The gleam is the Hangsa, which is the luminous energy (tejas) of the Para Bindu, in its aspect as Nirvā*n*ā Shakti (Nirvā*n*a-shaktyātmaka). The Parama Shiva shines with it.

We now describe how the joy of Liberation is brought about.

The Devī by dissolving Ku*nd*alinī in the Para Bindu effects the liberation of some Sādhakas through their meditation upon the identity of Shiva and Ātmā in the Bindu. She does so in the case of others by a similar process, and by meditation on Shakti.[1314] In other cases, again, this is done by the concentration of thought on the Parama Puru*sh*a, and in other cases by the meditation of the Sādhaka on the union of Shiva and Shakti.

The Māyā Tantra says[1315]: "Those who are learned in Yoga say that it is the union of Jīva and Ātmā. According to the experience of others it is the knowledge of the identity of Shiva and Ātmā. The Āgama-vādīs proclaim that Yoga[1316] is the knowledge (Jnāna) relating to or of Shakti. Other wise men say that the knowledge of the Purā*n*a Puru*sh*a is Yoga, and others, again, the Prak*r*iti-vādīs, declare that the

---

[1311] Lotuses grow in the mud, and these Lotuses grow in the blood and fat of the body. The process described is Ku*nd*alinī-yoga, or, as it is called in the Tippanī of Shangkara, Bhūta-shuddhi.

[1312] As the Sādhaka, who has taken the Jīvātmā from the heart to the Mūlādhāra, and thus identifies himself with Ku*nd*alinī, it is he who enters.

[1313] That is, the Nā*d*ī.

[1314] Shaktyātmakachintana; or it may mean meditation on the union of Shiva and Shakti.

[1315] These verses also occur in Ch. XXV., vv. 1, 2, of Shāradā Tilaka.

[1316] Shaktyātmakajnāna.

union of Shiva and Shakti is Yoga."[1317] By "union of Jīva and Ātmā" is meant Samādhi. By Yoga is meant that by which oneness is attained with the Paramātmā. Having spoken of Samādhi, he then deals with the different kinds of Yoga in Dhyāna. By "union (Sāmarasya) of Shiva and Shakti" is meant the sense of enjoyment arising from the union of male and female.[1318]

The B*ri*hat Shrīkrama speaks of the manner in which this is to be meditated upon: "They with the eye of knowledge[1319] see the stainless Kalā, who is longing to be united with Chidānanda[1320] on Nāda. He is the Mahādeva, white like a pure crystal, and is the effulgent first cause (Vimba-rūpanidāna),[1321] and She is the lovely woman of beauteous body[1322] whose limbs are listless by reason of Her great passion."[1323]

By Kalā in the above is meant Ku*nd*alinī. Vimba-rūpanidāna qualifies Para-shiva or Chidānanda. Chidānanda is the Bindu-rūpa-shiva or Para-shiva.

It has also been said elsewhere: "Having united Ku*nd*alī with the Shūnya-rūpa[1324] Parashiva, and having caused the Devī to drink the excellent nectar from their union, she by the same way should be brought back to the Kula cavity."[1325]

"Having brought them together and meditated upon Their union,[1326] let the Deha-devatā[1327] be satisfied with the nectar which flows from such a union."

The Gandharva-mālikā speaks of a different process: "The Sahasrāra is the beautiful and auspicious place of Sadāshiva. It is free from sorrow and divinely beautiful with trees bearing and adorned by flowers and fruits. The Kalpa Tree[1328] adds to its beauty. This tree contains all the five "elements," and is possessed of the three gu*n*as. The four Vedas are its four branches. It is laden with beautiful unfading flowers which are yellow, white, black, red, green, and of variegated color. Having meditated on the Kalpa Tree in this manner, then

---

[1317] Sāmarasyātmakam jnānam. Tantrāntāra says that Sāmarasa is the Dhyāna of a Kulayogī.

[1318] Stripungyogāt yat saukyhang.

Sāmarasyang prakīrtitam. In other words, the bliss of Union of Shiva and Shakti, of which sexual union is the material type.

[1319] Jnāna-chak*sh*u*h*.

[1320] Chidānanda is Consciousness and Bliss.

[1321] A variant reading is Bindu-rūpa-nidāna, the First Cause in the Bindu form.

[1322] Vāmoru—lit., beautiful thighs, the part being selected as an example of the whole.

[1323] Madālasa-vapu.

[1324] Shūnya-rupa. Shūnya means "the void" or space within the Bindu—the Shiva who is That, the Supreme Shiva.

[1325] Kula-gahvara; the Mūlādhara.

[1326] Sāmarasya; *v. ante.*

[1327] That is, the body of the Sādhaka considered as Devatā.

[1328] A celestial wishing-tree which grants all fruit.

meditate upon the jeweled altar below it. O Beauteous One, on it is a beautiful bed adorned with various kinds of cloth and Mandāra flowers, and scented with many kinds of scents. It is there that Mahādeva constantly stays. Meditate upon Sadāshiva, who is like the purest crystal, adorned with all kinds of gems, long-armed,[1329] and of enchanting beauty. He is ever gracious and smiling. In His ears are ear-rings, and a chain of gems goes round His neck. A garland of a thousand lotuses resting on his neck adorns His body. He has eight arms and three eyes like the petals of the lotus. On His two feet He wears a tinkling toe-ornament, and His body is Shabda-Brahma (Shabda-Brahma-maya). O Lotus-eyed One, meditate thus on His Great Body (Sthūla-vapu*h*). He is the quiescent, corpse-like[1330] Deva within the Lotus who is void of all action."

Also: "Meditate upon the Devī Ku*nd*alinī who encircles the Svayambhū Lingga. Lead the Devī with the aid of the Hangsa Mantra to the Sahasrāra, where, O Parameshvarī, is the great Deva Sadāshiva, who is gladdened by the scent of Her Lotus-like mouth. And then place there the beautiful Ku*nd*alinī, who is excited by Her desire. Ku*nd*alinī, O Beloved, then kisses the lotus-mouth of Shiva, and, O Deveshi, She enjoys Sadāshiva but a very little while when immediately, O Devī, O Parameshvari, there issues nectar. This nectar issuing from their union is of the color of lac.[1331] With this nectar, O Deveshi, should the Para-Devatā[1332] be satisfied. Having thus satisfied the Devatās in the six Chakras with that ambrosial stream, the wise one should by the same way bring Her back to Mūlādhāra. The mind should in this process of going and coming be dissolved there.[1333] O Pārvati, he who practices this Yoga day by day is freed from decay and death, and is liberated from the bondage of this world."

Other similar processes should be looked for in other Tantras.

VERSE 52.

The wise and excellent Yogī rapt in ecstasy,[1334] and devoted to the Lotus feet of his Guru, should lead Kula-ku*nd*ali along with Jīva to Her Lord the Parashiva in the abode of liberation within the pure Lotus, and meditate upon Her who grants all desires as the Chaitanyarūpā Bhagavatī.[1335] When he thus leads Kula-Ku*nd*alinī, he should make all

---

1329 Associated with the idea of strength.

1330 Shiva without Shakti is Shava (corpse): Devībhāgavata, and v. 1 of the Ānandalaharī.

1331 Red, which is the color of lac, is also that of the Rajas guna.

1332 Ku*nd*alinī.

1333 In the Shivasthānam.

1334 Samādhi. *Vide* Introduction, and *post*, Commentary.

1335 The Devī who is the Chit in all bodies.

things absorb into Her.

COMMENTARY.

Having spoken of the Dhyāna-yoga of Ku*nd*alinī, he now speaks of the Samādhiyoga of Ku*nd*alinī. The substance of this verse is that the wise (Sudhī) and excellent Yogī (Yogīndra) should for the attainment of Samādhi first of all lead Her who has been roused, who then, taking with Her Jīva, reaches the Brahmadvāra, causing the absorption into Herself of everything as She moves along. When She who is the Ishtadevatā and the giver of all good fruits is led up to Her Lord and is united with Him, the Para Bindu, she should be meditated upon as supreme (Parā) Para Bindu (Para bindu svarupām). When She has been led to Her Lord Shiva, the Para-Bindu, and has been united with Him, She should be meditated upon as the I*sht*adevatā who grants good fruit.

He should there (in the Sahasrāra) dissolve the Para-Bindu in the Chidātmā,[1336] which is in the void within the Bindu, and should meditate upon Her (Ku*nd*alinī) as Shuddhachaitanyarūpā.[1337] He thus realizes the identity of Jīva and Ātmā, being conscious within himself that "I am He" (So 'ham); and having dissolved the Chitta he remains unmoved, by reason of his full and all-pervading Knowledge.

The Revered Preceptor (Shrīmat Āchāryya)[1338] has said: "The wise one should absorb the Kāra*na*[1339] of Ma-kāra into the Chidātmā, and realize: 'I am Chidātmā, I am eternal, pure (Shuddha), enlightened (Buddha), liberated (Mukta); I am That which alone exists (Sat), without a second (Advaya); I am Supreme Bliss wherein is all bliss, and Vāsudeva's very self I am—Om.'[1340] Having realized that the mind (Chitta) is the discriminator, he absorbs it into its witness.[1341] Let not the mind (Chitta) be distracted when it is absorbed into Chidātmā. Let the Sādhaka rest in the fullness of his illumination like a deep and motionless ocean."

"Ma-kāra."[1342]: This is said for those who are Sādhakas of the Pra*n*ava. By Kāra*n*a is here meant Para-Bindu. By "I am Vāsudeva" (Vāsudevo'ham) the Vāi*shn*avas are alluded to (*vide ante*, vv. 44, 49).

We thus see that the worshipper of any particular Devatā should realize that he is one with the object of his worship. In Pra*n*ava worship, for instance, the worshipper realizes his identity with the

1336 The Brahman as Chit.

1337 Pure Chit.

1338 That is, Shangkarāchāryya.

1339 That is, the Bindu.

1340 Chidātmāhang nitya-shuddha-buddha-mukta-sadadvaya*h*
Paramānanda-sandohang vāsudevo' ham om iti.

1341 That is, the Ātmā, of which it is said Ātmā sāk*sh*īcheta*h* kevalo nirgu*n*ashcha.

1342 The Bindu is the Ma-kāra.

Ongkāra; in other forms of worship he realizes his identity with Ku*nd*alinī, who is embodied by all the Mantras of different worshippers.

The Tantrāntara says: "The King among Yogīs becomes full of Brahma-bliss by making his mind the abode of the great void which is set in the light of the Sun, Moon, and Fire."[1343]

"*Lead Kundali along with Jīva*" (Jīvena sārddhang nītvā).—The Jīvātmā which is the Hangsa, in form like the tapering flame of a light, should be brought to the Mūlādhāra from its place in the heart, and then led along with Ku*nd*alinī.

"*Abode of liberation*" (Mok*sh*e dhāmani).—This qualifies Pure Lotus (Shuddhapadma).[1344] It is here that liberation is attained.

"*Devoted to the two Lotus feet of his Guru*" (Guru-pāda-padma-yugalālambī).—This qualifies Yogīndra (excellent yogī). The Author means that Siddhi can only be attained by the instructions of the Guru. The Sādhaka should therefore seek shelter at his feet.

"*Rapt in Samādhi*" (Samādhau yata*h*).—The Kulār*n*ava Tantra (ix. 9) defines Samādhi thus: "Samādhi is that kind of contemplation[1345] in which there is neither 'here' nor 'not here,' which is illumination and is still like the ocean, and which is the Void Itself."[1346]

Also elsewhere: "The Munis declare that the constant realization of the identity of the Jīvātmā (with the Paramātmā) is Samādhi, which is one of the eight limbs (Angga) of Yoga."[1347] Patanjali defines "Yoga to be the control of the modifications (or functions) of Chitta (Yogashchitta v*ri*ttini-rodha*h*)."

Rapt (Yata*h*)—*i.e.*, he who constantly and with undivided attention practices it.

"*When he leads Kula-Kundali, he should make all things absorb into her*" (Laya-vashāt nītvā).[1348] Below is shown the process of absorption:

"O Deveshī, the Lang-kāra[1349] should next be meditated upon in the triangle; there should also Brahmā and Kāma-deva be contemplated. Having fixed Jīva there with the utterance of the Pra*n*ava, let him lead the Woman, who is longing for the satisfaction of Her passion,[1350] to the place of Her husband,[1351] O Queen of the Devas. O Great Queen, O beloved of my life, let him think of Ghrār*n*a (P*ri*thivī), and meditate on the adorable Shakti *D*ākinī. O Daughter of

---

[1343] That is, in the region of the Sahasrāra. See v. 4 of the Pādukā panchaka.

[1344] Shangkara reads it as Shuklapadma, white lotus.

[1345] Dhyāna.

[1346] Svarūpa-Shūnya.

[1347] This is from Shāradā Tilaka, Ch. XXV., v. 26.

[1348] Vishvanātha reads it as Naya-vashāt.

[1349] Bīja of P*ri*thivī.

[1350] Visarga-nāsha-kāminī.

[1351] That is, the Bindu in Sahasrāra.

the Mountain, O Queen of the Ga*n*as,[1352] O Mother, all these should be led into P*ri*thivī."

Also: "Then, O Great Queen, the blessed P*ri*thivī should be absorbed into Gandha, and then, O Daughter of the Mountain King, the Jīvātmā should be drawn (from the heart) with the Pra*n*ava (Mantra), and the Sādhaka should lead Prā*n*a,[1353] Gandha,[1354] and Ku*nd*alinī, into Svādhi*shth*āna with the Mantra So'ham."

And also: "In its pericarp (Svādishthāna) should Varu*n*a and Hari[1355] be meditated upon. And, O Beauteous One, after meditating on Rāki*n*ī[1356] all these and Gandha (smell) should be absorbed into Rasa (taste), and Jīvātmā, Ku*nd*alinī, and Rasa, should be moved into Ma*n*ipūra."

And again: "O thou of beautiful hips[1357] (Sushro*n*i), in its[1358] pericarp the Sādhaka should meditate upon Fire, and also on Rudra, who is the destroyer of all, as being in company with the Shakti Lākinī and beautiful to behold. And, O Shiva, let him next meditate on lustrous vision, and absorb all these and Rasa (taste) into Rūpa (sight), and thereafter lead Jīvātmā, Ku*nd*alinī, and Rūpa, into Anāhata."

And again: "Let him meditate in its pericarp[1359] on Vāyu, who dwells in the region of Jīva, as also on the Yoni-Ma*nd*ala, which is made beauteous by the presence of the Bā*n*a-Lingga and Kākinī.[1360] Let him there also meditate on Vāyu and touch (Tvagindriya or Sparsha), and there, O Thou who purifiest, Jīva, Ku*nd*alinī, and Rūpa, should be placed in Sparsha (touch), and then Jīva, Ku*nd*alinī, and Sparsha, should be placed in the Vishuddha."

And again: "Let him meditate in its[1361] pericarp on the Ethereal region,[1362] and on Shiva accompanied by Shākinī; and having placed speech (Vāk), and hearing (Shrotra), in Ether, let him, O daughter of the Mountain, place all these and Sparsha in Shabda (sound), and place Jīva, Ku*nd*alinī, and Shabda, in the Ājnā Chakra."

The above passages are from Kangkālamālinī Tantra.

"Triangle" in the above is the triangle in the Mūlādhāra, from which the commencement is made. Lang-kāra should be meditated upon as within this triangle. Leading of Jiva with the use of the Pranava is a variant practice. "Visarga-nāshakāminī": By Visarga is meant the

---

1352 Attendant (Upadevatā*s*) on Shiva, of whom Ga*n*esha is the Lord.

1353 *Sic* in text *Quaere* ghrar*n*a or Prā*n*a in sense of Hangsa.

1354 *I.e.*, Gandha Tanmātra.

1355 *I.e.*, Vi*shn*u.

1356 Purā*n*akāri*n*ī—one of her names.

1357 *I.e.*, one who has a beautiful figure, the part being selected for the whole.

1358 "Its"—*i.e.*, of Ma*n*ipūra padma.

1359 "Its"—*i.e.*, of Anāhatapadma.

1360 The text has Rāki*n*ī, but this is an error.

1361 Vishuddhapadma.

1362 Ākāsha.

agitation caused by an access of Kāma (desire). The compound word means She who is striving to satisfy Her desire (Kāma). The bringing of Jīva by the Hangsa Mantra is according to the teaching of some. "Place of her husband" (Patyau pade): This is the Bindu, the Shiva in the Lotus of a thousand petals. Sādhaka should lead Her there.

The Bīja Lang, Brahmā, Kāmadeva, *D*ākinī-Shakti, and the sense of smell (Ghrā*n*endriya)—all these are absorbed into P*r*ithivī, and P*r*ithivī is absorbed into the Gandha-tattva. Jīvātmā, Ku*nd*alinī, and Gandha-tattva, are drawn upward by the Pra*n*ava, and brought into the Svādhi*shth*āna by the So'ham Mantra. This is the process to be applied right through. After leading Jīva, Ku*nd*alinī, and Shabda-tattva, into Ājnā Chakra, Shabda-tattva should be absorbed into Ahangkāra which is there, and Ahangkāra into Mahat-tattva, and Mahat-tattva into Sūks*h*ma-prak*r*iti, whose name is Hira*n*ya-garbha, and Prak*r*iti again into Para-bindu.

The Mantra-tantra-prakāsha says: "Let Vyoma (Ether) be absorbed into Ahangkāra, and the latter with Shabda into Mahat, and Mahat, again, into the unmanifest (Avyakta) supreme (Para) Cause (Kāra*n*a) of all the Shaktis. Let the Sādhaka think attentively that all things beginning with P*r*ithivī are absorbed into Vi*sh*nu,[1363] the cause who is Sat, Chit, and Ānanda."

That is, Mahat, which is all Shaktis (Sarvashakti), should be absorbed into Sūk*sh*ma-prak*r*iti, who is known by the name of Hira*ny*a-garbha, and that Prak*r*iti should be absorbed into Para, by which is meant the Cause in the form of Parabindu. In this connection the Āchāryya has laid down the rule that the gross should be dissolved into the subtle.[1364] *Cf.*: "It should be attentively considered and practiced that the gross is absorbed into the subtle, and all into Chidātmā." The absorption of all things, beginning with P*r*ithivī and ending with Anāhata,[1365] takes place in the aforesaid manner; that being so, the feet and the sense of smell (Ghrā*n*endriya) and all pertaining to P*r*ithivī are dissolved in the place of P*r*ithivī, as they inhere in P*r*ithivī.

Similarly, the hands, the sense of taste (Rasanendriya), and all that pertains to water, are dissolved in the region of Water. In the region of Fire (Vahni-sthāna) are dissolved the anus, the sense of vision (Chak*sh*urindriya), and all that pertains to fire. In the region of Air (Vāyu-sthāna) the genitals, the sense of touch (Tvāgindriya), and all that pertains to Vāyu, are dissolved. In the place of Ākāsha are dissolved the sense of speech (Vāk) and hearing (Shrotendriya) and all that pertains to Ākāsha (Ether).

In the Ājnā Chakra the dissolution of Ahangkāra, Mahat,

[1363] Vi*sh*nu is specified by this particular Tantra, but it may be any other Devatā who is the I*sht*adevatā of the Sādhaka (see p. 299).

[1364] *Vide* v. 40 and Commentary under it.

[1365] This seems an error, for the last Mahābhūta Ākāsha is dissolved in Vishuddha.

Sūk*sh*maprak*ri*ti, and so forth, takes place, each dissolving into its own immediate cause. The letters of the alphabet should then be absorbed in the reverse order (Viloma), beginning with K*sh*a-kāra and ending with A-kāra. By "all things" it is meant that "Bindu," "Bodhinī," and so forth, which have been shown above to be causal bodies (Kāra*n*a-Sharīra), should be dissolved in a reversed order (Vilomena) into the Primordial Cause (Ādikāra*n*a)—the Para-bindu. Thus the Brahman alone remains.

The process is thus described: "The Sādhaka, having thus made his determination (Sangkalpa), should dissolve[1366] the letters of the Alphabet in the Nyāsa-sthāna.[1367] The dissolution of K*sh*a is in La, and La in Ha; Ha, again, is dissolved into Sa, and Sa into *Sh*a, and thus it goes on till A is reached. This should be very carefully done."

Also[1368]: "Dissolve the two letters into Bindu, and dissolve Bindu into Kalā. Dissolve Kalā in Nāda, and dissolve Nāda in Nādānta,[1369] and this into Unmanī, and Unmanī into Vi*sh*nuvaktra[1370]; Vi*sh*nuvaktra should be dissolved into Guruvaktra.[1371] Let the excellent Sādhaka then realize that all the letters are dissolved in Parama Shiva."

By Vi*sh*nuvaktra is meant Pung-bindu. "The Sūryya-bindu is called the Mouth, and below are Moon and Fire." "Bindu is said to be the Male, and Visarga is Prak*ri*ti."[1372]

All these authorities imply the same thing, and go to prove that it is the "mouth of Vi*sh*nu" (Vi*sh*nu-vaktra) where dissolution should take place. The following from Keshavāchāryya also leads to the same conclusion: "Lead Her (Unmanī) into the Male, which is the Bindu; lead Bindu into Parātmā, and Parātmā into Kālatattva, and this latter into Shakti, and Shakti into Chidātmā, which is the Supreme (Kevala), the tranquil (Shānta), and effulgent."

We have seen that each dissolves into its own immediate cause. Nādānta is therefore dissolved in Vyāpikā Shakti, the Vyāpikā Shakti in Unmanī, and Unmanī in Samanī,[1373] and Samanī in Vi*sh*nuvaktra. When the letters have been thus dissolved, all the six Chakras are dissolved, as the petals of the Lotuses consist of letters.[1374]

The Vishvasāra Tantra says: "The petals of the Lotuses are the

[1366] Sangharet.

[1367] The places where the Var*n*a have been placed in Māt*ri*kā Nyāsa.

[1368] Here is shown the Anuloma process.

[1369] *I.e.*, that which is beyond Nāda. See Introduction.

[1370] Pung-Vindu; *v. post.*

[1371] That is, the mouth of the Supreme Bindu (cited from Shāradā Tilaka, Ch. V., vv. 134-136). Also *cf.* Shāradā, Ch. XII., 123, and Kularnava IV., 76.

[1372] *Cf.* Shāradā, Ch. XXV., v. 51.

[1373] *Sic.* This is in conflict with other passages, according to which Unmanī is above Samanī.

[1374] Padmadalānāng var*n*a mayatvāt.

letters of the Alphabet, beginning with A."[1375] The Sammohana Tantra[1376] describes the dissolution[1377] of the Lotuses and the petals thus: "Dissolve the letters Va to Sa of the petals in Brahmā,[1378] and dissolve Brahmā in the Lotus of six petals which contains the letters Ba to La, and which is called Svādhi*shth*āna. Do this as the Guru directs." And so forth. And ending with:—

"The wise one should then dissolve it (Vishuddha) in the Lotus of two petals which contains the two letters Ha and K*sh*a, and dissolve the two letters which are in the latter lotus into Bindu, and dissolve Bindu into Kalā."[1379]

We thus see that the four letters in the Mūlādhāra are dissolved and Mūlādhāra is dissolved in Svādhi*shth*āna. Proceeding in this way till the Ājnā Chakra is reached, the letters Ha and K*sh*a which are there are also dissolved at this place. Then the Lotus itself is dissolved into Bindu, Bindu into Bodhinī, and proceeding in this way as already shown everything is dissolved into Parabindu. When the Ājnā-chakra is dissolved all that it contains in its pericarp—Hākinī, Itara lingga, Pra*n*ava—are unable to exist without support, and therefore after the dissolution into Prak*ri*ti these also are dissolved into Para Bindu.

VERSE 53.

The beautiful Ku*nd*alī drinks the excellent red[1380] nectar issuing from Parashiva, and returns from there where shines Eternal Bliss[1381] in all its glory along the path of Kula,[1382] and again enters the Mūlādhāra. The Yogī who has gained steadiness of mind makes offering (Tarpa*n*a) to the I*sht*a-devatā and to the Devatās in the six centers (Chakra), Dākinī and others, with that stream of celestial nectar which is in the vessel[1383] of Brahmā*nd*a, the knowledge whereof he has gained through the tradition of the Gurus.

COMMENTARY.

He now speaks of what should be done after all the different kinds of Yoga have been understood. The meaning of this verse is that the beautiful Ku*nd*alī drinks the excellent nectar issuing from Parashiva,

---

1375 Ādivar*n*ātmakam patram padmānām parikīrtitam.

1376 The passage cited also occurs in Shāradā Tilaka, Ch. V., vv. 129-134.

1377 Vilaya.

1378 That is, Mūlādhāra.

1379 That is, the Bindu of the Ājnā Chakra is dissolved into Ku*nd*alinī.

1380 Shangkara says it is so colored because it is mixed with the menstrual fluid, which is symbolic, like the rest of this erotic imagery. Red is the color of the Rajogu*n*a.

1381 Brahman is Eternity and Bliss.

1382 The Channel in the Chitri*n*īnādī.

1383 "The vessel is Ku*nd*alinī.

and having emerged from the place of Eternal and Transcendental Bliss, She passes along the path of Kula and re-enters Mūlādhāra. The Yogī, after having understood the different matters mentioned (Tat-tad-dhyānā-nantaram), should think of the union[1384] of Shiva and Shakti, and with the excellent nectar produced from the bliss of such union with Parashiva make offering (Tarpa*n*a) to Ku*nd*alinī.

"*Path of Kula*" (Kula-patha).—The path of Brahman, the channel in Chitri*n*ī.

Ku*nd*alī drinks the nectar with which Tarpa*n*a is made to her. The following authority says: "Having effected their union and having made (Her drink)," etc. It follows, therefore, that She is made to drink.

"*From there where shines Eternal and Transcendent Bliss*" (Nityānanda-mahodayāt)—that is, She returns from the place where eternal and transcendental Bliss is enjoyed—*i.e.*, where the Brahman is clearly realized.

"*Again enters Mūlādhāra*" (Mūle vishet).—She has to be brought back in the same way as She was led upward. As She passed through the different Chakras in their order (Chakra-bheda-krame*n*a) when going upward, so does She when returning to the Mūlādhāra.

The Revered Great Preceptor says: "Kuhari*n*ī,[1385] Thou sprinklest all things with the stream of Nectar which flows from the tips of Thy two feet; and as Thou returneth to Thy own place Thou vivifieth and maketh visible all things that were aforetime invisible, and on reaching Thy abode Thou dost resume Thy snake-like coil and sleep."[1386]

"As Thou returneth Thou vivifieth and maketh visible." This describes the return of Ku*nd*alī to Her own place. As She returns She infuses Rasa[1387] into the various things She had previously absorbed into Herself when going upward, and by the infusion of Rasa She makes them all visible and manifest. Her passage was Layakrama,[1388] and Her return S*r*ish*t*i[1389]-krama. Hence it has been said: "Ku*nd*alī, who is Bliss,[1390] the Queen of the Suras,[1391] goes back in the same way to the Ādhāra[1392] Lotus."

The Bhūta-shuddhi-prakara*n*a has the following: "Let the Tattvas

---

1384 Sāmarasya.

1385 Kuhara is a cavity; Kuhari*n*ī would then be She whose abode is a cavity—the cavity of the Mūlādhāra.

1386 Cited from the celebrated Ānandalaharī Stotra, Wave of Bliss Hymn, attributed to Shangkarāchāryya. See "Wave of Bliss," a translation, by A. Avalon.

1387 Rasa: sap, sap of life—that is, She re-vitalizes them.

1388 See v. 52 and next note.

1389 That is, She recreates or revives as She returns to her own abode; just as She "destroys" or absorbs all things on Her upward progress.

1390 Mudrākārā—that is, Ānandarūpi*n*ī; for Mudrā = Ānandadāyinī. Mudrā is derived from Mud = ānanda (bliss) + Rāti = dadāti (gives): Mudrā therefore means that which gives bliss.

1391 Sura = Deva.

1392 *I.e.*, Mūlādhāra.

P*ri*thivī, etc., in their order, as also Jīva and Ku*nd*alinī, be led back from Paramātmā and each placed in its respective position." She is then particularly described: "She is lustrous when first She goes, and She is ambrosial[1393] when She returns."

"*Stream of celestial nectar*" (Divyāmr*i*tadhārā).—This is the excellent nectar which, as has already been shown, is produced by the union[1394] of Shiva and Shakti, and runs in a stream from the Brahmarandhra to the Mūlādhāra. It is for this reason that the Author says in v. 3 that "the Brahmadvāra which shines in Her mouth is the entrance to the place sprinkled by ambrosia."

"*Knowledge whereof he has gained through the tradition of the Gurus*" (Yoga-paramparā-viditayā).—This qualifies "Stream of Nectar." It means that the knowledge is gained from instructions handed down traditionally through the succession of Gurus.

"*Which is in the vessel of Brahmā*nda" (Brahmā*nd*a-bhā*nd*a-sthitam).—This qualifies Am*r*ita (nectar).[1395] The vessel or support (Bhā*nd*a) on which the Brahmā*nd*a (universe) rests is Ku*nd*alinī. Ku*nd*alinī is the Bhā*nd*a as She is the Source (Yoni) of all.

Daivatam[1396] is the Ish*t*adevatā and *D*ākinī and others in the six Chakras. It has been said: "O Deveshī, with this nectar should offering (Tarpa*n*a) be made to the Paradevatā, and then having done Tarpa*n*a to the Devatās in the six Chakras," and so forth.

VERSE 54.

The Yogī who has, after practice of Yama, Niyama, and the like,[1397] learnt this excellent method from the two lotus feet of the auspicious Dīk*sh*ā-guru,[1398] which are the source of uninterrupted joy, and whose mind (Manas) is controlled, is never born again in this world (Sangsāra). For him there is no dissolution even at the time of Final Dissolution.[1399] Gladdened by constant (realization of) that which is the source of Eternal Bliss,[1400] (he becomes) full of peace and foremost among all Yogīs.[1401]

[1393] Because ambrosia (Am*r*ita) gives life.

[1394] Sāmarasya.

[1395] Vishvanātha reads this as an adjective qualifying Daivatam, and this seems more in consonance with the text. The Brahmā*nd*a is compared to a Bhā*nd*a, and the Devatās are in that. The offering is then made with that stream of nectar to the Devatās who are in the Universe. Or, according to Kālīchara*n*a, offering is made to the Devatās of the Am*r*itā which Ku*nd*alī has drunk.

[1396] Daivatam is the collective form of Devatās.

[1397] See Introduction.

[1398] The Guru who has given him initiation.

[1399] Sangk*sh*aya = Pralaya.

[1400] Nityānanda = Brahman.

[1401] Satām—lit., "of the Good."

COMMENTARY.

He here speaks of the good to be gained by knowing the method of Yoga practice.

"*From the lotus feet of his auspicious Dīkshā-guru, which are the source of uninterrupted joy*" (Shrī-dīk*sh*ā-guru-pāda-padma-yugalāmoda-pravāhodayāt).—Āmoda means joy or bliss; and by Pravāha is meant uninterrupted and continuous connection. Āmoda-pravāha therefore means Nityānanda, or "Eternal Bliss." Bliss such as this comes from the Lotus feet of the Guru, which also lead to a knowledge of Yoga practice.

The Dīk*sh*ā-guru is here spoken of as he is the first to initiate, and also by reason of his pre-eminence. But in his absence refuge may be sought with other Gurus. It has therefore been said: "As a bee desirous of honey goes from one flower to another, so does the disciple desirous of knowledge (Jnāna) go from one Guru to another."[1402]

"*Gladdened by constant* (*realization*) (*of that which is the source of*) *Eternal Bliss*" (Nityānanda-paramparā-pramudita)—*i.e.*, who is united with the Stream of Eternal Bliss.

"*Foremost among the good*" (Satām agra*n*ī)—*i.e.*, he is counted to be among the good who are the Yogīs.

VERSE 55.

If the Yogī who is devoted to the Lotus feet of his Guru, with heart unperturbed and concentrated mind, reads this work which is the supreme source of the knowledge of liberation, and which is faultless, pure, and most secret, then of a very surety his mind[1403] dances at the Feet of his I*sh*ta-devatā.

COMMENTARY.

He here speaks of the good to be gained by the study of the verses relating to the six Chakras.

"*Heart unperturbed*" (Svabhāva-sthita)—*i.e.*, engrossed in his own true spiritual being.

"*Concentrated mind*" (Yatāntarmanā*h*)—*i.e.*, he who by practice of Yoga has steadied and concentrated his mind on the inner spirit (Antarātmā).

The rest is clear.

[1402] This is from Ch. XII. of Niruttara Tantra.

[1403] Chetas or Chitta.

Here ends the Eighth Section of the Explanation of the Verses descriptive of the Six Chakras, forming part of the Shrītattvachintāma*n*i, composed by Shrī-Pūr*n*ānandayati.

The Fivefold Footstool[1404] (*Pādukā-Panchaka*)

INTRODUCTORY VERSE.[1405]

I meditate on the Guru in the Lotus of a thousand petals, who is radiant like the cool rays of the full moon, whose lotus hands make the gestures which grant blessing and dispel fear. His raiment, garland, and perfumes, are ever fresh and pure. His countenance is benign. He is in the Hangsa in the head. He is the Hangsa Himself.

VERSE 1.

I adore the wonderful White Lotus of twelve letters[1406] which is within the womb (Udare) of, and inseparable from, the pericarp of the Lotus in which is the Brahmarandhra, and which covers the top of the channel of Ku*nd*alī.[1407]

COMMENTARY.

The hymn Pādukā-panchakam, composed by Him of the Five Faces,[1408] destroys all demerit.[1409] Kālī-chara*n*a by his *Tī*kā called Amalā (Stainless) makes patent its beauty.

Sadāshiva, the Liberator of the three Worlds, being desirous of speaking of Gurudhyāna-yoga[1410] in the form of a hymn (Stotra), first of all describes the place of the Guru.

The verb Bhaje is First Person Singular, Ātmanepada, showing that Shiva Himself adores or worships. He says, "I adore or worship." By saying so He expresses the necessity that all worshippers (Upāsakas) of the Mantras revealed by Him should adore this wonderful twelve-petalled Lotus. He thus shows the necessity of His worship.

The meaning of this verse in brief is this: I adore the twelve-

---

1404 The meaning of this is explained in v. 7, *post*.

1405 This verse is inserted as it was found in a manuscript belonging to the late Achalānanda Svāmī, now in the possession of the Varendra Anusandhāna Samiti.

1406 Dvādashār*n*a—that is, twelve petals. The petals of the lotus are not independent of the letters thereon.

1407 That is, the Chitri*n*ī Nā*d*ī.

1408 Shiva. See as to the five faces the citation from the Linggārchana Tantra, v. 7, *post*. There is also a concealed sixth face, "like the color caused by deadly poison," known as Nilaka*nth*a.

1409 Anghas—sin and sorrow, pain and penalty.

1410 Yoga with the Supreme known as the Guru.

petalled Lotus which is within the pericarp of the Sahasrāra.

"*Wonderful*" (Adbhuta).—It excites our wonder by reason of its being pervaded by the luster (tejas) of Brahman, and for other reasons.

"*Lotus of twelve letters*" (Dvādashār*n*a-sarasīruha)—*i.e.*, the Lotus which contains twelve letters. The twelve letters, according to those learned in the Tantras, are the twelve letters which make the Gurumantra; they are Sa, ha, kha, phreng, ha, sa, k*sha*, ma, la, va, ra, yang. Some say that by Dvādashār*n*a is meant the twelfth vowel, which is the Vāgbhava-bīja.[1411] But that cannot be. If it were so, the authority quoted below would be tautologous: "(Meditate on) your Guru who is Shiva as being on the lustrous Hangsapī*th*a, the substance of which is Mantra (Mantramaya), which is in the pericarp of the Lotus of twelve letters, near the region of the Moon[1412] in the pericarp, and which is adorned by the letters ha, la, and k*sh*a, which are within the triangle A-ka-tha."

The above passage speaks of the Mantramayapī*th*a. The Mantra substance of this Pī*th*a is the Gurumantra in the form of Vāgbhava-bīja.[1413] There would therefore be a repetition of the same Mantra.[1414] Dvādashār*n*a is made up by Bahuvrīhi Samāsa—that in which there are Dvādasha (twelve) Ar*n*as (letters). This lotus has therefore twelve petals, on which are the twelve letters.

It is true that the letters are not here specified, and there has been nothing said as to where they are placed; but the Gurugītā says[1415] that "the letters Hang and Sa surround (that is, as petals) the Lotus," wherein the Guru should be meditated. This leads us to the conclusion that the letters Hang and Sa*h* are repeated six times, thus making twelve, and so the number of petals becomes clearly twelve, as each petal contains one letter. This is fit subject of meditation for the wise.

"*Inseparable from*" (Nitya-lagnam).—That is, it is connected with the Sahasrāra in such a way that the one cannot be thought of without thinking of the other.

"*The pericarp of the Lotus in which is the Brahmarandhra*" (Brahmarandhra-sarasīruhodara).—That is, the Sahasrāra. The thousand-petalled lotus in which is the Brahmarandhra; within its womb; that is to say, within it (Tanmadhye); that is to say, within its pericarp (Tat kar*n*ikāyām).

The Kangkāla-Mālinī, in describing the Lotus of a thousand petals, thus speaks of the place of the Brahmarandhra: "In its (Sahasrāra)

1411 *I.e.*, Bīja of Sarasvatī—Aing.

1412 Chandra-ma*nd*ala, by the Commentator (reading the locative as Sāmīpye saptamī).

1413 Aing.

1414 That is, if we understand that the body of both the Pī*th*a and the petals is Aing. The Vāgbhava Bīja Aing is the Guru Bīja also.

1415 This verse is quoted in full under v. 6, *post*.

pericarp, O Deveshī, is Antarātmā, and above it is the Guru; above him is the Sūryya Ma*nd*ala and Chandra Ma*nd*ala and Mahāvāyu, and above it is Brahma-randhra."

Some say that by Udara (belly or interior) is meant within the triangle in the pericarp. The word Udara here means "interior" or "center." The interior of the Lotus contains its pericarp, but the text does not mean the interior of the triangle in the pericarp, because the triangle is not here mentioned. The Shyāmā-saparyyā quotes the following:

"The Lotus of twelve petals (or Letters) is within the pericarp of the White Lotus of a thousand petals, which has its head turned downward, and the filaments of which are of the color of the rising sun, and which is adorned by all the letters of the alphabet."

"*Covers the top of the channel of Ku*nd*alī*" (Ku*nd*alī-vivara-kā*nd*a-ma*nd*itam).—The Vivara (Channel) is that by which Ku*nd*alinī goes to Shiva in the Sahasrāra. The Chitri*n*ī contains within it this passage or channel. Chitri*n*ī is the tube (stalk), as it were, through which the passage runs, and Chitri*n*ī is adorned by this Lotus. As a Lotus rests on its stalk, so does the twelve-petalled Lotus rest on Chitri*n*ī, and is made beautiful by its stalk, the Chitri*n*ī.

VERSE 2.

I adore the abode of Shakti in the place where the two pericarps come together. It is formed by the lines[1416] A, Ka, and Tha; and the letters Ha, La, and K*sh*a, which are visible in each of its corners, give it the character of a Ma*nd*ala.[1417]

COMMENTARY.

The Guru should be meditated upon as in the triangle within the pericarp of the Lotus before-mentioned. He now wishes to describe the triangle so that an adequate conception of it may be formed.

"*The abode of Shakti*" (Abalālayam).—By Abalā is meant Shakti. Here She is Kāmakalā (triangular) in form, and the three Shaktis, Vāmā, Jye*shth*ā, and Raudrī, are the lines (of the triangle). These three Shaktis emanate from the three Bindus.[1418] Kāmakalā is the abode of Shakti.

The Yāmala speaks of the identity of Kāmakalā with this abode. The passage begins, "I now speak of Kāma-kalā," and proceeding

---

[1416] Akathādi—*i.e.*, the lines formed by the letters A to A*h*, Ka to Ta, and Tha to Sa. These letters placed as three lines form the three sides of the triangle.

[1417] *I.e.*, the diagram where the Divinity is summoned and worshipped.

[1418] Vindutrayāngkurabhūta—that is, they have the three Bindus as their sprouting shoot.

says[1419]: "She is the three Bindus. She is the three Shaktis. She is the threefold Manifestation. She is everlasting." That is, Kāmakalā is composed of the three Shaktis spoken of (Trishaktirūpā). He next speaks of the attributes of Abalālaya (abode of Shakti).

"*Come together*" (Kandalita).—Kandala ordinarily means a quarrel in which one attacks the other with words. Here its significance is merely that one (the twelve-petalled lotus) is included within the other (Sahasrāra).

"*Formed by the lines A, Ka, and Tha*" (K*l*ipta-rekham-akathādirekhayā).—The sixteen vowels beginning with A form the line Vāmā, the sixteen letters beginning with Ka form the line Jye*shth*ā, and the sixteen letters beginning with Tha form the line Raudrī. The Abode of Shakti is formed by these three lines.

The B*ri*hat Shrīkrama, in dealing with Kāmakalā, says: "From the Bindu as the sprouting root (Angkura) She has assumed the form of letters."[1420]

"*The letters ha, la, and* ksha, *which are visible in its corners, give it the character of a Ma*ndala" (Ko*n*a-lak*sh*ita-ha-la-k*sh*a-ma*nd*alī-bhāva-lak*sh*yam).—In its corners—*i.e.*, in the inner corners of the aforesaid triangle. The three corners of the triangle are at the apex,[1421] the right, and the left. The letters ha, la, and k*sh*a, which are visible there, give the place the character of a Ma*nd*ala.

One cannot form an adequate conception (Dhyāna) of this triangle without knowing it in all its particulars, and that is why other authorities are quoted. This triangle should be so drawn that if one were to walk round it would always be on one's left.[1422]

The Shāktānanda-tarangg*in*ī says: "Write the triangle A-ka-tha so that walking outside it is always on one's left."

Kālī Ūrddhvāmnāya: "The Tri-bindu[1423] is the Supreme Tattva, and embodies within itself Brahmā, Vi*sh*nu, and Shiva (Brahmavi*sh*nushivātmakam). The triangle composed of the letters has emanated from the Bindu." Also: "The letters A to Visarga make the line Brahmā, which is the line of Prajāpati; the letters Ka to Ta make the most supreme (Parātparā) line of Vi*sh*nu. The letters Tha to Sa make the line of Shiva. The three lines emanate from the three Bindus."

The Tantra-jīvana: "The lines Rajas, Sattva, and Tamas, surround the Yoni-Ma*nd*ala." Also: "Above is the line of Sattva; the line of Rajas

1419 Trivindu*h* sā trishakti*h* sā trimūrti*h* sā sanātanī.

1420 Var*n*āvayava-rūpi*n*ī. Bindu appears in the form of letters by germinating as a sprout. The letters are sprouts from Bindu; that is, the Universe is evolved from Bindu.

1421 The triangle, it should be remembered, has its apex downward.

1422 Vāmāvartena vilikhet. The drawing is made in the direction which is the reverse to that of the hands of a watch.

1423 *I.e.*, the three Bindus considered as one and also separately.

is on its left, and the line of Tamas is on its right."[1424]

By a careful consideration of the above authority, the conclusion is irresistible that the letters A-ka-tha go in the direction above-mentioned.

The Svatantra Tantra says: "The lines A-ka-tha surround the letters Ha, La, and K*sh*a." It therefore places them within the triangle.

It is needless to discuss the matter at greater length.

VERSE 3.

In my heart I meditate on the Jeweled Altar (Ma*n*ipī*th*a), and on Nāda and Bindu as within the triangle afore-spoken. The pale red[1425] glory of the gems in this altar shames the brilliance of the lightning flash. Its substance is Chit.

COMMENTARY.

The place of the Guru is on the jeweled altar within the triangle. He therefore describes the jeweled altar (Ma*n*ipī*th*a).

"*On the Jeweled Altar and on Nāda and Bindu*" (Nāda-bindu-ma*n*ipī*th*ama*nd*alam).—The compound word may be formed in two ways: Ma*n*ipī*th*ama*nd*alam along with Nāda and Bindu (Nāda-bindubhyāng saha), or Nāda and Bindu and Ma*n*ipī*th*ama*nd*alam—*i.e.*, all these three. Some interpret this to mean that Nāda and Bindu are the Ma*n*ipī*th*a. But that cannot be. Nāda is white, and Bindu is red; and the pale red glory whereby the Ma*n*ipī*th*a shames the luster of the lightning flash is neither red nor white.

The Shāradātilaka says: "This Bindu is Shiva and Shakti,[1426] and divides itself in three different ways; its divisions are called Bindu, Nāda, and Bīja." If this be interpreted to mean, as it ought to be, that Bindu is Parashaktimaya, and Bīja, Nāda, and Bindu, are respectively Fire, Moon, and Sun, then Nāda being the Moon is white, and Bindu being the Sun is red. Pūr*n*ānanda also speaks[1427] of Nāda as being white like Baladeva, etc.

The B*ri*hat Shrīkrama also says: "There was the imperishable Bindu, lustrous like the young Sun."

Now, as one is white and the other red, they can never be the pale red gem. The meaning given by us is therefore correct. The solution is that Nāda is below, and Bindu above, and Ma*n*ipī*th*a in between the two—thus should one meditate. This has been clearly shown in the Gurudhyāna in Kangkālamālinī Tantra: "Meditate on the excellent

[1424] That is, on the left and right of the Yoni or the right and left of the spectator.

[1425] Pā*t*ala.

[1426] Sāk*sh*ātparashaktimaya.

[1427] V. 35, *Shat*-chakra-nirūpa*n*a.

Antarātmā[1428] in the (region of the) Lotus of a thousand petals, and above it (Antarātmā) meditate on the resplendent throne[1429] between Nāda and Bindu, and on this throne (meditate) upon the eternal Guru, white like a mountain of silver."

"*The pale red glory of the gems in this altar shames the brilliance of lightning*" (Pa*t*u-ta*d*it-ka*d*ārima-sparddhamāna-ma*n*ipā*t*ala-prabham).—This qualifies Ma*n*ipī*th*a-ma*nd*alam. To be "pa*t*u" is to be able to fully do one's work. Now, lightning wants to display itself. Here the idea is that the pale red luster of the Pī*th*a shames the uninterrupted brilliance of the reddish-yellow lightning flash, inasmuch as the Ma*n*ipī*th*a is covered all over with gems.

"*Its substance is Chit*" (Chinmayang vapu*h*).—The Chinmaya or Jnānamaya body. The body of Nāda, Bindu, and Ma*n*ipī*th*a, is Chinmaya or Jnāna-maya.[1430] Others interpret it to mean, "I meditate on the Chinmaya body of the twelfth vowel,[1431] the Bīja of Sarasvatī, which is the Gurumantra." But that is wrong. The Guru is white, and his Bīja is also white; to attribute to it a pale red luster would be incongruous.

VERSE 4.

I intently meditate on the three lines above it (Ma*n*ipī*th*a), beginning with the line of Fire, and on the brilliance of Ma*n*ipī*th*a, which is heightened by the luster of those lines. I also meditate on the Hangsa,[1432] which is the all-powerful Great Light in which the Universe is absorbed.[1433]

COMMENTARY.

On Hangsa-pī*th*a, which is within the triangle on Ma*n*ipī*th*a, between Nāda and Bindu, is the place of the Guru. He now wishes to describe Hangsa and the triangle in order that a clear conception of these two may be gained.

The meaning of this verse is, shortly, this: I meditate on the primordial Hangsa,[1434] I meditate on the three lines, beginning with the line of Fire, above the place of Ma*n*ipī*th*a. The verb "I meditate" occurs once in this verse, and governs three nouns in the objective case.

[1428] This Antarātmā is Hangsa. Unless the words in the text, "in the lotus of a thousand petals," be read Sāmīpye saptamī, then the view here expressed differs from that adopted by Kālichara*n*a, that Hangsa is in the twelve-petalled lotus.

[1429] Singhāsanā—lit., lion seat, the seat of the honored one, the King's seat.

[1430] That is, their substance is Chit in association with Māyā.

[1431] The Bīja of Sarasvatī or Vāgbhava Bīja is Aing. Ai is the twelfth vowel.

[1432] That is, the Paramahangsa which is both Prak*r*iti and Puru*sh*a.

[1433] Lit., "Light which devours the Universe."

[1434] *I.e.*, the union of Hang and Sa*h* whereby the Hangsa is formed.

"*I intently meditate*" (Vyāmrishāmi).—That is, I think with mind undisturbed, excluding all subjects likely to interfere with my thoughts.

"*Above it*" (Ūrddhvam asya)—that is, above Manipītha.

"*The three lines (beginning with the line of Fire)*" (Hutabhūk-shikhā-trayam).—This compound word is made up according to the rule known as Shāka-pārthiva, by which the word Ādi which comes in between two words is dropped. Ādi means "and others." The Line of Fire,[1435] which is called the Line Vāmā, emanates from Vahni Bindu in the South, and goes to the North-East Corner; and the Line of Moon emanates from Chandra Bindu in the North-East Corner, and goes towards the North-West Corner: this is the line Jyeshthā. The Line of Sun emanates from Sūryya Bindu in the North-East Corner, and reaches Vahni Bindu: this is the Line Raudrī. The triangle which is formed by the three lines uniting the three Bindus is Kāmakalā (Kāmakalārūpam).

The Brihat Shrīkrama says: "She whose form is letters is coiled up in the Bindu and comes out thereof as a sprouting seed from the South. From there[1436] She goes to the Īshāna corner (N.E.). She who thus goes is the Shakti Vāmā. This is Chitkalā Parā and the line of Fire. The Shakti which has thus gone to the Īshāna corner then goes in a straight line (that is, to the N.W.). This line, O Parameshvarī, is the line of Jyeshthā, who is Tripurā, the Sovereign Mistress. Again turning left[1437] She returns to the place of sprouting. She is Raudrī, who by Her union with Ichchhā and Nāda makes the Shringāta."[1438]

The Māheshvarī-sanghitā says: "Sūryya, Chandra, and Vahni, are the three Bindus, and Brahmā, Vishnu, and Shambhū, are the three lines."

The Prema-yoga-taranggini, in describing the Sahasrāra, quotes an authority which is here cited, clearly showing that the place of the Guru is within this triangle. "Within it is the excellent lightning-like triangle. Within the triangle are two imperishable Bindus in the form of Visarga. Within it, in the void, is Shiva,[1439] known by the name of Parama." Shangkarāchāryya also has shown this clearly in his Ānandalaharī. The Author of the Lalitā-rahasya also speaks of the Guru as seated on Visarga. Visarga is the two Bindus Chandra and Sūryya at the upper

[1435] Here Fire is the origin of life, and is therefore associated with Brahmā. Moon is associated with Vishnu. And the Sun spoken of here stands for the twelve suns (Āditya) which rise to burn the world at dissolution (Pralaya).

[1436] Yasmāt is according to the reading given in the original. The same passage is quoted elsewhere reading yāmyāt (from the south) in place of yasmāt.

[1437] Reading vakrībhūtā punarvāme for vyaktibhūya punarvāme.

[1438] According to another reading, "By the union of Ichchhā and Jnāna Raudrī makes the Shringāta." The passage above quoted shows that the Kāma-kalā is a subtle form of Kundalinī, more subtle than the Akatha triangle. *Cf.* Ānanda Lahari, v. 21, where the Sūkshma dhyāna of Kundalinī is given.

[1439] Shiva is Guru.

angles of the (down-turned) triangle.

"*On Hangsa*" (Ādihangsayor yugam).—Literally interpreted it would mean the union of[1440] the primordial Hang and Sa*h*. By Ādi (first) is implied the Parama-hangsa, which is also known as Antarātmā, and not the Jīvātmā, which resembles the flame of a lamp. The Hangsa here is the combination of Prak*ri*ti and Puru*sha*.

In Āgama-kalpadruma it is said: "Hangkāra is Bindu, and Visarga is Sa*h*. Bindu is Puru*sha*, and Visarga is Prak*ri*ti. Hangsa is the union of Pung (male) and Prak*ri*ti (female). The world is pervaded by this Hangsa."

Some interpret Asya ūrddhvam to mean "above Ma*n*ipī*tha*," and say that the verse means: "I meditate on the union of the two who constitute the primordial Hangsa above Ma*n*ipī*tha*." This is wrong. The Kangkāla-Mālinī speaks of the Ma*n*ipī*tha* as above Hangsa and between Nāda and Bindu. So how can these be below Hangsa? This is impossible. This also shows the impossibility of the reading adopted by some—namely, *Huta-bhuk-shikhā-sakham*[1441] in place of *Huta-bhuk-shikha-trayam*. If this reading were accepted, then the words *Ūrddhvam asya* (above it) have no meaning. The interpretation "I meditate on the union of," as given above, may, however, be understood in the following sense. We have seen that the Kangkālamālinī speaks of the Hangsa as below the Ma*n*ipī*tha*, which is between Nāda and Bindu. The interpretation mentioned is in great conflict with the view of Kangkāla-Mālinī. But if Huta-bhuk-shikhā-trayam be read as qualifying Hangsa, then the difficulty may be removed. Then the meaning would be: "Below Ma*n*ipī*tha* is Hangsa, and above it is the triangular Kāmakalā which is formed by the Hangsa."[1442]

"*Which is the all-powerful Great Light in which the Universe is absorbed*" (Vishva-ghasmara-mahochchidotka*t*am).—"Bhaks*h*" and "Ghas" mean the same thing. The root "Ghas" means "to devour," and the roots "Chid," "Hlād," and "Dip," all mean "to shine." The Great Light (Mahochchit) which is the Devourer (Ghasmara) of the Universes: By that is meant that it is all-powerful (Utka*t*a). Utka*t*a, which literally means very high, here means very powerful.

[1440] *I.e.*, Hang and Sa*h*. The union of the two makes Hangsa*h*.

[1441] Huta-bhuk-shikhā-sakha—the friend of the flame of Fire. By this is meant Vāyu (air). As there is no Vāyu in this region, therefore Vāyu cannot be above the triangle or above Ma*n*ipī*tha*.

[1442] Tasya parī*n*atasya. Apparently the sense is that the three Bindus, or Hangsa, are below, but that the triangle which they collectively form, or the Kāmakalā, is above, and in this sense the Hangsa is both above and below Ma*n*ipī*tha*.

VERSE 5.

The mind there contemplates the two Lotuses which are the Feet of the Guru, and of which the ruby-colored nectar is the honey. These two Feet are cool like the nectar of the Moon, and are the place of all auspiciousness.

COMMENTARY.

Having described the place where the two Lotus Feet of the Guru should be meditated upon, he now speaks of the union by meditation (Dhyāna) on them, in this and the following verse.

"*There*" (Tatra)—*i.e.*, in the triangle on the Ma*n*ipī*th*a. The meaning of this verse, in short, is: "The mind there, within the triangle on the Ma*n*ipī*th*a, contemplates upon the Lotus Feet of the Guru."

"*Of which the ruby-colored nectar is the honey*" (Kungkumāsavaparī-marandayo*h*).—This qualifies "the lotuses." Kungkuma means red, the color of lac. The excellent nectar which is of the color of lac is the honey of the Lotus Feet of the Guru. Some read "Jharī" for "Pan"; the meaning would then be: "from which flows like honey the ruby-colored nectar."

"*Cool like the nectar of the Moon*" (Indu-makaranda-shītalam)—*i.e.*, they are cool as the nectar-like beams of the Moon. As the beams of the Moon counteract heat, so does devotion at the Feet of the Guru overcome sorrow and suffering.

"*Place of all auspiciousness*" (Manggalāspadam).—It is the place where one gets all one desires. The sense is that by devout concentration on the feet of the Guru all success is attained.

VERSE 6.

I adore in my head the two Lotus Feet of the Guru. The jeweled footstool on which they rest removes sin. They are red like young leaves. Their nails resemble the moon shining in all her glory. Theirs is the beautiful luster of lotuses growing in a lake of nectar.

COMMENTARY.

He says here: "I adore the two Lotus Feet of the Guru, resting on the footstool already described in my head."

"*The jeweled footstool on which they rest removes all sin*" (Nishakta-ma*n*i-pādukā-niyamitāgha-kolāhalam).—That is, all the multitude of sins are removed by devotion to the jeweled footstool which serves as the resting-place of His Feet. Or it may be interpreted thus: "The footstool which is studded with gems—that is, the Ma*n*ipī*th*a-ma*nd*ala which is the footstool—removes all the multitude of sins. By meditating on the Feet of the Guru as resting on this stool all sins are destroyed." Or it may be thus interpreted: "The five footstools with which are inseparably connected the gems (by which are meant the Chintama*n*i-like feet of the Guru) destroy all the multitude of sins." By meditating first on the fivefold footstool, and then on the feet of the Guru as resting thereon, sin is removed. As the removal of sins is effected by meditation on the fivefold footstools, it is the cause which effects such removal.

"*They are like young leaves*" (Sphurat-kishalayāru*n*am).—That is, the feet of the Guru possess the red color of newly opened leaves. The leaves of the Mango and Kenduka[1443] tree when newly opened are of a red color, and comparison is made with them.

"*Their nails resemble the moon shining in all her glory*" (Nakha-samullasachchandrakam)—*i.e.*, the toe-nails are like so many beautifully shining moons.

"*Theirs is the beautiful luster of lotuses growing in a lake of nectar*" (Parām*r*ita-sarovarodita-saroja-sadrochis*h*am).—That is, they have the clear luster of lotuses growing in a lake of nectar. He means to say that the excellent nectar drops constantly from the Lotus Feet of the Guru. Pūr*n*ānanda has said the same thing in v. 43 of the S*hat*-chakra-nirūpa*n*am. The excellent nectar is the lake on which the Feet show like lotuses. It has been said that the place of the Guru is in the pericarps of both the Lotuses afore-mentioned. Now, a question may be raised as to whether it is in the pericarp of the twelve-petalled lotus below, or in that of the Sahasrāra above. To solve this the following passages are quoted:

B*r*ihat Shrīkrama: "Then meditate upon the Lotus which with its head downward is above all, and which drops nectar on the Shakti of the Guru in the Lotus."

Yāmala: "The Lotus of a thousand petals is like a canopy[1444]; it is above all, and drops red nectar."

Gurugītā: "In your own Guru meditate according to your powers on the (divine) Guru as having two arms in the Lotus whose petals have the letters Hang and Sa*h*. Although He is Himself the cause of the Universe, He is without and beyond the Universe. On His will there are no limitations.[1445] From Him emanates the Light of knowledge. The Devatā is the Guru. The letters of the mantra[1446] are Devatā."

The Shyāmā-saparyyā quotes the following: "The Lotus Sahasrāra downward turned, in the head, is white. Its filaments are of the color of

---

[1443] *Diospyros glutinosa.*

[1444] Which, is an emblem of supremacy.

[1445] Svachchhandam ātmechchhayā.

[1446] *Cf.* Mantrār*n*ā devatāh proktā Devatāguru-rūpi*n*ī.

the rising sun; all the letters of the Alphabet are on its petals. In the pericarp of the Sahasrāra is Chandra-Ma*nd*ala, and below the pericarp is the lustrous lotus of twelve petals which contains the triangle A-ka-tha, marked out by the letters Ha, La, and K*sh*a. Meditate there on your Guru who is Shiva, seated on the Hangsa-pī*th*a which is composed of Mantras."

The above and similar passages indicate that the place of the Guru is in the pericarp of the Lotus of twelve petals.

The Kangkāla-Mālinī says: "Meditate on the excellent Antarātmā in the Lotus[1447] of a thousand petals, and on the shining throne which is between Nāda and Bindu, and on it (the throne) meditate constantly upon your own Guru, who is like a Mountain of Silver," etc.

The Yāmala says[1448]: "Meditate (on your Guru) in the Lotus of a thousand petals. His cool beauty is like that of the full moon, and His Lotus hands are lifted up to grant boons and to dispel fear."

The Purashchara*n*a-rasollāsa has the following dialogue: "Shrī Mahādeva said: 'There in the pericarp of the wonderful everlasting Lotus of a thousand petals meditate always on your own Guru.' Shrī-Pārvatī said: 'The head of the Great Lotus of a thousand petals, O Lord, is always downward turned; then say, O Deva, how can the Guru constantly dwell there?' Shrī Mahādeva said: 'Well hast thou asked, O Beloved. Now listen whilst I speak to Thee. The great Lotus Ṡahasrāra has a thousand petals, and is the abode of Sadāshiva and is full of eternal bliss. It is full of all kinds of delightful fragrance, and is the place of spontaneous bliss.[1449] The head of this Lotus is always downward, but its pericarp is always upward,[1450] and united with Him is Ku*nd*alinī in the form of a triangle.'"

The Bālā-vilāsa Tantra has the following: "Shrī Dak*sh*i*n*āmūrti said: 'As you awake in the morning remember your Guru in the White Lotus of a thousand petals, the head of which great Lotus is downward turned, and which is decorated with all the letters of the Alphabet. Within it is the triangle known by the name of A-ka-tha, which is decked by the letters Ha, La, and K*sh*a. He of the smiling countenance is on the Hangsa-pī*th*a,[1451] which is in the region of the Chandra Mandala within it (the Sahasrāra).' Shrī Devī said: 'O Lord, how does the Guru stay there when its head is turned downwards?' Shrī Dak*sh*i*n*āmūrti said: 'The Chandra Ma*nd*ala in the pericarp of the Lotus of a thousand petals is turned upward; the Hangsa is there, and there is

[1447] Or in the region of the lotus of a thousand petals.

[1448] The Commentator does not say from which of the different Yāmalas he has quoted this and the passage in the first group.

[1449] Sahajānanda—that is, the bliss springs up itself. This bliss is Svabhāva.

[1450] That is, apparently, if we regard that portion of the pericarp which is attached to the lotus as its head.

[1451] Kāmakalā.

the Guru's place.'"

These and similar passages speak of the place of the Guru as in the pericarp of the Lotus of a thousand petals.

As there are two distinct methods, one should follow the instruction of the Guru and adopt one of the two in his Sādhanā (Anu*shth*āna). For it has been laid down in the Kulār*n*ava Tantra, Ch. XI.: "Beloved, Vedas and Tantras handed down to us by tradition, as also Mantras and usages, become fruitful if communicated to us by the Guru, and not otherwise."

VERSE 7.

This hymn of praise of the Fivefold Footstool was uttered by Him of Five Faces. By (the hearing of) it is attained that good which is gained by (the hearing of) all the hymns in praise of Shiva. Such fruit is only attainable by great labor in the Wandering (Sangsāra).

COMMENTARY.

He now speaks of the good gained by listening to this Stotra.

"*Hymn of praise of the Fivefold Footstool*" (Pādukā-panchaka-stotram).—Pādukā means a footstool (Padaraksh*an*ādhāra). The five of these are: (1) The (twelve-petalled) Lotus; (2) the triangle A-ka-tha in its pericarp; (3) the region of the Nāda, Bindu, and Ma*n*ipī*th*a in it; (4) the Hangsa below, and (5) the triangle on, the Ma*n*ipī*th*a. Or they may be counted thus: (1) The Lotus (*i.e.*, twelve-petalled); (2) the triangle (A-ka-tha); (3) Nāda-Bindu; (4) the Ma*n*ipī*th*a Ma*nd*ala; (5) the Hangsa—which taken collectively form the triangular Kāmakalā.[1452] Stotra is a hymn of praise. This hymn, including the verse which speaks of the benefit to be gained by listening to it, is one of seven verses.

"*Uttered by Him of Five Faces*" (Pancha-vaktrādvinirgatam).—The Five Faces of Shiva as given in the Linggārchana Tantra are: "On the West[1453] (*i.e.*, back) is Sadyojāta; on the North (*i.e.*, left) is Vāmadeva; on the South (right) is Aghora; and on the East (front) is

[1452] These two accounts appear to agree as to the position of the following in the order stated—viz., twelve-petalled Lotus with A-ka-tha triangle in which are Ma*n*ipī*th*a, with Bindu above and Nāda below. There remains then to be considered the position of Hangsa and the Kāmakalā which they form. Both are one and the same, the first being the three Bindus, and the second the triangle they make (Kāmakalā), from which emanates (and in this sense forms part of it) the lower A-ka-tha triangle (for this is Var*n*amaya). In the second classification the three Bindus and the triangle (Kāmakalā) which they form are treated as one, and placed above the Ma*n*ipī*th*a. In the first classification, apparently with a view to gain accordance with the Kangkālamālinī Tantra cited in v. 4, the Hangsa and the triangle which they form are taken separately, the first being placed below and the other above Ma*n*ipī*th*a.

[1453] Shiva is seated facing the East.

Tat-puru*sh*a. Īshāna should be known as being in the middle. They should thus be meditated upon in a devout spirit. Vinirgata means uttered—that is, uttered by these Five Faces.

"*By listening to it is attained that good*" (*Shad*āmnāyaphala-prāptam).—This literally means: "by it is obtained the fruit of what has been spoken by the Six Mouths." The Six Faces are the five given above and a sixth concealed one which is below, called Tāmasa. This is alluded to in *Shad*vaktranyāsa in the Shiva Tantra thus: "Ong Hang Hrīng Aung Hrīng tāmasāya svāhā"; as also in the meditation (Dhyāna) there given, thus: "The lower face, Nīlaka*nth*a, is of the color caused by poison."

*Shad*āmnāya is what has been spoken by these Faces—that is, all the hymns of praise to Shiva. By the fruit of this is meant the benefit gained by reciting or listening to all these Mantras, and practicing the appropriate Sādhanā. This is what is gained through this hymn.

"*It is attainable by great labor in this Wandering*" (Prapanche chātidurlabham).—By Prapancha is meant this Sangsāra (Wandering or World), comprising the Universe from all effects up to Brahmā, and which is shown by Māyā. It is difficult of attainment (Durlabha), as it is the result of manifold merit acquired by the practice of laborious endeavor (Tapas) in previous births.

End of the Commentary (*T*ippanī) of the Name of Amalā (Stainless), written by Shrīkālīchara*n*a on the Pādukāpanchaka Stotra.

THE END

Plates

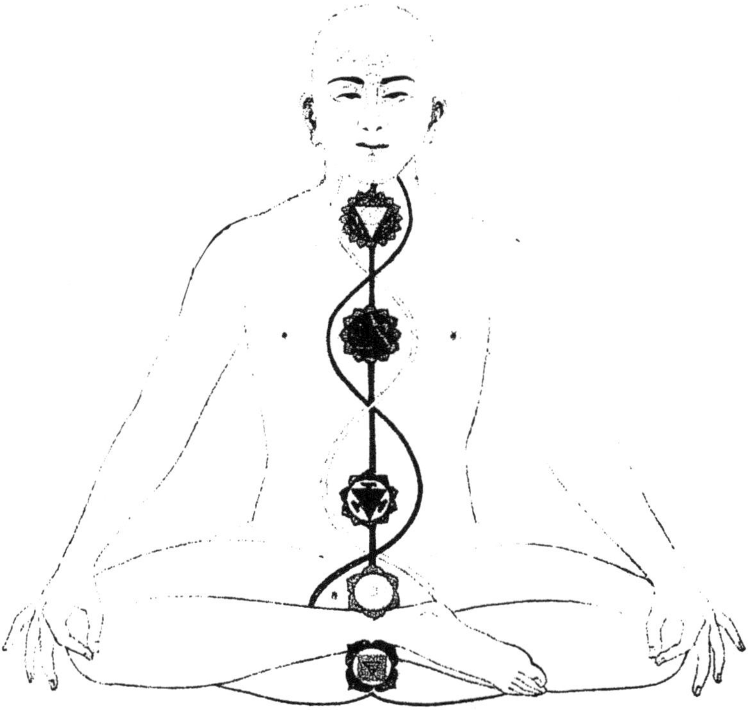

PLATE 1.

PLATE 2.

PLATE 3.

PLATE 4.

PLATE 5.

PLATE 6.

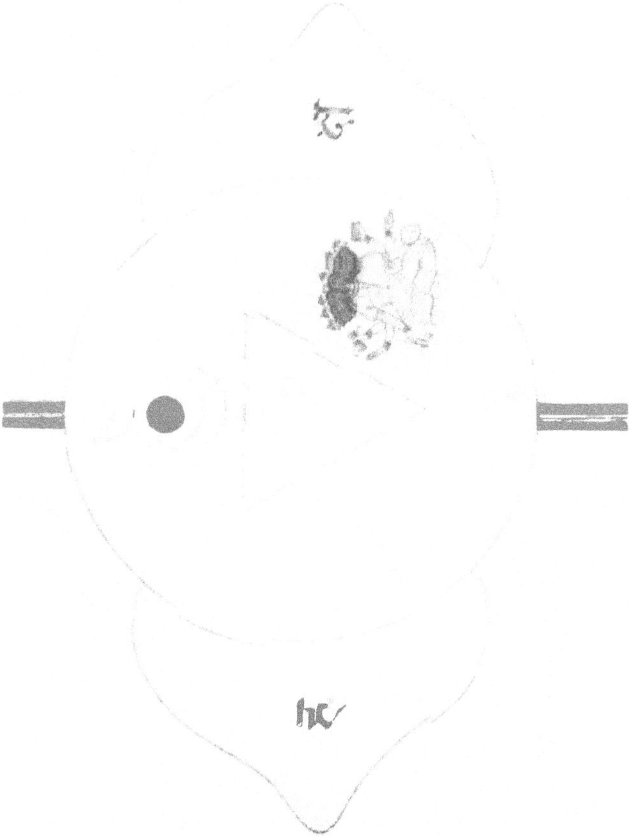

PLATE 7.

PLATE 8.